WORLD TRADE
COMPETITION

WORLD TRADE COMPETITION

Western Countries and Third World Markets

Edited by

Center for Strategic and International Studies

PRAEGER

PRAEGER SPECIAL STUDIES • PRAEGER SCIENTIFIC

Published in 1981 by Praeger Publishers
CBS Educational and Professional Publishing
A Division of CBS, Inc.
521 Fifth Avenue, New York, NY 10175 USA

Library of Congress Catalog Card Number: 81-11930
ISBN: 0-03-059671-8

123456789 145 987654321
Printed in the United States of America

ACKNOWLEDGMENTS

A special word of thanks is due to a number of colleagues and friends who contributed to the U.S. Export Competitiveness Project and its studies: Penelope Hartland-Thunberg, Robert A. Kilmarx, Raymond F. Mikesell, and Robert A. Sammons for offering useful criticism of all or part of the studies contained in this two-volume text; Nancy Eddy and Jean Newsom for their editorial assistance; and Desiree Blackwell, Steve Cibull, Patricia Dodson, Sheila Payne, John Pauley, and Patricia Pefley for typing and proofing assistance.

Jennifer J. White
Project Editor
U.S. Export
  Competitiveness Project

Michael A. Samuels
Executive Director
U.S. Export
  Competitiveness Project

CONTENTS

INTRODUCTION

Many factors shape the strategic balance. The commercial competitive posture of a nation, that which strengthens its currency and provides impetus to its economic growth, is, however, often overlooked as an integral element of national power. In the 1980s, the United States will face increasing competition from all quarters. In this period, the strategic balance will be shaped by more than military might and strategic competence. It will also be influenced by the nation's economic strength and resilience.

For a nation to function as a great power, national economic growth and national profitability must be at the core of the power base. Yet in recent years we have witnessed relative national economic decline, frequent unwillingness and inability to compete, and a reactionary, defensive approach to world trade. At home, the existence of entire industries is being challenged by successful marketing from other countries; abroad, U.S. global market shares in key product areas have been eroded by competitors. U.S. productivity gains are close to nil, ranking the United States sixth among the world's top seven industrial nations. Oil imports continue to drain the U.S. economy of foreign exchange and contribute to the large balance of trade deficits witnessed throughout the decade.

Given these alarming trends, there are fundamental questions that must be addressed. What role do U.S. exports play in the U.S. national power equation? If they are indeed an important element, can the U.S. afford to ignore the declining competitiveness of U.S. products? What has caused the erosion of U.S. export performance? What approaches can government and industry take to revitalize the export drive? Are there lessons to be learned from our competitors? These are the basic questions that must be answered to launch an actively internationalistic, offensive approach to the challenges of the 1980s and beyond.

Three years ago, the Georgetown University Center for Strategic and International Studies set out to investigate these compelling questions. Through its U.S. Export Competitiveness Project, 20 studies were commissioned to examine the various components of U.S. export needs and policy directions. The study has proceeded from the hypothesis that one of the distortions in the U.S. national power base is that U.S. policy, in contrast to that of other major developed countries, has discouraged rather than encouraged exports. Faced with excessive export controls, financial and legal constraints, and active promotion by U.S. competitors, U.S. exporters have suffered serious loss of market shares. Consequently, not only has U.S. industry suffered but the prestige of the nation in the world economy has been severely challenged.

The seriousness of the U.S. export competitiveness problem must be understood not just by the normal observers of export and trade policy, the economists, and the businessmen, but more importantly by all Americans concerned with the overall economic and political strength of the United States domestically and internationally.

This two-volume work brings together the results of three years of research on the decline of U.S. export competitiveness. Volume One, <u>The Export Performance of the United States</u>, examines the political and strategic importance of exports and their role in the U.S. economy. Consideration is given to the effect of U.S. foreign direct investment on U.S. export performance and an examination is made of the U.S. regulatory, financial, and political environment for exports. The impact of recent multilateral agreements on U.S. exports is also evaluated.

Volume Two, <u>World Trade Competition</u>, examines the extent to which U.S. market shares have been lost vis-à-vis U.S. competitors and reviews the export experience of certain key U.S. trading partners. The outlook for trade competition in the 1980s is also addressed.

In both volumes, particular attention is given to trade competition with the industrialized world in the markets of the developing world. U.S. exports to the Third World, the fastest growing world market, represent a larger share of total U.S. exports than Europe and Japan combined. The objective here is to concentrate on U.S. export performance vis-à-vis other major exporting countries, given the developing world import market as a constant.

The study is also limited to manufactured exports since the U.S. competitive position in agricultural products has been fairly well maintained and, in the short run, agricultural exports are largely affected by worldwide crop variations. Moreover, international trade in nonmanufactures generally is subject to influences that cannot be explained by short-run changes in the measures of export competitiveness.

We hope that this two-volume work will serve to increase public understanding of the current export problem and will stimulate public concern for the direction of U.S. export policy. There are times when a nation must consciously change its course. Both empirical observation and economic facts say that time is now. The U.S. government and the nation must come of age, see the challenge and the opportunity, and take the offensive with a coordinated national export policy.

Jennifer J. White
Project Editor
U.S. Export Competitiveness
  Project

Michael A. Samuels
Executive Director
Third World Studies

1

THE UNITED STATES, WESTERN EUROPE, AND THE THIRD WORLD: ALLIES AND ADVERSARIES

Simon Serfaty

CONTENTS

I. INTRODUCTION

A complex and fluid triangular relationship of security, economic issues, and problems with the less developed countries (LDCs) has been a constant feature of U.S. ties with allied states. The linkages among these arenas, the precise interplay of national interests and perspectives, and the relative leverage of governments from one arena to another, have varied significantly in the past; they are likely to evolve further in the future, although the direction of this evolution is difficult to predict at a time when the international system is more uncertain, and allied interests and policies more fragmented, than at any moment in the postwar era.[1]

The general unfolding of U.S.-allied relationships since the formation of the western security system in the late 1940s strongly suggests that economic issues will continue to expand their weight and influence in shaping overall allied politics during the years ahead. In this context, the growing competition of advanced industrial states for markets and profitable economic ties in the LDCs is only a subordinate aspect of interallied relations. Yet, such competition is bound to exacerbate already existing conflicts over the more central issues of a weakened American security guarantee and the continued unraveling of an American-dominated international economic order. Thus, the United States, beset by chronic economic weaknesses, which include a persistent and enormous balance of trade deficit, will be engaging in further economic competition with its allies in the Third World at the very time the security it provides for such allies is deemed to be either less desirable or, if as desirable as ever, less effective than has been the case.

II. THE U.S. - ALLIED RELATIONSHIP

Our allies in Europe depend on many states for
many services. To achieve physical security, they rely
primarily on the military constraints imposed on the
Soviet Union by the U.S. deterrent; secondly, they rely
on Soviet goodwill that may be generated further by the
diplomatic initiatives of some European states. To
achieve economic security and well-being, they have
needed a stable U.S. dollar and a strong U.S. economy
to provide an adequate framework within which their
supply of raw materials is guaranteed at a fair price,
while foreign markets (often stabilized and protected
by the United States) remain open to their manufactured
products and service exports. Throughout the past
decade, they have also come to accept, however hesi-
tantly, a special role for the German deutschmark (with
or without an integrated European monetary system) and
the German economy. Finally, to achieve political
stability, the states of Europe assume an orderly
manipulation of those factors (U.S. protection, Soviet
benevolence, and LDC accessibility) on which they are
so heavily dependent, as sudden disruptions in their
respective reliability are bound to have significant
political consequences.

This variety of dependencies is not new. A U.S.
guarantee of the physical security of Europe has been
central to the postwar history of Europe, even if, at
first, there seemed to be much confusion as to whether
such a guarantee was being sought against a renewal of
German militarism, an outburst of Soviet imperialism,
or anticolonial forces at work throughout the fast
declining European empires. In dealing with such
threats, however defined, the Europeans have consistently remained security consumers. Repeatedly, they
have stressed their military impotence by pointing to
such factors as their economic limitations, their
political fraility, the Soviet conventional capabilities, the U.S. strategic superiority, or the
horrors of nuclear technology.

Any one, or any combination, of these factors has
been used, regardless of the contradictions inherent
in their successive or simultaneous presentation by one or several European countries. Even
isolated, national efforts in Europe to produce

4

security by waging colonial war or by developing an independent nuclear deterrent have been initiated and pursued to integrate such a war within the framework of the East-West conflict, or permit the perceived coupling of such a deterrent with the American deterrent.[2]

Accordingly, although persistently questioned, the credibility of the U.S. commitment has never declined to the point of incredibility, either from the standpoint of the allies or the Soviet Union. In numerous instances, it has provided successive administrations in Washington with much leverage in other areas (monetary, economic, and political) as issues have been conveniently linked to force the allies into an acceptance or a rejection of U.S. leadership in toto.

Such explicit linkage of general politico-economic issues to military issues could be seen, for example, during the years that preceded the formation of the Atlantic Alliance when a high and effective measure of dollar diplomacy was used by the Truman administration to insure Europe's endorsement of its various initiatives on the continent.[3] It could also be seen in the 1950s, when the U.S. request for a rearmament of Germany was explicitly tied to the continuation of U.S. economic aid and trade privileges; and in the 1960s, in a reverse fashion, when the U.S. bargaining posture during the negotiations of the Kennedy Round was very much affected by Washington's interests in areas other than trade, while the maintenance of U.S. troops in Germany was linked to a continued willingness of the Bonn government to accumulate unwanted dollars and accept offset payments. A linkage policy in ally relationships, readily visible in Kissinger's proposed Year of Europe in 1973 -- the U.S. predilection for it, the allies' objections to it -- has been dramatized further by the overall circumstances of the 1970s.[4]

An intrinsic feature of the U.S. leadership package has been its economic and monetary dimension. Thus, the Atlantic Alliance originally emerged as a subsidiary to the key economic concerns that were the focus of the evolving Atlantic relations after World War II. Following an early underestimation of the destruction of the European economies by the war, the policymakers in Washington concluded that recovery could be achieved only to the extent that the

United States was willing, as recommended by Assistant Secretary of State for Economic Affairs, Will Clayton, "to run the show."[5]

A consequence of international circumstances as well as a matter of U.S. choice, the postwar monetary system soon became an hegemonial system that left the United States with an apparently unlimited freedom of monetary action in return for making available the resources needed by the Europeans for an instant economic recovery. Once recovery had been launched, a long phase of European growth began and was subsequently stimulated by the semiprotectionist clauses of the Rome Treaty in 1957. The European Economic Community (EEC) permitted substantial trade expansion from within the Community, primarily to the benefit of German industry and French agriculture, but also to the general gain of all member states. By exposing European companies to the advantages of an economy of scale within an expanding market, however, the EEC also improved Europe's competitiveness vis-a-vis other industrial states, now hampered by the higher external tariffs surrounding the EEC.[6]

That the consequences for the United States of such additional competitiveness would have been accepted at a time when the dollar was beginning to show distinct signs of wear and tear (the first dollar crisis dates back to November 1960) was due to three considerations. First and foremost, in the cold war era it was reasoned that the political and strategic gains that would result from a unification of Europe would outweigh any loss of disadvantage that might afflict the U.S. economy. Second, these losses were in any case likely to be minimal, it was then argued, because of the marginal importance of foreign trade to the U.S. economy (about 7 percent of GNP in 1960, as compared to approximately 40 percent for the countries then in the Common Market), because of the overwhelming U.S. competitiveness in a number of key trade areas, and because of the ability of U.S. capital to bypass tariff restrictions through massive direct investments into the Community. Third, it was thought that whatever small trade diversion there might be would be compensated for, from the standpoint of U.S. economic interests, by the large amount of trade creation that would follow the emergence of Europe as one thriving trade unit.[7]

Accordingly, the resulting American strategy of the 1960s simply assumed, in the name of the allies, that a fresh infusion of economic interdependence would serve to strengthen the political and strategic bonds required to contain Soviet expansion in Europe and elsewhere. Increasing U.S. trade surpluses would balance the capital outflows generated by military expenditures and rapidly growing direct investments in Europe, and thus alleviate an ever larger balance of payments deficit, already seen by President Kennedy as a threat second only to the threat of nuclear war.[8]

Linkages between the costs and rewards of U.S. Atlantic leadership were made all too obvious: committed to a trading partnership with the United States, an integrated Western Europe would further shift the global balance of power to the side of freedom. European unity continued to be seen as the logical extension of the postwar Atlantic bargain, and the temporary consequences of high external tariffs (which the Dillon Round tried to dismantle even before they were actually applied) were discounted as secondary to the benefits that would accrue to NATO if the nations of Europe, including the United Kingdom, were to form a political unit based on the U.S. model of federalism and supranational institutions.

For most Europeans, however, a continuing relationship based on American primacy and European dependence was tolerated by default only, and with considerable reservations. In France and in the United Kingdom -- increasingly in West Germany as well -- what was feared from the U.S. leadership was a volatile mixture that included a presumed virginity in world affairs, an obsession with poorly understood communist ideology and an excessive commitment to global military superiority, a cultural influence seen as a threat to Europe's intellectual heritage, and a series of ulterior motives that were especially directed against Europe's colonial possessions. "If we only pushed on and developed Africa," contended Foreign Secretary Ernest Bevin in 1948, "we could have the U.S. dependent on us, and eating out of our hands in four or five years." Churchill also deplored: "Poor England! They have become so big and we are now so small."[9]

That such reluctance (most forcefully and most persistently articulated in France) was nevertheless overcome resulted from an obvious lack of alternatives: only in the United States could the policymakers of Europe find the necessary economic aid, the sizeable markets, and the protection required by growing tensions within the international system.[10] In the end, such a choice undoubtedly served Europe and the United States well.

Relying as it did on a policy that mixed military instruments, economic tools, and cultural appeal for the masses, the United States constrained the communist and procommunist forces in several countries where those forces were seen as a real threat to the continuity or resumption of democratic processes, helped build an anti-Soviet alliance that effectively denied the expansion of the Eastern bloc into Western Europe, facilitated the recovery of West Germany within an integrating Western Europe while postponing if not cancelling the dangerous issue of German reunification, and satisfied U.S. economic interests through the availability of large outlets for excess capacity and excess capital.

Similarly, from the standpoint of Europe, the Atlantic policy of the United States facilitated a rapid economic recovery though the availability of U.S. monetary aid, the opening of U.S. markets, and the preservation of low prices for raw materials coming from developing countries where a measure of U.S. influence promptly replaced European imperial control. It also helped stabilize the political relationships of forces within Western Europe by making sustained economic growth the presumed solvent of social conflicts, eliminated or contained the threats of Germany's military revival and Soviet military expansion, and provided a ready-made rationale for the initial efforts at European integration.

Nevertheless, even during those years when the "bargain" worked best, European states continued to doubt the long term credibility and desirability of U.S. leadership. As Chancellor Adenauer warned in 1956 before the Suez crisis, "Vital necessities for European states are not always ... vital necessities for the United States, and vice versa; there may result differences in political conceptions that may lead to independent political actions."[11] Not surprisingly, the Atlantic partnership has had a troubled history of

8

collaboration and discord: described as cracked, unhinged, and complex, even while it endured.[12]

Indeed, nearly every decade discord has triumphed for a time over collaboration, resulting in a short phase of European self-assertiveness. That phase, however, is then checked by an external event over which the Europeans have found themselves without recourse other than a renewed reliance on U.S. leadership. So it was, for example, with the EEC challenge that followed the Hague meeting of 1969, contained and rolled back after the oil crisis of 1973-1974. As Henry Kissinger said in 1965 of the earlier Gaullist challenge, "A united Europe is likely to insist on a specifically European view of world affairs -- which is another way of saying that it will challenge American hegemony in Atlantic policy. This may well be a price worth paying for European unity; but American policy has suffered from an unwillingness to recognize that there is a price to be paid."[13]

III. ALLIED INTERESTS IN THE THIRD WORLD: THE POSTWAR ECONOMIC ORDER

Interestingly enough, the most bitter interallied disputes have arisen over clashes of ambivalent and often contradictory interests in peripheral areas of the globe, that is to say, outside the NATO area proper: over the decolonization process, the Middle East wars, numerous African conflicts, Indochina, and, more generally, the presence and influence of industrial states in developing countries. Indeed, there never has been a political, economic, or strategic consensus in the West regarding the structure of their ties with the Third World. Even when the Atlantic area was the center of East-West confrontation, competition rather than cooperation has been the rule for allied policies in this region, as the imperatives of world responsibilities for the United States, and the necessities of domestic politics for the European states, have prevented the subordination of American or European policies to purely Atlantic concerns.[14]

While the Third World has not been the focus of U.S. economic and strategic interests, it would be foolish to dismiss the important place it has held in Western relations throughout the postwar era. In assessing this area, due consideration must be made for the historical experiences that have shaped America's and Europe's respective views of (and, as will be seen, dependence on) the Third World. The Third World's legacy of colonialism stands in sharp contrast with the American legacy of a liberal tradition that has grown out of a unique national experience -- the Puritan migration to an affluent, new world.[15] At times, this tradition influenced American policies in a way that went against, or at least delayed, the promotion or preservation of specific U.S. interests, and, as Europeans often had it, Western interests too. This is not to say that U.S. policies toward the Third World were in all instances benevolent. In effect, these combined, more or less properly and more or less effectively, the traditional objectives of self-preservation (hence the favorable disposition toward the stabilization of regimes overtly hostile to communist ideology) and self-expansion (hence the emphasis on a strategy of economic development that would help make these countries open for U.S. goods and capital) with less traditional aspirations of self-abnegation.[16]

That Europe's vision of the Third World would have been different is not hard to comprehend. European imperialism was an effort to bypass the natural limitations imposed on the continent by geographic circumstances. Initially the leading industrial region in the world because it could draw from its own soil the coal, the iron ore, the zinc, the copper it needed, Europe found itself faced with the obligation to secure access to such materials when its own resources approached depletion. With its markets often unable to keep pace with improvements in technology and productivity, the continent looked elsewhere for outlets that were at first conquered by force, and then preserved or regained by more orderly means. Because it sought to satisfy some of the former colonial objectives, the diplomacy of trade represented the continuation of empires by other means. The continent became a region engaged in processing raw materials imported from other continents, and reselling them as finished goods.

Yet, even within the more limited context of Atlantic trade relations, strains between the United States and the European countries clearly preceded the economic crisis of the 1970s. Although much in evidence during the years of the Kennedy Round, such strains were nevertheless tempered by an overall willingness in Europe to pay the price for U.S. leadership, matched by a willingness in the United States to pay the price for the exercise of such leadership. Even during the Gaullist challenge of the 1960s, there remained an Atlantic interest that repeatedly superseded the interests of the nation-states that comprised the Atlantic area. Nevertheless, over the years, several factors steadily eroded this mutual willingness on the part of the allies to accommodate each other, and progressively made of the United States and Europe adversary brothers of sorts. These have included an ambiguous reaction to the growth of U.S. investment in Europe, the instability of the U.S. dollar, the effects of sustained inflation and reduced rates, the energy crisis and the new role played by the LDCs vis-a-vis the industrialized countries, and the evolution of the military balance between the two superpowers.

During the ten-year period that followed the formation of the Common Market, U.S. direct investments in the EEC increased six times in book value: coming at a time when misgivings over the U.S. connection were fed throughout Europe by a vocal and public debate over the so-called défi américain, they added significantly to European grievances, grievances that had theretofore focused on the more traditional issues of physical security. From the standpoint of many in Europe, the U.S. multinational corporations (MNCs) were just too big, too mobile, and too American. They preempted European credit markets to aggrandize their own assets, maneuvered around national credit control policies and national plans, escaped the surveillance of national banking institutions, distorted intra-European trade patterns through intracorporate transfers, denied much needed tax receipts to national authorities by transfer pricing, fueled a politically dangerous inflation, fostered price wars at the expense of the smaller and less competitive national companies, and disrupted traditional social relationships. In sum, the U.S. MNCs, many argued in Europe, were sapping the ability of the various national governments in Europe to conduct an independent and effective macroeconomic policy of their own, thereby affecting national production, employment, prices, and income. Coming at a time when an overvalued dollar permitted the cheap acquisition of vital European assets in several key national industries as well as in banking, U.S. investments made the displacement of power from Europe to America irreversible. They disarmed the state in the midst of an international economic environment that was growing increasingly unstable and precarious.

The same question of national control has been at stake in the repeated offensives launched by the allies against the dollar. Started by the French in early 1965, gold conversions were designed to show the unworkability of a system based on a single national reserve currency. Yet, what was most significant in the 1968 agreement over the creation of Special Drawing Rights was less the emergence of a new international unit of account other than the dollar (a proposition readily accepted by the United States) that its actual management by the previously formed Group of Ten, a group within which Europe enjoyed a veto power on decision, thereby diluting the controlling influence exerted by the United States at the International Monetary Fund.

Subsequently, at the December 1969 Hague Summit of the EEC countries, post-de Gaulle France, fearful of the consequences that currence instability might have on the delicate structure of the Common Agricultural Policy, sought a European Monetary Union that might reduce Europe's dependence on the dollar and shield it from the destabilizing transmissions of the Eurodollar glut. But even the first modest steps that were agreed upon at the Hague, principally between the French and the Germans, could not survive the monetary storms of 1971.

For those who might have missed it in 1971, the energy crisis that erupted following the 1973 Middle East war exposed further the impotence of Europe in the face of a manipulation of economic and monetary parameters by foreign countries or foreign-based multinationals alike. "It is inadmissible," complained West Germany's Minister of Commerce Hans Friderichs in April 1974, "that we should be kept in the dark about sales, policies, prices, and profits of the international petroleum companies, which are operating in our territory and which are behaving like a state within a state."[17]

Although the reaction in 1974-1976 was initially one of accommodation (France and the rest of Europe to West Germany, but also West Germany to the United States) by 1977 it evolved into one of revived rebellion. The general inconsistencies of Carter's foreign policy, including the cancellation of the B-1 bomber, the Turkish arms embargo, the wavering and waffling over the neutron bomb, the pressure on sales of arms and nuclear reactors, and the debate over SALT II added sharply to perennial European misgivings over the durability and reliability of U.S. leadership.[18]

While attention was focused on economic and monetary differences within the West, the East-West military balance was reversed slowly but steadily following the 1962 Cuban missile crisis. At the time, Western Europe's full and immediate support for Kennedy's demand that Soviet missile installations be dismantled reflected a concern over the effects the displacement of about half of the Soviet strategic capabilities would have on the military balance in the midst of a difficult Berlin crisis. European support, however, was all the more easily extended as U.S. superiority was unquestioned. Eleven years later, with similar if not greater European interests at stake in the Middle East, the Nixon-Kissinger policies toward the Arab states and the related warnings against any unilateral intrusion of Soviet power in the region met with much skepticism in Europe. In 1979 the "uncovering" of a military brigade in Cuba faced general indifference from the allies.

Apparently, a trend in the military balance that seemed to favor the Soviet Union has also progressively enhanced Europe's sensitivity to the consequences of any provocation of the Kremlin, be it through a strategy of human rights, the playing of an ever elusive Chinese card, or the challenging of well-established or new Soviet presences in Third World countries. In this context, Europe's clear support for SALT II has reflected less the endorsement by the European states of the terms of the treaty proper than a genuine fear that rejection of the treaty might cause a renewal of Cold War tensions in a period of Soviet military ascendance. To Europe, SALT II might buy enough time either for a U.S. effort to redress its compromised strategic posture, or for European initiatives to confront the consequences of growing Soviet capabilities and diminished U.S. will.

All in all, Europe displays an obvious crisis of confidence in U.S. leadership. Going beyond consider-ations of strictly military issues, this new Atlantic crisis is the culmination of 15 years of doubts enter-tained by the distant contemplation of U.S. violence at home (Kennedy's and King's assassinations, civil disobedience and urban riots) and abroad (Vietnam and Chile), constitutional crises (Johnson's withdrawal from the presidential race, Watergate), executive impotence in dealing with congressional constraints and pressure groups, and executive ineffectiveness in dealing with the economic and monetary problems of the past few years.

In sum, the U.S. ability to provide Europe with the measure of security to which it has become accustomed since World War II has diminished, while the

U.S. potential for eroding Europe's economic and monetary stability has significantly increased. A chief culprit here has been, of course, the U.S. dollar. "What is necessary," in the words of Chancellor Helmut Schmidt, "is to shield the Common Market ... against monetary turbulence which stems from outside Europe. We must not let our growth policies be destroyed piecemeal by monetary ruptures and uncertainties."[19] There have been other culprits as well, not the least being an excessive U.S. consumption of raw materials (including, but not limited to, oil) that helps drive prices up to a level increasingly difficult for the European nations to manage.

Consequently, the United States is now seen on the continent as part of the threat to Europe's economic security at the very time it has lost some of its relevance to the physical security of Europe. Accordingly, special relationships have been sought more and more pressingly with the former colonies and new influentials in the Third World, thereby returning to former historical patterns. As Claude Cheysson, has put it, "We European countries, with our limited geographic space, do not have the opportunities of the Americans and cannot find at home our essential supplies, markets and the bases of our economy. We must always remember how vulnerable we are. More than others, we must seek to find an order of cooperation and joint development with the 'South' of this world."[20]

IV. THE THIRD WORLD AND THE GLOBAL ECONOMY: IMPLICATIONS FOR THE UNITED STATES AND WESTERN EUROPE

The degree of the European Community's dependence for its supplies of industrial raw materials has been estimated at an overall 75 percent (as compared to 15 percent for the United States and 90 percent for Japan). Although the Community produces enough iron ore and aluminum to meet one fourth of its requirements, all its other essential minerals are imported (see Table 1).

Similarly, its dependence on imports for nonessential minerals range from 90 to 100 percent.[21] Yet, save for oil, the Europeans have surprisingly minimized the prospects of a generalized interruption of commodity supplies from the LDCs.[22] For one, in spite of such dependence on external sources of raw materials (only one third of which come from the developing countries), Europe perceives very few areas for which the threat of an OPEC-like cartel would be serious. Reasons for such wholesale dismissal of the potential for additional cartels are well-known. To be effective, a cartel requires a substantial control of the world's exports, adequate political cohesion, sufficient reserves of foreign exchanges, the absence of quickly available substitutes, and limited stocks in consuming countries. In effect, a realistic threat of cartel action by the LDCs is said to exist for a very few products, including uranium, bauxite, tin, copper, and manganese.

To reduce such threat even further, some European states (particularly France) have effectively preserved their pre-independence political influence in a few Third World countries that produce such materials, especially in Africa. Thus far, these efforts have been significantly free of domestic constraints or even international inhibitions, the expression perhaps of colonial impulses that over two decades of independence have not broken yet. The support shown by the French populace to the increasing militarization of Giscard d'Estaing's policy in Africa is a case in point.

Nor are French interventions in Chad, Gabon, Zaire, and the Central African Republic new within the

TABLE 1

EEC, JAPAN, AND U.S. DEPENDENCE ON IMPORTED
PRIMARY COMMODITIES

(Import as percent of consumption)

	EEC(a)	USA(b)	Japan(c)
Aluminum	61	85	100
Copper	81	-	90
Lead	53	4	76
Nickel	100	71	100
Tin	87	75	97
Zinc	68	64	80
Iron ore	79	29	94
Manganese	100	99	90
Antimone	95		
Cadmium	36(plus) close to 100 with iron ore		
Chrome	100	91	100
Cobalt	100	98	
Mercury	33	73	
Molybdenum	100	-	
Platinum	100	80	
Selenium	100	42	
Tantalum	100	95	
Titanium	100		
Tungsten	99	54	
Vanadium	99	36	
Zirconium	100		
Uranium	59		
Phosphate	99		100
Potassium	20		
Sulfer	43		
Amianthus	100	83	100

(a) Average 1974-76
(b) 1974
(c) 1972

Source: Commission of the European Communities, "Instruments of Mining
and Energy Cooperation with the ACP Countries," COM(79) 130,
March 14, 1979, Appendix 3.

17

context of French policies and objectives. After liquidating the impossible Algerian adventure, de Gaulle was able to emerge as a self-appointed spokesman for Third World aspirations. By relying effectively on a sharp criticism of U.S military policy in Indochina, de Gaulle rapidly erased the stigma of France's colonial legacy and bolstered her claims to serve as a bridge between the industrial and developed world. Although meant to preserve neocolonialist relationships based on the poverty and weakness of regimes that continue to depend on Paris for political survival, cultural aid, and financial support, French interventionism has played a generally stabilizing role in Africa, especially in the face of recent Soviet Cuban aggressiveness and American disabilities. What has been added over the past few years is a marked interest on the part of Giscard d'Estaing to expand French influence and presence in LDC countries other than former French colonies.

When dealing with commodities, European countries seem to be especially concerned with price stability, as rises in prices significantly affect the economic and political landscapes of Europe. Such vulnerability is particularly evident in the case of oil. A March 1979 EEC study estimated that every dollar per barrel above the December 1978 price of $12.70 would result in a $3.6 million annual increase in the Community's oil bill, a $3 billion worsening in its balance of payments on current account, a 0.4 percent reduction in economic growth, and a 0.3 percent increase in inflation.[23] But in the case of other commodities as well, sudden price increases, likely to occur during a period of general upswing, reinforce inflationary trends, thereby forcing governments to enforce deflationary policies even while the economy continues to work below capacity. The political significance of such measures is all too obvious as existing government coalitions are destabilized by the fluctuation of vital economic parameters over which they have limited control.

Generally, U.S. conflicts with leading Atlantic allies over Third World issues have reflected broad differences over the organization of the postwar economic order that are still the source of sharp tensions. Policymakers in Washington have traditionally favored an open, liberal global economy with free trade, and equal access to markets and investment opportunities for all actors. The assumption under-lying American policy was that superior American technology, marketing, and financial power would give the United States decisive advantages in this kind of system. As it is well known, the European states fought this approach: at first, they resisted decolo-nization; later, they substituted privileged and generally closed economic communities linking them to their former colonies, communities into which American business and banks were to be denied sustained access.

The British Commonwealth and the French Union (subsequently Community) were the institutional expres-sions of the successor policies to overt colonialism. With the formation of the EEC and eventual British membership (long delayed over -- in part at least -- the modalities of Commonwealth participation in the agreements that would be reached between Great Britain and the Common Market countries) this strategy of maintaining more or less exclusive economic ties with former dependencies was converted into broader multi-lateral agreements linking Western Europe with Third World regions, to the advantage of Europe and to the relative disadvantage of outside parties such as the United States (see Table 2).

Initially, French interests in Africa were mainly responsible for the special economic arrangements between the EEC and some developing states. The two successive Yaounde agreements between the EEC and nine associated African and Malagache countries set up a regime of financial assistance and regional trade preferences. British membership in the Community and the generalized preferences system for underdeveloped economies, instituted in 1971, necessitated a more inclusive set of negotiations between the EEC and 46 Third World countries. These culminated in the Lomé Convention of February 1975, a convention that granted a generous system of nonreciprocal tariff conces-sions to the African, Caribbean, Pacific (ACP) countries, including most of independent Black Africa. In addition, Lomé devised a so-called STABEX mechanism that was meant to protect the ACP and the European countries against sudden fluctuations in the market prices of raw materials, and, finally, pledged finan-cial, technical, and other forms of EEC economic assistance to the ACP states. The following year, the tendency of the EEC to develop a broad, all-embracing

TABLE 2

THE LARGEST EXPORTERS TO LDCs, BY REGIONS
(in percent)

Origin	LDCs		Oil Producing LDCs		Nonoil Producing LDCs	
	1970	1977	1970	1977	1970	1977
North America	25.0	18.8	23.3	18.8	25.3	18.8
EEC	28.0	28.3	40.2	41.6	25.6	21.8
Japan	12.0	13.7	10.3	14.8	12.3	13.1
Total industrialized countries	70.3	66.3	79.4	82.5	68.3	58.4
Oil exporting developing countries	5.3	12.3	1.1	1.5	6.1	17.6
Other developing countries	14.3	13.8	10.1	10.4	15.1	15.5
State trading area	7.7	5.7	8.1	4.5	7.6	6.3

Source: Commission of the European Communities, Dossiers, "Europe and the Third World," 1978, p. 60; GATT, International Trade, 1977-78.

policy of privileged economic cooperation with a significant portion of the Third World was furthered by the 1976 agreement between the European Community and the Mahgreb states (Algeria, Morocco, and Tunisia). The signing of the Lomé II agreement (now extended to 57 states) is a clear sign that this strategy is being sustained despite many substantial difficulties in revising the agreement, and despite a shift in the interests and attention of the industrialized states away from the poorer supplies of raw materials (except oil) in favor of the more rapidly expanding economies of the newly industrializing countries (NICs).

Indeed, given their past successes with organized and protected marketing arrangements, the Europeans may wish to encourage further a North-South trade structure based on interregional agreements, various forms of mutually beneficial protectionism, and more or less overt discrimination against third parties (including the United States and Japan). With the financial power of West Germany theoretically available to support European efforts in both old and new Third World markets, EEC interests might reasonably expect to benefit by acquiring stable, guaranteed sources of raw materials (the ACP countries remain the EEC's biggest source of raw materials among the LDCs) in return for concessions such as privileges granted to Third World manufacturers (over 99 percent of total ACP exports to the EEC, by value, have gained duty free and nearly unrestricted entry).[24] Such an approach to North-South issues was behind the French proposals for the unproductive Conference on International Economic Cooperation, and characterized related themes of "organized free trade" or "orderly growth of trade," both viewed with natural and legitimate suspicion by proponents of free trade in the United States.

To be sure, intra-European differences should not be overlooked. However unwilling it may be to speak with one Atlantic voice, the EEC finds it difficult to speak with one European voice. Increasingly weary of any dirigiste scheme, satisfied with the national and international experience of the past 30 years, with no colonial ties to preserve but numerous emotional concerns to manage, West Germany continues to stand farthest away from LDC demands. Unlike the Dutch, who have sought the implementation of the integrated program adopted at UNCTAD IV "as quickly as possible,"

21

and unlike the French, who have on occasion asked that the world move toward a new international economic order, the Germans have insisted that any "new" order remain based on the steering principles of the free market, a free hand to the multinationals, and unhindered commodity supplies. Thus, the government in Bonn has objected to the creation of a common fund for commodities, opposed indexation, ruled out a debt moratorium, supported the additional capitalization of multilateral financial institutions, and dismissed the feasibility of automatic transfers of technology.[25] Accordingly, even the occasional "joint positions" reached by the Commission have usually been followed by so-called "explanations" that all but reject the resolution commonly agreed upon.[26]

In this regard, the Lomé agreements are especially significant. By limiting the Lomé benefits to economic exchanges between the ACP countries and the EEC only, the Europeans have clearly strengthened their control for the ACP markets, and the principal beneficiaries of the Lomé trade provisions have been the main EEC exporters. Thus, as shown in Table 3, exports to the ACP states rapidly doubled during the post-Lomé years (rising from 6,065 million European units of account (EUA) in 1974 to 12,460 million in 1977) even while ACP exports to the Nine fell enough to give the EEC and approximate trade equilibrium at first, then a trade surplus, that contrasted with the pre-Lomé trade deficit of the EEC with the ACP states. Furthermore, with a stabilization fund kept small (now amounting to 550 million EUA for agricultural commodities, and 280 million EUA for minerals, i.e., $372 million), the price for such a privileged relationship has proved to be rather moderate; by 1 July 1979, 270 million EUA had been transferred to 31 ACP states, including 22 grants worth 160 million EUA.[27]

Ultimately, Lomé might even permit in the future the legitimation of low prices for raw materials should, for example, a period of protracted crisis force prices down for several years in a row. As the price that is stabilized in a given year is the average price of the previous five years, a few years of sustained decline brings the average down in an orderly fashion. Concurrently, EEC concessions to third countries, at Lomé and elsewhere, have also had a serious and significant impact on U.S. exports of commodities

TABLE 3

EEC-ACP TRADE

'000 million EUA*

TREND OF EEC-ACP TRADE	1973	1974	1975	1976	1977	1978
Imports (extra-EEC) from the developing countries	31.9	61.4	55.0	70.0	75.2	71.2
of which OPEC	15.3	38.9	33.4	41.8	42.3	38.2
of which ACP	6.2	10.5	8.7	10.5	12.5	11.9
Annual grown (ACP)	+28%	+70%	-17%	+20%	+19%	- 5%
ACP share of extra-EEC imports	7.4%	8%	6.7%	6.6%	7.3%	6.7%
Exports (extra-EEC) to the developing countries	22.9	35.2	44.1	50.9	61.8	66.5
of which OPEC	6.6	11.4	18.4	24.1	29.7	31.1
of which ACP	4.4	6.1	8.1	9.8	12.5	12.7
Annual growth (ACP)	+10%	+37%	+33%	+22%	+27%	+2%
ACP share of extra-EEC exports	5.5%	5.3%	6.7%	7%	7.6%	7.3%
EEC-ACP trade balance	-1.7	-4.4	-0.6	-0.6	-0.0	+0.8

*EUA: European Unit of Account

Source: Statistical Office of the European Community.

such as tobacco, citrus products, and other processed fruits and vegetables. At times, they have virtually shut U.S. exporters out of EEC markets.[28]

The growing significance of the Third World in the global economy and for the domestic economies of industrial states accounts for the new agenda that places this issue in the forefront of allied concerns.[29] By 1977, EEC exports to all developing countries, including oil exporting states, had grown to 37.6 percent of total exports (43 percent of capital good exports), versus only 28.5 percent in 1973. By comparison, the United States took only 12.5 percent of EEC exports in 1977, and Eastern Europe only 8.9 percent. The lion's share of this Third World trade (also accounting for 44 percent of EEC imports in 1976) was concentrated in the oil-rich countries (18.1 percent) of EEC exports in 1977) and in the NICs, which represent the most rapidly expanding markets in the world, as well as the latest competitors for more traditional European products.[30] With the instability of markets in the industrialized countries of the West during the 1970s, the more constant growth of demand in those countries has been an important counter-cyclical factor in buoying up the economies of the EEC states. Thus, in 1975 while EEC exports to the United States fell by 17 percent and those to the EFTA countries by 3.3 percent, EEC exports to LDCs increased by 25 percent, those to the ACP countries alone by 33 percent.

The importance of this trade for individual allied countries is readily apparent: 25 percent of total exports from Great Britain and France go to the LDCs, 22 percent from Italy, and 17 percent from West Germany. In 1977, the Third World accounted for two-thirds of the EEC's surplus in the trade of manufactures even though the EEC exported more industrial products to the industrialized countries that same year.

France's surplus of industrial exports to developing economies (plus Eastern Europe) more than covered her mounting oil import bills. The traditional focus on French trade in the franc zone has given way to a strategy of market diversification throughout the developing world, even though by 1977 former colonies or protectorates still took 40 percent of all French exports to LDCs.[31]   This trend (also true of Great Britain) toward less concentration on ex-colonial and other traditional trading partners in the Third World is symptomatic of the diversification of market activities, and the expansion of competition into former "hunting preserves" of one industrial state or the other, and, therefore, the intensification of economic conflict among these states.

The implications for the United States are obvious, particularly as the Europeans (led by the Germans), and the Japanese as well, move into key Latin American markets such as Brazil and Mexico, even while the United States moves into such former European grounds as Algeria and Nigeria. It causes American concern for the future that Latin American markets would remain generally less protected from European penetration than African markets remain protected from American penetration (in spite of earlier U.S. programs of so-called tied aid), and that various political forces at work in Latin America would help welcome further the entry of non-U.S. interest in that region.[32]   In this respect, global interdependence has tended to create a ricochet effect as new competition in one regional market encourages firms to move into other areas as competitors of established foreign interests. Similarly, protectionist agreements between industrial states can encourage disadvantaged firms to compensate with more aggressive inroads into established export markets of the allied rival. Such has been the case, it seems with Japanese expansion into Latin America following antidumping agreements with the United States (or for that matter, the pressure on Japan to export more cars into the United States following the quantitative restrictions put on Japanese car imports into Great Britain).

Thus depressed and uncertain prosperity among industrialized states has encouraged them to seek relief among the more rapidly growing economies of the NICs and the oil rich. There are, to be sure, inconveniences and costs associated with this strategy. The most politically explosive one has been the loss of production and employment to competition in certain manufacturing sectors (textiles and clothing, leather goods and footwear, ceramics, woodwork, basic electronics, watches and clocks, bicycles and motorcycles, and some steel products). Although this is an awkward problem, and programs for massive transfers and retraining of workers are difficult to manage in practice, the overall net loss or gain in employment from Third World trade is hard to estimate. Belgium, Germany, and the Netherlands are probably experiencing small overall losses, while French studies estimate that there has been a net gain or 100,000 jobs between 1970 and 1976, and smaller gains are likely to continue (depending on the global economic scenario).[33]

In this expanding competition among industrialized countries for the benefits of trade with the Third World, the United States, Canada, and the United Kingdom have until recently been losing to the more aggressive and successful strategies of Japan and West Germany, as well as to those of Italy and France in a lesser degree. The U.S. share of developing country markets was down to 18.8 percent by 1977 (as compared to 25 percent in 1970), while more agile competitors have increased their share -- led by the Japanese gain from 12 percent to 13.7 percent of the market, including a $10 billion surplus with the key NIC group in 1977. More recently, however, this trend may have been reversed (or only sidetracked by the continuing devaluation of the dollar) as overall U.S sales to developing countries jumped by 11 percent in 1978 as a major boost to American exports. American business has, however, continued to concentrate on traditional U.S. trading partners in Latin America (49.1 percent of all exports to LDCs in 1978), where OECD competitors are making determined new efforts.[34] Future competition among industrial states for Third World markets is likely to be concentrated in the advanced technology sectors of new products and processes where the United States had once had many advantages but today finds formidable rivals in the Japanese and some European states.

V. COMPETITION FOR THIRD WORLD MARKETS: IMPLICATIONS FOR U.S. AND WESTERN EUROPE SECURITY INTERESTS

The likelihood of enhanced competition among industrial states for markets in the profitable Third World seems assured. What is less clear is the nature of the competition and the effect it may have on the relations these stages have with each other as political-military allies with networks of mutual security interests that span the globe.

In the economic arena these industrial states have been increasingly competitive with one another since the early 1960s, and their relations have been subject to numerous -- often bitter -- confrontations, negotiations, and agreements or understandings that seem to unravel shortly after they are reached. These conflicts and shifts in relative power have not, however, irreparably damaged the complex web of interdependence and mutual interest that binds these societies and economies together, no matter what particular configuration of interests and issues divide them at a given time.

The future course of economic competition in the Third World is likely to reflect the essentially ambivalent characteristic of the interallied political system as well, unless the world economy takes such a disastrous turn that contradictions are sharpened unbearably, while established ties and patterns of political behavior are fatally dismembered. Barring this most pessimistic scenario, however, industrial competitors will probably find it desirable to set limits and restraints on their economic conflicts in the 1980s for the sake of their broader collective interests as interdependent states and societies. Thus, for example, governments of industrial states realize that (despite the rhetoric they sometimes use) their competition in the Third World is mitigated by a common interest in resisting, whittling away, or diluting the Third World's more radical demands for "new economic orders" and a politically unacceptable (and domestically unmanageable) redistribution of global wealth from North to South. Whereas unrestricted competition among industrial states tends to divide them and assist radical forces (found at home as

27

well) in their aims, thus far the overwhelming common interest in blocking the immoderate goals of the "77" has in fact prevailed -- especially as the "moral legitimacy" of the Third World to unearned and unmerited rewards meets with growing skepticism.

If there are natural restraints and mutual concerns that mitigate economic competition, this situation is even more characteristic of the security arena where allied interests remain important despite the transformations in the nature and significance of allied ties discussed earlier. Security issues will probably become more visible and controversial among Atlantic governments in the next few years, including questions about security in the unstable areas of the Third World, especially the Middle East, the Indian Ocean, and Southern Africa (and possibly North Africa as well). Economic conflicts in such areas might, therefore, have to be restrained or controlled for the sake of an overall strategy of enhancing the West's presence and influence against mounting internal disorder and external penetration.

In some instances, to be sure, the immediate reconciliation of strategic interests in these areas may be difficult. This was seen most recently in Iran, for instance, a case in which Europe's support for the United States was muted by its concern over the implications a confrontation between Teheran and Washington over past and present U.S. policies toward Iran might have on Europe's well-being. In this regard, it should be noted that Atlantic unity in the Third World has occasionally been the prelude to fragmentation following the crisis, and vice versa. Thus, following the Cuban missile crisis, the Europeans were sharply critical of risks incurred under circumstances that were not of their own making -- even though they had been fully supportive of the U.S. position during the crisis. Conversely, a reluctance on the part of most European states to cooperate with the United States during the Middle East War of 1973 was followed by an Atlantic rapprochement immediately thereafter.

In instances when differences cannot be easily bridged, the United States must remain able and willing to act alone without prejudicing the balance of its relationship with allied states (including Japan) for the immediate future. Yet, in numerous other instances, when differences can indeed be bridged, there is room for effective cooperation in managing or preventing a crisis, as seen implicitly with the French in Zaire (and, most recently, in Tunisia), and explicitly with the British in Zimbabwe.

In many respects, Western Europe's role in the future world political economy, including its relationship to the United States and the Third World, remains ambiguous and characterized more by potential and ambitious rhetoric than by the immediate impact of any one concrete development. Allied resentment, however, is unabated at the U.S. government's inability to manage its domestic economy and especially to control the inflation that surplus dollars are said to carry throughout the international economy. As perceived in Europe, this privileged and destabilizing role for the dollar, undisciplined and inconvertible since the 1971 shock, has posed growing inconveniences for the European economies even if there are some substantial compensations, such as the reduced oil bills for allies who pay in devalued dollars. The European Monetary System (EMS), launched in early 1979, represents an attempt to restore some stability to EEC currency markets and create a basis for harmonizing the domestic economic policies of Community members.

This rather ambitious and as yet untested extension of European economic cooperation may prove to be no more than a device to create some coherence among European national economies by imposing German-style deflationary policies on the more inflation-prone systems of Italy, France, and Britain. It is still too early to ascertain whether the EMS and its proposed common currency unit may also emerge as a comprehensive challenge to the dollar and, therefore, to American domination of the international monetary system. Based on the past performance of the Europeans though, a measure of skepticism over their ability to mount successfully such a clear challenge may be appropriate. In any event, the American government's own inability to stabilize the dollar and control domestic inflation will continue to bear primary responsibility for this currency's declining role as an international medium of exchange and the ad hoc emergence of multiple alternatives such as SDRs, stronger marks or Swiss francs, and gold.

Modest expectations, if not outright skepticism, should perhaps also be a leitmotif for the future of a European Community expanded to include Greece and -- almost certainly -- Portugal as well as Spain. The political sentimentality that insists on extending EEC membership to emerging democracies in southern Europe may prove quite costly as the Community is saddled with a burgeoning diversity of social systems, political cultures, and economic problems of regional development and the like. Rather than stimulate the political progress of European unity, as many hope, the expansion may well debilitate unity further and reinforce visible European tendencies to turn inward to try to cope with the mounting social and economic problems that threaten the stability of states and often fragile societies.

Thus Western Europe's ability to enhance its own political and economic unity -- its will to assert further its own regional interests -- in reaction to the many issues plaguing the Atlantic and global systems is uncertain. Yet, it must not be dismissed out of hand simply because similar phases of self-assertiveness in the past proved to be inconclusive. To be sure, a more auspicious occasion was probably passed up during the 1960s, when the environment of rapid economic growth, spreading prosperity, and apparent domestic stability might have been mobilized in the service of structural cohesion or even confederation.

At the time, the effort failed for a number of reasons, including the resistance of other European countries (and the United States as well) to Gaullist-style leadership and abrasive French preten-sions. One underlying fear then was that France was fundamentally too weak and unstable, thus making West Germany inevitably the dominant power in any integrated European enterprise. This latter concern has, of course, been confirmed over the past few years, as the Federal Republic has remained a determining senior partner of the West European enterprise. The persistent reluctance to encourage unity as a vehicle for West German (or even Franco-German) hegemony remains one of the factors that seem to erode whatever logic there might otherwise be to stressing a separate West European identity from the United States. In this situation, and the inconvenient annoying -- although neither authoritarian nor usually arrogant --

leadership of a more distant and somewhat debilitate "superpower" is tolerable and even preferable as a counterweight to the unrelenting vitality and (now restrained) ambitions of German power in Europe.

The paradox of this situation -- probably convenient for all concerned, East as well as West -- is that the strongest economic and political power in Western Europe is also the one most dependent on the United States and NATO for psychological as well as physical security. Bonn is thus an unlikely leader of a rebellion, even if West Germany's new power and enhanced status must occasionally be asserted more forcefully than necessary by its leadership.

Finally, the contradictions and inconveniences of Europe's unenviable situation are exacerbated by the possibility that trends in the global economic division of labor have overtaken the EEC and may finally scuttle remaining European pretensions to economic unity or coherence. Thus, at best, the Community might act to protect some European interests and forge or strengthen some privileged ties to the Third World or the oil rich. But most key economic developments will in fact have to be guided by more flexible national governments on bilateral terms, by the multinationals for whom Western Europe is only one base for worldwide operations, and by broad-membership international organizations (including the OECD) capable of managing some sectors of the truly global economy that emerged during the 1970s.

In many ways, therefore, the factors transcending the European dimensions have reinforced the long-standing and extensive ties that bind together the fates of industrialized states that have survived the numerous and dramatic conflicts littering the history of U.S.-allied relations. The practice of regular summit meetings to establish joint priorities is only the most visible (and perhaps least effective) symbol of institutionalized cooperation and the continuing need of these states to manage jointly the economic challenges to their growth and well-being. The many common interests of the partially integrated "trilateral" economies do somehow seem to prevail over periodic crises and to defy worrisome trends such as growing protectionism and mercantilism.

The community of economic, political, and security interests that ties the United States to its allies may thus rule out coherent and decisive challenges to the United States based on a separate European (or Japanese) identity. It does not, however, exclude the possibility, even the likelihood, of selective issue by issue or sectoral collaboration in competition with the United States. This pattern has, in fact, been most characteristic of the partial and fragmented scope of European unity; it certainly applies to the arena of European relations with the Third World and reactions to aggressive American inroads into certain privileged markets or sectors (the sales of nuclear technology, for example).

Given the past inability of allies to mount consistent and successful challenges to the United States in the arena of political economy, and because of their continued dependence on the United States of security, one widespread expectation has been that this dependence can still be manipulated to secure advantages or concessions on economic issues. It seems, however, that this kind of leverage across conflicting areas is both less available and less susceptible to successful manipulation because of structural transformations in the allied security systems and, furthermore, because of an incapacity of beleaguered and bewildered governments to wield cumbersome foreign policy instruments for purposeful and sustained leverage. The two factors most responsible for the weakened American security leverage probably supersede administrative and leadership problems because they are embedded in the very nature of the contemporary international system. They are the partial, incomplete, but persistent long-range decline in the perception of the Soviet threat on the part of American allies, and the steady erosion in the value of the superpower defense guarantee that underlay the original bargains struck at the creation of these alliance systems.

Although detente has its limitations, the Soviet violations of Western expectations (in Africa, Afghanistan, and elsewhere) regularly dispel the illusions of Pollyannas, the West European political investment in detente is substantial enough to ensure that these governments will bend over backwards to avoid any significant revival of East-West tensions in

Europe. Important domestic forces have numerous
interests in sustaining the sense of a declining or
dormant threat from the East.   The dominant economic
and political power represented in the Federal Republic
has, through Ostpolitik, forged an overwhelming
national commitment to detente as the vehicle for
peacefully resolving the problems of Germany's division
and the slow development of new ties between the two
halves of this divided nation.

To be sure, this West European commitment does not
prevent Alliance members from devoting new resources to
bolster the theater balance in Western Europe, a
balance that is in any case perceived as a prerequisite
for sustaining detente.   But a revived concern over
Soviet military capabilities in Europe should not be
confused with the creation of Cold War-type tensions
that might resuscitate the Atlantic Alliance as an
American instrument capable of structuring and managing
a range of Western policies beyond the security arena.
It seems more likely that the increased attention paid
to common defense problems will bear limited returns
and will not undermine the more independent political
or economic wills of allied states, or their ability to
challenge American policies and actions when required
by individual or collective interests.   Only if such
distancing is allowed can the Alliance endure.

The other factor reducing American leverage is the
evolution of the strategic balance between the United
States and the Soviet Union.   This new balance (if not
marginal Soviet superiority) is unlikely to change
significantly in the foreseeable future.   In the
context of this discussion, it means that the United
States is less able to guarantee the security of its
allies in Europe (or Asia) because the surplus of
strategic nuclear power essential to extending assured
protection to distant allies has evaporated.   Whatever
the course of detente, this situation cannot be altered
except by long-range and expensive defense programs,
whose enactment remains doubtful at this time.   Thus,
American allies are to some extent victims of declining
American power, because Washington has an obvious
interest in qualifying its external strategic commitments and retaining a maximum amount of freedom to make
crisis decisions that are bound at times to put allied
interests behind those of the United States.   In war,
of course, there are sanctuaries and there are

battlefields -- and underlying the dialectic of American-allied conflicts since the late 1950s (if not earlier) is that when choices have to be made, Europe is bound to be the battlefield while presidents struggle to keep North America a sanctuary.

West Europeans can therefore be excused for a certain schizophrenia, regretting and fretting over the long-declining validity of the nuclear guarantee, while simultaneously rejoicing that the combined effect of devalued American protection and a seemingly reduced Soviet threat is one of more freedom and flexibility for American allies. This is an anomalous situation. The frustrations and conflicts inherent in the trans- formed Western system are enhanced by the fact that, regardless of their capability, neither Western Europe nor Japan are willing to provide for their own security, individually or collectively. They must calculate their opposition or accommodation to American interests according to basically incalculable estimates of the present and future relevance of military dependence.

The logical alternative to this unwelcome and uncomfortable situation might be attempts by the allies to establish stronger defense capabilities that would be more independent of the United States. In the case of Japan, however, constitutional and political restrictions seem likely to continue restraining the growth of Japanese defense forces. The nuclear option, which is the sine qua non of independent security, seems unavailable because of Japan's unique experience in innoculating the population against nuclear weapons. For Western Europe, periodic attempts to move European cooperation into the defense realm as a basis for independence have been frustrated by the persistence of intra-European rivalries that make it difficult at best to conceive of a multilateral West European defense system that would institutionalize the decision-making input of a number of states so as to ensure all of them that their interests would be protected, and, finally, would create the illusion of multilateral equality while somehow constraining West Germany and preventing German fingers from reaching nuclear triggers.

The inability to design or promote a mutually acceptable defense arrangement was fatal to the

European Defense Community, to the Multilateral Force, and for the Gaullist schemes. It is also true that no plan providing for European nuclear independence could attempt the United States to support the dangerous transition from an American-dominated Atlantic system to an autonomous European one. Despite periodic speculation and the often compelling logic of further European autonomy in this arena as well, it remains unlikely that the basic Atlantic solution to problems of West European defense and deterrence will be challenged with success in the foreseeable future (that is, in the 1980s).[35]

The arguments advanced here do not imply that the security dimension of the interallied politics has lost its significance, that NATO and bilateral defense agreements will cease to have some influence over a wider range of issues and allied behavior, or that the Atlantic defense system will not experience revived antagonisms that are not so evident at this time. It does seem clear, however, that military alliances and security dependence are unlikely and unwieldy instruments for forcing government into line on matters largely extraneous to joint military defense and security. It is true, as Henry Kissinger insisted during the "Year of Europe," that issues and interests are linked and economic conflicts can obviously affect political and defense relations among allies. But the most significant lesson of recent experiences with explicit linkages and trade-offs is that it is preferable not to encourage or exploit the natural tendency of issues to "spill over" and poison the broader pool of allied relations.

In particular, the more pluralistic structures of contemporary Western defense ties are relatively unsusceptible to this kind of manipulation, up to a point, regardless of the administration that is in power in Washington at a given time. The multilateral structure of security ties with the United States serves a useful and even indispensable variety of purposes for its allies, but the inherent fragility of these relationships in the evolving international system suggest that they should not be subject to extraneous and ill-conceived pressures that might unravel a mutually beneficial security arrangement.

This conclusion is perhaps not a very dramatic guideline for relating intra-alliance problems with the often confusing mixture of competition and cooperation that increasingly characterize allied affairs in the Third World. In an international system where relationships based on a genuine (however transformed) community of interests are rare and therefore quite valuable, it seems imperative to order one's priorities toward stabilizing the obviously beneficial ties while still permitting the broad flexibility, freedom of action, and diversity reflective of the member states today. Indeed, this global flexibility and pluralism within a recognized community of interests -- what Henry Kissinger used to call "the boundaries of permissible differences" -- has been the major source of vitality and strength for the West. The management of this type of loose allied structure has never been more difficult or more challenging that it is today; nor has the required skill and talent ever seemed so indispensible to the mutual well-being and security of allied governments.

Unfortunately, such flexibility has provided to be singularly lacking of late, as a decade of detente between the superpowers has come to an end, while a troubled decade of renewed tensions and possible military clashes à la Fashoda appears to have begun. For, if anything, the crisis in Iran and the Soviet invasion of Afghanistan have confirmed the realities of intra-allied differences over issues that are of vital importance to all.

Vis-à-vis Iran, an uneven dependence of the United States and the European states on Iranian oil naturally made the coordination of policy especially difficult when the implementation of specific sanctions against the Khomeini regime was considered following the seizure of the U.S. embassy. With much of their oil coming from Iran, France and West Germany are more vulnerable than the United States to the counter-reprisals that might follow such sanctions. That it was nevertheless possible to achieve the semblance of a consensus on sanctions following many weeks of assiduous consultations is a tribute to the persistence of the Carter administration. That such sanctions were then put aside by Washington without much consultation, thereby leaving some of the European states with the distinct feeling that they were left in the unenviable position of being more American than the Americans, promises a new wave of recriminations against the unreliability of a partner who all too often says what it wants, but then fails to do what it says.

Even before the end of the crisis, therefore, it is apparent that there will be a bitter trial in Europe of the U.S. policies before, during, and after the capture of American hostages, with the implicit support of the Iranian government. The focus of such criticism is easy to foresee. To the states of Western Europe, Iran may have shown once more -- and in the most vivid fashion -- that the American connection is not so desirable in the Third World where European interests are threatened by the consequences of uncertain U.S. policies. The theme -- annihilation wthout consultation -- is one that was popular after the Cuban missile crisis in the early 1960s: it applied then primarily to issues of physical security. In the early 1980s it may regain new popularity after Iran, and will apply primarily to issues of economic security.

In a sense the allies may come to see the events in Iran and in Afghanistan as the latest expressions of the decline, or even irrelevance, of the U.S. deterrent. That the Carter administation would have been sufficiently moved by these events to adjust its policies to "the world as it is," and in effect run a presidential campaign against its own record, may have swayed an American public anxious to close ranks under the pressure of adverse international circumstances. It does little, however, to assuage the anxieties entertained in Paris and in Bonn. There, widespread calls for a "division of labor" that would avoid the vain and self-defeating search for a coordinated, all-or-nothing attitude of all alliance partners may well open the door to a formal redistribution of roles in a way that will expose further the growing separation between the two sides of the Atlantic doomed to remain, at one and the same time, allies and adversaries in search of a mutual balance of satisfaction in the Third World.[36]

[1]I am especially indebted to my friend and colleague at SAIS, Professor Michael Harrison, for his assistance in defining and clarifying some of the ideas developed in this essay.

[2]Consider, for example, the French contention, shortly after the outbreak of the Korean war, that their colonial war in Indochina was "the same war against the same enemy, for the same cause and at the same price of the same sacrifices," as stated by General de Lattre de Tassigny, then commander of the French forces, during an official visit in Washington, D.C., in September 1950. French Embassy Service de Presse et d'Information (20 September 1959), p. 2. For an analysis of the effectiveness of a national nuclear force within the framework of the Alliance see such early writing of General Andre Beaufre as Deterrence and Strategy (New York: Praeger, 1965).

[3]As Herbert Feis noted in early 1947: "We are using [our command over the dollar] regularly to do the work done during the war by the Lend Lease program. We are favoring the countries which we trust; using loans to prove our good will to rulers inclined to bargain; encouraging countries that are denying those we fear." "Diplomacy of the Dollar," Atlantic Monthly, vol. 179, January 1947, p. 26.

[4]The juxtaposition of economic concessions to Europe by the United States versus political acceptance of the United States by Western European states should not be extended too far. For instance, it is just too simple to argue, as some observers have, that the Truman administration "bought" de Gasperi's decision to expel the communists from his government in late May 1947. As I have tried to show elsewhere ("An International Anomaly: the United States and the Community Parties in France and in Italy, 1945-1947," Studies in Comparative Communism, Spring/Summer, 1975), it is quite likely instead that de Gasperi himself used the need for U.S. aid as a justification for a decision otherwise imposed upon him by domestic circumstances that remained independent of U.S. pressures. After May 1947, the national delegitimization of the Italian

and other West European communist parties was the result of the policies which they themselves chose to follow, at home and abroad.

[5]As reported by Dean Acheson, Clayton's memorandum (27 May 1947) began by stating: "It is now obvious that we have grossly underestimated the destruction of the European economy by the war." The memorandum concluded: "We must avoid getting into another UNRRA. The United States must run this show." Dean Acheson, Present at the Creation: My Years at the State Department (New York: Norton, 1969), p. 231.

[6]Initially, the EEC's common tariff was averaged arithmetically without consideration of the value of goods imported in each case. Thus the two low tariff countries (the Benelux, regarded as one single unit, and West Germany) counted as much as the two high tariff countries (France and Italy) even though they represented about two thirds of the Community's imports. In addition, such calculations did not take into account some earlier tariff reductions in Germany and in Italy, and, in a number of instances, pushed up the arithmetic average no matter how calculated. This conveniently placed the EEC in a stronger position to bargain with any state seeking to negotiate mutual tariff reductions, as would be seen subsequently.

[7]U.S. merchandise exports to the EEC grew from $4 billion in 1960 to $8.4 billion in 1970. During those years, U.S. merchandise imports grew at about the same pace, from $3.2 billion to $6.6 billion.

[8]As quoted in Arthur M. Schlesinger, Jr., A Thousand Days: John F. Kennedy in the White House (Boston: Houghton Mifflin, 1965), pp. 654-55.

[9]Bevin's remark is quoted in R. B. Manderson-Jones, The Special Relationship: Anglo-American Relations and Western European Unity, 1947-1956 (New York: Crane, Russak, 1972), p. 23. Churchill's comment is found in Alfred Grosser, Les Occidentaux: Les Etats Unis et l'Europe Depuis la Guerre (Paris: Fayard, 1978).

[10]"Not the result of enthusiasm," Georges Bidault said of the North Atlantic Pact during the debates at the French National Assembly, "but the fruit of a very

grave disappointment and ... a very heavy fear." See my France, de Gaulle and Europe: The Policy of the Fourth and Fifth Republics Toward the Continent (Baltimore: Johns Hopkins University Press, 1968), p. 33. See also Michael Harrison, The Reluctant Ally (forthcoming, 1980).

[11]Quoted in Gerald Freund, Germany Between Two Worlds (New York: Harper & Row, 1961), p. 115.

[12]Louis Halle, "The Cracked Alliance." New Republic, 23, 1963, pp. 17-20; Robert Pfaltzgraff, The Atlantic Community: A Complex Imbalance (New York: Van Nostrand Reinhold, 1969); Robert Shaetzel, The Unhinged Alliance: America and the European Community (New York: Harper & Row, 1975); and Anton de Porte, Europe Between the Superpowers: The Enduring Balance (New Haven and London: Yale University Press, 1979).

[13]Henry Kissinger, The Troubled Partnership. A Reappraisal of the Atlantic Alliance (New York: McGraw Hill, 1965), p. 40.

[14]Stanley Hoffman, Gulliver's Troubles, or the Setting of American Foreign Policy (New York: McGraw Hill, 1968), p. 475.

[15]Robert A. Packenham, Liberal America and the Third World (Princeton, New Jersey: Princeton University Press, 1973), p. 318.

[16]Vietnam is a case in point. Yet to explain the war, as Gabriel Kolko does, as "an American intervention against a nationalist, revolutionary agrarian movement which embodies social elements in incipient and similar forms of development in numerous other Third World nations, "--to make, in other words, of the Vietnam war the expression of a consistent reality said to be, by Harry Magdoff for example, "nothing less than keeping as much as possible of the world open for trade and investment by the giant multinational corporations," is to misunderstand the evolution of postwar U.S. foreign policy, neglect inconsistencies written into the very manner in which such policies were conceptualized and implemented, and misrepresent the realities and perceptions of U.S. interests in those years. (Gabriel Kolko, The Roots of American

Foreign Policy, Boston: Beacon Press, 1969, p. 89; and Harry Magdoff, The Age of Imperialism, New York: Monthly Review Press, 1969, p. 14.)

[17]Cited in Romano Prodi and Alberto Clo, "Europe," Daedalus, Fall 1975, p. 104.

[18]See my "Une Politique Etrangère Introuvable," Politique Internationale, Winter 1979-1980, and "Brzezinski: Play It Again, Zbig," Foreign Policy, Fall 1978.

[19]Reported in the Washington Post, 20 April 1978.

[20]Claude Cheysson is the European commissioner responsible for development. See his "The Policy of Europe Towards Development: Generalized Preferences and the Lomé Convention," in Pierre Uri, ed., North-South: Developing a New Relationship (Paris: Atlantic Institute for International Affairs, 1975), p. 39.

[21]See Commission of the European Communities, "Instruments of Mining and Energy Cooperation with the ACP Countries," COM (79) 130, 14 March 1979, p. 3, and "The Raw Materials Dossier," Background Paper, 1976, p. 12; see also Michael Noelke, "Europe and the Third World. A Study on Interdependence," Dossiers, Commission of the European Communities, Series Development No. 2 (Brussels: February 1979), and Wolfgang Hager, Europe's Economic Security: Non-Energy Issues in the International Political Economy (Paris: Atlantic Institute for International Affairs, 1975), p. 43.

[22]Of late, however, following the Shaba crises and the revolution in Iran, European countries have shown an increasing interest in strategic mineral stock-piling. Started in 1975, the French stock is believed to exceed $70 million, with an additional $12 million scheduled to be spent annually for five years beginning in 1980. Since early 1979, West Germany too has been investigating various stockpiling schemes, especially for chromium, manganese, and asbestos (ranked 1, 2, and 3 in a "danger list" that lists a number of key minerals on a risk factor scale) and cobalt (in shortage since the escalation of Zaire's political problems). While a coordinated European commodity stockpile seems a long way off, the European

Commission is nevertheless looking into this question. See the Wall Street Journal, 26 February 1979, and the German Tribune, 8 April 1979.

[23]Commission of the European Communities, "Community Energy Policy," 7 March 1979. Cited in Robert J. Lieber, "Les Malentendus Transatlantiques et la Seconde Crise de l'Energie," Politique Etrangère, October 1979, p. 95.

[24]Although France has provided the lion's share of unharmonized EEC official development aid (about $2.25 billion in 1977), West Germany has been in clear second place (about $1.4 billion in 1977). See The Economist, 27 October 1979.

[25]See my "Conciliation and Confrontation: A Strategy for North-South Relations," Orbis, Spring 1978, pp. 47-61.

[26]In theory, France has remained the country most willing to differ publicly with its EEC partners. But in practice, where Bonn has offered pre-emptive explanations, Paris has often offered confusing contradictions: now against, now for, resolutions which, whatever the technicalities involved, state essentially the same thing.

[27]Commission of the European Communities, Information, "A New Cooperation Contract," Brussels 1979. Also, Europe Information, "EEC-ACP Trade Relations," December 1978. Notice that EEC trade represents approximately 40 percent of total ACP trade, as compared to ACP's 7 percent share of total EEC trade. The results of the first four months of 1979 show the reappearance of the community's trade deficit.

[28]Omero Sabatini, "The EEC and its Special Third Country Partnerships," Foreign Agriculture, 21 February 1977, p. 3.

[29]Between 1963 and 1977, total OECD exports of manufacturers to NIC markets increased from $5 billion to $49 billion. The NICs share of OECD exports rose from 7.6 percent to 9.2 percent during the same period, whereas the rest of the nonoil rich developing world fell from 14.2 percent of the OECD export market to 8.7 percent.

[30]Europe and the Third World, op. cit., p. 53; see also The Impact of the Newly Industrialized Countries in Production and Trade in Manufactures, Report by the Secretary General for the OECD, Paris, 1979.

[31]Yves Berthelot and Gerard Tardy, Le Défi Economique du Tiers Monde (Paris: La Documentation Francaise, 1979).

[32]Notice also the growing interest of the EEC in the ASEAN countries. With the Community's share in ASEAN external trade down from over 20 percent in 1960 to under 15 percent in 1976, the EEC countries are seeking new agreements that, as the EEC Commission seets it, would permit the five ASEAN states "to achieve a better balance as between different economic partners." See "The European Community and ASEAN," Europe Information Commission of the European Communities, 16/79, February 1979.

[33]Berthelot and Tardy, op. cit. See also the discussion found in the appendix of the OECD study, op. cit., and Europe and the Third World, op. cit., p. 82. To this day, the issue of safeguard remains the only unfinished piece of business of the Tokyo Round. Worried that selective safeguards would be applied against them systematically, the NICs (and other LDCs) argue for a general safeguard that the EEC countries (as well as Japan and the United States) are more reluctant to accept.

[34]Thus, French exports to such key markets in Latin America as Argentina, Brazil, and Mexico have grown substantially faster than U.S. exports during the period 1973-1978.

Importing Country	Percent Increase, 1973-1978	
	France	United States
Argentina	124	87
Brazil	91	55
Mexico	171	127

Source: As calculated from IMF, <u>Direction of Trade</u> by
Lawrence G. Franko and S. Stephenson, "French
Export Competitiveness in Third World
Markets," <u>Significant Issues Series</u>, vol. 2,
no. 6, (Washington, D.C.: Center for
Strategic and International Studies 1980).

[35]For an example of such speculation, see my
<u>Fading Partnership: American and Europe after Thirty
Years</u> (New York: Praeger, 1979), pp. 36-42.

[36]<u>Washington Post</u>, 31 January 1980, p. 16.

2

U.S. EXPORT COMPETITIVENESS IN MANUFACTURES IN THIRD WORLD MARKETS

Raymond F. Mikesell
Mark G. Farah

CONTENTS

Introduction

I. An Overview of U.S. Export Performance, 1962 to 1978

Regional Distribution of Exports of Manufactures to the LDCs, 1970-1978

II. The Commodity Structure and Market Distribution of U.S. Export Performance

Changes in U.S. Shares of Individual Commodity Exports in the Overall LDC Market

Shifts in U.S. Export Shares: Technology-Intensive vs. Non-technology-Intensive Commodities

Commodity Structure of U.S. Exports and Exports of its Principal Competitors by LDC Region

Central America
South America
The Caribbean
Far East and South Asia
Middle East/Non-OPEC and Africa/Non-OPEC
OPEC

III. Measures of Price and Cost Competitiveness in U.S. Export Performance

Relative Price and Cost Indexes

Comparisons of Measures of Price and Cost Competitiveness

Relative Price and Cost Indexes and U.S. Export Shares in Manufacturing

IV. An Analysis of U.S. Export Competitiveness in Manufactures in the LDC Market

Introduction

This study examines U.S. export performance in manufactured commodities in the less developed countries (LDCs) during the 1970s by a disaggregated analysis of changes in U.S. market shares in the LDC markets.[1] The analysis is designed to reveal the areas of weakness and strength in U.S. export performance relative to that of its major competitors and to suggest the causal factors in the deterioration of U.S. export performance. This study is limited to manufactured exports since the U.S. competitive position in agricultural products has been fairly well maintained, and in the short run exports are largely affected by worldwide crop variations. Moreover, international trade in nonmanufactures generally is subject to influences that cannot be explained by short-run changes in the measures of export competitiveness.

U.S. export performance in manufactures is affected both by developments within particular markets and by changes in U.S. competitive strength relative to that of competing exporting countries. The former include shifts in consumer demand within the LDCs, import-substituting production, and import restrictions. Our objective here, however, is to concentrate on U.S. export performance vis-a-vis other exporting countries, given the LDC import market environment within which exporters operate. For this reason, our analysis is in terms of export shares in particular commodities and in particular LDC markets. It should be noted that LDC markets are greatly influenced by the activities of foreign firms. Market penetration in the LDCs by foreign firms may take the form of exports of finished products, the establishment of producing affiliates in the LDC markets, and by the transfer of technology to nonaffiliate firms by licensing or construction and engineering contracts. Both foreign investments and technology transfer to nonaffiliated firms may constitute a form of export marketing strategy, since they may facilitate the creation of a market for components of production in the LDC market. Moreover, multinational firms not only export commodities, but technology, management, and other productive factors. This dimension of export competitiveness is explored in a companion study in this series by Jack N. Behrman and Raymond F. Mikesell, entitled "The Impact of U.S. Foreign Direct Investment on U.S. Export Competitiveness in LDC Markets."[2]

The primary measure of U.S. export performance employed in this study is the U.S. export share in the LDC market. Changes in export shares are independent of changes in the size of the overall LDC market. We do distinguish, however, between export performance and export competitiveness in that the latter takes account of differential rates of growth in individual regional LDC markets. If the United States maintains its export share in each of the LDC regional markets over a given period, but the individual regional markets grow at different rates over the period, U.S. export competitiveness does not change. Nevertheless, U.S. overall export performance in the LDC market as measured by its export share may change.

The decline in the U.S. export share of the LDC markets during the 1960s and 1970s, and the year-to-year changes in U.S. market shares during periods since 1962, raise the central questions with which this study is concerned. In which commodities and in which LDC regional markets did the United States lose or gain export shares? Which competing exporting countries gained and which ones lost as measured by their export shares? What were the production characteristics (e.g., technology intensity, physical capital intensity or human capital intensity) of the commodities for which U.S. export shares showed substantial shifts? How much of the year-to-year changes in U.S. export shares can be explained by changes in U.S. relative prices and costs? These and other explanations for the changes in U.S. export performance in the LDCs constitute the primary objective of this study.

An important long-term factor accounting for shifts in shares in the export markets among countries is structural changes in the world economy. Since World War II the Western European economies and Japan have grown much faster than the U.S. economy. This is partly a consequence of the reconstruction of their wartime economies, but there were also other factors such as the creation of the European Community and the

social and political changes within Japan that have
resulted in a high rate of growth in that country
necessarily accompanied by a rapid expansion of trade.
Some of the developing countries have also had high
growth rates during the post-World War II period, and
have been transformed from largely primary producing
economies to economies with large modern industrial
sectors. It is inevitable that these structural
changes in the world economy would be reflected in the
loss of U.S. export shares. Despite differences in
national rates of growth, both overall and among
sectors, relative changes in national wealth and
sectoral distribution take place slowly. Moreover, we
are concerned with a relatively short period,
1970-1978, during which the United States had a
merchandise deficit in six of the nine years, as
contrasted with merchandise surpluses in every year of
the post-World War II period prior to 1971. The
dramatic changes in U.S. export performance during the
1970s cannot be attributed in any significant degree to
world structural changes of the kind referred to above.
Differential rates of growth among exporting countries
can account for no more than a small portion of the
year-to-year changes in U.S. shares of the export
markets of the LDCs during the 1970-1978 period.

A unique characteristic of this study is the
relatively high degree of disaggregation employed. We
have based our export commodity analysis on 73 manufactured commodities exported to 76 countries that we have
grouped into seven LDC regions. In addition to U.S.
exports to these countries, we analyze those of Japan,
Western Germany, the United Kingdom, France, and Italy,
plus five other OECD countries and four LDC exporting
countries (Brazil, Hong Kong, Mexico, and South Korea).
The latter nine countries are referred to in the text
as the "residual group" and in the tables as "other."
The four LDC exporting countries are referred to as the
NICs (Newly Industrialising Countries). The data for
this degree of disaggregation is only available for the
1970-1978 period and was made available through the
Georgetown University Center for Strategic and International Studies in Washington, D.C. Overall data on
manufactures to the LDCs by major exporting country for
the 1962-1977 period was obtained from the Organization
for Economic Cooperation and Development (OECD) in
Paris.

I. AN OVERVIEW OF U.S. EXPORT PERFORMANCE, 1962-1978

In 1978 total world exports reached just over $1.3 trillion, of which $788 billion represented exports of manufactures. Total U.S. exports in 1978 were $138 billion, of which nearly $93 billion represented manufactures. Of the total world exports of manufactured goods, Third World countries (OPEC and other developing countries) imported nearly $200 billion in 1978, and nearly $36 billion of that market was supplied by manufactured exports from the United States.

The U.S. share of total world exports was 13.8 percent in 1962, but declined to 13.2 percent in 1978. The U.S. share of total exports of manufactured goods to the world was 15.2 percent in 1962, declining to 11.8 percent in 1978; this represents a decline of 22.4 percent. The U.S. share of world exports of manufactures to the LDCs was 24.3 percent in 1962, but declined to 17.9 percent in 1978; this represents a decline of 26.3 percent. It may be seen that although the share of U.S. exports of world manufactured goods to the LDCs has been consistently higher than the U.S. shares of both total world exports and world exports of manufactures, the decline in the U.S. share of world exports of manufactured exports to the LDCs has been relatively greater than the decline in the U.S. share of either total world exports or of world exports of manufactures to all areas.[3]

The U.S. share of manufactured exports by the OECD countries to the LDCs declined from 36.4 percent in 1962 to 22.3 percent in 1977, and related data show a further decline to about 22.0 percent in 1978.[4] The largest decline in the U.S. market share occurred between 1962 and 1965, and there was a further substantial decline in the U.S. market share after 1968. The U.S. share of OECD countries manufactured exports to the LDCs declined from 29.2 percent in 1968 to 21.8 percent in 1978, or by about 25.4 percent (Table I-1).

The data bank on exports of manufactures to 76 LDCs prepared for this study covers the exports of the United States plus those of ten other developed

TABLE I.1

MARKET SHARE ANALYSIS OF MANUFACTURED EXPORTS OF OECD COUNTRIES TO LDCS
(1962-1978)
(percentages)

	United States	Japan	FRG	United Kingdom	France	Italy
1962	36.39	11.43	10.94	14.95	9.24	4.20
1963	35.63	12.77	10.94	14.76	9.78	4.41
1964	35.12	13.66	10.91	13.62	9.66	4.47
1965	29.18	16.47	11.94	14.49	9.70	4.99
1966	29.33	16.94	11.98	13.51	9.24	5.12
1967	29.40	17.93	12.08	12.19	9.44	5.25
1968	29.22	19.21	11.60	11.38	9.34	5.64
1969	28.65	20.72	11.40	11.90	8.95	5.43
1970	27.05	20.72	11.22	11.35	8.90	4.97
1971	24.70	23.14	11.34	12.33	8.52	4.98
1972	22.72	23.78	11.31	11.30	8.73	5.70
1973	23.61	24.89	12.30	9.54	8.74	4.78
1974	24.18	26.03	12.96	8.21	8.11	5.28
1975	24.65	23.26	12.32	8.98	9.57	5.85
1976	24.40	23.96	12.78	8.35	9.24	5.47
1977	22.29	25.13	13.21	9.06	9.45	6.35
1978	21.8	n.a	n.a	n.a	n.a	n.a

Source: OECD data, Paris, 1979.

countries and four NICs for the period 1970-1978. Manufactured exports to the LDCs covered in our data bank constitute about 80 percent of all imports of manufactured goods by the LDCs in 1978.[5] Between 1970 and 1978 the U.S. market share of exports of manufactures to the 76 LDCs covered by our data bank declined from 28.3 percent to 22.1 percent, or by 21.9 percent. Japan's share, on the other hand, rose from 21.8 percent in 1970 to 26.1 percent in 1978, or by 19.7 percent (see Table I-2). The decline of 6.2 percentage points in the U.S. market share over this period was nearly matched by the 4.3 percentage point rise in the Japanese share plus the 1.7 percentage point rise in the share of the four NICs. This left only 0.2 of a percentage point to be accounted for by the increase in aggregate shares of the other developed countries. Italy was the largest gainer after Japan with an increase of 1.5 percentage points, whereas the United Kingdom was the largest loser after the United States with a loss of 1.8 percentage points. Germany was also a substantial gainer by about 1.3 percentage points, whereas significant losses in relative terms occurred for Canada and Australia (see Table I-2).

Even if we assume there were structural factors in both Japan and the four NICs that accounted in part for the combined 6 percentage point rise in their share of the LDC market over the 1970-1978 period, it would be difficult to demonstrate that these same structural factors were responsible for virtually the same percentage point decline in the U.S. share of the LDC market over this period. The index of industrial production in the United States rose by 34.5 percent during the 1970-1978 period as contrasted with 32.8 percent for Japan, 16.5 percent for Germany, 10.1 percent for Italy, and 35.6 percent for Canada.[6] There is no basis for believing that structural factors prevented other countries as a group from absorbing their proportionate share of the increased share of the LDC market captured by Japan and the four NICs.

TABLE I-2

MARKET SHARES FOR MANUFACTURED EXPORTS TO THE LDCS
BY 15 SELECTED COUNTRIES, 1970 and 1978
(percentages)

Country	1970	1978
United States	28.3	22.1
Japan	21.8	26.1
FRG	12.4	13.7
United Kingdom	11.6	9.8
France	8.0	8.2
Italy	5.2	6.7
Other Developed Countries		
Canada	2.4	1.5
Netherlands	2.3	2.4
Sweden	1.8	1.7
Switzerland	2.6	3.0
Australia	0.9	0.5
NICs		
Brazil	0.6	0.8
South Korea	0.2	1.7
Mexico	0.4	0.2
Hong Kong	1.4	1.6

Source: CSIS Data Bank prepared for U.S. Export Competitiveness Proj

Regional Distribution of Exports of Manufactures
to the LDCs, 1970-1978

During the 1970-1978 period there were substantial shifts in the regional distribution of manufactured exports by the 15 exporting countries to the LDCs. The percentage of total manufactured exports to LDCs in our sample declined significantly between 1970 and 1978 for Central America, South America, Caribbean, and Africa/ Non-OPEC, but the percentage of total exports going to OPEC countries rose from 21.1 percent in 1970 to 41.1 percent in 1978. The percentage going to the Far East and South Asia declined moderately over the period while the percentage of exports to the Middle East/ Non-OPEC region remained virtually unchanged (see Table I-3 and Figure I-1). This pattern suggests that any country that maintained the same market share in each of the regional markets in 1978 that it had in 1970, but had a relatively small share of the OPEC market would have lost a substantial portion of its market share in the seven LDC regions taken as a group. Although the United States lost market shares in percentage terms between 1970 and 1978 in every region but the Caribbean -- its largest losses in market shares in terms of percentage points were in South America and the OPEC countries, followed by the Far East and South Asia (Table I-4). These three regions accounted for 76.3 percent of total manufactured exports of all exporting countries to all LDCs in 1978 as against 66.9 percent in 1970. The major single reason for the overall U.S. loss in its market share for manufactured exports in the LDCs was the failure of U.S. exports to the OPEC region to grow in line with the overall growth of exports to those countries. The loss of U.S. export shares in South America and the Far East and South Asia were also important contributing factors.

In 1970 over 52 percent of U.S. manufactured exports to all LDCs in our sample went to the Western Hemisphere LDCs, with another 22 percent going to the Far East and South Asia (see Table I-5 and Figure I-2). By 1978 Western Hemisphere LDCs accounted for only 37 percent of U.S. exports to all LDCs, but U.S. exports to the OPEC countries had risen from about 17 percent in 1970 to nearly 34 percent in 1978. The OPEC market, however, grew more rapidly than U.S.

TABLE I-3

MANUFACTURED EXPORTS BY ALL EXPORTING COUNTRIES TO EACH REGION AS A PERCENTAGE OF TOTAL MANUFACTURED EXPORTS TO ALL LDCS (1970-1978)
(percentage)

Region	1970	1971	1972	1973	1974	1975	1976	1977	1978
1. Central America	11.03	9.59	10.24	10.08	10.03	8.76	8.71	7.29	8.05
2. South America	16.56	16.26	16.10	14.76	16.22	13.06	10.62	9.92	9.29
3. Caribbean	3.73	3.36	3.16	2.66	2.09	1.87	1.70	1.51	1.43
4. Far East & South Asia	29.32	29.12	28.20	29.98	26.94	21.82	22.24	22.79	26.00
5. Middle East/ Non-OPEC	8.18	8.24	8.29	8.32	8.24	8.66	8.66	8.39	8.01
6. Africa/ Non-OPEC	10.08	11.20	9.81	9.62	8.74	8.15	7.73	7.49	6.12
7. OPEC	21.10	22.23	24.20	24.58	27.74	37.68	40.34	42.61	41.10
TOTALS	100.00	100.00	100.00	100.00	100.00	100.00	100.00	100.00	100.00

Source: CSIS Data Bank prepared for the U.S. Export Competitiveness Project.

FIGURE I-1

MANUFACTURED EXPORTS BY ALL EXPORTING COUNTRIES TO
EACH REGION AS A PERCENTAGE OF TOTAL MANUFACTURED EXPORTS
TO ALL LDCs (1970-1978)
(PERCENTAGE)

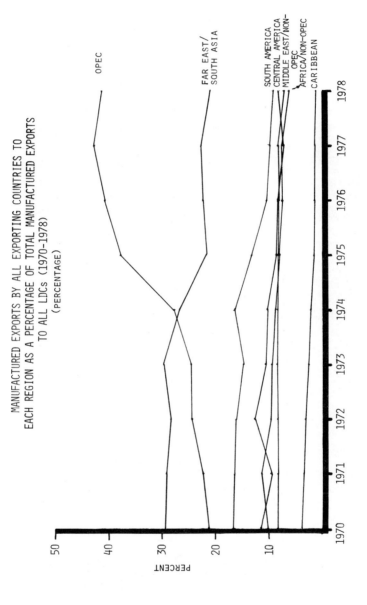

TABLE I-4

MARKET SHARES FOR U.S. MANUFACTURED EXPORTS
BY REGION (1970-1978)
(percentage)

Region	1970	1971	1972	1973	1974	1975	1976	1977	1978
1. Central America	57.13	53.13	50.93	52.99	52.80	53.33	53.07	51.95	53.10
2. South America	40.10	34.94	33.40	33.49	34.45	35.16	37.01	34.33	34.32
3. Caribbean	47.69	47.75	44.92	47.71	53.42	55.41	54.19	53.70	52.92
4. Far East & South Asia	21.27	19.45	18.37	19.12	20.43	21.89	21.23	19.60	18.41
5. Middle East/ Non-OPEC	17.32	18.61	14.84	17.18	16.08	17.68	18.05	15.60	15.05
6. Africa/ Non-OPEC	9.79	7.70	6.52	7.10	6.94	8.16	6.58	6.31	6.18
7. OPEC	23.31	21.79	21.08	19.01	19.20	21.11	22.18	19.04	18.17

Source: CSIS Data Bank prepared for U.S. Export Competitiveness Project.

TABLE I-5

U.S. MANUFACTURED EXPORTS TO EACH REGION AS
A PERCENTAGE OF U.S. MANUFACTURED EXPORTS TO
ALL LDCS (1970-1978)
(percentage)

Region	1970	1971	1972	1973	1974	1975	1976	1977	1978
1. Central America	22.29	20.15	21.58	22.18	21.39	18.52	18.33	16.93	19.39
2. South America	23.49	22.47	22.25	20.54	22.57	18.20	15.58	15.22	14.45
3. Caribbean	6.29	6.34	5.87	5.28	4.50	4.12	3.67	3.65	3.45
4. Far East & South Asia	22.05	22.40	21.44	23.81	22.23	18.92	18.73	19.97	21.68
5. Middle East/ Non-OPEC	5.00	6.07	5.09	5.93	5.35	6.07	6.20	5.85	5.47
6. Africa/ Non-OPEC	3.49	3.41	2.65	2.84	2.45	2.64	2.02	2.11	1.72
7. OPEC	17.39	19.16	21.12	19.42	21.51	31.53	35.47	36.27	33.84
TOTALS	100.00	100.00	100.00	100.00	100.00	100.00	100.00	100.00	100.00

Source: CSIS Data Bank.

59

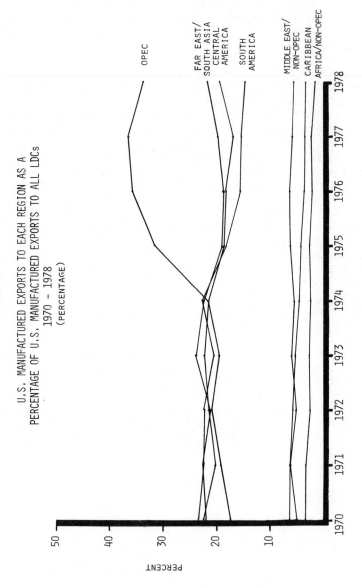

FIGURE I-2

U.S. MANUFACTURED EXPORTS TO EACH REGION AS A
PERCENTAGE OF U.S. MANUFACTURED EXPORTS TO ALL LDCs
1970 - 1978
(PERCENTAGE)

OPEC

FAR EAST/
SOUTH ASIA
CENTRAL
AMERICA

SOUTH
AMERICA

MIDDLE EAST/
NON-OPEC
CARIBBEAN
AFRICA/NON-OPEC

50   40   30   20   10

PERCENT

1970   1971   1972   1973   1974   1975   1976   1977   1978

exports to that market so that the U.S. share of the OPEC market declined from 23.3 percent in 1970 to 18.2 percent in 1978. The countries with the largest gains in the OPEC market were Japan (14.8 percent to 20.7 percent) and Germany (15.2 percent to 18.0 percent). The United Kingdom and France lost market shares in OPEC over the period, while Italy's share rose from 7.8 to 9.8 percent.

Although the U.S. market share declined in all seven LDC regions except one (the Caribbean), Japan's share rose in all regions except one (Africa/Non-OPEC). The U.S. loss of market share was largest for the South American region (40.1 percent in 1970 to 34.3 percent in 1978), although this was one of the regions in which Japan's gain in market share was highest (9 percent in 1970 to 15.3 percent in 1978). Japan also increased its market share substantially in Central America (10.3 percent in 1970 to 19.7 percent in 1978). Thus, Japan was a substantial gainer in two of the regions in which U.S. market shares have traditionally been highest. Germany's market shares declined in both Central and South America as did those of the United Kingdom; but France's share of the South American market rose over the period (see Figures I-3 through I-9 and Appendix Table I-A). Brazil's market share in South America rose from 2.6 percent in 1970 to 4.8 percent in 1978.

Japan increased its dominant share position in the Far East and South Asia market (42.2 percent in 1970 to 47.3 percent in 1978). The U.S. share of this market declined from 21.3 percent in 1970 to 18.4 percent in 1978, and the German and U.K. market shares also declined in this region. Hong Kong and South Korea doubled their market share in this region from a combined 2.8 percent in 1970 to 5.5 percent in 1978.

Figure 1-3: Export Market Shares of Manufactures
to the LDCs: Central America

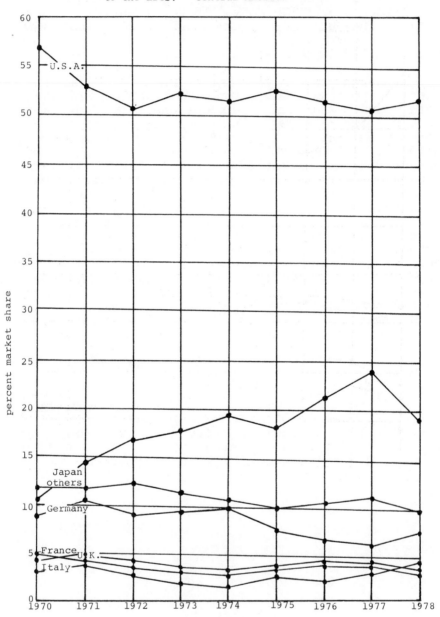

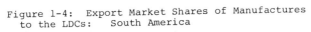

Figure 1-4: Export Market Shares of Manufactures
to the LDCs: South America

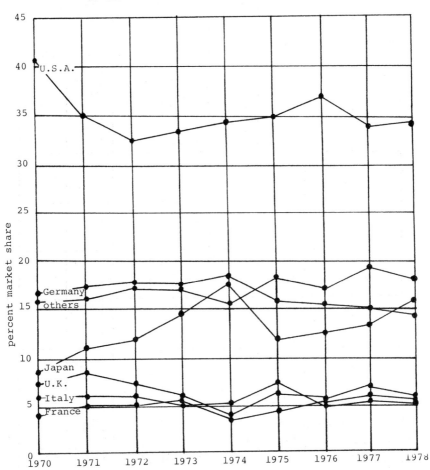

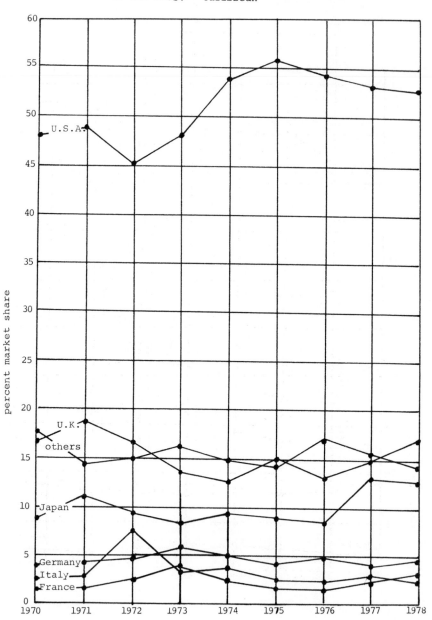

Figure 1-5: Export Shares of Manufactures
to the LDCs: Caribbean

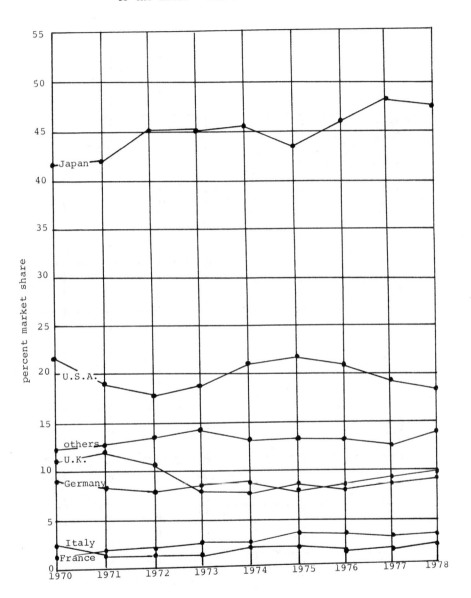

Figure 1-6: Export Market of Manufactures
to the LDCs: Far East & South Asia

65

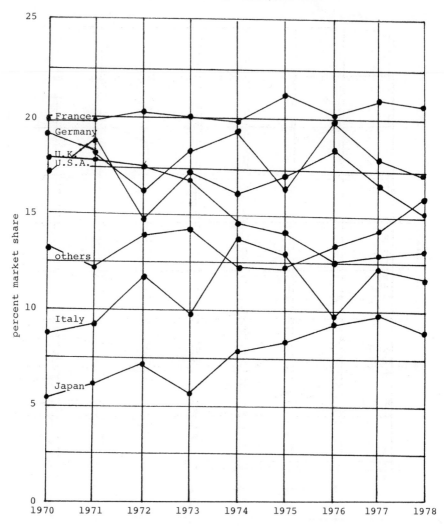

Figure 1-7: Export Market Shares of Manufactures
to the LDCs: Middle East/Non-OPEC

Figure 1-8: Export Market Shares of Manufactures
to the LDCs: Africa/Non-OPEC

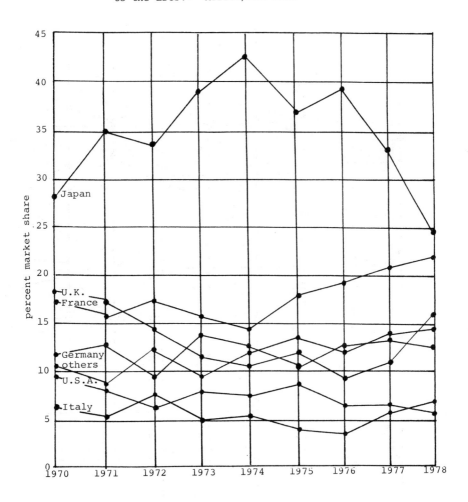

Figure 1-9: Export Shares of Manufactures
to the LDCs: OPEC

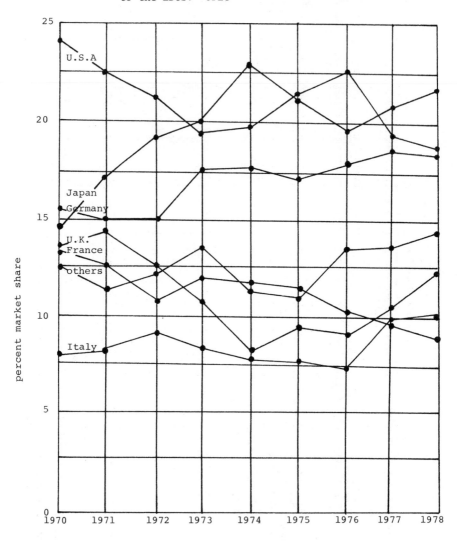

APPENDIX TABLE I-A

MARKET SHARES FOR MANUFACTURED EXPORTS TO THE LDCS BY 15 SELECTED COUNTRIES, 1970-1978
(percentages)

Country	Central America		South America		Caribbean		Far East & South Asia		Middle East/ Non-OPEC		Africa/ Non-OPEC		OPEC	
	1970	1978	1970	1978	1970	1978	1970	1978	1970	1978	1970	1978	1970	1978
United States	57.2	53.1	40.1	34.3	47.8	52.9	21.3	18.4	17.3	15.0	9.8	6.2	23.3	18.2
Japan	10.3	19.7	9.0	15.3	9.6	10.9	42.2	47.3	5.5	8.1	28.6	24.8	14.8	20.7
FRG	9.3	7.8	16.7	14.6	4.1	4.1	9.0	8.0	18.6	17.4	10.8	12.1	15.2	18.0
United Kingdom	4.2	2.6	7.8	6.1	16.6	14.3	11.0	7.9	17.5	12.1	17.3	15.3	13.4	11.7
France	4.9	3.2	4.4	6.1	1.5	3.2	2.1	3.1	19.9	20.3	16.8	21.0	13.3	8.7
Italy	2.8	3.5	6.0	5.9	2.9	2.6	2.6	2.0	9.0	11.4	6.3	6.7	7.8	9.8
Other Developed Countries														
Canada	2.7	1.6	3.9	2.1	6.9	3.3	2.1	1.1	0.6	0.9	0.5	1.2	2.2	1.7
Netherlands	1.5	1.0	2.4	2.6	6.8	3.5	1.5	1.6	3.0	3.5	2.5	3.6	2.8	2.7
Sweden	2.4	1.6	2.5	1.8	0.6	0.6	0.8	1.3	2.5	1.8	3.9	4.2	1.5	1.6
Switzerland	2.5	2.5	3.2	3.7	1.2	1.0	2.3	2.3	5.0	6.8	1.5	2.2	2.3	2.8
Australia	0.1	0.1	0.1	0.2	0.5	0.3	2.2	1.3	0.1	0.1	0.4	0.2	0.7	2.7
NICS														
Brazil	0.7	1.0	2.6	4.8	0.1	0.9	0.1	0.1	0.3	0.3	0.0	0.3	0.3	0.5
South Korea	0.1	1.0	0.0	0.3	0.0	0.5	0.5	2.3	0.0	1.2	0.2	1.3	0.3	2.0
Mexico	0.7	0.6	1.2	1.5	0.3	0.5	0.0	0.0	0.0	0.0	0.0	0.0	0.4	0.1
Hong Kong	0.7	0.8	0.2	0.3	1.2	1.4	2.3	0.3	0.8	1.0	1.4	1.0	1.2	1.3

Source: CSIS Data Bank prepared for U.S. Export Competitiveness Project.

II.   THE COMMODITY STRUCTURE AND MARKET
DISTRIBUTION OF U.S. EXPORT PERFORMANCE

In this chapter we analyze U.S. export performance
in the LDC market during the 1970-1978 period in terms
of its commodity composition and of the regional
distribution of exports. As in the case of aggregate
exports, we measure relative export performance of the
United States and of competing exporting countries by
market shares for individual commodities, i.e., the
ratio of U.S. exports of commodity k to total exports
of commodity k by all 15 exporting countries, either to
all LDCs or to a particular regional market.

Annual   U.S.   market   shares   for   each   of   the
73 commodity groups are given in Table II-1.[7] We shall
not be able to discuss U.S. export performance in terms
of all 73 commodities, but will summarize the developments with respect to the U.S. position in a number of
the   more   important   ones   on   both   an   overall   and   a
regional   basis.   In   addition,   we   shall   analyze   the
export   performance   of   major   competing   exporting
countries in some of the commodity groups.

Changes in U.S. Shares of Individual Commodity
Exports in the Overall LDC Market

In 1970 the U.S. market share was larger than that
of any of the 14 competing exporting countries in the
LDC market in 44 out of 73 commodity groups, and for
eight of these commodity groups the United States had
over half the entire LDC market. By 1978 the number of
commodity groups in which the U.S. share was larger
than that of any of its competitors had declined to 25,
and the United States accounted for more than half of
the total LDC market in only three commodity groups,
namely, aircraft, office machines, and other nonferrous
manufactures.

Of the 73 commodity classifications in our sample,
the U.S. export share in the total LDC market rose by
more than 5 percent between 1970 and 1978 for 11 items,
did not change by more than 5 percent for six items,
declined by more than 5 percent but less than 22 percent for 24 items, and fell by more than 22 percent

70

TABLE II-1

U.S. MARKET SHARES IN THIRD WORLD COUNTRIES
(1970-1978)
(percentages)

CODE	COMMODITY	1970	1971	1972	1973	1974	1975	1976	1977	1978
1	Chemical Elements, Comp.	37.95	34.49	33.29	33.77	35.94	36.50	36.74	37.57	37.51
2	Synthetic Organic Dyes	11.05	9.35	8.78	8.30	9.75	8.80	9.06	9.85	9.95
3	Medicinal & Pharm. Prod.	23.55	19.96	19.41	17.54	17.66	16.50	18.60	16.43	16.06
4	Oils and Perfume	26.01	24.52	24.03	23.21	24.94	23.81	24.17	20.95	24.17
5	Fertilizers, Manufactured	45.14	44.59	47.97	41.54	37.98	46.30	44.03	45.88	36.52
6	Plastic Materials	25.82	22.55	22.16	24.57	26.25	21.57	31.05	22.22	23.20
7	Other Chemicals	36.31	34.41	33.28	34.42	36.35	34.20	34.20	33.77	28.51
8	Leather Manufactures	34.62	28.87	24.05	22.71	22.64	20.99	21.33	21.23	26.09
9	Rubber Manufactures	18.47	16.58	15.61	11.72	16.51	15.46	15.69	18.40	23.87
10	Wood, Cork Manufactures	30.73	26.58	29.07	31.43	30.62	25.60	23.21	25.56	23.98
11	Paper, Paperboard	32.43	32.74	32.74	30.37	30.75	32.26	34.02	29.50	28.90
12	Yarn Thread	6.41	4.66	4.05	7.99	10.57	8.76	10.30	10.01	11.77
13	Textile Fabrics	8.74	8.13	8.65	9.30	10.03	8.00	8.46	7.56	9.03
14	Other Textile Products	20.24	18.61	17.75	17.31	19.89	18.67	20.39	19.50	18.50
15	Diamonds	33.38	32.60	31.03	49.22	26.63	24.70	22.26	22.29	21.70
16	Glassware, Pottery	22.99	17.97	17.22	17.90	19.28	16.53	17.49	18.68	21.86
17	Mineral Manufactures	20.03	20.51	16.69	14.87	12.74	12.09	11.61	9.86	11.86
18	Pig Iron	41.57	25.34	16.15	9.08	13.85	10.40	18.18	12.85	33.75
19	Iron, Steel Manufactures	17.73	11.76	10.52	12.30	13.32	14.05	10.56	8.24	9.14
20	Unwrought Copper	60.70	58.22	33.93	48.32	28.68	55.15	11.34	4.68	10.54
21	Unwrought Aluminum	51.85	27.82	26.01	41.51	31.99	20.76	20.04	16.22	29.17
22	Other Unwrought Nonferr.	13.73	7.70	4.16	11.39	13.15	9.14	3.89	5.50	9.76
23	Copper Manufactures	11.19	12.03	10.37	11.54	12.23	9.99	10.28	7.21	9.91
24	Aluminum Manufactures	30.35	21.70	23.13	28.47	26.35	28.35	28.53	21.46	15.32
25	Other Nonferrous Manu.	39.19	29.78	23.98	32.86	38.92	37.74	39.98	39.78	60.81
26	Cutlery, Household Equip.	14.06	12.33	11.68	11.63	11.73	10.29	11.03	9.17	12.14
27	Hand Tools	30.11	29.05	27.42	26.04	28.55	30.18	28.71	25.84	24.30
28	Other Metal Manufactures	23.18	18.71	16.82	19.88	20.81	18.86	18.28	15.79	14.94
29	Non-electric Power Mach.	19.25	18.37	21.03	26.44	29.58	24.74	26.04	14.80	19.25
30	Internal Combustion Engines	37.44	36.23	32.23	31.74	29.47	28.60	26.86	24.71	28.51
31	Aircraft Engines	52.04	55.51	47.15	46.73	47.12	34.29	41.94	38.16	37.32
32	Tractors	57.60	50.04	53.73	46.70	46.01	46.39	46.92	42.36	45.74
33	Other Agricultural Mach.	41.34	35.61	36.12	31.89	30.08	31.02	31.90	29.09	49.06
34	Office Machines	51.78	51.98	55.60	52.96	53.80	48.09	47.13	48.44	57.88
35	Computers	41.53	35.43	26.60	23.16	26.76	27.57	23.07	27.11	33.43

TABLE II-1 (Cont.)

CODE	COMMODITY	1970	1971	1972	1973	1974	1975	1976	1977	1978
36	Metal Working Machinery	25.62	27.36	22.30	21.66	18.65	23.01	27.15	16.15	20.30
37	Textile, Leather Machinery	13.28	10.58	9.72	10.78	12.02	11.35	10.07	9.91	9.50
38	Construction, Mining Mach.	59.83	56.34	56.99	56.46	51.43	52.47	53.17	49.51	49.86
39	Other Industrial Machinery	29.28	28.12	25.56	26.57	26.74	24.33	23.40	21.71	18.94
40	Heating, Cooling Equipment	43.07	35.48	36.88	36.86	39.73	38.78	36.66	31.86	28.87
41	Pumps, Centrifuges	45.91	39.73	38.57	36.79	38.24	35.70	34.92	30.64	29.16
42	Fork Lift Trucks	42.85	36.62	31.27	34.04	36.28	38.13	38.83	30.55	48.64
43	Parts, Accessories Machines	31.83	31.28	25.48	23.86	23.54	25.40	25.20	23.34	21.00
44	Electric Power Machinery	25.35	27.84	25.69	27.62	28.90	26.81	28.34	26.66	22.21
45	Television Receivers	31.55	29.69	31.74	31.56	30.43	36.24	31.25	19.62	26.25
46	Radio Receivers	4.19	5.42	3.20	3.34	3.53	3.94	3.56	4.16	4.96
47	Telecommunications Equip.	25.52	23.57	26.69	25.15	26.33	25.84	29.68	30.81	24.13
48	Domestic Electrical Equip.	27.16	26.53	27.06	26.75	29.78	27.40	28.21	26.08	18.78
49	Medical Electrical Appar.	31.74	31.87	34.22	33.42	33.43	33.13	29.80	30.57	34.20
50	Transistors, Photocells	70.29	67.31	63.19	63.33	69.43	68.72	65.06	63.57	28.12
51	Electrical Measuring Equip.	44.99	40.10	39.65	38.58	40.66	39.09	38.24	38.70	47.41
52	Other Elec. Machinery App.	20.61	20.08	20.46	20.91	23.88	22.92	20.98	20.04	15.95
53	Railway Vehicles	32.30	50.77	40.28	38.61	40.27	43.66	35.87	27.88	23.65
54	Passenger Motor Cars	16.26	16.87	16.47	17.14	17.85	19.40	18.73	15.60	14.59
55	Trucks, Buses	33.13	27.96	23.74	23.02	20.77	24.28	22.12	18.76	21.32
56	Motor Vehicles Parts	35.49	34.97	37.52	31.95	31.27	30.82	30.38	22.89	14.38
57	Motorcycles	1.64	1.38	1.47	1.07	5.94	1.31	1.68	1.52	4.08
58	Trailers, Bicycles	16.23	16.82	15.56	11.89	19.01	25.82	26.63	17.66	14.96
59	Aircraft	65.30	64.93	60.76	67.48	73.19	70.82	72.25	71.72	59.52
60	Ships, Boats	4.91	3.00	2.32	3.13	3.62	2.80	2.89	2.21	2.61
61	Furniture	31.69	25.98	14.67	22.83	21.45	18.19	19.90	13.90	16.19
62	Clothing	34.95	31.97	30.22	41.78	31.23	27.61	25.89	22.03	22.70
63	Footwear	9.25	8.82	8.53	11.34	9.29	8.78	9.15	7.33	7.18
64	Optical Instruments	17.41	12.89	13.33	14.20	16.10	18.94	17.04	15.94	17.53
65	Cameras & Equipment	29.44	31.10	31.75	32.02	31.27	28.80	26.14	22.26	21.94
66	Other Scientific Instru.	44.29	39.52	39.31	35.17	34.21	34.77	34.87	32.25	21.63
67	Movies, Photographic Film	45.03	40.14	38.11	37.57	38.09	37.21	34.54	33.00	36.67
68	Watches, Clocks	2.11	2.07	1.98	3.11	3.04	4.52	10.68	7.65	6.06
69	Phonographs, Musical Instr.	27.38	23.23	22.41	18.40	23.68	26.32	24.12	22.38	21.71
70	Books, Magazines	30.10	20.91	25.40	24.83	27.25	21.44	19.95	20.28	22.93
71	Toys, Sporting Goods	28.06	30.61	35.73	36.34	38.09	29.60	28.52	26.90	30.71
72	Jewelry, Art	18.23	15.49	15.03	20.79	17.66	14.70	9.73	6.11	5.74
73	Other Manufactured Goods	25.89	24.18	23.26	22.84	23.62	22.63	22.88	20.67	15.58

Source: CSIS Data Bank.

(i.e., the average for all 73 commodities) for 32 items (see Table II-2).

The most important commodities (in terms of the value of exports) for which U.S. export shares in the total LDC market rose by more than 5 percent between 1970 and 1978 were rubber manufactures; electrical measuring equipment; other agricultural machinery (excluding tractors); office machinery; and fork lift trucks. In the case of only two of these items, office machinery and fork lift trucks, was the value of U.S. exports in 1970 in excess of $100 million (see Appendix Table II-C).

Of the six commodity groups for which U.S. export shares did not change by more than 5 percent between 1970 and 1978, the chemical elements and compounds group was by far the most important in terms of value in 1970 ($418 million), followed by radio receivers ($98 million) and textile fabrics ($85 million).

Of those U.S. exports for which export shares declined by more than 5 percent but less than 22 percent between 1970 and 1978, the most important were manufactured fertilizers; plastic materials; other chemicals; wood, cork manufactures; paper and paperboard; copper manufactures; tractors; construction, mining machinery; electric power machinery; telecommunications equipment; passenger motor cars; and aircraft -- each of which had a 1970 export value in excess of $100 million.

Of those commodity classifications for which the U.S. export share declined by more than 22 percent (the average percentage decline for all 73 commodities) between 1970 and 1978, the most important were medicinal and pharmaceutical products; iron, steel manufactures; other metal manufactures; internal combustion engines; other industrial machinery; heating, cooling equipment; pumps, centrifuges; parts, accessories machinery; transistors, photocells; other electrical machinery apparatus; trucks, buses; motor vehicle parts, clothing; and other scientific instruments -- each with an export value of over $100 million. It will be noted from Table II-2 that of the commodity groups just enumerated, the decline in U.S. export shares was in excess of 30 percent for

TABLE II-2

PERCENTAGE CHANGES IN U.S. EXPORT SHARES OF LDC MARKET
BETWEEN 1970 AND 1978, BY 73 COMMODITY CLASSIFICATIONS

Code	Commodity	Percentage Change
A.	Commodities for which U.S export share did not change by more than 5 percent:	
1	Chemical Elements, Compounds	-1.2
13	Textile Fabrics	+3.3
16	Glassware, Pottery	-4.9
29	Nonelectric Power Machinery	+0.0
46	Radio Receivers	-0.7
64	Optical Instruments	+0.6
B.	Commodities for which U.S. export share declined by more than 5 percent, but less than 22 percent:	
2	Synthetic Organic Dyes	-10.0
4	Oils and Perfume	-7.0
5	Fertilizers, Manufactured	-19.1
6	Plastic Materials	-10.1
7	Other Chemicals	-21.5
10	Wood, Cork Manufactures	-22.0
11	Paper, Paperboard	-10.9
14	Other Textile Products	-8.5
18	Pig Iron	-18.8
23	Copper Manufactures	-11.5
26	Cutlery, Household Equipment	-13.6
27	Hand Tools	-19.2
32	Tractors	-20.6
35	Computers	-19.5
36	Metalworking Machinery	-20.8
38	Construction, Mining Machinery	-16.7
44	Electric Power Machinery	-12.4
45	Television Receivers	-16.8
47	Telecommunications Equipment	-5.4
54	Passenger Motor Cars	-10.3
58	Trailers, Bicycles	-7.9
59	Aircraft	-8.8
67	Movies, Photographic Film	-18.6
69	Photographs, Musical Instruments	-20.7
C.	Commodities for which U.S. export share declined by more than 22 precent:	
3	Medicinal & Pharmaceutical Products	-31.8
8	Leather Manufactures	-24.6
15	Diamonds	-35.0
17	Mineral Manufactures	-40.7
19	Iron, Steel Manufactures	-48.4
20	Unwrought Copper	-82.6

Code	Commodity	Percentage Change
21	Unwrought Alumium	-43.7
22	Other Unwrought Nonferrous	-28.8
24	Aluminum Manufactures	-49.5
28	Other Metal Manufactures	-35.5
30	Internal Combustion Engines	-23.8
31	Aircraft Engines	-28.3
37	Textile, Leather Machinery	-28.4
39	Other Industrial Machinery	-35.3
40	Heating, Cooling Equipment	-33.0
41	Pumps, Centrifuges	-36.5
43	Parts, Accessories Machinery	-34.0
48	Domestic Electrical Equipment	-30.8
50	Transistors, Photocells	-60.0
52	Other Electrical Machinery Apparatus	-22.6
53	Railway Vehicles	-26.8
55	Trucks, Buses	-35.6
56	Motor Vehicle Parts	-59.5
60	Ships, Boats	-46.8
61	Furniture	-49.0
62	Clothing	-35.0
63	Footwear	-22.3
65	Cameras and Equipment	-25.5
66	Other Scientific Instruments	-51.2
70	Books, Magazines	-23.8
72	Jewelry, Art	-68.5
73	Other Manufactured Goods	-39.8

D. Commodities for which U.S. export share rose by over 5 percent:

Code	Commodity	Percentage Change
9	Rubber Manufactures	+29.2
12	Yarn Thread	+83.5
25	Other Nonferrous	+55.1
33	Other Agricultural Machinery	+18.7
34	Office Machines	+11.8
42	Fork Life Trucks	+13.5
49	Medical Electrical Apparatus	+7.7
51	Electrical Measuring Equipment	+5.4
57	Motorcycles	+149.4
68	Watches, Clocks	+187.6
71	Toys, Sporting Goods	+9.4

Source: Table II-1.

all but two, internal combustion engines and other
electrical machinery apparatus.

Shifts in U.S. Export Shares: Technology-Intensive vs. Nontechnology-Intensive Commodities

Since the United States traditionally has had a
comparative advantage in technology-intensive commodities, it is useful to analyze the shifts in U.S. export
shares between 1970 and 1978 for these two classes of
commodities.[8] Table II-3 shows U.S. market shares for
leading technology-intensive exports to the LDC market
for 1970, 1974, 1977, and 1978.

Of the 44 commodity classifications for which the
U.S. market share in the LDC market was larger than any
of its 14 competitors in 1970, 15 are classified as
technology-intensive. By 1977, the U.S. dominant
position in technology-intensive exports had declined
to 13 product groups; and by 1978 this number fell to
11 product groups. Between 1970 and 1978 the United
States lost its dominant position in electric power
machinery, transistors, and photocells to Japan. It
lost its dominant position in computers to Japan in
1977, but regained market superiority in 1978. The
United States also lost its dominant position in
medicinal and pharmaceutical products and in manufactured fertilizers to the residual group of exporting
countries (composed of Canada, Netherlands, Sweden,
Switzerland, Australia, and four NICs).

The U.S. market share in its highest value export
(aircraft) declined significantly between 1977 and
1978. Although the United States increased its exports
of aircraft to the LDCs by 3.5 percent in value terms
between 1977 and 1978, its market share declined from
71.7 percent to 59.5 percent. This was primarily the
result of a rapid rise in exports of aircraft to the
LDCs by the United Kingdom, which became the major U.S.
competitor in this commodity in the LDC market.

Although the United States lost its dominant
market position in four of the 15 technology-intensive
product groups between 1970 and 1978, the decline in
the U.S. dominant positions in the nontechnology-
intensive commodity groups was substantially greater.

TABLE II-3

U.S. MARKET SHARES FOR LEADING TECHNOLOGY-INTENSIVE EXPORTS
TO THE LDC MARKET, 1970, 1974, 1977 and 1978
(percentages)

Code	Commodity	1970	1974	1977	1978
1	Chemical Elements, Comp.	37.95	35.94	37.57	37.51
3	Medicinal & Pharm. Products	23.55	17.66	16.43	16.06
5	Fertilizers, Manufactured	45.14	37.98	45.88	36.52
7	Other Chemicals	36.31	36.35	33.77	28.51
30	Internal Combustion Engines	37.44	29.47	24.71	28.51
31	Aircraft Engines	52.44	47.12	38.16	37.32
34	Office Machines	51.78	53.80	48.44	57.88
35	Computers	41.53	26.76	27.11	33.43
44	Electric Power Machinery	25.35	28.90	26.66	22.21
47	Telecommunications Equipment	25.52	26.33	30.81	24.13
50	Transistors, Photocells	70.29	69.43	63.57	28.12
51	Electrical Measuring Equipment	44.99	40.66	38.70	47.41
59	Aircraft	65.30	73.19	71.72	59.52
66	Other Scientific Instruments	44.29	34.21	32.25	21.63
67	Movies, Photographic Film	45.03	38.09	33.00	36.67

Source: Table II-1

77

By 1978, the U.S. market share had fallen behind its competitors in 16 product groups classified as non-technology-intensive (Table II-4). Over the same period, the United States achieved market dominance in only one new product category in the nontechnology-intensive group, namely, toys and sporting goods. Japan achieved market dominance in 10 of the 16 non-technology-intensive commodity groups for which the United States lost its major share of the LDC market between 1970 and 1978. Of the remaining six commodity groups, dominant market shares were achieved by:

Commodity Group	Major Exporting Country
Other Industrial Machinery	Germany
Furniture	Italy
Books and Magazines	United Kingdom
Paper and Paperboard	Canada and Sweden
Unwrought Aluminum	Canada
Clothing	Hong Kong and South Korea

Of the remaining 35 nontechnology-intensive commodity groups, the United States maintained a dominant position in 15. Of the 20 nontechnology-intensive product groups in which the United States did not maintain a dominant market share during the period 1970-1978, Japan had the dominant share in 13 in 1978.

In 1970 Japan maintained the largest market share in 18 commodity groups and was second to the United States in 15 others. By 1978 Japan had a dominant position in 31 commodity groups and was the leading U.S. competitor in market shares in 17. Therefore, Japan is clearly the major U.S. competitor for market dominance in Third World markets. Moreover, once Japan secures a dominant market position in a commodity, it rarely loses it.

Substantial gains in market shares were made by the residual group countries when they are considered as a group in comparison with the major OECD exporting countries. In 1970, the residual group maintained the largest market share in only two commodity groups: watches and clocks (Switzerland) and other unwrought nonferrous manufactures (Canada, Australia and Mexico).

TABLE II-4

DECLINE IN U.S. MARKET SHARES FOR
LEADING NONTECHNOLOGY-INTENSIVE EXPORTS TO THE LDC MARKET
(1970 and 1978)
(percentages)

		1970		1978	
Code	Commodity	U.S. Share	Share of Leading U.S. competitor	U.S. Share	Share of Leading U.S. Competitor
8	Leather Manufactures	35.05	Japan 18.74	26.09	Japan 35.07
11	Paper, Paperboard	32.74	Other 29.17	28.90	Other 32.25
20	Unwrought Copper	60.77	Japan 14.87	10.54	Japan 52.36
21	Unwrought Aluminum	52.41	Other 40.88	29.17	Other 34.53
24	Aluminum Manufactures	31.20	Japan 17.32	15.32	Japan 25.25
28	Other Metal Manufactures	23.49	Japan 19.64	14.94	Japan 22.12
39	Other Industrial Mach.	29.54	FRG 25.22	18.93	FRG 30.38
43	Parts, Access. Mach.	32.09	U.K. 16.67	21.00	Japan 26.77
48	Domestic Elect. Equip.	31.85	Japan 23.79	18.78	Japan 29.64
53	Railway Vehicles	32.31	France 26.12	23.64	Japan 24.11
55	Trucks, Buses	33.15	Japan 10.43	21.32	Japan 34.93
56	Motor Vehicle Parts	35.52	FRG 19.79	14.38	Japan 23.90
61	Furniture	32.43	U.K. 17.41	16.19	Italy 35.77
62	Clothing	40.94	Japan 17.77	22.71	Other 33.17
70	Books, Magazines	31.78	France 20.05	22.93	U.K. 29.94
73	Other Manufactured Goods	28.47	Japan 19.21	15.58	Japan 19.49

Source: Table II-1 and Appendix Table II-A.

By 1978, the residual group maintained the largest market shares in the following commodity groups:

| | Major Exporting Country within the |
Commodity Group	Residual Group
Medicinal and Pharmaceutical Products; Diamonds; Trailers and Bicycles	Switzerland
Paper and Paperboard; Unwrought Aluminum, Other Nonferrous Metals	Canada
Paper and Paperboard	Sweden
Manufactured Fertilizers	Netherlands
Manufactured Fertilizers; Other Textile Products, Clothing	South Korea
Clothing	Hong Kong

In 1978, the residual group had the second largest market share in seven other product categories, including synthetic organic dyes; aluminum manufactures; jewelry, art; ships, boats; yarn thread; textile fabrics; and other manufactured goods.

Commodity Structure of U.S. Exports and Exports of its Principal Competitors by LDC Region

Central America

Although Central America is not a major market for most leading exporting countries and its relative importance as a market for both U.S. exports and the exports of all exporting countries has declined over the 1970-1978 period, it is the market in which the United States maintains the largest market share relative to that of its competitors (see Table II-5). The United States also has the largest share in many of the commodities it exports to Central America and actually increased its market share for a number of them. Among the 23 technology-intensive product categories, the United States maintained the dominant market share in all but two commodity groups, namely, radio receivers and clocks, and watches. In the 50 nontechnology-intensive product categories, the

TABLE II-5

MARKET SHARES BY EXPORTING COUNTRY
TO CENTRAL AMERICA (1970-1978)
(percentages)

	1970	1971	1972	1973	1974	1975	1976	1977	1978
U.S.	57.13	53.13	50.93	52.99	52.79	53.33	53.07	51.95	53.10
Japan	10.31	14.29	17.17	17.78	19.21	18.40	20.51	23.39	19.72
FRG	9.31	10.41	9.62	9.80	10.09	7.98	7.18	6.54	7.84
U.K.	4.19	4.22	3.98	2.95	2.62	3.85	3.25	2.65	2.61
France	4.89	3.51	3.47	2.85	2.67	3.87	3.77	2.76	3.17
Italy	2.80	3.29	2.58	2.00	1.76	2.36	1.88	2.14	3.49
Other	11.37	11.15	12.25	11.63	10.86	10.21	10.34	10.57	10.07

Source: CSIS Data Bank.

TABLE II-6

MARKET SHARES BY EXPORTING COUNTRY
TO SOUTH AMERICA (1970-1978)
(percentages)

	1970	1971	1972	1973	1974	1975	1976	1977	1978
U.S.	40.10	34.94	33.40	33.49	34.45	35.16	37.01	34.33	34.33
Japan	8.97	11.12	11.67	14.76	17.41	13.33	13.45	14.35	15.32
FRG	16.66	17.15	17.49	17.20	17.85	15.49	15.48	15.06	14.59
U.K.	7.84	9.22	7.92	6.34	4.72	6.12	5.64	7.02	6.29
France	4.37	5.25	5.85	5.84	4.44	4.82	5.63	5.70	6.08
Italy	6.02	6.01	6.52	5.21	5.12	6.55	5.34	4.89	5.92
Other	16.04	16.31	17.15	17.16	16.01	18.53	17.45	18.65	17.47

Source: CSIS Data Bank.

United States maintained largest market shares in 40 product classifications in 1970 and increased this number to 42 by 1978. Moreover, the United States increased its market share for more than half of these 42 product groups between 1970 and 1978.

The commodity groups for which the United States market share had been reduced significantly in Central America since 1970 include television receivers; cameras and equipment; and movies, photographic film. In the first two commodity groups, Japan increased its market share from 24 to 28 percent and 24 to 34 percent respectively. In movies and photographic film, the leading competitor (second to the United States) is the residual group, primarily the Netherlands and Brazil.

For all product categories the United States maintained a dominant market share in nearly 90 percent of the 73 commodity groups. In 1970 the residual group of countries constituted the leading U.S. competitor in 19 product categories; followed by Japan with 18; Germany with 17; and the United Kingdom with 7. By 1978, Japan was the leading U.S. competitor in 24 product groups; followed by the residual group with 20; Germany with 12; and the United Kingdom with 2. Within the residual group of countries, the leading U.S. competitors include:

Code	Commodity	Major Exporting Country
2	Synthetic Organic Dyes	Switzerland, Mexico
3	Medicinal and Pharmaceutical Products	Switzerland, Mexico
5	Fertilizers, Manufactured	Netherlands
11	Paper, Paperboard	Canada
14	Other Textile Products	Korea, Hong Kong
21	Unwrought Aluminum	Sweden
26	Cutlery, Household Equipment	Brazil, Korea
33	Other Agricultural Machinery	Canada, Australia
44	Electric Power Machinery	Sweden, Switzerland, Brazil

Code	Commodity	Major Exporting Country
47	Telecommunications Equipment	Sweden
53	Railway Vehicles	Canada
62	Clothing	Korea, Hong Kong, Brazil
71	Jewelry, Art	Hong Kong
73	Other Manufactured Products	Hong Kong

South America

U.S. exports to South America as a proportion of total U.S. exports to LDCs declined by more than one-third between 1970 and 1978, reflecting the slow growth in the market size of this region relative to other regional markets in the Third World. The proportion of manufactured exports by all exporting countries to South America also declined from just over 16 percent in 1970 to less than 10 percent in 1978. The U.S. share of the South America market also declined, from 40.1 percent in 1970 to 34.9 percent in 1971 and, except for a 2 percentage point rise in 1976, has remained stable over the 1971-1978 period (see Table II-6).

Among the 23 technology-intensive products, the United States increased its dominant market share from 16 to 17 commodity classifications between 1970 and 1978, with the additional product being telecommunications equipment. In this latter commodity the United States experienced strong competition from Sweden during the early 1970s, but in recent years Japan has emerged as the leading U.S. competitor in this commodity in South America. Among the 17 technology-intensive products noted above, Germany was the leading competitor in nine product groups in 1970; followed by Japan with two; and the United Kingdom with one (aircraft engines). By 1978, Japan was the leading U.S. competitor in seven product groups; followed by Germany with six; and the United Kingdom with two.

In 1970 Japan, Germany, and the residual group maintained market domination in two commodity groups each. By 1978, Japan and Germany had market domination in three and two product categories respectively.

In the nontechnology-intensive product categories, the United States maintained a dominant market share in South America in 35 commodity groups in 1970 and 31 commodity groups in 1978. Of the 31 U.S. dominant market shares in 1978, nearly two-thirds had declined over the period. Japan and Germany were the principal U.S. competitors in the South American market in the 1970-1978 period. In 1978, Japan had a dominant market share in seven product groups, namely, textile fibers; iron and steel manufactures; heating, cooling equipment; passenger cars; motorcycles; trailers, bicycles; and ships, boats. Germany had the dominant market share in five product groups, namely, leather manufactures; copper manufactures; metalworking machinery; textile, leather machinery; and other industrial machinery. Among the residual group, Canada and Sweden were the leading exporters of paper and paperboard.

The Caribbean

As a proportion of total exports to the Third World, the Caribbean market is of only marginal significance for both the United States and all 15 exporting countries. Moreover, the Caribbean market has been expanding more slowly than other regional markets in the Third World during the 1970-1978 period. The United States increased its share of the Caribbean export market between 1970 and 1978 from about 48 percent to nearly 53 percent. Japan's share of the Caribbean market increased only marginally while the share of the United Kingdom declined, and there was a significant decline in the share of the residual group.

In the technology-intensive category, the United States held the dominant market shares in all but five products in 1970 and in all but three product categories in 1978, namely, radio receivers; watches, clocks; and aircraft. (The U.K. share of the aircraft market increased dramatically between 1977 and 1978, but this may be a temporary condition arising from relatively few sales to the region.) Japan maintained the dominant position in radio receivers while Switzerland and Hong Kong accounted for roughly 40 percent of the exports of watches and clocks to the Caribbean.

Between 1970 and 1978 the United States increased its market share in more than half of the

FIGURE II-1

EXPORT MARKET SHARES BY EXPORTING COUNTRY
TO CENTRAL AMERICA

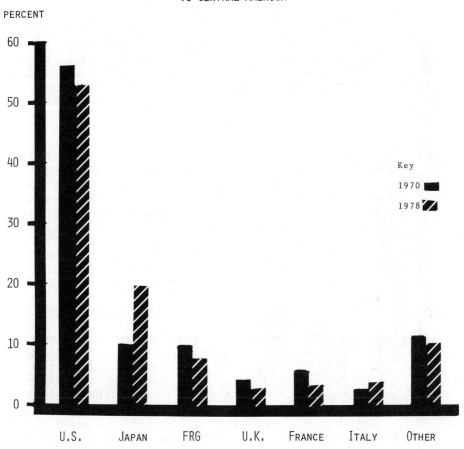

FIGURE II-2

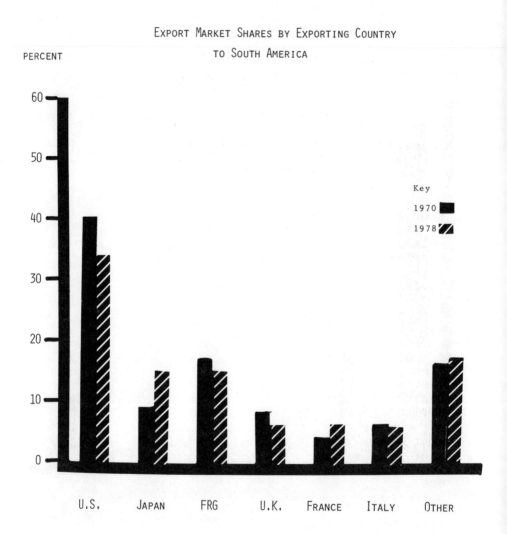

Export Market Shares by Exporting Country
to South America

86

technology-intensive categories in which it maintained the largest market share. The United States also had a dominant market share in more than three-quarters of the nontechnology-intensive categories and was able to increase its market share in nearly two-thirds of these groups between 1970 and 1978. The United Kingdom was the leading U.S. competitor in 18 of the nontechnology-intensive groups in 1978, and had the largest market share in three commodities, namely, unwrought copper; copper manufactures; and motor vehicle parts. Japan had the largest share in iron, steel manufactures; passenger cars; and motorcycles. (See Table II-7.)

Far East and South Asia

About one-fifth of all U.S. manufactures exported to the LDCs and roughly one-fourth of manufactured exports of all 15 exporting countries go to the Far East and South Asia, which is second only to OPEC in importance as a regional market in the Third World. As might be expected, Japan has by far the highest overall market share in this region, 47 percent as contrasted with 18 percent for the United States. Japan's market share rose significantly between 1970 and 1978, while the shares of the United States, Germany, and the United Kingdom declined (Table II-8).

In the technology-intensive group, the product markets dominated by the United States declined from 12 to 5 between 1970 and 1978, while Japan increased the number of commodities in which it was the largest exporter from 9 to 14. The United States lost its dominant position in chemical elements, compounds; manufactured fertilizers; other chemicals; computers; telecommunications equipment; other scientific instruments; and movies, photographic film. Among the five commodities in which the United States maintained the dominant position, its market share declined in aircraft engines; office machines; and transistors, photocells, but its market share rose in electrical measuring equipment and aircraft.

In the nontechnology-intensive category, the markets dominated by the United States declined from ten to two between 1970 and 1978, while Japan increased the markets it dominated from 36 to 42. In this category, the United States lost its dominant position

TABLE II-7

MARKET SHARES BY EXPORTING COUNTRY
TO CARIBBEAN (1970-1978)
(percentages)

	1970	1971	1972	1973	1974	1975	1976	1977	1978
U.S.	47.69	47.75	44.92	47.71	53.42	55.41	54.19	53.70	52.92
Japan	9.56	10.56	9.64	8.46	9.07	8.79	8.28	11.48	10.92
FRG	4.13	4.32	4.57	6.10	4.91	4.16	4.78	3.74	4.10
U.K.	16.60	18.40	16.60	14.38	12.47	13.91	12.33	12.74	14.34
France	1.48	1.49	2.12	3.49	1.90	1.85	1.79	2.42	3.22
Italy	2.92	2.77	7.19	3.44	3.25	2.26	2.02	2.59	2.65
Other	17.62	14.71	14.95	16.42	14.98	13.62	16.61	13.33	11.85

Source: CSIS Data Bank.

TABLE II-8

MARKET SHARES BY EXPORTING COUNTRY TO
THE FAR EAST AND SOUTH ASIA (1970-1978)
(percentages)

	1970	1971	1972	1973	1974	1975	1976	1977	1978
U.S.	21.27	19.45	18.37	19.12	20.43	21.89	21.23	19.60	18.41
Japan	42.24	42.79	45.13	45.10	45.94	43.81	45.81	47.46	47.34
FRG	9.02	8.57	3.42	8.86	8.93	7.78	7.67	7.73	8.02
U.K.	10.95	12.20	10.58	8.62	7.80	8.34	7.30	7.37	7.92
France	2.10	2.35	2.43	2.62	2.32	3.48	3.41	3.21	3.13
Italy	2.63	2.26	1.93	1.88	2.10	2.09	1.71	1.84	2.03
Other	11.79	12.38	13.14	13.80	12.48	12.61	12.87	12.79	13.16

Source: CSIS Data Bank.

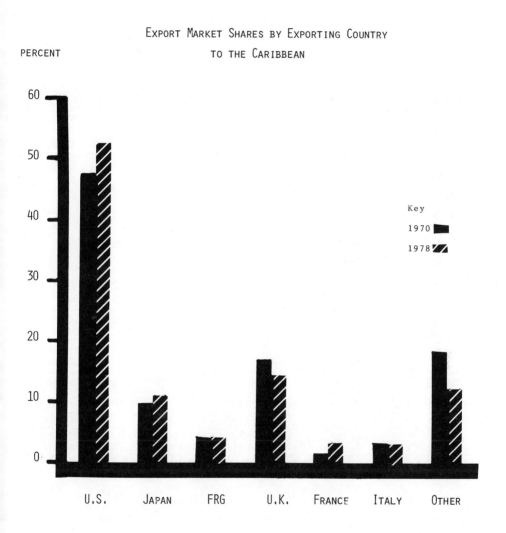

FIGURE II-3

EXPORT MARKET SHARES BY EXPORTING COUNTRY
TO THE CARIBBEAN

PERCENT

Key
1970
1978

U.S.   JAPAN   FRG   U.K.   FRANCE   ITALY   OTHER

89

FIGURE II-4

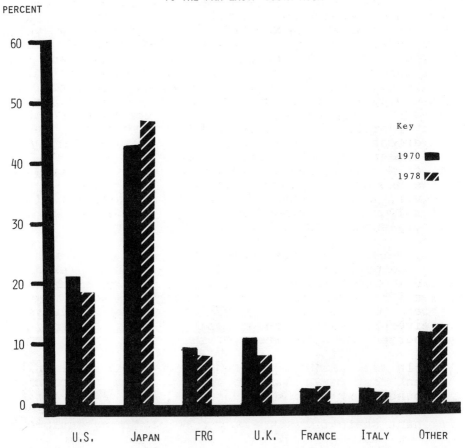

Export Market Shares by Exporting Country
to the Far East/ South Asia

PERCENT

Key

1970 ■■

1978 ▨▨

U.S.   Japan   FRG   U.K.   France   Italy   Other

90

in leather manufactures; unwrought copper; unwrought aluminum; tractors; construction, mining machinery; pumps, centrifuges; clothing; and books, magazines. It maintained its dominant share in diamonds and medical electrical apparatus. By 1978, Japan maintained the largest market share in more than three-quarters of the 73 commodity classifications.

Middle East/Non-OPEC and Africa/Non-OPEC

Tables II-9 and II-10 show the market shares of the major exporting countries to the Middle East/Non-OPEC and Africa/Non-OPEC countries for the years 1970-1978. The market share of the United States declined in both regions. Japan, Italy, and the residual group were the major gainers in shares in the Middle East/Non-OPEC region, while Germany, France, and the residual category were the major gainers in Africa/Non-OPEC. Japan's share in the Africa/Non-OPEC group rose rapidly from 29 percent in 1970 to nearly 39 percent in 1976, but then declined sharply to 25 percent in 1978. Japan's increased share in the Africa/Non-OPEC region was primarily the result of large exports of ships, and boats. In recent years, however, Japan's share of the market declined almost entirely as a consequence of the decrease in that country's exports of this product category.

In the Middle East/Non-OPEC region, France was the more competitive in nontechnology-intensive exports, while Germany was more competitive in the technology-intensive products. Japan was highly competitive in rubber manufactures; textile fabrics; television receivers; radio receivers; ships, boats; and phonographs, musical instruments.

In the technology-intensive products, the United States lost the dominant market share in chemical compounds and aircraft that it held in the Africa/Non-OPEC region in 1970, and by 1978 maintained a dominant share only in electrical measuring equipment. In the nontechnology-intensive category, the United States maintained the dominant market share in 1970 in tractors; construction, mining machinery; heating, cooling equipment; and fork lift trucks. But by 1978, the United States had lost its dominant position in heating and cooling equipment.

91

TABLE II-9

MARKET SHARES BY EXPORTING COUNTRY TO
THE MIDDLE EAST/NON-OPEC (1970-1978)
(percentages)

	1970	1971	1972	1973	1974	1975	1976	1977	1978
U.S.	17.32	18.61	14.83	17.18	16.08	17.68	18.05	15.60	15.05
Japan	5.50	5.84	6.99	5.76	7.30	7.55	9.11	9.62	8.13
FRG	18.56	17.92	16.34	17.71	19.24	16.96	19.31	17.76	17.44
U.K.	17.50	17.86	17.54	16.76	13.79	13.62	11.96	11.99	12.10
France	19.86	18.67	20.06	19.94	19.58	20.91	19.38	20.46	20.32
Italy	9.03	9.37	11.33	9.81	12.49	11.88	9.68	11.51	11.44
Other	12.23	11.73	12.91	12.84	11.52	11.41	12.51	13.06	15.52

Source: CSIS Data Bank.

TABLE II-10

MARKET SHARES BY EXPORTING COUNTRY TO
AFRICA/NON-OPEC (1970-1978)
(percentages)

	1970	1971	1972	1973	1974	1975	1976	1977	1978
U.S.	9.79	7.70	6.52	7.10	6.94	8.16	6.57	6.31	6.18
Japan	28.63	35.11	34.47	39.37	41.10	37.03	38.60	32.83	24.76
FRG	10.85	11.87	9.19	12.83	11.62	10.19	11.21	12.40	12.12
U.K.	17.35	16.37	14.03	10.70	10.21	10.90	9.55	10.20	15.26
France	16.75	15.25	16.65	15.53	13.45	17.02	18.42	20.26	20.97
Italy	6.28	5.76	7.64	5.22	5.44	4.66	4.46	5.54	6.68
Other	10.35	7.94	11.50	9.25	11.24	12.04	11.19	12.46	14.03

Source: CSIS Data Bank.

FIGURE II-5

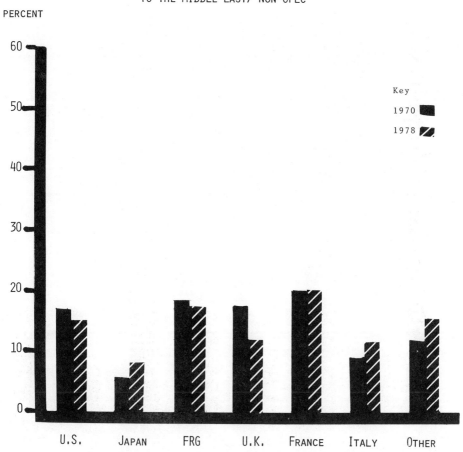

Export Market Shares by Exporting Country
to the Middle East/ Non-OPEC

PERCENT

Key
1970 ■
1978 ▨

60

50

40

30

20

10

0

U.S.   Japan   FRG   U.K.   France   Italy   Other

FIGURE II-6

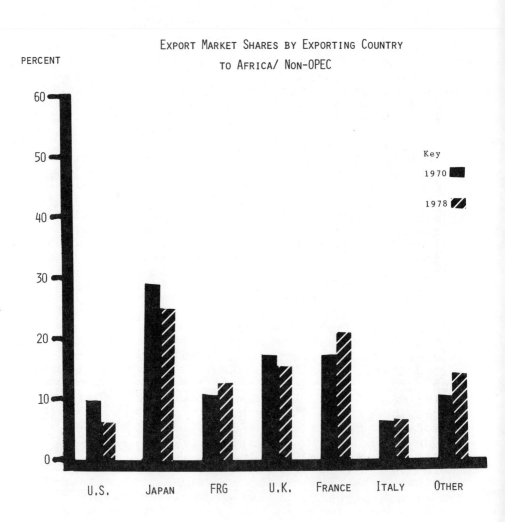

EXPORT MARKET SHARES BY EXPORTING COUNTRY
TO AFRICA/ NON-OPEC

PERCENT

Key
1970 ▮
1978 ▨

OPEC

Exports of manufactures to the OPEC countries
constitute the most important share of the LDC market
and have increased rapidly in importance during the
1970-1978 period. As was noted earlier, the U.S. share
of the OPEC market has declined, although the OPEC
market constitutes an increasing proportion of total
U.S. exports of manufactures to the LDCs.

In the technology-intensive products, the United
States had a dominant share in 14 product groups in
1970, but this number declined to 10 by 1978. By 1978,
the United States had lost its dominant position in
other chemicals; electrical power machinery; transistors, photocells; other scientific instruments;
watches, and clocks. In 1978, it gained the dominant
market share in telecommunications equipment. Of the
technology-intensive commodities in which the United
States maintained its dominant market share between
1970 and 1978, its share was substantially increased in
manufactured fertilizers; office machines; electrical
measuring equipment; and aircraft. Of the technology-
intensive commodities in which the United States lost
dominant market shares between 1970-1978, the United
Kingdom achieved leadership in chemicals and other
scientific instruments, and Germany achieved the
dominant position in electrical power machinery,
transistors, and photocells.

In the nontechnology-intensive categories the
United States had a dominant market share in 14 in
1970, but this number declined to eight by 1978. The
United States lost its dominant share in the market in
paper, paperboard; other nonferrous manufactures; hand
tools; domestic electrical equipment; railway vehicles;
trucks, buses; and other manufactured goods. Among the
commodities in which it maintained its dominant share
in the OPEC market, the U.S. market share increased
significantly only for other agricultural machinery and
there were substantial losses in construction, mining
machinery; heating, cooling equipment; pumps, centrifuges; and parts, accessories machines. Oddly enough,
the only commodity in which the United States gained a
dominant market share between 1970 and 1978 was glassware, pottery. Japan assumed the dominant market share
in place of the United States in railway vehicles;
trucks, buses; France in other nonferrous manufactures;

Germany in hand tools; and Italy in domestic electrical equipment.

Japan and Germany were the leading U.S. competitors in the OPEC market. Japan gained the largest overall share (21 percent) between 1970 and 1978, while Germany's share rose from 15 percent to 18 percent over the same period, approximately equaling the U.S. share in 1978 (see Table II-11).

TABLE II-11

MARKET SHARES BY EXPORTING COUNTRY
TO OPEC (1970-1978)
(percentages)

	1970	1971	1972	1973	1974	1975	1976	1977	1978
U.S.	23.31	21.79	21.08	19.01	19.20	21.11	22.18	19.04	18.17
Japan	14.79	17.11	18.97	19.88	22.94	21.11	19.57	20.46	20.70
FRG	15.22	15.01	15.07	16.88	17.10	16.84	17.21	18.34	17.99
U.K.	13.37	14.27	12.64	10.95	9.31	10.03	9.82	10.45	11.67
France	13.26	12.21	10.70	11.71	11.55	11.34	10.13	9.50	8.73
Italy	7.77	8.08	9.06	8.45	8.59	8.55	8.43	9.56	9.76
Other	12.28	11.53	12.48	13.12	11.31	11.02	12.66	12.65	12.98

Source: CSIS Data Bank.

FIGURE II-7

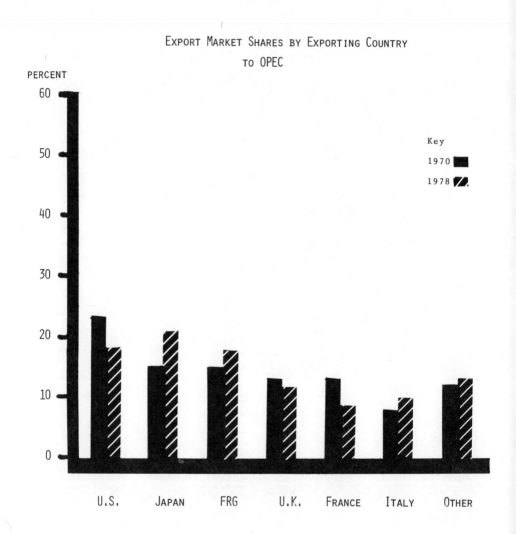

EXPORT MARKET SHARES BY EXPORTING COUNTRY
TO OPEC

APPENDIX TABLE II-A

SAMPLE OF 15 EXPORTING COUNTRIES
AND REGIONAL GROUPINGS OF
76 LESS DEVELOPED COUNTRIES

I.   EXPORTING COUNTRIES

   A.   Major OECD Exporting Countries:

        1.   United States
        2.   Japan
        3.   Federal Republic of Germany
        4.   United Kingdom
        5.   France
        6.   Italy

   B.   Other Exporting Countries:

        1.   Canada
        2.   Netherlands
        3.   Sweden
        4.   Switzerland
        5.   Australia
        6.   Brazil
        7.   Republic of Korea
        8.   Mexico
        9.   Hong Kong

II. REGIONAL GROUPINGS OF LESS DEVELOPED COUNTRIES

   A.   Central America:

        1.   British Honduras (Belize)
        2.   Costa Rica
        3.   El Salvador
        4.   Guatemala
        5.   Honduras
        6.   Mexico
        7.   Nicaragua
        8.   Panama

   B.   South America:

        1.   Argentina
        2.   Bolivia
        3.   Brazil
        4.   Chile
        5.   Colombia
        6.   Ecuador

B.　South America:

    7.　Guyana
    8.　Paraguay
    9.　Peru
  10.　Surinam
  11.　Uruguay

C.　Caribbean:

    1.　Bahamas
    2.　Dominican Republic
    3.　Jamaica
    4.　Netherlands Antilles
    5.　Trinidad-Tobago
    6.　U.S. Virgin Islands

D.　The Far East and South Asia:

    1.　Bangladesh
    2.　Hong Kong
    3.　India
    4.　Malaysia
    5.　Pakistan
    6.　Phillipines
    7.　Singapore
    8.　South Korea/ROK
    9.　Sri Lanka
  10.　Taiwan
  11.　Thailand

E.　The Middle East/Non-OPEC:

    1.　Afghanistan
    2.　Bahrain
    3.　Egypt
    4.　Israel
    5.　Jordan
    6.　Lebanon
    7.　Morocco
    8.　Syria
    9.　Tunisia

F.　Africa/Non-OPEC:

    1.　Cameroon
    2.　Congo-Brazzaville
    3.　Ethiopia
    4.　Ghana
    5.　Guinea

F. Africa/Non-OPEC:

     6.   Ivory Coast
     7.   Kenya
     8.   Liberia
     9.   Malawi
    10.   Mali
    11.   Senegal
    12.   Sierra Leone
    13.   Somalia
    14.   Sudan
    15.   Swaziland
    16.   Tanzania
    17.   Uganda
    18.   Zaire
    19.   Zambia

G. OPEC:

     1.   Algeria
     2.   Ecuador
     3.   Gabon
     4.   Indonesia
     5.   Iraq
     6.   Iran
     7.   Kuwait
     8.   Libya
     9.   Nigeria
    10.   Saudi Arabia
    11.   United Arab Emirates
    12.   Venezuela

STANDARD INTERNATIONAL TRADE
CLASSIFICATION INDEX

I. SITC 5--CHEMICALS:

Code	Commodity	SITC Code
01	Chemical Elements, Compounds	51
02	Synthetic Organic Dyestuff	53
03	Medicinal and Pharmaceutical Products	54
04	Oils and Perfume	55
05	Fertilizers, Manufactured	56
06	Plastic Materials	58
07	Other Chemicals	52, 57, 59

II. SITC 6--MANUFACTURED GOODS CLASSIFIED BY MATERIAL

Code	Commodity	SITC Code
08	Leather Manufactures	61
09	Rubber Manufactures	62
10	Wood, Cork Manufactures	63
11	Paper, Paperboard	64
12	Yarn Thread	651
13	Textile Fabrics	652, 653
14	Other Textile Products	654, 655, 656, 657
15	Diamonds	667
16	Glassware, Pottery	664, 665, 666
17	Mineral Manufactures	661, 662, 663
18	Pig Iron	671
19	Iron, Steel Manufactures	(exc. 671) 67
20	Unwrought Copper	6821
21	Unwrought Aluminum	6841
22	Other Unwrought Nonferrous	681, 6831, 6851 6861, 6871
23	Copper Manufactures	6822
24	Aluminum Manufactures	6842
25	Other Nonferrous Manufactures	6832, 6852, 6862 6872, 688, 689
26	Cutlery, Household Equipment	696, 697
27	Hand Tools	695
28	Other Metal Manufactures	691, 692, 693 694, 698

III. SITC 7--MACHINERY AND TRANSPORT EQUIPMENT

Code	Commodity		SITC Code
29	Non-electric Power Machinery	(Exc. 7114 & 7115)	
			711
30	Internal Combustion Engines		7115
31	Aircraft Engines		7114
32	Tractors		7125
33	Other Agricultural Machinery	(Exc. 7125)	712
34	Office Machines		7141, 7149
35	Computers		7142, 7143
36	Metal Working Machinery		715
37	Textile, Leather Machinery		717
38	Construction, Mining Machinery		7184
39	Other Industrial Machinery	(Exc. 7184)	718
		7194, 7195, 7196,	7198
40	Heating, Cooling Equipment		7191
41	Pumps, Centrifuges		7192
42	Fork Lift Trucks		7193
43	Parts, Accessories Machinery, nes.*		7199
44	Electric Power Machinery		722
45	Television Receivers		7241
46	Radio Receivers		7242
47	Telecommunications Equipment		724
48	Domestic Electrical Apparatus		725
49	Medical Electrical Apparatus		726
50	Transistors, Photocells		7293
51	Electrical Measuring Equipment		7295
52	Other Electrical Machinery Apparatus	7291,	7292
		7296, 7297, 7299,	723
53	Railway Vehicles		731
54	Passenger Motor Cars		7321
55	Trucks, Buses	7322, 7323, 7324,	7325
56	Motor Vehicle Parts	7326, 7327, 7328,	7294
57	Motocycles		7329
58	Trailers, Bicycles		733
59	Aircraft		734
60	Ships, Boats	7355, 7358,	7359

IV. SITC 8--MISCELLANEOUS MANUFACTURED ARTICLES

Code	Commodity	SITC Code
61	Furniture	82
62	Clothing	84
63	Footwear	85
64	Optical Instruments	8611, 8612, 8613
65	Cameras & Equipment	8614, 8615, 8616
66	Other Scientific Instruments	8617, 8618, 8619

IV. SITC 8--MISCELLANEOUS MANUFACTURED ARTICLES (CONT.)

Code	Commodity	SITC Code
67	Movies, Photographic Film	862, 863
68	Watches, Clocks	864
69	Phonographs, Musical Instruments	891
70	Books, Magazines	892
71	Toys, Sporting Goods	894
72	Jewelry, Art	896, 897
73	Other Manufactured Goods	81, 83, 893, 895, 899

*
not elsewhere specified

APPENDIX TABLE II-C

EXPORTS BY COMMODITY BY ALL 15 EXPORTING COUNTRIES
TO ALL LDCS, 1970 and 1978
(millions of dollars)

Code	Commodity	United States 1970	United States 1978	Japan 1970	Japan 1978	Germany 1970	Germany 1978	United Kingdom 1970	United Kingdom 1978	Total of 15 Countries 1970	Total of 15 Countries 1978
1	Chemical Elements, Compounds	418	2,037	171	1,213	173	758	80	323	1,102	5,431
2	Synthetic Organic Dyes	38	135	36	236	110	374	56	219	347	1,356
3	Medicinal & Pharmaceutical Prods.	168	379	24	81	125	399	104	434	714	2,359
4	Oils and Perfume	60	277	16	100	26	116	52	256	232	1,148
5	Fertilizers, Manufactured	111	401	22	71	35	94	0	16	246	1,098
6	Plastic Materials	158	776	198	890	108	534	43	217	610	3,346
7	Other Chemicals	208	635	36	252	92	367	75	399	571	2,228
8	Leather Manufactures	22	137	12	184	5	28	7	60	62	524
9	Rubber Manufactures	57	350	102	453	22	125	45	122	306	1,467
10	Wood, Cork Manufactures	16	133	5	26	6	111	4	53	51	556
11	Paper, Paperboard	212	587	101	292	26	119	53	165	655	2,030
12	Yarn Thread	35	150	269	472	65	150	35	101	546	1,275
13	Textile Fabrics	85	278	576	1,647	43	167	76	187	974	3,083
14	Other Textile Products	53	229	60	244	17	99	33	137	263	1,237
15	Diamonds	84	351	11	18	3	21	116	450	252	1,616
16	Glassware, Pottery	41	180	37	172	19	75	22	108	179	824
17	Mineral Manufactures	45	215	46	468	26	230	58	166	226	1,808
18	Pig Iron	12	28	1	15	4	11	1	2	28	67
19	Iron, Steel Manufactures	399	1,018	946	5,732	200	1,341	202	577	2,250	11,139
20	Unwrought Copper	64	13	16	63	6	24	7	4	106	121
21	Unwrought Aluminum	51	100	1	53	1	26	1	7	99	344
22	Other Unwrought Nonferrous	19	25	13	61	7	32	15	42	137	260
23	Copper Manufactures	17	62	35	284	18	86	29	73	150	626
24	Aluminum Manufactures	33	91	18	151	11	74	11	44	109	597
25	Other Nonferrous Manufactures	20	171	5	36	6	17	6	19	52	281
26	Cutlery, Household Equipment	17	71	21	134	14	53	20	60	120	585
27	Hand Tools	63	229	21	154	41	195	29	110	211	944
28	Other Metal Manufactures	181	850	152	1,258	78	670	128	698	782	5,687

APPENDIX TABLE II-C (cont.)

Code	Commodity	United States 1970	United States 1978	Japan 1970	Japan 1978	Germany 1970	Germany 1978	United Kingdom 1970	United Kingdom 1978	Total of 15 Countries 1970	Total of 15 Countries 1978
29	Nonelectric Power Machines	64	536	60	883	69	595	46	205	335	2,785
30	Internal Combustion Engines	205	775	63	692	78	440	101	406	547	2,717
31	Aircraft Engines	75	259	1	1	3	40	39	152	145	695
32	Tractors	207	559	19	255	24	93	75	205	359	1,223
33	Other Agricultural Machines	42	265	5	33	14	72	18	53	101	540
34	Office Machines	112	583	11	120	28	89	17	62	216	1,007
35	Computers	83	242	24	205	16	55	16	57	199	723
36	Metal Working Machinery	86	457	42	603	90	607	30	141	337	2,250
37	Textile, Leather Machinery	99	223	190	676	183	560	92	188	743	2,349
38	Construction, Mining Machinery	317	1,711	44	452	28	291	60	402	529	3,431
39	Other Industrial Machinery	406	1,395	126	1,017	347	2,238	178	799	1,388	7,365
40	Heating, Cooling Equipment	210	922	70	916	62	420	30	208	488	3,192
41	Pumps, Centrifuges	244	964	56'	636	62	447	55	355	530	3,308
42	Fork Lift Trucks	186	1,834	49	515	42	423	54	259	433	3,771
43	Parts, Accessory Machines	114	426	49	543	36	284	59	209	357	2,030
44	Electric Power Machinery	226	1,467	159	1,705	107	1,006	97	788	892	6,608
45	Television Receivers	38	217	58	444	10	92	3	17	120	826
46	Radio Receivers	98	42	122	691	6	15	1	4	243	839
47	Telecommunications Equipment	192	978	105	926	85	559	112	470	752	4,053
48	Domestic Electrical Equipment	44	185	38	292	9	60	15	74	162	987
49	Medical Electrical Apparatus	14	131	3	32	16	84	3	27	45	382
50	Transistors, Photocells	163	423	36	653	8	117	7	37	232	1,504
51	Electrical Measuring Equipment	79	577	26	159	19	108	18	114	176	1,217
52	Other Electrical Mach. Appar.	128	702	149	1,023	94	1,408	104	449	620	4,389
53	Railway Vehicles	59	190	31	193	19	89	13	80	183	802
54	Passenger Motor Cars	125	742	117	1,731	154	696	123	492	769	5,088
55	Trucks, Buses	318	1,417	157	2,322	156	1,166	139	382	959	6,648
56	Motor Vehicle Parts	375	580	93	964	209	925	191	596	1,057	4,035
57	Motorcycles	1	20	50	397	1	5	2	51	81	489
58	Trailers, Bicycles	15	130	21	232	12	141	23	109	95	871
59	Aircraft	476	2,529	11	22	5	142	107	699	729	4,249
60	Ships, Boats	61	176	783	4,445	77	341	34	271	1,232	6,741
61	Furniture	23	152	5	46	7	129	12	121	72	938

APPENDIX TABLE II-C (cont.)

Code	Commodity	United States 1970	United States 1978	Japan 1970	Japan 1978	Germany 1970	Germany 1978	United Kingdom 1970	United Kingdom 1978	Total of 15 Countries 1970	Total of 15 Countries 1978
62	Clothing	115	366	50	83	11	71	28	218	330	1,611
63	Footwear	5	19	7	16	2	17	10	33	62	269
64	Optical Instruments	10	63	22	105	12	72	2	31	60	358
65	Cameras and Equipment	37	166	49	346	22	94	6	40	126	755
66	Other Scientific Instruments	136	299	31	254	48	251	36	213	307	1,382
67	Movies, Photographic Film	68	216	17	132	21	68	15	66	150	590
68	Watches, Clocks	7	126	73	715	13	63	3	37	334	2,080
69	Phonographs, Musical Instru.	52	228	77	558	21	43	8	66	190	1,048
70	Books, Magazines	53	156	14	46	10	55	28	204	176	681
71	Toys, Sporting Goods	27	145	28	119	5	18	12	43	96	471
72	Jewelry, Art	17	57	2	23	8	37	5	43	95	1,002
73	Other Manufactured Goods	98	320	66	400	44	239	49	267	378	2,051

Source: CSIS Data Bank.

III. MEASURES OF PRICE AND COST COMPETITIVENESS IN U.S. EXPORT PERFORMANCE

Price and cost competitiveness are important factors determining the export performance of a country. Not only does their role differ from country to country and from period to period, but the influence on export performance of changes in prices and costs in a country relative to those in competing countries involves complex analytical issues which need to be explored.[9] A firm selling a commodity in a foreign market may quote a price on the basis of its domestic price for the same commodity or it may adjust its export price in accordance with the competitive conditions that exist in the foreign market. Domestic prices for exported products will be determined on the basis of both costs and competitive conditions in the domestic market. If a firm desires to maintain or expand a particular foreign market for its product, however, it may quote export prices that differ from its domestic market price or from the prices that it quotes for the same product in other foreign markets. In some cases a firm may find that it can maximize its profits by charging a higher price in a particular foreign market than its domestic price, but this depends upon the competitive conditions in the market in question.

Pricing policies will depend in considerable measure upon the degree of product differentiation as well as on the proportion of a particular market represented by the sales of a firm, whether foreign or domestic. A firm that is selling a relatively homogeneous product in a foreign market in which the firm's share is no more than, say, 5 or 10 percent, will have little choice but to sell at the world market price. On the other hand, a firm selling a highly differentiated product or one for which it controls half of the total sales in a particular market will have considerable discretion in setting the price of its product in that market. In the former case, the firm is a price taker, while in the latter case the firm is within limits a price maker. Nevertheless, in both cases the firm's costs will have an impact on how much it is willing to supply (or aggressively compete for) in the foreign market. If a firm finds that in order to penetrate a foreign market it must sell its products at prices that do not fully cover costs, it will have less interest in penetrating or even maintaining sales in the foreign market as contrasted with selling in the domestic market or in an alternative foreign market.

It is clear from the above discussion that price competitiveness in foreign markets involves three types of measures: (a) export prices or the prices actually quoted in foreign markets; (b) domestic prices of products sold in foreign markets; and (c) production costs. Although over time these measures may tend to move together, they may change at different rates or even diverge widely in the short run. Moreover, aggregate measures of costs, domestic wholesale prices, and export prices will have different significance for export competitiveness with respect to different types of products or markets. No single measure captures all the relevant elements in the relationship between relative prices and costs on the one hand, and export competitiveness on the other.

For measuring a country's overall price-cost competitiveness in foreign markets, we use aggregative measures such as overall export price indexes, domestic wholesale price indexes, and indexes of costs of manufactures. Admittedly, aggregate measures of price-cost competitiveness do not indicate the conditions relevant for individual commodities and markets, but they provide a broad indicator of changes in the price-cost environment within which exporters operate. Since a country's export performance is a relative matter, the indexes must measure a country's prices or costs relative to those of competing exporting countries. Finally, since we are concerned in this study with the explanation for changes in U.S. export performance over time, we must employ indexes that measure changes in relative price and cost competitiveness for the United States and other countries over time from a common base period, and relate these changes to the export performance of the United States and competing exporting countries.

Measures of changes in prices and costs in one country relative to those in other countries must take account of the fact that we live in a world of floating exchange rates. Hence, relative changes in a country's prices or costs must be adjusted for changes in the exchange value of that country's currency in terms of

the currencies of competing exporting countries over
the relevant period. A change in the exchange value of
a country's currency in terms of a composite index of
the exchange values of other currencies is known as a
change in the effective rate of exchange. The effective rate of exchange is expressed as an index that
measures the change in the value of a currency in terms
of a number of other currencies from a common base
period.[10]

Relative Price and Cost Indexes

In this study we employ three indexes published on
an annual and quarterly basis by the International
Monetary Fund (IMF): (a) the relative wholesale price
index, (b) the relative export unit value index, and
(c) the relative unit labor cost index --all adjusted
for the effective rate of exchange.[11] The IMF publishes these three indexes for the United States and
13 other industrial countries. The relative price or
cost index for each country is the ratio of the index
of prices or costs of manufactures of that country to
the trade-weighted average of the corresponding indexes
for 13 competing countries; each index is adjusted for
the effective rate of exchange for that country and all
indexes employed in its calculation have a common base
year.[12]

The relative wholesale price index adjusted for
the effective rate of exchange provides a method for
measuring changes in domestic wholesale prices in one
country relative to those in 13 competing countries in
terms of a common currency. The relative export unit
value index is calculated by dividing the export unit
value index (of manufactures) for a given country by
the average of the corresponding export unit value
indexes for a number of competing countries. This
provides a measure of relative changes in a country's
export prices of manufactures.[13] The relative unit
labor cost index is the ratio of the index of compensation of employees per unit of output in the
manufacturing sector to trade-weighted averages of the
corresponding indexes for competing countries on a
common base. Unit labor costs capture relative changes
in productivity, which are exceedingly important in
export competitiveness. These three indexes together

110

with a fourth index, the relative value-added deflator, are shown in Appendix Table III-A for the United States, Japan, Germany, and the United Kingdom covering the years 1968-1978.[14] Figures III-1 and III-2 show movements of indexes of relative unit labor costs, relative wholesale prices, and relative export unit values for the United States and Japan, respectively, for the 1968-1976 period.

Each of the indicators of price or cost competitiveness described above has its weakness, either statistical or conceptual, and its relative advantages or disadvantages with respect to other indicators. Comparisons among these idexes may reveal certain aspects of export competitiveness among the countries whose indexes are compared.

Comparisons of Measures of Price and Cost Competitiveness

Between 1970 and 1978, the U.S. relative unit labor cost index for manufacturing (adjusted for the effective rate of exchange) declined by nearly 39 percent while the U.S. relative wholesale price index for manufactures (adjusted) declined by only 21 percent. The relative export unit value index for manufactures (adjusted) declined by less than 14 percent over the same period (see Appendix Table III-A). To a major degree these decreases in U.S. relative price and cost measures were influenced by the 21 percent decline in the effective rate of exchange for the dollar as measured by the IMF (MERM) index. How can we explain the disparities in the changes in these three indexes over the 1970-1978 period?

From 1970-1978 the U.S. industrial wholesale price index (absolute index) rose by about 90 percent while the U.S. unit labor cost index rose by only 66 percent. This difference can be explained largely by the increases in prices of fuel and raw material imports. The much wider disparity in changes between the relative U.S. wholesale price index and the relative unit labor cost index can be explained in considerable part by the relative movements of these indexes abroad. For example, Japanese wages rose three-fold between 1970 and 1978 whereas the Japanese wholesale price index rose by only 53 percent. Some, but not all, of the disparity between these two Japanese indexes may be explained by increased Japanese productivity.

Perhaps more significant from the standpoint of U.S. price competitiveness is the behavior of the U.S. relative export unit value index, which declined by only 14 percent over the 1970-1978 period, as contrasted with a 21 percent decline in the U.S. relative wholesale price index. In part, the behavior of these indexes may be explained by the fact that the absolute U.S. wholesale price index increased by 90 percent as against an increase of 109 percent in the absolute U.S. export unit value index between 1970 and 1978. Again, however, the behavior of the relative indexes was greatly influenced by the fact that the Japanese absolute export unit value rose by only 41 percent between 1970 and 1978, although the absolute Japanese wholesale price index rose by 53 percent. By contrast, the German absolute unit value index rose by 48 percent, although the German industrial wholesale price index rose by 46 percent over the 1970-1978 period. The corresponding U.K. indexes exhibited a similar pattern. We find that although the U.S. export unit value index rose by a higher percentage than the U.S. wholesale price index, as was also the case of the United Kingdom and Germany for the 1970-1978 period, the Japanese export unit value index rose by substantially less than the Japanese wholesale price index over the same period. Whether the cause of this phenomenon is to be found in the fact that productivity increased more rapidly in Japan's export industries than in industries producing nontrade goods, or whether it is to be found in Japan's export pricing methods is not known to the authors. It is worth investigating. It would also be useful to know why U.S. export prices have been rising relative to both the U.S. general wholesale price index and the U.S. wholesale price index of industrial goods.

Relative Price and Cost Indexes and U.S. Export Shares in Manufacturing

Figure III-1 shows the changes in the U.S. relative unit labor cost index, the relative wholesale price index, and the relative export unit value index

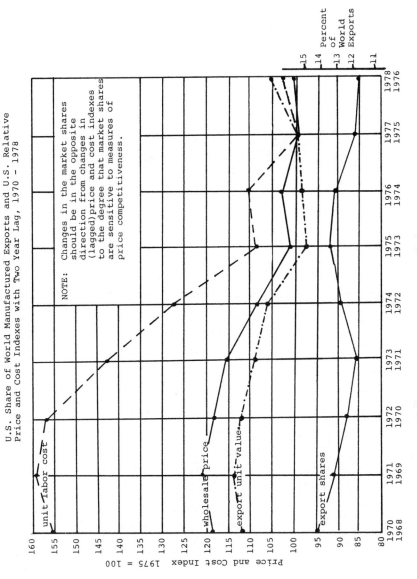

FIGURE III-1

U.S. Share of World Manufactured Exports and U.S. Relative
Price and Cost Indexes with Two Year Lag, 1970 - 1978

NOTE: Changes in the market shares
should be in the opposite
direction from changes in
(lagged) price and cost indexes
to the degree that market shares
are sensitive to measures of
price competitiveness.

Dates from 1970-1978 refer to the U.S. share of world manufactured exports;
1969-1976 refers to U.S. relative price and cost indices.
Source: Appendix Tables III-A and III-B.

113

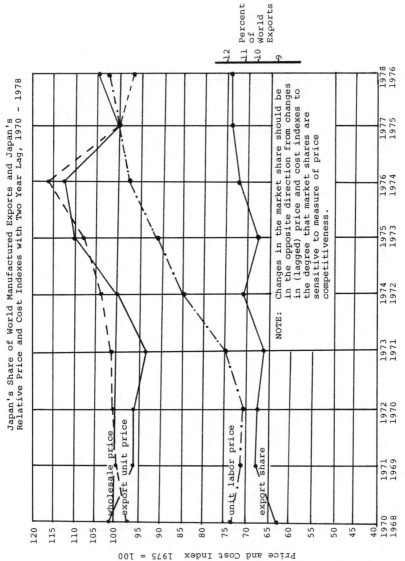

FIGURE III-2

Japan's Share of World Manufactured Exports and Japan's
Relative Price and Cost Indexes with Two Year Lag, 1970 – 1978

Dates from 1970-1978 refer to Japan's share of world manufactured exports;
1969-1976 refers to Japan's relative price and cost indices.
Source: Appendix Tables III-A and III-C.

NOTE: Changes in the market share should be
in the opposite direction from changes
in (lagged) price and cost indexes to
the degree that market shares are
sensitive to measure of price
competitiveness.

114

APPENDIX TABLE III-A

INDEXES OF RELATIVE COSTS AND PRICES FOR MANUFACTURES
VIS-A-VIS OTHER INDUSTRIAL COUNTRIES, 1968-1978
(1975=100)

	1968	1969	1970	1971	1972	1973	1974	1975	1976	1977	1978
Relative Unit Labor Costs											
United States	155.7	160.4	157.0	142.9	126.5	113.2	115.0	100.0	105.0	103.5	96.1
Japan	75.2	72.4	69.7	74.9	84.9	91.8	98.4	100.0	101.8	108.9	120.9
Germany	78.9	80.8	92.2	95.9	99.0	110.5	108.7	100.0	98.6	100.8	104.3
United Kingdom	96.5	100.5	103.9	106.8	103.1	90.2	94.1	100.0	94.1	92.8	100.6
Relative Value Added Deflators											
United States	146.0	145.7	141.0	134.7	121.6	98.1	106.2	100.0	105.7	105.0	95.5
Japan	81.7	82.1	80.3	83.6	90.5	93.1	95.7	100.0	97.0	99.6	114.4
Germany	84.5	83.6	93.5	97.2	97.0	106.4	106.3	100.0	100.9	104.2	105.6
United Kingdom	94.9	98.1	101.1	105.1	103.5	92.5	96.1	100.0	93.5	91.6	93.7
Relative Wholesale Prices											
United States	119.8	120.6	118.2	115.0	106.7	98.0	99.8	100.0	103.1	100.9	93.9
Japan	100.2	99.0	97.7	94.1	100.3	111.1	113.7	100.0	103.8	107.3	119.7
Germany	103.8	82.5	89.7	93.4	94.1	102.4	103.0	100.0	101.6	103.7	104.9
United Kingdom	105.5	106.6	107.6	112.9	110.1	96.5	96.8	100.0	93.9	100.5	105.0
Relative Export Unit Values											
United States	110.7	113.2	112.1	109.7	103.5	95.4	96.0	100.0	105.8	103.0	96.6
Japan	99.0	99.4	99.7	100.3	104.4	108.9	116.2	100.0	96.6	98.2	108.5
Germany	89.6	90.0	94.5	96.4	96.6	104.7	100.6	100.0	100.0	100.8	101.7
United Kingdom	103.4	102.9	104.7	105.9	107.5	99.3	98.1	100.0	96.8	103.3	109.7

Source: International Financial Statistics Yearbook, 1979, p. 53.

APPENDIX TABLE III-B

U.S. AND WORLD EXPORTS OF MANUFACTURES
1970-1978

(billions of dollars)

Year	United States	World	Percent
1970	28.8	201.7	14.3
1971	29.8	226.0	13.1
1972	33.2	270.7	12.3
1973	42.7	363.9	11.7
1974	62.3	483.8	12.8
1975	69.3	519.5	13.3
1976	74.8	565.6	13.2
1977	77.8	647.8	12.0
1978	92.6	788.0	11.8

Source: International Trade, 1978/79, General Agreement on Tariffs and Trade, Geneva, 1979 (and earlier issues).

116

APPENDIX TABLE III-C

JAPANESE AND WORLD EXPORTS OF MANUFACTURES
1970-1978

(billions of dollars)

Year	Japan	World	Percent
1970	18.1	201.7	9.0
1971	22.6	226.0	10.0
1972	27.1	270.7	10.0
1973	34.8	363.9	9.6
1974	52.4	483.8	10.8
1975	53.2	519.5	10.2
1976	63.9	565.6	11.3
1977	76.8	647.8	11.8
1978	93.2	788.0	11.8

Source: International Trade, 1978/79, General Agreement on Tariffs and Trade, Geneva, 1979 (and earlier issues).

IV.   THE ANALYSIS OF U.S. EXPORT
COMPETITIVENESS IN MANUFACTURES IN THE LDC MARKET

We have measured changes in U.S. export performance by changes in U.S. shares in the LDC market for manufactures. For purposes of analysis we may distinguish among three sources of changes in U.S. market shares: (a) changes in the relative demand for particular products in the LDC market; (b) changes in the relative sizes among the regional LDC markets; and (c) changes in U.S. competitiveness in particular products and in particular markets. This analytical breakdown implies that a relative decline in demand for those products for which the United States is a major supplier, or a decline in the relative size of the regional markets to which the United States is a major supplier, could result in a decline in the U.S. overall market share for LDC imports of manufactures, even though U.S. competitiveness in particular commodities and in regional markets for these commodities may not change. This analysis, therefore, isolates changes in export market shares arising from shifts in product demand and changes in the relative sizes of regional markets from changes in market shares arising from U.S. competitiveness in particular commodities and markets.[16]

In the broadest sense, U.S. competitiveness should encompass the ability of U.S. exports to adjust to changes in the relative rates of growth of foreign markets as well as to the shifts in world demand for particular commodities. For example, a country that increased its share of the world market for buggy whips and horse collars between 1910 and 1920, or a country that increased its share of the import market for Burma during the 1950s should scarcely be given high marks for export competitiveness! Nevertheless, for some purposes, including that of relating measures of price competition to export market shares, it is useful to decompose changes in export shares in the LDC market to distinguish between what we shall call the market size effect and the competitive effect. It would also be possible to isolate the effects on U.S. export performance arising from shifts in the total LDC and regional demand pattern for the 73 commodity classifications in our sample, but this exercise was rejected for three reasons. First, the ability of a country to adjust its supply of exports to shifts in the world demand for individual commodities is an important element of export competitiveness; hence, it is included in our measure of export competitiveness. Second, statistical problems arise in isolating the effects of both changes in market size and changes in demand patterns, since the interaction between the two effects tend to create a large residual. Third, the percentage year-to-year changes in U.S. competitiveness are not greatly affected by the isolation of year-to-year changes in the relative demand for individual manufactures in the LDC market.[17]

The statistical method employed for decomposing U.S. export shares is detailed in Technical Appendix I to this study and only the results will be summarized here. The methodology is a variant of the constant market share analysis based on that employed in a study by Bert G. Hickman, et al.[18] This approach statistically decomposes sources of export performance with respect to (a) the competitive effect; (b) the market size effect; and (c) the interaction effect. The competitive effect measures changes in the U.S. export share in each of the regional markets for the period 1970-1978, holding constant the relative size of each LDC regional market. This effect isolates the influence of changes in the competitiveness of U.S. exports in specific LDC markets. The market size effect measures the net effect of shifts in the size of the various regional markets, holding constant the U.S. share in each of the LDC regional markets. The market size effect will be positive in its influence on the annual percentage change in U.S. export shares when the markets that are of above average importance for U.S. exports in the base period grow more rapidly than the rate of growth in total imports of all LDCs. If these markets grow less rapidly than total LDC imports, the effect on the change in U.S. market shares in the total LDC market will be negative. Consequently, the U.S. share in total exports to the LDCs may increase without any change in U.S. competitiveness, provided the markets that are of relatively greater importance to the United States grow more rapidly than the rate of growth of total LDC imports.

The sum of the competitive effect and the market size effect is not equal to the total percentage year-to-year changes in the U.S. export share in the

LDC market. Changes in market shares in the individual regions and in the relative market sizes of the regions give rise to what is called the interaction effect. The interaction effect is a residual term that accounts for changes that cannot be attributed exclusively to either the competitive effect or the market size effect. This residual tends to be small, and for the overall period 1970-1978 accounted for a negligible portion of the total change in the U.S. export share of the LDC market.

Table IV-1 shows the decomposition of the annual percentage changes in U.S. export shares to the LDC market over the 1970-1978 period, according to the three component effects. For the entire period, the cumulative 23.4 percent decline in the total U.S. export share is attributed mainly to the competitive effect (14.9 percent), with virtually all the remainder (8.4 percent) attributed to the market size effect. The negative market size effect can be explained mainly by the fact that the Western Hemisphere markets in which U.S. market shares were highest did not grow as rapidly as the OPEC market. The negative competitive effect can be explained mainly by the failure of the United States to maintain its market shares in the South American and OPEC markets.

Table IV-2, Column 3, disaggregates the cumulative percentage change in U.S. export performance by regional market for the periods 1970-1974, 1974-1977 and 1977-1978. The column totals indicate a marked decline in U.S. export performance in all three periods. In the 1970-1974 period the total percentage change in U.S. export shares (-12.4 percent) can be largely explained by the decline in U.S. competitiveness (-9.5 percent) and to a much lesser degree by the market size effect (-2.0 percent). By contrast, during the 1974-1977 period when U.S. export shares declined by 9.7 percent, the decrease in competitiveness (-1.9 percent) was only a minor factor compared with the market size effect (-8.0 percent). During the final period, 1977-1978, the decline in U.S. competitiveness (-2.8 percent) was substantially offset by a gain in the market size effect (+1.5 percent) (see Table IV-2).

Over the 1970-1978 period, the decline in U.S. market shares is concentrated in the regional markets

TABLE IV-1

ANNUAL PERCENTAGE CHANGES IN U.S. EXPORT PERFORMANCE
IN THE LDC MARKET (1970-1978)
(Measured in percentage terms)

Year	Total Change in U.S. Export Share	Competi- tiveness Effect	Market Size Effect	Inter- action Effect
1970-71	-10.59	-7.96	-2.75	+0.13
1971-72	-4.44	-5.85	+1.36	+0.04
1972-73	-0.36	+1.15	-1.45	-0.06
1973-74	+2.86	+2.52	+0.55	-0.21
1974-75	+1.90	+5.54	-3.97	+0.33
1975-76	-0.07	+1.41	-1.43	-0.05
1976-77	-11.30	-8.93	-2.22	-0.15
1977-78	-1.37	-2.81	+1.49	-0.05
TOTAL CHANGE:	-23.37	-14.93	-8.42	-0.02

Source: Technical Appendix I.

TABLE IV-2

COMPONENTS OF CUMULATIVE PERCENTAGE CHANGES IN U.S. EXPORT PERFORMANCE
WEIGHTED FOR SEVEN REGIONAL MARKETS IN THE THIRD WORLD DURING THREE PERIODS
(1970-1974, 1974-1977, and 1977-1978)

(measured in percentage terms)

Region (1)	Period (2)	Cumulative Percentage Change in U.S. Export Share (3)	Components of Cumulative Percentage Change			Base Period Export Weights (7)
			Competi- tiveness Effect (4)	Market Size Effect (5)	Inter- action Effect (6)	
Central America	1970-1974	-3.56	-1.69	-2.02	+0.153	22.28
South America	1970-1974	-3.73	-3.31	-0.48	+0.069	23.49
The Caribbean	1970-1974	-2.35	+0.76	-2.77	-0.332	6.29
South Asia & Far East	1970-1974	-2.58	-0.86	-1.79	+0.070	22.05
Middle East/ Non-OPEC	1970-1974	-0.32	-0.36	+0.04	-0.002	5.01
Africa/ Non-OPEC	1970-1974	-1.35	-1.02	-0.47	+0.136	3.49
OPEC	1970-1974	+1.45	-3.06	+5.47	-0.965	17.39
TOTALS:		-12.44	-9.54	-2.01	-0.871	100.00

TABLE IV-2 (Cont.)

Region (1)	Period (2)	Cumulative Percentage Change in U.S. Export Share (3)	Components of Cumulative Percentage Change			Base Period Export Weights (7)
			Competitiveness Effect (4)	Market Size Effect (5)	Interaction Effect (6)	
Central America	1974-1977	-6.10	-0.34	-5.85	+0.093	21.39
South America	1974-1977	-8.82	-0.08	-8.78	+0.030	22.56
The Caribbean	1974-1977	-1.21	+0.02	-1.23	-0.006	4.50
South Asia & Far East	1974-1977	-4.20	-0.91	-3.43	+0.140	22.23
Middle East/ Non-OPEC	1974-1977	-0.07	-0.16	+0.10	-0.003	5.35
Africa/ Non-OPEC	1974-1977	-0.54	-0.22	-0.35	+0.032	2.45
OPEC	1974-1977	+11.25	-0.19	+11.53	-0.100	21.51
TOTALS:		-9.69	-1.88	-8.01	+0.186	100.00

TABLE IV-2 (Cont.)

Region (1)	Period (2)	Cumulative Percentage Change in U.S. Export Share (3)	Components of Cumulative Percentage Change			Base Period Export Weights (7)
			Competitiveness Effect (4)	Market Size Effect (5)	Interaction Effect (6)	
Central America	1977-1978	+1.71	+0.38	+1.78	+0.039	16.93
South America	1977-1978	-0.96	-0.004	-0.96	+0.0002	15.22
The Caribbean	1977-1978	-0.25	-0.05	-0.20	+0.003	3.65
South Asia & Far East	1977-1978	+1.43	-1.21	+2.81	-0.171	19.97
Middle East/ Non-OPEC	1977-1978	-0.46	-0.21	-0.26	+0.009	5.85
Africa/ Non-OPEC	1977-1978	-0.42	-0.04	-0.38	+0.008	2.11
OPEC	1977-1978	-2.90	-1.66	-1.30	+0.059	36.27
TOTALS:		-1.37	-2.81	+1.49	-0.053	100.00
TOTAL CHANGE/1970-1978:		-23.49	-14.22	-8.53	-0.738	

Source: Technical Appendix I.

of the Western Hemisphere and the Far East/South Asia. The base period export weights (see Column 7) for the first two periods reveal that these four regions constitute nearly three-fourths of all U.S. exports to LDCs. Consequently, the decline in U.S. export performance between 1970 and 1977 reflects in large part a deterioration in U.S. export shares in its major markets in the Third World.

An examination of the component effects during the first period (1970-1974) reveals the decline in U.S. export performance is primarily the result of a general decline in the competitive effect across all regions. More than two-thirds of this decline is concentrated in the regional markets of South America and OPEC. This result reflects a significant reduction in U.S. market shares for these regional markets since the base period. At the same time, the market size effect indicates that the markets where U.S. exports are most highly concentrated grew more slowly than regional markets in the Middle East/Non-OPEC, Africa/Non-OPEC, and OPEC. The decline in U.S. export performance measured by the competitive effect, however, is more than four times as large as the decline in U.S. export performance by the market size effect.

An examination of the component effects during the second period (1974-1977) reveals that the decline in U.S. export performance measured by the market size effect is more than four times the decline measured by the competitive effect. This result is exactly the reverse of that obtained during the first period. During the second period there is only a marginal reduction in U.S. market shares in each of the regional markets. The negative measures for the market size effect in major U.S. markets reflect the fact that these markets grew much less rapidly than other markets where U.S. exports are less concentrated.

The decline in U.S. export performance during the final period (1977-1978) is exclusively attributable to a further deterioration in the U.S. competitive effect. The decline in the competitive effect is most significant in the Far East/South Asia and OPEC. The corresponding market size effect is positive and concentrated in the regional markets of Central America and the Far East/South Asia.

Table IV-2 yields three important results. First, the decline in U.S. market penetration (i.e., the competitive effect) was greatest during the first period (1970-1974). Second, the major component of decline in U.S. export growth during the second period (1974-1977) was the market size effect. Third, the decline in U.S. export performance has continued during the final period (1977-1978). Thus, U.S. exports of manufactures to LDCs have increased more slowly than its major competitors and have remained concentrated in those markets that have increased in size less rapidly throughout the period 1970-1978.

The Role of U.S. Price Competitiveness in
U.S. Export Performance in the LDC Market

The measures of relative U.S. price and cost competitiveness described in Chapter III are undoubtedly important determinants of U.S. export performance in the LDC market. The influence of relative prices and costs on export shares can best be measured on a commodity-by-commodity basis, but unfortunately, export prices for individual commodity groups are only available over the relevant period for a few of these commodity groups. In this study, therefore, we have attempted to relate aggregate measures of changes in relative U.S. prices and costs as independent variables to measures of changes in U.S. export competitiveness in the LDC market. It must be emphasized that changes in these measures account for only a minor portion of U.S. export performance, and there are problems in interpreting the relationships between these two sets of variables. Relating aggregate measures of prices and costs to aggregate measures of export competitiveness are not the same as relating prices and costs of individual commodities to exports of individual commodities. Demand and supply functions for individual commodities cannot be aggregated to yield a demand and supply function for all commodities. Each commodity has its own demand and supply function in the international market derived from complex functions in each of the exporting and importing countries. Moreover, relative prices and costs are only two among several important factors determining U.S. export performance, including changes in the structure of the U.S. and the world economy, the availability of government export credits and guarantees, and the U.S. tax system as it affects exports, among others. Nevertheless, it is useful to explore just what influence overall price and cost measures have had on U.S. export competitiveness in recent years.

In the case of the measures of relative cost competitiveness, we found no significant correlation with overall U.S. export competitiveness in the LDC markets. We did find, however, a significant relationship for the two measures of price competitiveness.

In this analysis we seek to show the relationship between annual percentage changes in the competitive effect discussed above, or that portion of changes in U.S. shares in the LDC market that cannot be explained by changes in the relative sizes of the regional LDC markets, and each of our two measures of price competitiveness, namely, the relative wholesale price index and the relative export unit value index. The relative price measures as the independent or explanatory variables were lagged two years, since it normally requires a period of time before changes in prices have an effect on trade. The pooled regression model presented in this section combines cross-section and time-series data over the period 1970-1978. The pooled regression technique increases the number of observations for the period by utilizing the competitive effect measures for each of the seven regional markets for each year (see Table IV-2). The statistical results and methodology of this investigation are described in Technical Appendix II.

The empirical results of the pooled regression model indicate that about 18 percent of the year-to-year changes in U.S. shares in the LDC market over the 1970-1978 period accounted for by the competitive effect can be explained by year-to-year changes in the U.S. relative wholesale price index (adjusted for the effective rate of exchange), lagged by two years; and about 21 percent can be explained by year-to-year changes in the U.S. relative export unit value index (adjusted), lagged two years.[19]

A similar regression analysis was conducted for Japan, Germany, and the United Kingdom for the 1970-1978 period. The results for the United Kingdom showed that 24 percent of the year-to-year changes in United Kingdom shares in the LDC market accounted for by the competitive effect could be explained by year-to-year changes in the U.K. relative wholesale price index (adjusted), lagged by two years; and about 29 percent could be explained by changes in the U.K. relative export unit value index (adjusted), lagged by two years. For Germany the explanatory power of the two price competitiveness measures was much lower: only 5 percent for the German relative wholesale price index (adjusted), and 13 percent for the German relative export unit value index (adjusted). For Japan we found no relation between changes in that country's export share accounted for by the competitive effect and changes in Japan's relative export unit value index, and only 7 percent for changes in Japan's relative wholesale price index. Although the regression results were statistically significant for all four countries, only for the United States and the United Kingdom was the explanatory power of the two price competitiveness measures high enough to attach much credibility to the results.[20]

V.   COMPARATIVE ADVANTAGE OF U.S. EXPORTS
IN THE LDC MARKET

In analyzing U.S. export performance in the LDC market, it is instructive to know the products in which the United States has a comparative advantage and what changes have taken place in U.S. comparative advantage over time. Comparative advantage is a fundamental concept in economics and is easy to understand, but there is no satisfactory way of identifying those manufactures in which the United States has a comparative advantage. The United States as well as other industrialized countries are both exporters and importers of virtually the same industrial commodity classifications, and the relationships between a country's exports and imports of the same commodity classification shift from year to year with dynamic changes in the pattern of world supply and demand, the introduction of new products or variants of old products, and of improved technology for producing them. Also, a country may have a relatively large share of the export market in one country or region and a relatively small share (or none at all) in another country or region, depending upon proximity to the markets and other factors.

Although we shall not attempt to identify the commodities in which the United States has a comparative advantage in the conventional sense, we shall employ a measure for ranking U.S. exports to the LDC market in terms of what Bela Balassa calls "'revealed' comparative advantage."[21] For purposes of this study this measure is calculated by weighting the U.S. market share of each commodity in the LDC market by the ratio of U.S. exports of all manufactures to the LDC market to total LDC imports of manufactures from the 15 exporting countries in our sample.[22] The weighted market share for each commodity can be expressed as an index number such that a value greater than unity indicates that the U.S. market share of the commodity is larger than the U.S. share of total imports of manufactures by the LDCs. Where the index number is less than unity, it indicates that the U.S. share of the LDC market for the commodity is less than the U.S. share of total imports of manufactures by the LDCs. We shall refer to the weighted market share measure as the relative export share and to the unweighted market share as simply the export share or market share. We shall regard the United States as having a revealed comparative advantage in those commodities for which the weighted market share index is greater than unity. Changes in U.S. relative export shares (or in the indexes described above) over time reveal shifts in U.S. revealed comparative advantage among commodities. Appendix Table V-A shows U.S. relative export shares (expressed as indexes) in the LDC market for 73 commodities for the years 1970-1978.

About two-thirds of the U.S. technology-intensive commodity groups in our sample demonstrated a revealed comparative advantage for the years between 1970 and 1978. These product groups included the following:

Code	Commodity	1978 Relative Export Share
59	Aircraft	2.70
34	Office Machines	2.62
51	Electrical Measuring Equipment	2.15
1	Chemical Elements, Compounds	1.70
31	Aircraft Engines	1.69
67	Movies, Photographic Film	1.66
5	Fertilizers, Manufactured	1.66
35	Computers	1.52
7	Other Chemicals	1.29
30	Internal Combustion Engines	1.29
50	Transistors, Photocells	1.27
45	Television Receivers	1.19
47	Telecommunications Equipment	1.09
6	Plastic Materials	1.05
44	Electric Power Machinery	1.01

Among the technology-intensive commodity groups, only two -- cameras and equipment, and other scientific instruments -- lost their revealed comparative advantage between 1970 and 1978.

In 1970, 50 percent (or 25) of the nontechnology-intensive products in our sample demonstrated a revealed comparative advantage, but by 1978 this number had declined to 40 percent (or 20 product groups). The leading commodity groups in the nontechnology-intensive products in which the United States had a comparative advantage in 1978 included:

Code	Commodity	1978 Relative Export Share
25	Other Nonferrous Manufactures	2.76
38	Construction, Mining Machinery	2.26
33	Other Agricultural Machinery	2.22
42	Fork Lift Trucks	2.20
32	Tractors	2.07
49	Medical Electrical Apparatus	1.55
17	Pig Iron	1.53
71	Toys, Sporting Goods	1.39
41	Pumps, Centrifuges	1.32
21	Unwrought Aluminum	1.32
11	Paper, Paperboard	1.31
40	Heating, Cooling Equipment	1.31

This analysis suggests that U.S. revealed comparative advantage is concentrated in the technology-intensive products. In these products comparative advantage is most evident in aircraft, chemicals, and high-technology machinery. In the nontechnology-intensive products, comparative advantage lies in heavy equipment machinery and capital intensive mineral manufactures.

The Basis for U.S. Comparative Advantage in Manufactures

The basis for a country's comparative advantage in trade, or the commodity structure of its exports and imports under conditions of trade equilibrium, has been a major subject of inquiry among economists for over 150 years. Commodities that a country may actually export or import in any particular year may differ significantly from that country's basic comparative advantage structure as a consequence of trade disequilibrium, disequilibrium arising from currency overvaluation or undervaluation, countercyclical movements in business activity among countries, trade barriers and other interferences with international competition, and short-run shifts in demand and supply for particular commodities in world markets. In recent years the leading theories of comparative advantage have been based on the relationship between the production characteristics of commodities on the one

131

hand, and the relative abundance or scarcity of inputs for the production of these commodities among trading countries on the other. If a country has a relative abundance of unskilled labor and is poor in capital and land, it is expected to have a comparative advantage in labor-intensive manufactures. Originally, this hypothesis, called the Heckscher-Ohlin theorem in most economics textbooks, was applied and tested with respect to the traditional factors of production -- land, labor, and capital. Most of the empirical tests of the Heckscher-Ohlin theorem, however, have given puzzling results. For example, in a famous study by Leontief, first published in 1947 and later revised with more recent data, it was found that the United States tended to export relatively-labor intensive commodities and to import relatively capital-intensive commodities.[23] Although the U.S. economy is richly capital abundant, the commodity composition of its exports was not capital-intensive relative to the composition of its imports. This finding, which became known as the Leontief Paradox, led to investigations involving a greater disaggregation of the inputs into the production of individual commodities, including the quality of labor in terms of education and training, and the amount of investment in R&D that went into their production.

By means of regression analysis we have investigated the relationship between U.S. relative export shares in index form (revealed comparative advantage) in the LDC market for 73 commodity groups, and four independent or explanatory variables reflecting the production characteristics of the individual industries producing these commodities. The four independent variables are: (1) physical capital intensity per worker; (2) human capital intensity per worker; (3) the ratio of professional and technical workers to total employment in the industry; and (4) the ratio of R&D expenditures to total net sales of the industry.

The statistical results and methodology of this investigation are given in Technical Appendix III. In our regression analysis of the relationships between the relative export shares on the one hand and each of the four independent variables indicated above on the other, we found the most significant correlation for the R&D intensity variable, i.e., the ratio of R&D

expenditures to total net sales of the industry. It was found that about 20 percent of the variation in U.S. relative market shares in the LDCs among the 73 commodity groups is explained by the R&D intensity variable for the particular industry. Our regression equation for the physical capital-intensity per worker variable, however, yielded a negative (though not significant) regression coefficient. This result, which is in conformity with the Leontief Paradox, suggests that those commodities produced with high physical capital-intensity may on the average have a lower ranking in terms of U.S. relative export shares or revealed comparative advantage in the LDC market. Although by their very nature the three variables, human capital intensity per worker, the ratio of professional and technical workers to total employment in the industry, and the ratio of R&D expenditures to total net sales of the industry, are closely related, our regression analysis described in Technical Appendix III reveals that the latter variable has the highest explanatory power for ranking U.S. exports to the LDC market according to revealed comparative advantage.

Although this finding leaves much of the variation in relative U.S. market shares among the commodities to be explained by other factors, it is in conformity with the well-known product-cycle hypothesis, which holds that the United States has an initial advantage in exporting new and technology intensive products, but that this advantage disappears as other countries acquire the technology for producing the same or similar products.[24] The empirical evidence presented in Chapter II shows that although U.S. market shares declined in a number of technology-intensive products over the 1970-1978 period, the loss of U.S. market shares was relatively highest in the nontechnology-intensive product categories.

The policy implications of these findings are difficult to assess. Since U.S. revealed comparative advantage is highest in technology-intensive commodities, it seems to suggest that a high level of R&D in the United States promotes U.S. export competitiveness, and that a relative decline in R&D works against U.S. export competitiveness. Aggregate measures of R&D, however, do not reveal how much goes into the development of commodities of importance for the export

133

market. For example, much U.S. R&D goes into military production and aero-space experiments. There is some evidence that the Japanese channel their R&D, and the technical knowledge obtained from abroad, more specifically into their export industries. There is also some evidence that the lead time between the development of new products and new technologically advanced processes in the United States -- which gives the United States a temporary export advantage in these products -- and the acquisition and application of these innovations by other countries, is declining. This suggests that U.S. industries must innovate faster to maintain the same U.S. export share in the export market.

APPENDIX TABLE V-A

U.S. RELATIVE EXPORT SHARES TO THIRD WORLD COUNTRIES
(1970-1978)
(index number form)

Code	Commodity	1970	1971	1972	1973	1974	1975	1976	1977	1978
1	Chemical Elements, Comp.	1.3421	1.3639	1.3779	1.4029	1.4517	1.4469	1.4572	1.6801	1.7003
2	Synthetic Organic Dyes	0.3909	0.3697	0.3635	0.3450	0.3940	0.3488	0.3594	0.4405	0.4510
3	Medicinal & Pharm. Prod.	0.8329	0.7893	0.8034	0.7288	0.7132	0.6538	0.7376	0.7350	0.7280
4	Oils and Perfume	0.9196	0.9695	0.9945	0.9642	1.0072	0.9438	0.9586	0.9367	1.0957
5	Fertilizers, Manufactured	1.5963	1.7632	1.9856	1.7258	1.5338	1.8350	1.7464	2.0521	1.6554
6	Plastic Materials	0.9132	0.8919	0.9173	1.0209	1.0601	0.8550	1.2317	0.9946	1.0518
7	Other Chemicals	1.2841	1.3605	1.3775	1.4300	1.4682	1.3557	1.3568	1.5101	1.2923
8	Leather Manufactures	1.2242	1.1416	0.9955	0.9436	0.9145	0.8320	0.8462	0.9494	1.1829
9	Rubber Manufactures	0.6531	0.6555	0.6462	0.4868	0.6670	0.6128	0.6224	0.8229	1.0821
10	Wood, Cork Manufactures	1.0865	1.0510	1.2032	1.3057	1.2366	1.0148	0.9205	1.1431	1.0869
11	Paper, Paperboard	1.1468	1.2945	1.3550	1.2616	1.2418	1.2786	1.3496	1.3192	1.3102
12	Yarn Thread	0.2267	0.1844	0.1678	0.3319	0.4269	0.3471	0.4087	0.4478	0.5333
13	Textile Fabrics	0.3090	0.3216	0.3580	0.3865	0.4051	0.3173	0.3356	0.3383	0.4094
14	Other Textile Products	0.7156	0.7358	0.7347	0.7192	0.8033	0.7402	0.8086	0.8723	0.8385
15	Diamonds	1.1803	1.2890	1.2844	2.0450	1.0756	0.9788	0.8831	0.9971	0.9837
16	Glassware, Pottery	0.8129	0.7107	0.7129	0.7438	0.7788	0.6553	0.6937	0.8353	0.9907
17	Mineral Manufactures	0.7081	0.8108	0.6909	0.6176	0.5145	0.4792	0.4605	0.4409	0.5379
18	Pig Iron	1.4698	1.0021	0.6685	0.3772	0.5592	0.4121	0.7210	0.5745	1.5301
19	Iron, Steel Manufactures	0.6268	0.4648	0.4356	0.5110	0.5380	0.5567	0.4190	0.3687	0.4144
20	Unwrought Copper	2.1464	2.3020	1.4044	2.0075	1.1583	2.1860	0.4497	0.2093	0.4777
21	Unwrought Aluminum	1.8334	1.1001	1.0769	1.7244	1.2922	0.8227	0.7950	0.7253	1.3221
22	Other Unwrought Nonferrous	0.4855	0.3044	0.1721	0.4731	0.5313	0.3624	0.1544	0.2459	0.4427
23	Copper Manufactures	0.3958	0.4758	0.4291	0.4796	0.4938	0.3958	0.4077	0.3223	0.4491
24	Aluminum Manufactures	1.0733	1.1774	0.9575	1.1829	1.0643	1.1237	1.1315	0.9597	0.6944
25	Other Nonferrous Manu.	1.3856	1.1774	0.9925	1.3653	1.5719	1.4960	1.5860	1.7788	2.7564
26	Cutlery, Household Equipment	0.4974	0.4875	0.4835	0.4834	0.4738	0.4078	0.4376	0.4101	0.5504
27	Hand Tools	1.0647	1.1487	1.1351	1.0819	1.1531	1.1963	1.1390	1.1561	1.1016
28	Other Metal Manufactures	0.8197	0.7399	0.6961	0.8258	0.8404	0.7473	0.7250	0.7063	0.6774
29	Non-electric Power Mach.	0.6805	0.7266	0.8704	1.0984	1.1946	0.9807	1.0331	0.6618	0.8727
30	Internal Combustion Engines	1.3238	1.4325	1.3340	1.3185	1.1903	1.1336	1.0656	1.1049	1.2923

APPENDIX TABLE V-A (Cont.)

Code	Commodity	1970	1971	1972	1973	1974	1975	1976	1977	1978
31	Aircraft Engines	1.8403	2.1947	1.9514	1.9413	1.9032	1.3589	1.6636	1.7068	1.6917
32	Tractors	2.0369	1.9785	2.2238	1.9400	1.8584	1.8388	1.8613	1.8945	2.0736
33	Other Agricultural Mach.	1.4619	1.4079	1.4950	1.3248	1.2150	1.2294	1.2654	1.3011	2.2242
34	Office Machines	1.8308	2.0556	2.3015	2.2001	2.1729	1.9060	1.8694	2.1662	2.6238
35	Computers	1.4685	1.4008	1.1010	0.9623	1.0809	1.0929	0.9151	1.2126	1.5154
36	Metal Working Machinery	0.9061	1.0819	0.9228	0.9000	0.7532	0.9120	1.0769	0.7224	0.9203
37	Textile, Leather Mach.	0.4696	0.4185	0.4024	0.4477	0.4853	0.4498	0.3996	0.4433	0.4309
38	Construction, Mining Mach.	2.1155	2.2276	2.3588	2.3456	2.0772	2.0796	2.1091	2.2144	2.2601
39	Other Industrial Mach.	1.0352	1.1117	1.0578	1.1037	1.0799	0.9643	0.9283	0.9707	0.8584
40	Heating, Cooling Equipment	1.5231	1.4028	1.5265	1.5312	1.6044	1.5369	1.4542	1.4250	1.3089
41	Pumps, Centrifuges	1.6233	1.5709	1.5965	1.5285	1.5446	1.4151	1.3852	1.3704	1.3219
42	Fork Lift Trucks	1.5151	1.4480	1.2945	1.4141	1.4654	1.5111	1.5402	1.3665	2.2049
43	Parts, Accessor. Machines	1.1254	1.2368	1.0546	0.9913	0.9509	1.0068	0.9994	1.0436	0.9520
44	Electric Power Machinery	0.8966	1.1007	1.0635	1.1474	1.1673	1.0627	1.1243	1.1923	1.0067
45	Television Receivers	1.1155	1.1740	1.3138	1.3110	1.2288	1.4366	1.2396	0.8772	1.1899
46	Radio Receivers	0.9025	0.2144	0.1327	0.1388	0.1425	0.1561	0.1411	0.1859	0.2247
47	Telecommunications Equipment	0.9025	0.9320	1.1045	1.0448	1.0634	1.0240	0.1776	1.3777	1.0939
48	Domestic Electrical Equipment	0.9605	1.0490	1.1199	1.1111	1.2028	1.0858	1.1190	1.1665	0.8515
49	Medical electrical Appar.	1.1225	1.2601	1.4165	1.3885	1.3501	1.3132	1.1821	1.3674	1.5504
50	Transistors, Photocells	2.4855	2.6615	2.6156	2.6311	2.8038	2.7237	2.5807	2.8429	1.2746
51	Electrical Measuring Equip.	1.5909	1.5857	1.6410	1.6027	1.6421	1.5493	1.5170	1.7310	2.1493
52	Other Elec. Mach. Appar.	0.7289	0.7940	0.8470	0.8689	0.9647	0.9084	0.8324	0.8963	0.7232
53	Railway Vehicles	1.1422	2.0074	1.6671	1.6044	1.6265	1.7306	1.4229	1.2468	1.0719
54	Passenger Motor Cars	0.5751	0.6669	0.6819	0.7122	0.7208	0.7690	0.7428	0.6978	0.6615
55	Trucks, Buses	1.1716	1.1055	0.9826	0.9564	0.8389	0.9625	0.8775	0.8392	0.9664
56	Motor Vehicle Parts	1.2551	1.3826	1.5529	1.3273	1.2630	1.2214	1.2049	1.0236	0.6517
57	Motorcycles	0.0579	0.0546	0.0610	0.0467	0.0240	0.0520	0.0668	0.0678	0.1851
58	Trailers, Bicycles	0.5741	0.6650	0.6438	0.4939	0.7677	1.0232	1.0561	0.7899	0.6781
59	Aircraft	2.3091	2.5676	2.5149	2.8037	2.9561	2.8069	2.8621	3.2074	2.6981
60	Ships, Boats	0.1737	0.1187	0.0958	0.1299	0.1462	0.1108	0.1147	0.0988	0.1185
61	Furniture	1.1207	1.0275	0.6073	0.9484	0.8662	0.7208	0.7893	0.6215	0.7338
62	Clothing	1.2360	1.2645	1.2508	1.7357	1.2614	1.0945	1.0271	0.9854	1.0294
63	Footwear	0.3269	0.3488	0.3532	0.4712	0.3751	0.3480	0.3631	0.3279	0.3255
64	Optical Instruments	0.6158	0.5097	0.5518	0.5900	0.6501	0.7505	0.6759	0.7128	0.7946
64	Cameras and Equipment	1.0412	1.2298	1.3141	1.3304	1.2628	1.1415	1.0368	0.9956	0.9944

APPENDIX TABLE V-A (Cont.)

Code	Commodity	1970	1971	1972	1973	1974	1975	1976	1977	1978
66	Other Scientific Instru.	1.5663	1.5627	1.6270	1.4610	1.3816	1.3782	1.3832	1.4424	0.9806
67	Movies, Photographic Film	1.5923	1.5871	1.5775	1.5610	1.5383	1.4748	1.3701	1.4759	1.6623
68	Watches, Clocks	0.0746	0.0817	0.0821	0.1293	0.1229	0.1790	0.4237	0.3421	0.2749
69	Phonographs, Musical Ins.	0.9683	0.9186	0.9274	0.7644	0.9562	1.0432	0.9568	1.0009	0.9840
70	Books, Magazines	1.0645	0.8269	1.0515	1.0315	1.1005	0.8498	0.7912	0.9068	1.0396
71	Toys, Sporting Goods	0.9924	1.2105	1.4788	1.5096	1.5382	1.1732	1.1311	1.2029	1.3919
72	Jewelry, Art	0.6447	0.6123	0.6219	0.8638	0.7133	0.5827	0.3859	0.2734	0.2601
73	Other Manufactured Goods	0.9154	0.9561	0.9628	0.9489	0.9538	0.8968	0.9075	0.9243	0.7064

Source: CSIS Data Bank.

VI. SUMMARY AND CONCLUSIONS

Had the United States maintained the same share of the total (all commodities) LDC export market in 1978 that it had in 1962, U.S. exports of manufactures to that market in 1978 would have been $14 billion larger than they actually were. This would have reduced the U.S. overall trade deficit for all commodities in 1978 by about 41 percent. For our sample of 73 manufactured commodities and 15 exporting countries, the U.S. share of the LDC market declined from 28.3 perdent in 1970 to 22.1 percent in 1978. Had the U.S. market share of exports of manufactures to the LDCs covered by our sample remained the same in 1978 as in 1970, U.S. exports would have been greater by about $10 billion in 1978.

The decline of 6.2 percentage points in the U.S. market share over the 1970-1978 period was nearly matched by a 4.3 percentage point rise in the Japanese share of the LDC market plus a 1.7 percentage point rise in the share of the four NICs, leaving only 0.2 of a percentage point to be accounted for by the increase in the net shares of the other developed countries. Although the United States lost market shares in percentage terms between 1970 and 1978 in every region but the Caribbean, its largest losses were in South America and OPEC, followed by the Far East and South Asia. Moreover, the Western Hemisphere LDC markets, which traditionally have accounted for the largest share of U.S. exports going to the LDC market, did not grow nearly as rapidly as the OPEC market, whose share of total imports to the LDCs as a group rose from 21 percent in 1970 to 41 percent in 1978. The principal gainer in nearly all the regional markets was Japan. Germany's share of the Third World market increased by 1.3 percentage points, while Britain's share declined by 1.8 percentage points. Italy's share rose to 1.5 percent, while France's share remained almost the same. Among the residual group of countries, the Netherlands, Switzerland, Brazil, South Korea, and Hong Kong were gainers; whereas Canada, Australia, and Sweden were losers in terms of market shares.

Of the 73 commodity classifications in our sample, the U.S. export share in the total LDC market rose by

138

more than 5 percent between 1970 and 1978 for 11 items, did not change by more than 5 percent for 6 items, declined by more than 5 percent but less than 22 percent for 24 items, and fell by more than 22 percent (i.e., the average for all 73 commodities) for 32 items. The two most important items for which the U.S. share in the LDC market rose by more than 5 percent were office machines and fork lift trucks. The commodities in which the U.S. lost market shares cover a very wide range, but included several important technology-intensive as well as nontechnology-intensive commodities. In 1970 the U.S. market share in the LDC market for technology-intensive commodities was larger than that of any of its 14 competitors for 15 commodities, but by 1978 this number fell to 11 product groups. The United States lost its dominant position in such important commodities as medicinal and pharmaceutical products; electric power machinery; transistors, photocells; and manufactured fertilizers. The decline in U.S. dominant shares in the nontechnology-intensive commodity groups, however, was considerably larger; by 1978 the United States had lost its dominant position in 16 product groups classified as nontechnology-intensive.

A major conclusion of this study is that the loss of U.S. shares in the LDC market over the 1970-1978 period cannot be attributed to a decline in U.S. overall price and cost competitiveness as measured by the relative wholesale price index, the relative export unit value index, and the relative unit labor cost index, all adjusted for the effective rate of exchange. The U.S. relative unit labor cost index declined sharply (about 38 percent) between 1968 and 1978, and the U.S. relative wholesale price index and relative export unit value index declined by 22 percent and 14 percent respectively over the same period. For Japan on the other hand, price and cost competitiveness in terms of all three measures declined, largely as a consequence of the appreciation of the yen since 1970. Japan's relative unit labor cost index rose by 64 percent over the 1968-1978 period, that country's relative wholesale price index rose by 19 percent, and its relative export unit value index rose by about 9 percent. Germany's relative unit labor cost index rose by about 24 percent over the 1968-1978 period, its relative wholesale price index remained about the same, and its relative export unit value index rose by about

12 percent. Britain's relative unit labor cost index rose by about 5 percent; its relative wholesale price index also remained about the same, and its relative export unit value index rose by about 6 percent (see Appendix Table III-1).

Although the U.S. export unit value index (absolute index) rose by 109 percent between 1970 and 1978, the U.S. wholesale price index (absolute index) increased by only 90 percent over the same period. During the same period, the Japanese (absolute)/export unit value index rose by only 41 percent, whereas the Japanese (absolute) wholesale price index rose by 53 percent. The German (absolute)/export unit value index rose by 48 percent, whereas, the industrial wholesale price index rose by 46 percent over the 1970-1978 period. The corresponding United Kingdom indexes exhibited a similar pattern.

Various explanations might be put forward for the unique behavior of the Japanese indexes. One is that the Japanese held down their export prices relative to their domestic prices of manufactures. Another is that productivity increased more rapidly in Japan's export industries than in industries producing nontraded goods. Only an examination of the domestic prices and export prices of individual Japanese commodities could determine which interpretation is correct. Unfortunately, it is exceedingly difficult to obtain data on the domestic prices of many Japanese commodities. (The U.S. Treasury has encountered this problem in trying to determine whether Japan has been dumping commodities in the U.S. market.)

It would also be useful to know why the U.S. export unit value index rose more rapidly than the U.S. wholesale price index. In Germany and the United Kingdom these indexes have risen by about the same percentage during the 1970-1978 period. In the case of Japan the export unit value index rose substantially less than the wholesale price index. A study of the U.S. export prices of individual commodities in relation to U.S. wholesale prices of these same commodities will be possible with the publication of new export price data for a number of U.S. commodities by the Bureau of Labor Statistics.

An exporting country may lose its share in the export market as a consequence of (a) a decline in the relative size of the country or regional markets that normally import the largest share of that country's exports (the market size effect); or (b) a decline in the exporting country's market share in individual markets (the competitive effect). Both of these effects on U.S. export shares to the LDC market were strongly evident during 1970-1978. For the period as a whole, about 64 percent of the cumulative year-to-year percentage decline in U.S. export shares of the LDC market can be attributed to the competitive effect and most of the remainder to the market size effect.

Since U.S. price and cost competitiveness may be expected to be an important determinant of the competitive effect on U.S. market shares, we analyzed by means of a regression model the relationship between the annual percentage changes in the competitive effect and the annual percentage changes in each of our two measures of price competitiveness -- the relative wholesale price index and the relative unit value index. The relative price measures -- the independent or explanatory variables -- were lagged by two years since it normally requires a period of time before changes in prices have an effect on trade. It was found that about 18 percent of the year-to-year changes in U.S. shares in the LDC market over the 1970-1978 period accounted for by the competitive effect can be explained by year-to-year changes in the U.S. relative wholesale price index (lagged by two year); and about 21 percent can be explained by year-to-year changes in the U.S. relative export unit value index (lagged by two years). These results show that, although for the entire period 1970-1978 the U.S. share of the LDC market declined (despite a marked improvement in U.S. price and cost competitiveness), year-to-year changes in the two measures of overall price competitiveness had some impact on changes in U.S. export shares in the LDC market accounted for by the competitive effect.

A similar regression analysis was conducted for Japan, Germany, and the United Kingdom for the 1970-1978 period. Results for the United Kingdom showed that 24 percent of the year-to-year changes in U.K. shares in the LDC market accounted for by the competitive effect can be explained by year-to-year changes in the U.K. relative wholesale price index (lagged two years), and about 29 percent can be explained by changes in the U.K. relative export unit value index (lagged by two year). For Germany the explanatory power of the two price competitiveness measures was much lower: only 5 percent for the German relative wholesale price index and 13 percent for the German relative export unit value index. For Japan we found no relationship between changes in that country's export share accounted for by the competitive effect and changes in Japan's relative export unit value index -- and only 7 percent for changes in Japan's relative wholesale price index. These findings for Japan support the conclusion that there is little correlation between measures of Japan's price competitiveness on the one hand and that country's export performance on the other.

Our analysis of changes in market shares was conducted in terms of current prices, and, of course, export performance as it affects the balance of payments and the domestic economy is also measured in current prices. Although no attempt was made to determine changes in U.S. market shares in constant prices, it appears that during the 1970-1974 period the decline in the U.S. share of the LDC market in real terms was less than the decline in current prices. This raises the question of whether the substantial depreciation of the dollar over this period contributed to the decline in the U.S. market share in current prices or whether it prevented the decline in U.S. market share from being greater than it actually was. A disaggregated analysis of the market for each major commodity would be required to shed light on this question. Nevertheless, it is interesting to note that the 14 percent decrease in the relative U.S. export unit value index (adjusted for the effective rate of exchange on the dollar) between 1970 and 1974 was approximately the same as the percentage depreciation (effective) of the dollar during this period.

The question is frequently asked whether or not the large U.S. trade deficits during the latter part of the 1970s and the decline in U.S. export share of manufactured products in the world market between the early 1960s and the late 1970s reflect a structural change in U.S. comparative advantage. Although our detailed commodity data cover only the 1970-1978 period and are confined to export of manufactures to the LDC market, we do not find evidence of a change in U.S. comparative advantage in the manufacturing sector over the period. To rank the 73 manufactured commodity exports in our sample according to comparative advantage, we calculated the U.S. share of each commodity in the LDC market weighted by the ratio of U.S. exports of all manufactures to the LDC market to total LDC imports of manufactures from the 15 exporting countries in our sample. This gave us an index number for each commodity and for each year. An index number greater than unity indicates that the U.S. market share of the commodity is larger than the U.S. share of total imports of manufactures by the LDCs. By ranking each commodity according to this measure, which we call revealed comparative advantage, we are able to identify changes in the rankings or revealed comparative advantage among the 73 commodities over the 1970-1978 period and to determine whether the changes in ranking reflected a change in product characteristics. Although quite a number of changes took place in revealed comparative advantage among the 73 commodities over the period, there is no evidence of a fundamental change in the structure of U.S. comparative advantage over the 1970-1978 period. For example, the commodities with the highest ranking have remained those characterized by technology-intensity. There is also evidence that fewer U.S. technology-intensive exports lost their dominant share in the LDC market than was the case for nontechnology-intensive exports.

In our analysis of the basic determinants of the comparative advantage structure of U.S. exports to the LDC market, we investigated the relationships between revealed comparative advantage in the LDC market for each commodity group and four independent or explanatory variables reflecting the production characteristics of the individual industries producing these commodities. The four independent variables are: (1) physical capital intensity per worker, (2) human capital intensity per worker, (3) the ratio of professional and technical workers to total employment in the industry, and (4) the ratio of R&D expenditures to total net sales of the industry. Our regression analysis of these relationships revealed the most significant correlation for the R&D intensity variable. It was found that about 20 percent of the variation in the rankings according to revealed comparative advantage among the 73 commodity groups is explained by the

R&D intensity variable for the particular industry. Our regression equation for the physical capital intensity per worker variable yielded a negative regression coefficient. This result, which is in conformity with the earlier findings of Wassily Leontief, suggests that those commodities whose production is characterized by high physical capital intensity have on the average a lower ranking in terms of revealed comparative advantage in the LDC market. At least it can be said that U.S. comparative advantage does not lie in those commodities produced with a high ratio of physical capital to labor.

The question arises whether the importance of R&D intensity in determining revealed comparative advantage of U.S. commodity exports establishes a link between the slower growth in U.S. R&D on the one hand and the deterioration in U.S. export performance on the other.[25] We lack empirical evidence to answer this question satisfactorily. Not only do technology-intensive products continue to maintain a high rank in terms of revealed comparative advantage, but these commodities appear to have lost less in terms of reduced U.S. share in the LDC market between 1970 and 1978 than have the nontechnology-intensive products. Moreover, export performance is not determined simply by the total volume of R&D expenditures but by how R&D effort is channeled. Japan's success in capturing the dominant share of the export market for a number of products originally developed in the United States has arisen from the ability of that country to obtain U.S. technology and apply it to production for exports. One possible explanation for the decline in U.S. export performance is that other exporting nations, and Japan in particular, have been able to reduce the time between the development of a U.S. product or production process and the adoption of the U.S. innovations for production in competition with U.S. exports. This suggests that the product cycle may have been substantially shortened as a consequence of the increased flow of technology among countries through both licensing and foreign direct investment.[26]

If the reasons for the deterioration in U.S. export performance in the LDC market are not to be found in an overall decline in U.S. price and cost competitiveness, or in a change in the comparative advantage structure of U.S. exports, we must look

144

elsewhere for the explanation. In a companion study in this series we reject the hypothesis that U.S. foreign direct investment in the LDCs has had a significant negative effect on direct U.S. exports to these countries; much of this investment has been induced by competition from manufacturing affiliates of other developed countries in the LDCs.[27] One explanation for the deterioration in U.S. export performance is a reduction in the incentive to export. The incentive to export is a function of both the structure of the U.S. economy and U.S. government policies that promote or discourage exports. For example, in an overheated domestic economy producing at relatively full capacity, there is less incentive to compete in world markets than there is when the domestic economy is producing at well under full capacity. During the period under investigation, 1970-1978, however, the U.S. economy experienced both recession and expansion. Yet there was a more or less continuous deterioration of U.S. export performance in the LDC market.

Production for foreign markets involves greater uncertainties and risks than production for the domestic market and may require special incentives that are generously provided by most governments. A relative lack of incentive to exploit foreign markets on the part of the U.S. producers might, therefore, be explained by the fact that U.S. government taxation, export credits, and other policies and programs relating to exports are less favorable than those found in competing countries. It would be important to determine, however, whether these policies and programs had changed significantly over the period when U.S. export performance was deteriorating. Evidence regarding U.S. government export policies and the policies and programs of other countries is provided in other studies in this series.[28]

TECHNICAL APPENDIX I

THE DECOMPOSITION OF U.S. EXPORT PERFORMANCE

The decomposition of U.S. export performance is based on a method developed by Hickman.[29] This approach statistically decomposes the sources of export performance and distinguishes between changes in the degree of market penetration (i.e., market share) and changes in the size of these markets (i.e., market size).

This version of constant market share analysis uses aggregate export data to measure the difference between the constant-share norm and actual export performance. This procedure assumes export performance is invariant regarding commodity disaggregation. Some authors include a commodity-composition effect indicating the extent to which a country's exports are concentrated in commodity classes that are increasing at a faster than average rate for world exports as a whole.[30] Junz and Rhomberg found the commodity-composition effect to be quite small even when exports were disaggregated by one-digit SITC manufactured classifications.[31] Nevertheless, the commodity-composition effect may increase in importance at higher levels of disaggregation.[32]

It should be emphasized that constant market share analysis is merely a measurement technique for decomposing the growth of a variable and should not be viewed as a behavioral relationship. The overall measure of export competitiveness obtained from the constant market share calculations serves as the basis of the regression model presented in Technical Appendix II.

In order to decompose U.S. export performance in the LDC market into its essential components, it is necessary to introduce the following definitions:

$$X_{ijt} = \text{Exports from country } i \text{ to region } j \text{ in year } t.$$

$$M_{jt} = \sum_{i=1}^{m} X_{ijt} = \text{total exports of country i to all regions in year t.}$$

$$W_t = \sum_{i=1}^{m} X_{it} = \sum_{j=1}^{m} M_{jt} = \text{total exports and total imports for the LDC market by all exporting countries to all regions in year t.}$$

$$\alpha_{ijt} = \frac{X_{ijt}}{M_{jt}} = \text{the market share of exporting country i in region j in year t.}$$

$$\beta_{jt} = \frac{M_{jt}}{W_t} = \text{the import share of region j of total imports by all regions in year t.}$$

$$\gamma_{it} = \frac{X_{it}}{W_t} = \text{the market share of country i in terms of total exports to all regions in year t.}$$

$j = \quad 1,\ldots,n$ where $n=7$ regional markets in the Third World.

$i = \quad 1,\ldots,m$ where $m=15$ exporting countries to the Third World.

$0 = \quad$ the subscript used to denote the base year.

Applying these definitions and summing over all seven regional markets yields expression (1) that decomposes total exports by country i in year t into four components:[33]

$$X_{it} = \sum_{j=1}^{7} X_{ijt} = \left[\sum_{j=1}^{7} \alpha_{ijo} \beta_{jo} \right] W_t +$$

$$\left[\sum_{j=1}^{7} \beta_{jo} \Delta\alpha_{ijt} \right] W_t + \left[\sum_{j=1}^{7} \alpha_{ijo} \Delta\beta_{jt} \right] W_t$$

$$+ [\sum_{j=1}^{7} \alpha_{ijt} \Delta\beta_{jt}] W_t \qquad [1]$$

1. The Constant Market Share

The first term gives the constant market share or the value of exports for country i in year t assuming the ith country's share of the LDC market has remained unchanged since the base period. To show this, we note that in the base period, $\Delta\beta_{jt} = \Delta\alpha_{ijt} = 0$, so [1] reduces to:

$$X_{io} = [\sum_{j=1}^{7} \alpha_{ijo}\beta_{jo}] W_o \qquad [2]$$

where:

$$\gamma_{io} = [\sum_{j=1}^{7} \alpha_{ijo}\beta_o]$$

is the base period market share of total exports for country i such that:

$$\gamma_{io} = \frac{X_{io}}{W_o} \qquad [3]$$

2. The Competitive Effect

The second term summarizes the effects of changes in the ith country's market shares ($\Delta\alpha_{ijt}$) for all regions since the base period, holding constant the relative size (β_{jo}) of the various importing regions. This term isolates the influence of changes in the competitiveness of country i in specific LDC markets.

3. The Market Size Effect

The third term measures the net effect of shifts in the size of the various regional markets, holding constant the ith country's share in each market. This effect will be positive if the markets that are important to country i in the base period grow more rapidly than the growth rate in total exports for all LDCs. If these markets grow less rapidly than total exports then this effect will be negative. As a result, the market share of country i in total exports may increase without any change in its export competitiveness provided that the markets that are of relatively greater importance to country i grow more rapidly than the rate of growth of total exports.

4. The Interaction Effect

Finally, the last term measures the interaction between changes in market shares and market sizes. This measure is generally less significant than either the competitive effect or the market size effect. The interaction effect serves largely as a residual term and takes into account changes that cannot be attributed exclusively to either the competitive effect or the market size effect.

The export share for country i of total exports to all LDCs may be obtained by dividing expression [1] by W_t:

$$\gamma_{it} = \frac{X_{it}}{W_t} = [\sum_{j=1}^{7} \alpha_{ijo}\beta_{jo}] + [\sum_{j=1}^{7} \beta_{jo}\Delta\alpha_{ijt}]$$

$$+ [\sum_{j=1}^{7} \alpha_{ijo}\Delta\beta_{jt}] + [\sum_{j=1}^{7} \Delta\alpha_{ijt}\Delta\beta_{jt}] \quad [4]$$

Since the first term on the right side is the base period market share, [4] may also be written as:

$$\Delta\gamma_{it} = \gamma_{it} - \gamma_{io} = [\sum_{j=1}^{7} \beta_{jo}\Delta\alpha_{ijt}]$$

$$+ [\sum_{j=1}^{7} \alpha_{ijo}\Delta\beta_{jt}] + [\sum_{j=1}^{7} \Delta\alpha_{ijt}\Delta\beta_{jt}] \quad [5]$$

where [5] decomposes the cumulative changes in the export share between the base period and year t into its three component effects.

It is convenient to express the cumulative change in the export share in the form of a ratio to the base period export share by dividing expression (5) through by γ_{i0}:

$$\frac{\Delta\gamma_{it}}{\gamma_{io}} = \frac{[\sum_{j=1}^{7}\beta_{jo}\Delta\alpha_{ijt}]}{[\sum_{j=1}^{7}\alpha_{ijo}\beta_{jo}]} + \frac{[\sum_{j=1}^{7}\alpha_{ijo}\Delta\beta_{jt}]}{[\sum_{j=1}^{7}\alpha_{ijo}\beta_{jo}]}$$

$$+ \frac{[\sum_{j=1}^{7}\Delta\alpha_{ijt}\Delta\beta_{jt}]}{[\sum_{j=1}^{7}\alpha_{ijo}\beta_{jo}]} \qquad [6]$$

Finally, [6] can be readily transformed to a weighted average of the cumulative relative changes in the α's and β's:

$$\frac{\Delta\gamma_{it}}{\gamma_{io}} = \sum_{j=1}^{7}\lambda_{ijo}\left[\frac{\Delta\alpha_{ijt}}{\alpha_{ijo}}\right] + \sum_{j=1}^{7}\lambda_{ijo}\left[\frac{\Delta\beta_{jt}}{\beta_{jo}}\right]$$

$$+ \sum_{j=1}^{7}\lambda_{ijo}\left[\frac{\Delta\alpha_{ijt}}{\alpha_{ijo}}\right]\left[\frac{\Delta\beta_{jt}}{\beta_{jo}}\right] \qquad [7]$$

where:

$$\lambda_{ijo} = \frac{\alpha_{ijo}\beta_{jo}}{\sum_{j=1}^{7}\alpha_{ijo}\beta_{jo}} = \frac{X_{ijo}}{X_{io}}$$

and:

$$\sum_{j=1}^{7}\lambda_{ijo} = 1$$

Thus the percentage change in country i's export share since the base period (γ_{i0}) is decomposed into weighted averages of the percentage changes in its market shares (competitive effect), the percentage changes in the

150

size of the various import markets (market size effect), and the product of the two (interaction effect). The weights (λ_{ij0}) represent the proportion of country i's total exports sold in each year of the j regional markets in the base period.

Utilizing Equation [7], the various component effects were calculated using Tables I-3 to I-5 in Chapter I. The competitive effect was calculated from Table I-4, the market size effect was calculated from Table I-3, and the base period export weights were calculated from Table I-5. The cumulative per-centage changes in U.S. export shares and the corresponding component effects are provided on an annual basis in Table IV-1, and for three separate periods using base years 1970, 1974, and 1977 in Table IV-2.

TECHNICAL APPENDIX II

RELATIVE PRICE COMPETITIVENESS AND EXPORT SHARES

An econometric model, based on a two-year lag structure, was developed using annual competitive effect measures between 1970-1978 for each of the regional markets. This measure served as the dependent variable in a multiple regression equation employing two measures (i.e., the relative wholesale price index and the relative export unit value index) of relative price competitiveness as the explanatory variables. The annual percentage change in the dependent variable was regressed on the annual percentage change in the independent variables, each lagged by two years.

Since the observations over nine years were too few to specify an appropriate time-series regression model, a single-equation system was developed that combined the cross-section observations across all nine years. This method of pooling cross-section and time series data is appropriate if the time series variables remain constant over the individual observations, but vary over time.[34] This is the case in the measures of price competitiveness employed here.

A. Empirical Results and Statistical Analysis

The actual regression equation assumes the following form:

$$Y_{ij} = \alpha + \beta_1 X_{1j} + \beta_2 X_{2j} + u_{ij}$$

where:

$Y_{ij} =$ the percentage change in the competitiveness effect for the ith regional market in the jth year

$X_{ij} =$ The percentage change in the relative wholesale price index in the jth year

$X_{2j} =$ the percentage change in the relative export unit value index in the jth year

and $i=1,\ldots,7$; $j=1,\ldots,8$.

By pooling the number of cross-section observations and the number of time periods, one large pooled regression may be run with (7x8=56) observations. Since two parameters are used in estimating the intercept and the means, the regression equation has (56-2=54) degrees of freedom. The correlation between the independent variables was very strong ($R^2 = 0.94562$) resulting in a high degree of multicollinearity when both measures were used in a single regression equation. When the measures of relative price competitiveness were run separately, the regression equations yielded regression coefficients significantly different from zero at the 99 percent confidence level.

The results of the regression model are presented in Technical Appendix II--Table 1 for four major OECD countries: the United States, Japan, FRG, and the United Kingdom. For the regression equations involving the relative wholesale price index, the F-statistic indicates the model is highly significant for the United States (11.85), the United Kingdom (17.05), and Japan (4.08), but only marginally significant for Germany (2.82). An examination of the t-statistics indicates the explanatory variable, X_{1j}^r, has the appropriate sign and is highly significant for the United States and the United Kingdom. The coefficient of determination (i.e., the square of the correlation coefficient) reveals that the proportion of the variance in the dependent variable, Y_{ij}, explained by the linear influence of the independent variable, X_{1j}, is greatest in the case of the United Kingdom (24 percent) and the United States (18 percent) and least in the case of Japan (7 percent) and Germany (5 percent). An analysis of the Durbin-Watson statistic (DW) indicates the presence of negative first-order auto-correlation in the model for the United States and Germany. The null hypothesis of zero autocorrelation was accepted in the case of Japan and the United Kingdom.

For the regression equations involving the relative export unit value index, the model is highly significant for the United States (14.64), the United Kingdom (21.85) and Germany (7.77). The F-statistic indicates the model is not significant in the case of Japan (0.12). The t-statistics for the explanatory variable, X_{2j}^r, are highly significant and possess the appropriate sign for the United States, the United Kingdom, and the FRG. Apparently, percentage changes in Japan's relative export unit value index are unrelated to percentage changes in Japan's competitive effect. The explanatory power of the model is greatest in the case of the United Kingdom (29 percent), the United States (21 percent), and least in the case of Germany (12 percent), and Japan (5 percent). The Durbin-Watson statistic indicates negative first-order autocorrelation for the regression equation involving the United States. The Durbin-Watson statistic yielded inconclusive results for Germany and the null hypothesis of zero first-order autocorrelation was accepted for both the United Kingdom and Japan.

An interpretation of the above findings suggests that exports of manufactures to LDCs by the United States, United Kindgom, and West Germany are somewhat more sensitive to price variations than is the case of exports from Japan. This is particularly true for price variations measured in terms of the relative export unit value index. Thus, to a significant degree, annual percentage changes in the relative price competitiveness of exports from the United States and United Kingdom vary inversely with annual percentage changes in the competitive effect for the seven LDC regional markets for the period 1970-1978.

B.   Secondary Regressions: Correcting for Problems

The pooled cross-section time-series procedure assumes the estimates of the intercept and slope parameters are constant across all regions. To relax this assumption, dummy variables were introduced into the model in order to allow for the intercept term to vary over the cross-section units and over the time periods as well. Because of the existence of extreme multicollinearity, the test for variations among the intercept terms was conducted separately for the cross-section regional intercepts and the time intercepts. The results of the model using dummy variables indicate no significant differences between the intercept terms with respect to either the cross-section observations or different time periods. Consequently, the model suggests the intercept terms are not significantly different from zero for the individual regions over time. This finding supports the assumption of constant intercepts across all regions.

In addition to constant intercepts, the pooled model assumes the estimated slope coefficients to be constant as well. If this assumption is violated and the slopes vary, then each separate regression would involve a distinct model and the use of pooled data would be inappropriate. A Chow Test was used to test the null hypothesis:

$$H_o : B_1 = B_2 = B_3 = \cdots = B_7$$

For the explanatory variable involving the relative wholesale price index, the Chow Test yielded a F-statistic:

$$F_{(6,49)} = 1.411$$

which is less than the table value ($F_{(6,50)} = 2.29$) at the 5 percent level of significance. Therefore, the null hypothesis is accepted and the slope coefficients are not significantly different across individual regions. A second Chow Test was calculated involving the relative export unit value index. For this explanatory variable, the Chow Test resulted in a F-statistic:

$$F_{(6,49)} = 1.100$$

Therefore, the estimated intercept and slope parameters do not vary over time or across regions and the pooled cross-section time-series procedure appears to be an appropriate specification of the model.

The negative first-order autocorrelation indicated by the Durbin-Watson statistic for the suggests the presence of omitted variables in the residuals. Certainly, many factors contribute to export competitiveness in addition to measures of relative price competitiveness. Nevertheless, results obtained in this study suggest that relative price competitiveness is a significant explanatory variable in determining U.S. export competitiveness in Third World markets.

REGRESSION EQUATIONS ANALYZING THE RELATIVE PRICE
COMPETITIVENESS FOR SELECTED COUNTRIES EXPORTS TO LDCS
(1970-1978)

Country	Dependent Variable	Constant Term	X^r_{ij}	X^r_{2j}	F-Value	R^2	D.W.
				Explanatory Variables			
U.S.	Y^{US}_{ij}	-0.03 -(2.95)**	-0.93 -(3.44)**		11.85**	0.1800	2.7517
U.S.	Y^{US}_{ij}	-0.02 -(2.08)*		-0.88 -(3.83)**	14.64**	0.2132	2.7112
Japan	Y^{J}_{ij}	+0.05 (2.81)**	-0.56 -(2.02)*		4.08**	0.0702	2.11
Japan	Y^{J}_{ij}	+0.05 (2.52)**		-0.11 -(0.35)	0.12	0.0022	2.18
FRG	Y^{FRG}_{ij}	+0.02 (1.13)	-0.67 -(1.68)+		2.82+	0.0496	2.60
FRG	Y^{FRG}_{ij}	+0.02 (1.23)		-1.19 -(2.79)**	7.77**	0.1257	2.52
U.K.	Y^{UK}_{ij}	-0.04 -(2.09)*	-1.45 -(4.13)**		17.05**	0.2400	1.9433
U.K.	Y^{UK}_{ij}	-0.04 -(2.28)*		-2.72 -(4.67)**	21.85**	0.2880	1.9432

NOTE: Numbers in parentheses are "t" coefficients.

* = 95 percent level of significance
** = 99 percent level of significance
\+ = 90 percent level of significance
r = U.S., Japan, FRG, U.K.

Source: CSIS Data Base.

TECHNICAL APPENDIX III

PRODUCTION CHARACTERISTICS AND RELATIVE EXPORT SHARES

The multiple regression equation used in analyzing production characteristics was estimated in a double-logarithmic form where the value of the estimated coefficients represent elasticities of the significant variables:

$$\log Y_{1kt}^{*U.S.} = \beta_0 + \beta_1 \log X_{1it-2}$$
$$+ \beta_2 \log X_{2it-2} + \beta_3 \log X_{3it-2}$$
$$+ \beta_4 \log X_{4it-2} + U_{it}$$

where: $Y_{1kt}^{*U.S.}$ = the U.S. trade-weighted export share (i.e., "revealed" comparative advantage) for the kth commodity group in the LDC market at time t

X_{1it-2} = the measure of <u>physical</u> capital intensity per worker in the ith industry in year t-2

X_{2it-2} = the measure of <u>human</u> capital intensity per worker in the ith industry in year t-2

X_{3it-2} = the calculated <u>skill ratio</u> for the ith industry in <u>year t-2</u>

X_{4it-2} = the <u>ratio of R&D expenditures</u> as a percentage of total net sales for the ith industry in year t-2

The results of the regression model using $Y_{1kt}^{*U.S.}$ as a dependent variable are presented in Technical Appendix III--Table 1.

The regression model presented in Table 1 is significant for all regression equations involving the dependent variable Y_1 based on market share data for both 1977 and 1978. [1] The significant variables for the model include the intercept term and the R&D variable, X_4. When all the explanatory variables are

157

TECHNICAL APPENDIX III
TABLE I

REGRESSION EQUATIONS

Eq. No	1977 Dependent Variable	Constant Term	1975 Independent Variables				F-Value	R^2	$\bar{R}^2$	D.W.
			X_1	X_2	X_3	X_4				
1	Y_1^*	1.015 (1.01)	-0.044 -(0.79)	-0.056 -(0.64)	0.188 (1.55)	0.252 (2.37)*	5.12**	0.2315	0.2095	1.9843
2	Y_1^*	0.212 (0.29)	-0.037 -(0.67)	-0.027 -(0.32)		0.330 (4.02)**	6.35**	0.2165	0.2055	1.9601
3	Y_1^*	1.657 (1.66)	-0.060 -(1.04)	-0.026 -(0.29)	0.434 (3.35)**		4.65**	0.1681	0.1564	2.0322

Eq. No	1978 Dependent Variable	Constant Term	1976 Independent Variables				F-Value	R^2	$\bar{R}^2$	D.W.
			X_1	X_2	X_3	X_4				
1	Y_1^*	-1.460 -(1.15)	-0.021 -(0.40)	0.183 (1.36)	0.038 (0.25)	0.163 (1.68)+	3.79**	0.1824	0.1590	2.0741
2	Y_1^*	-1.030 -(1.57)	-0.010 -(0.21)	0.108 (1.45)		0.193 (2.66)**	4.98**	0.1780	0.1664	2.0843
3	Y_1^*	-0.280 -(0.31)	-0.021 -(0.41)	0.109 (1.35)	0.226 (1.93)*		3.75**	0.1401	0.1280	2.1002

NOTE: Numbers in parentheses are "t" coefficients

* = 95 percent level of significance
** = 99 percent level of significance
+ = 90 percent level of significance

$\bar{R}^2 = 1 - (1 - R^2) \frac{N-1}{N-k}$ (See Pindyck and Rubinfeld, 1976, p. 59.)

included in the model, the significance levels of the regression coefficients are reduced. Since the variables X_2, X_3, and X_4 are highly correlated, we may conclude that a high degree of multicollinearity is present in the model.

Multicollinearity arises when two or more explanatory variables are (but not perfectly) correlated with each other. The correlation matrix for the variables in Table 1 is provided below:

	Y_1	X_1	X_2	X_3	X_4
Y_1	1.0000	-0.0421	0.1506	0.3870	0.4577
X_1		1.0000	0.3415	0.2151	0.0998
X_2			1.0000	0.5329	0.4516
X_3				1.0000	0.7192
X_4					1.0000

The most highly correlated variables are X_3 and X_4. Since both variables are considered to be measures of technology-intensiveness, the regression model was estimated by introducing these variables separately. Regression equations 2 and 3, using both 1977 and 1978 data, indicate the technology intensiveness measures are highly significant for all equations. This is particularly true for the variable X_4 and suggests that this variable is a superior measure of technology intensiveness. This is true since X_4 is specifically a measure of R&D while X_3 is a somewhat more general measure involving some degree of human skills. This conclusion is based on an examination of the correlation matrix involving X_2 and X_3 and X_2 and X_4.

An examination of the coefficient of determination ($\bar{R}^2$) for each equation reveals that the proportion of the variation in Y that is explained by the regression equation is quite small. This result suggests that the primary explanatory power of the regression model involves X_3 or X_4 exclusively. Moreover, the regression equations involving X_4 have relatively more explanatory power than those involving X_3. The low results obtained by the coefficient of determination in this model may be explained by the fact that the data are highly disaggregated relative to earlier studies and because the model contains only a single significant explanatory variable.[35]

A test for heteroscedasticity was made using the Goldfeld-Quandt test.[36] This test requires that the sample be partitioned and separate regressions be run for each sample. In this case, the sample was divided according to the significant variable, X_4, to test for structural differences in the sample of observations involving technology-intensive and nontechnology-intensive commodity groups. The Goldfeld-Quandt test for homoscedasticity requires that the ratio of the sum of squared residual (SSR) for both regressions be less than the critical F-value obtained from the table of the F-distribution. For the partitioned regression equation using 1977 data, the Goldfeld-Quandt null hypothesis for homoscedasticity yields:

$$\frac{SRR_2}{SRR_1} = \frac{6.787}{21.102} = 0.3216$$

Examination of the table F-value shows that the critical value at the 1 percent level of significance is:

$$F_{(46,19)} \cong 2.37$$

Therefore, the null hypothesis is accepted and we conclude that the regression model exhibits homoscedasticity.

A test for autocorrelation involving the Durbin-Watson statistic suggests that the null hypothesis ($\rho=0$) should be accepted.

[1]Export shares are in current dollars. As explained in Chapter IV, changes in export shares in constant prices (real export shares) may differ from changes in export shares in current dollars.

[2]Jack N. Behrman and Raymond F. Mikesell, "The Impact of U.S. Foreign Direct Investment on U.S. Export Competitiveness in Third World Markets," Significant Issues Series, Vol. II, No. 1, (Washington, D.C.: Center for Strategic and International Studies), 1980.

[3]Data derived from International Trade, 1978/79, General Agreement on Tariffs and Trade, (GATT) Geneva, 1979 (and earlier issues). World exports include exports of Eastern European countries.

[4]These percentages are based on data supplied by the OECD. The OECD coverage of LDCs and the commodity coverage is slightly different from that of the GATT data employed in the previous paragraph.

[5]GATT data show total imports of manufactures by the OPEC countries plus other developing countries in 1978 to be $198.5 billion, whereas the total exports of manufactures to 76 LDCs covered by our data bank total $157.5 billion. International Trade, 1978/79, op.cit., Appendix Table G.

[6] International Financial Statistics Yearbook, 1979, (Washington, D.C.: International Monetary Fund), 1980.

[7]The sample of 15 exporting countries and 6 importing countries, classified according to regional markets in the Third World, are presented in Appendix Table IIA. The three and four digit SITC classifications corresponding to our commodity codes are presented in Appendix Table II-B. Manufactured goods defined by these 73 product groups cover commodity categories five to eight of the Standard International Trade Classification Index (SITC).

[8]The identification of technology-intensive and nontechnology-intensive commodity groups employed in this section has been derived from a study by Regina K.

Kelly-Vargo entitled "The Impact of Technological Innovation on International Trade Patterns," Staff Economic Report, Office of International Economic Research, Industry and Trade Administration, U.S. Department of Commerce, Washington, D.C., December 1977, pp. 1-24. Kelly-Vargo's definition of technology-intensive exports includes those commodities that lend themselves most readily to innovation. Empirical justification for these product classifications is provided by tests that demonstrate a very high correlation between measures of R&D intensity and measures of technology intensity.

[9]For a more complete analysis of measures of relative costs and prices and their role in export performance, see Raymond F. Mikesell, "The Meaning and Significance of U.S. Price Competitiveness," CSIS Monograph (Washington, D.C.: Center for Strategic and International Studies), 1980.

[10]Several measures of the effective rate of exchange for the U.S. dollar are published, but in this study we use the MERM index published by the International Monetary Fund (monthly) in International Financial Statistics.

[11]See International Financial Statistics Yearbook, (Washington, D.C.: International Monetary Fund), 1979, p. 53 for annual indexes, and the (monthly) International Financial Statistics, also published by the IMF, for quarterly data.

[12]For a description of the derivation of the indexes, see International Financial Statistics, op.cit., November 1978, p. 412. For an analysis of these indexes and a comparison with other published indexes of relative prices and costs of manufactures, see Mikesell, "The Meaning and Significance of U.S. Price Competitiveness," op.cit.

[13]Export unit values, which are derived by dividing reported value data by reported volume data, have serious weaknesses as indicators of movements of export prices. A proper export price index should be based on actual prices of products entering into international trade. For a discussion of the methodology of determining export price indexes, see Irving B. Kravis and Robert E. Lipsey, Price

Competitiveness in World Trade, (New York: National Bureau of Economic Research), 1971.

[14]The relative value-added deflator provides a more comprehensive indicator of costs in manufactures, but there are difficulties in obtaining comparable data for this indicator among countries. Relative value-added deflator indexes are also published in International Financial Statistics.

[15]See, for example, Robert Brusca, "United States Export Performance," Federal Reserve Bank of New York, Quarterly Review, Winter, 1978-1979, p. 53.

[16]The literature on constant market share analysis is concerned with measuring these sources of change in market shares. See, for example, Edward E. Leamer and Robert M. Stern, Quantitative International Economics, (Boston: Allyn and Bacon), p. 174; Helen B. Junz and Rudolf R. Rhomberg, "Prices and Export Performance of Industrial Countries, 1953-1963," IMF Staff Papers, Washington, D.C., July 1965, p. 253.

[17]See Technical Appendix I.

[18]Bert G. Hickman, Yoshimi Kuroda, and Lawrence J. Law, "The Pacific Basin in World Trade: An Analysis of Changing Trade Patterns, 1955-1975," Vol. 4, Issue 1, Empirical Economics, Vienna, March 1979, pp. 63-85.

[19]Junz and Rhomberg, "Prices and Export Performance," op.cit., p. 245. Junz and Rhomberg found similar results when using relative price measures to explain short-run variations in market shares.

[20]The statistical results of the regression analysis for all four countries are given in Technical Appendix II.

[21]Bela Balassa, "Trade Liberalization and 'Revealed' Comparative Advantage," Manchester School of Economic and Social Studies, Vol. XXXIII, No. 2, May 1965, pp. 99-123.

[22]The weighted market share, Y_1, may be expressed in index form as follows:

$$Y_1 = \left[\frac{\dfrac{Y_k}{15}}{\displaystyle\sum_{y=1}^{15} Y_{ki}} \middle/ \frac{\displaystyle\sum_{i=1}^{73} Y_{ki}}{\dfrac{15}{\displaystyle\sum_{i=1}^{73}} \quad \dfrac{73}{\displaystyle\sum_{k=1}^{73} Y_{ki}}} \right]$$

where the ratio of the ith country's export share of the kth commodity is divided by the ratio of the ith country's export share for all k commodities.

[23]Wassily Leontief, "Domestic Production and Foreign Trade: The American Capital Position Reexamined," in R. E. Caves and H. J. Johnson (eds.), Readings in International Economics, (Homewood, Ill.: Irwin), 1968, Ch. 30; and "Factor Proportions and the Structure of American Foreign Trade," Review of Economics and Statistics, November 1956.

[24]For an explanation of the product cycle, see Raymond Vernon, "International Investment and International Trade in the Product Cycle," Quarterly Journal of Economics, May 1966.

[25]See Economic Report of the President, Council of Economic Advisors, (Washington, D.C.: Government Printing Office), 1979, p. 132.

[26]Behrman and Mikesell, "The Impact of U.S. Foreign Direct Investment," op.cit.

[27]Ibid.

[28]See the back of this booklet for a complete list of the U.S. Export Competitiveness Project studies.

[29]Hickman, et al, "The Pacific Basin," op.cit., pp. 67-69.

[30]Leamer and Stern, op.cit., p. 174; and Junz and Rhomberg, op.cit., pp. 229-230.

[31]Junz and Rhomberg found the commodity composition effect to be less significant than the market size effect. For this reason, it was not included in the overall analysis of relative price effects of major industrial countries.

[32]David B. Houston, "The Shift and Share Analysis of Regional Growth: A Critique," Southern Economic Journal, Vol. 34, April 1967, p. 580.

[33]Hickman, et al, "The Pacific Basin," op.cit., pp. 67-69.

[34]See Pindyck and Rubinfeld, Econometric Models, op.cit., pp. 202-211.

[35]Junz and Rhomberg, op.cit., pp. 244-245.

[36]Pindyck and Rubinfeld, 1976, pp. 105-106.

BIBLIOGRAPHY

Aho, C. Michael and Carney, Richard D., "An Econometric Analysis of the Structure of Manufactures Trade for the United States, Germany, Japan: 1964-1976," unpublished paper presented at the Econometric Society Meetings, Chicago, August 1978.

Balassa, Bela, "Trade Liberalization and 'Revealed' Comparative Advantage," The Manchester School of Economic and Social Studies, Vol. 32, No. 2, May 1965, pp. 99-123.

_____, "The Changing Pattern of Comparative Advantage in Manufactured Goods," The Review of Economics and Statistics, Vol. 61, No. 2, May 1979, pp. 259-266.

Baldwin, Robert E. "Determinants of the Commodity Structure of U.S. Trade," American Economic Review, March 1971.

Baranson, Jack, "The Competitiveness of U.S. High Technology Exports in World Markets," testimony before the Joint Hearing of the Science, Technology and Space Subcommittee, U.S. Senate, 94-1, May 16, 1978, pp. 1-6.

Behrman, Jack F. and Mikesell, R. F., "The Impact of U.S. Foreign Direct Investment on U.S. Export Competitiveness in LDC Markets," CSIS, 1980. Significant Issues Series, Vol. II, No. 1 (Washington, D.C.).

Branson, William H. and Juntz, H. B., "Trends in U.S. Trade and Comparative Advantage," Brookings Papers on Economic Activity, No. 2, Washington, D.C., 1971, pp. 285-346.

Branson, William H. and Monoyios, Nikolaos, "Factor Inputs in U.S. Trade," Journal of International Economics, Vol. 7, May 1977, pp. 111-131.

Brusca, Robert, "United States Export Performance," Federal Reserve Bank of New York, Quarterly Review, Winter, 1978-79, pp. 49-56.

Council of Economic Advisors, Economic Report of the President, (Washington, D.C.: Government Printing Office), 1979.

Deppler, Michael C., "Costs, Prices and Competitiveness in Manufacturing: Summary Indexes," International Financial Statistics, (Washington, D.C. Bureau of Statistics, International Monetary Fund), December 28, 1978.

Ford, J. L., "The Ohlin-Heckscher Theory of the Basis of Commodity Trade," The Economic Journal, September 1963, pp. 459-476.

Fox, Lawrence A. and Katz, Stanley, "Dollar Devaluation, Floating Exchange Rates and U.S. Exports," Business Economics, January 1978, pp. 14-24.

General Agreement on Tariffs and Trade, International Trade, 1978/79, Geneva, 1979.

Gilpin, Robert, "Technology, Economic Growth, and International Competitiveness," Subcommittee on Economic Growth of the Joint Economic Committee, 94-1, U.S. Congress, Washington, D.C., July 9, 1975.

Gruber, W., Mehta, D. and Vernon, R., "The R&D Factor in International Trade and International Investment of U.S. Industries," Journal of Political Economy, February 1967.

Hickman, Bert G., Kuroda, Y., and Lau, L. J., "The Pacific Basin in World Trade: An Analysis of Changing Trade Patterns, 1955-1975," Empirical Economics, Vol. 4, Issue 1, March 1979, Vienna, pp. 63-85.

Houston, David B., "The Shift and Share Analysis of Regional Growth: A Critique," Southern Economic Journal, Vol. 34, April 1967, pp. 577-581.

Hufbauer, Gary C., "The Impact of National Characteristics and Technology on the Commodity Composition of Trade in Manufactured Goods," in Raymond Vernon (ed.), The Technology Factor in

International Trade, New York: National Bureau of Economic Research, 1970, p. 184.

International Monetary Fund, International Financial Statistics Yearbook, 1979, Washington, D.C., 1979.

Johnston, J., Econometric Methods, 2nd edition, (New York: McGraw-Hill), 1972, pp. 32-35.

Junz, Helen B. and Rhomberg, Rudolf R., "Prices and Export Performance of Industrial Countries, 1953-1963," IMF Staff Papers, (Washington, D.C.: International Monetary Fund), July 1965, pp. 224-269.

Kelly-Vargo, Regina K., "The Impact of Technological Innovation on International Trade Patterns," Staff Economic Report, Office of International Economic Research, Industry and Trade Administration, U.S. Department of Commerce, Washington, D.C., December 1977, pp. 1-24.

_____, "Recent Trends in Technology-Intensive Trade," Staff Economic Report, U.S. Department of Commerce, Washington, D.C., March 29, 1978.

Kravis, Irving B. and Lipsey, Robert, Price Competitiveness in World Trade, (New York: Bureau of Economic Research), 1971.

Leamer, Edward E. and Stern, Robert M., Quantitative International Economics (Boston: Allyn and Bacon), 1970.

Leontief, Wassily, "Domestic Production and Foreign Trade: The American Capital Position Re-examined," in Caves and Johnson (eds.), Readings in International Economics (Homewood, Illinois: Richard D. Irwin, Inc.), 1968.

_____, "Factor Proportions and the Structure of American Foreign Trade," Review of Economics and Statistics, November 1956.

Lipsey, R. E., and Weiss, M. Y., Exports and Foreign Investment in Manufacturing Industries (New York: National Bureau of Economic Research Working Paper No. 131), May 1976.

Lowinger, Thomas C., "The Technology Factor and the Export Performance of U.S. Manufacturing Industries," Economic Inquiry, No. 13, June 1975, pp. 221-228.

Mikesell, Raymond F., "The Meaning and Significance of Price Competitiveness in the Export Market for Manufactures," CSIS Monograph (Washington, D.C.: Center for Strategic and International Studies), 1980.

National Science Foundation, "Research and Development in Industry, 1977: Technical Notes and Detailed Statistical Tables," NSF 79-313, Washington, D.C., January 1978.

Pindyck, Robert S. and Rubinfeld, Daniel L., Econometric Models and Economic Forecasts (New York: McGraw-Hill) 1976.

Sailors, J. W., Thomas, R. W., and Luciana, "Sources of Comparative Advantage of the United States, Economia Internazionale, Vol. 30, No. 2-3, May-August 1977, pp. 282-294.

U.S. Department of Commerce, "Total Research and Development and Total Net Sales for 3-Digit Manufacturing Industries, 1973," unpublished data by the Bureau of the Census, Washington, D.C.

_____, (ASM) Annual Survey of Manufactures: 1972-1976/Industry Profiles (M76-AS-7) (Washington, D.C.: Bureau of the Census), June 1978, p. 112.

U.S. Department of Labor, "Capital Stock Estimates for Input-Output Industries: Methods and Data," Bureau of Labor Statistics, Bulletin 2034, Washington, D.C., September 1979 (3-digit SIC industry information provided separately through the Office of Economic Growth (BLS).

Vernon, Raymond, "International Investment and International Trade in the Product Cycle," Quarterly Journal of Economics, May 1966.

3

FRENCH EXPORT BEHAVIOR IN THIRD WORLD MARKETS

Lawrence G. Franko
Sherry Stephenson

CONTENTS

I. INTRODUCTION

Since it overtook Great Britain in the mid-1960s, France has been number four among the world's largest exporting countries.[1] France's very rapid rate of export growth over the period 1973-1977 was exceeded (in dollar terms) only by Japan among the "big five" industrial exporters (Table I.1).

In part, this exceptional rate of export growth can be related to a reorientation and reinforcement of French export policy. The need for increased export earnings to pay for fuel imports pushed the French government to aggressive action for export promotion and altered the thrust of an already existing drive to shifting exports from traditional, but stagnating European markets, toward the increased purchasing power of Third World markets. Before 1974, France sold 70 percent of its exports in a radius of 1,500 kilometers around Paris.[2] In 1974, moves to secure new markets and to support exports were made first through government grants of special guarantees and additional export credits and, from 1976 through low-interest credits to capacity-enlarging investments in export-oriented enterprises.[3] The strategy was successful enough to cause temporary redressing of the trade balance in 1975 due to the increased sale of manufactured products, mainly to developing countries.

The geographical orientation of French exports has changed noticeably over the past half-dozen years. Until recently the development of French exports was concentrated on the European Economic Community (EC) market, but from 1973 to 1976, the share of exports going to Third World countries out of total French exports rose substantially. Tables I.2 and I.3 show that in 1977 and 1978 nearly a fourth of French exports were absorbed by the developing countries (OPEC, other Third World and the French-franc free trading zone[4]. The geographical shift of French exports from traditional developed-country markets to an increasing concentration on Third World customers is dramatically

TABLE I.1

TOTAL EXPORTS

(current $ billion)

	1973	1977	1978	Percent Increase 73/77	73/78
France	36.7	70.5	79.4	92%	116%
West Germany	67.6	118.0	142.3	74%	110%
Japan	37.0	81.1	98.4	119%	166%
United Kingdom	31.0	57.6	71.7	86%	131%
United States	71.3	120.2	143.7	69%	102%

Source: IMF, Direction of Trade, Annual 1971-1977 and 1979 issues.

shown by the growth of French exports to LDCs of 171 percent in dollar value terms over the period 1973 to 1978, while French exports to developed countries increased by 99 percent during this same period.

The product categories in which French exports have grown faster than the average are on the whole capital and technology-intensive. France has become a net importer of labor-intensive goods such as textiles, clothing, wood, furniture, leather, and footwear, but it has excelled in exporting more sophisticated capital-intensive goods such as mechanical and electrical equipment, armaments, aeronautic and naval construction, metals, and construction material. The latter have especially been directed to the Third World. The majority of French exports to LCDs in 1977 (51 percent) was made up of machinery and transport material and equipment, and France's positive trade balance with the developing countries in this product category was substantial. Other important French export items were constituted by glassware, chemicals, iron and steel works, and construction material.

The OPEC countries had the biggest appetite for French goods, followed by several nonoil Middle Eastern and African countries. Export sales to OPEC doubled in two years, from 4.1 percent of total exports in 1973 to 9.2 percent in 1975.[5] Export sales to OPEC countries increased by 45 percent in 1975 alone while those to nonoil LCDs increased by 20 percent. Substantial increases in (dollar-denominated) exports to industrial countries, however, reduced the percentage of French exports going to OPEC in 1978. (See Tables I.2 A and I.2 B.)

The non-OPEC developing countries represent one of the few geographic areas where France has both maintained a positive balance on its net export/ import transactions (see Table I.2) and has obtained rates of growth in exports above those of most competing OECD suppliers. Table I.3 shows that between 1973 and 1977 French exports to the nonoil LCDs increased by 104 percent, whereas the increases in Japanese, German, and U.S. exports to the nonoil LDCs were 102 percent, 72, and 70 percent respectively. A few large developing countries in this category -- Mexico, Brazil, and Argentina -- have been important absorbers of French goods.

TABLE I.2A

FRENCH EXPORTS BY GEOGRAPHICAL AREA: 1977

Geographical Area	Value of Exports ($ billion)	Percent Share in Total	Trade Balance ($ billion)
Developed Countries	45.3	70.0%	-4.1
Industrial Countries	40.5	62.4%	-4.3
Other Europe	4.1	6.3%	0.6
Australia, New Zealand, and South Africa	0.7	1.0%	-0.4
Socialist Countries	2.7	4.1%	0.4
Developing Countries	15.4	23.7%	-3.3
Oil Exporting Countries	5.6	8.6%	-5.9
Nonoil LDCs	9.8	15.1%	2.6
West Hemisphere	1.9	2.8%	0.1
Middle East	1.2	1.8%	0.7
Asia	1.5	2.3%	-0.1
Africa	5.3	8.2%	1.8
Special Categories	1.5	2.3%	1.6
TOTAL	64.9	100 %	-5.4

Source: IMF Direction of Trade Annual, 1971-1977.

TABLE I.2B

FRENCH EXPORTS BY GEOGRAPHICAL AREA: 1978

Geographical Area	Value of Exports ($ billion)	Percent Share in Total	Trade Balance ($ billion)
Developed Countries	56.0	70.5%	-3.9
Industrial Countries	50.4	63.5%	-3.7
Other Europe	4.7	5.9%	0.2
Australia, New Zealand, and South Africa	0.9	1.1%	-0.4
Socialist Countries	2.8	3.5%	0.2
Developing Countries	17.6	22.2%	-1.5
Oil Exporting Countries	6.2	7.8%	-5.3
Nonoil LDCs	11.4	14.4%	3.8
West Hemisphere	2.3	2.9%	0.4
Middle East	1.5	1.9%	1.0
Asia	2.0	2.5%	0.2
Africa	5.6	7.1%	2.2
TOTAL	76.4	96.2%	-5.2

Source: IMF Direction of Trade, May 1979.

France appears to have done less well in OPEC markets relative to other industrial exporters, even though its exports there increased faster than to nonoil LCDs in absolute terms. French exports to OPEC increased 229 percent between 1973 and 1977, compared to 381 percent for Germany, 341 percent for Japan, and 297 percent for the United States (see Table I.3). Comparisons between 1973 and 1978 also given in Table I.3 show only one major change in these trends: a major acceleration in Japanese exports to nonoil LDCs in 1978. French trade statistics with OPEC may, however, be understated. As far as we have been able to ascertain, reported French trade data do not include armaments sales. French armaments exports -- largely sales of combat aircraft and helicopters to OPEC members such as Libya, Iraq, and the United Arab Emirates -- were significant and growing rapidly during these years, as shall be seen below.

The relatively fast growth of French exports to nonoil LDCs took place in spite of a slight revaluation of the French franc against the dollar of 11 percent between 1973 and 1978 which placed French exporters at a price disadvantage on world markets with respect to their American competitors. For Germany the revaluation of the deutschmark against the dollar during this same period was 34 percent, and rapid growth of German exports to Third World markets (faster to OPEC than either French or U.S. exports) also occurred despite this unfavorable exchange rate movement.

Chart 1 shows the evolution of the French franc/U.S. dollar exchange rate over the period 1973 to the end of October 1979. Domestic price levels in both countries followed an inflationary path, as shown in Chart 2. From 1970 on, however, the rate of increase in consumer prices in France was actually higher than that in the United States and with an ever widening margin. Thus French exporters competed in world markets against U.S. suppliers under the double disadvantage of both higher internal prices and a stronger external currency. Clearly, the success of French exports on foreign markets in recent years is due to the competitiveness of French exporters (aided by strong government policies) who have had to overcome unfavorable price and exchange rate movements in competition with U.S. suppliers.

TABLE I.3

UNITED STATES, JAPANESE, FRENCH, GERMAN, AND TOTAL EC
EXPORTS TO LESS DEVELOPED COUNTRIES (LDCs)

1973 - 1978 ($bn)

From	To	1973	1974	1975	1976	1977	1978	Percent Increase 73/77	73/78
United States	Nonoil LDCs	17.5	26.3	28.8	28.2	29.7	36.8	70	110
	Oil LDCs	3.4	6.4	10.4	12.2	13.5	16.0	267	370
Japan	Nonoil LDCs	11.4	17.1	16.2	18.5	23.0	29.4	102	158
	Oil LDCs	2.7	5.4	8.3	9.2	11.9	14.2	341	426
France	Nonoil LDCs	4.8	6.2	8.2	8.3	9.8	11.4	104	138
	Oil LDCs	1.7	2.8	4.6	4.7	5.6	6.2	229	265
Germany	Nonoil LDCs	5.5	8.3	7.8	8.3	9.5	11.5	72	109
	Oil LDCs	2.2	4.0	6.8	8.2	10.6	12.7	381	477
EC	Nonoil LDCs	20.0	28.0	31.1	30.7	37.0	N.A.	85	
	Oil LDCs	8.1	13.4	22.7	25.9	33.5	N.A.	316	

Source: IMF, Direction of Trade, Annual 1971-1977 and May 1979.

179

Chart I

EVOLUTION OF CONSUMER PRICES IN FRANCE AND THE UNITED STATES

(Index 1970 = 100)

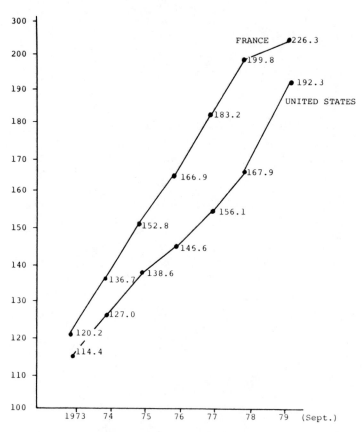

Source: U.N. Monthly Bulletin of Statistics,
December 1979

Chart II

FRENCH FRANC/ U.S. DOLLAR EXCHANGE RATE 1972 - 1979

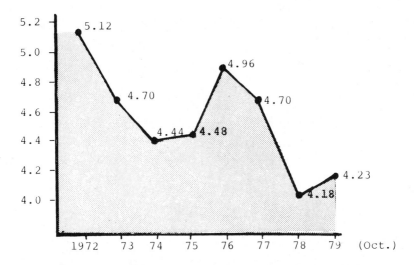

Source: IMF International Financial Statistics,
December 1979

The efficiency and competitiveness of French exporters has been substantially aided and backed by French government policy. In planning and policy objectives, promotion of exports is one of the very highest priorities in France and is explicitly embodied in the seventh French Economic Plan, where a vigorous expansion of the export sector is cited as the principal mechanism for offsetting a worsening trade deficit. Consequently, French government support for exports, in various forms, is quite active. Although in 1975 approximately 25 percent of all French exports received some official support, in 1976 this figure was 40 percent.[6] Support at home has been accompanied by active pursuit of "commercial diplomacy" abroad in potential export markets through the strengthening of foreign policy and economic ties. The next section focuses on this extremely important aspect in what has been the success story of French exporters over the past six years.

II. FRENCH GOVERNMENT POLICY TOWARD EXPORTS

Few Western governments are as directly and intensely involved in business decision making as is the French government. Moreover, whereas government involvement in business in the United States tends to mean control, regulation, or "bureaucratic interference" with business, in France it almost invariably means promotion and assistance to industry.[7] French business and government, particularly French big business and government, have long worked cooperatively together. Since World War II, they have done so in the context of drawing up seven successive indicative plans for the French economy. Although the plans have had little or nothing in common with the Soviet model of command decisions handed down from on high, they have specified guidelines and targets toward which industry and government propose jointly to work.

Perhaps as or more important than the specific content of the French plans (they are only indicative, easily revised, and often ignored), is the spirit they signify of a broad social consensus and close business-government cooperation. France's clear postwar goal of "catching up with Germany," and perhaps even with the United States in certain areas of industry fosters this commitment to cooperation. Indeed, although France's fragmented and partly Communist trade union structure precludes much direct participation by organized labor in the planning process, support for proindustry, protechnology goals is shared widely throughout French society. "Post" or "anti" industrial society groups are small and of minor political importance in France. Although "the left", for example, has all but brought nuclear power programs and the nuclear power industry to a halt in Germany and the United States, the massive French drive to use and export nuclear power and power equipment has few more staunch supporters than the French communist unions.

In light of the traditionally close relations between French business and government, it is no surprise that France has, and uses, one of the largest government batteries of explicit export promotion tools. The French government affects the performance of its export sector in several ways, ranging from state ownership positions in several of

France's leading industrial export firms, to the use of official export credits and assistance, cash grants, loans by the Ministry of Industry, financing by the Caisse Central through loans, grants, mixed credits, and insurance guarantees by the Coface, to more indirect measures such as tax-related incentives directly and indirectly tied to exports, and the political push to increase export orders provided by the disbursements of French aid in the form of official export credits, tied aid, technical assistance, and training programs.

A recent report by the U.S. Senate Subcommittee on International Finance states that France spent about six times the amount of the U.S. government for export promotion, which in the United States amounts to about 1/100th of 1 percent of the federal budget. In comparing the amount spent on export promotion for each million dollars of manufactured exports for fiscal year 1976, the French government spent $600, as opposed to $340 by the United States and $140 by the German government. The German figure is most likely understated, however, because German exports are promoted by trade associations and overseas German Chambers of Commerce which exporters are legally required to join and financially support.[8]

The close working relationship between business and government is accompanied by complete or partial state ownership of several of France's leading industrial export firms. Examples include 100 percent state-owned Renault in automobiles, trucks, machine tools, and consulting engineering; partly state-owned Framatome in nuclear power equipment; 100 percent state-owned Aerospatiale in helicopters and civil aircraft, and a consortium-leader for the Airbus; and partly state-owned Technip, one of the largest consulting-engineering firms.

The French government's current emphasis on export promotion, however, has stemmed from more than just habit. The French Economics Ministry, Industry Ministry, and Planning Commissariat executives are acutely aware of the contradiction between France's historic drive for independence, and its acute dependence on foreign materials and energy to (literally) fuel her industrial drive to "catch up with Germany."[9]

The aftermath of the oil-price shock convinced France that it could not have anything resembling energy independence in the near term, in spite of its having the only effectively continuing large-scale, nuclear-energy program in the industrialized world. Exports were necessary, and a diversified set of sources of energy imports and of markets for exports were to be sought to allow France some modicum of "independence." This point was written into the Seventh Plan.[10] Moreover, since very little oil could be paid for in French francs, and since any public borrowing from abroad to afford oil in the short run would have to be paid back by earnings from yet more exports, the French government saw no choice but to stimulate exports. This was especially the case since growth was needed to absorb France's baby-boom generation into the labor market. Unlike the United States, which was perhaps encouraged in the short run by the illusion that it did not have to export more by being able to pay for oil in dollars, France defined the constraint to growth imposed by the effect of the oil price increase on its balance of payments as its number one economic policy problem.

The result was that in 1974 the first priority of industrial policy in France shifted to promoting exports and export-oriented industries. (The second remained nuclear energy.) First came increased guarantees and credits, and then in 1976, a 10 billion francs ($2 billion) appropriation for low-interest loans for more capacity-enlarging investments by export-oriented enterprises. (These credits were in addition to the dramatic increases in export credits per se noted in Chart 3.)

Accompanying specific, financial incentives to exports were presidential and prime ministerial visits to oil LDCs and to the most rapidly growing nonoil developing countries, whose aims were clearly as oriented to selling airport construction, subway, power plant, and aircraft contracts as they were to geo-political ends. President Giscard d'Estaing's visit to Brazil in October 1978 had as one of its announced motives to encourage the establishment of French firms in Brazil in the form of joint ventures. Such corporate direct investment was seen to be an essential precondition for increasing French exports to this market.[11] The December 1978 tour of the French

Chart III

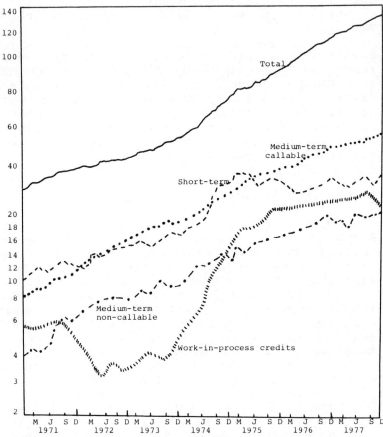

EXPORT CREDITS, BY TYPE,
1971-1977

(billion F, FR)

Source: Statistiques et Etudes Financières, Trente-deuxième rapport
annuel du Conseil National du Crédit, No. 340, Ministère de
l'Economie et des Finances, Paris, 1977, p. 181.

Secretary of State for Foreign Affairs, Mr. Olivier Stirn, in anglophone Africa was aimed in part at diversifying French export markets in Africa and to pick up "missed commercial opportunities" in an already strong area of French export success.[12] The same motivation prompted the April 1979 trips of Mr. Stirn to Colombia and Peru and of the French Budget Minister, Mr. Maurice Papon, to Argentina where France hopes to increase its exports of construction projects and public works such as harbors, railways, and metro systems.[13]

France's specific export incentives, subsidies, and promotional devices can be classed into two groups: nontax export incentives and tax-related export incentives. Nontax incentives include such programs as official credit assistance, insurance guarantees, and cash grants, while tax-related incentives refer to French income tax practices and to the remission of indirect taxes on goods destined for export.

Export Insurance Programs

A quasi-public corporation created in 1948 -- the Compagnie Francaise d'Assurance pour le Commerce Exterieur (Coface) -- provides French exporters with extensive insurance coverage.[14] The Coface insures about 27 percent of all exports and makes available preshipment coverage and export credit coverage as well. To be insured, goods must be made in France and have no more than 10-15 percent foreign content, with the exception of capital goods components of EC origin which may have up to 40 percent foreign content. Coface insurance covers the following risks:

- political risks (war, including civil war and revolution outside France, or a foreign government's decision to block the payment of a public buyer),

- risk of catastrophe (cyclone, flood, earthquake, volcanic eruption, tidal inundation -- all outside France),

- risk of nontransfer (a foreign government's blocking or retarding payment),

- commercial risks (insolvency case by case),

- inflation risk (abnormal increases in production costs due to inflation) can be covered for contracts with a duration of at least one year,

- exchange risk for fluctuations above 2.25 percent in certain currencies, and

- market development risk related to start-up expenses and the building up of inventory abroad.[15]

It may seem surprising that only about a quarter of total French exports are insured, but this is explained by the fact that the majority of shipments insured are those going to Third World or socialist destinations. How important a factor the availability of risk insurance is in encouraging exporters to choose these higher-risk destinations is difficult to assess. For commerical risks the exporter may insure his entire sale (excluding sales to foreign subsidiaries) or a minimum of 50 percent of his exports, although the exporter insured for political risks is obliged to insure all transactions with the country he selects. Both policies are available normally only for exports to private buyers, although there are exceptions by special agreement.

Insurance coverage is also available from the Coface for longer-term guarantees, and for sales to both private and public buyers for payments that extend up to five years from the date of delivery. In response to foreign competition, Coface has also guaranteed credits extending for more than five years. These policies may insure commercial and political risks together, or political risks alone. The exporter has the choice of taking preshipment and/or credit coverage separately. Moreover, exchange risk is now available from Coface for capital equipment contracts written in deutschmarks, sterling, guilders or dollars. The insurance covers risk of loss if the currency has fluctuated more than 2.25 percent (only losses due to fluctuations above 2.25 percent are insured).

Besides the insurance facility of the Coface destined specifically for exporters, the French government also uses its foreign investment insurance program to promote exports; however, the extent of this program in comparison with the use of export credits, or direct export insurance is small. Explicit eligibility requirements for investors seeking insurance coverage with Coface are that the investment must be linked to French exports. In 1975 nearly two-thirds of insured investments were located in developing countries.[16] Those seeking insurance coverage for investments [the institutions involved are the Banque Francaise du Commerce Exterieur (BFCE) or the Caisse Centrale de Cooperation Economique (CCCE)] must cite export expansion to be one of the major benefits anticipated by such investments.

Export Financing/Export Credits

Credit to buyers and suppliers is generally used to support both medium and long-term export transactions and goes overwhelmingly to finance capital goods. The BFCE deals with export financing. It primarily supports loans made by commercial banks through preferential rediscounting or interest rate subsidies. It can also make direct loans for maturities of more than seven years. Medium-term suppliers' credits are supported by the Bank of France (the Central Bank) through the refinancing of early maturities by special interest rates for export financing. Up to 90 percent of the contract value can be supported. The interest rates charged borrowers for such long-term credits are generally 7.5 percent. Interest subsidies for long-term loans distributed by the BFCE have doubled since 1975, amounting to 800 billion francs in 1976.[17]

The BFCE also provides for long-term "mixed loans" which are a combination of normal commercial terms with "soft terms" such as special long-term loans with extremely low interest rates. These "mixed credit" arrangements are used to finance capital goods exports to developing countries, in combining low-interest loans (3 percent) under official aid and commercial credit. These mixed credits amounted to 1.3 billion francs ($280 million) in the first half of 1977.[18]

Table II.1 shows a comparative summary of export credit agencies in the major industrial countries,

TABLE II.1

EXPORT CREDIT AGENCIES: SUMMARY DATA

Country	Agency	Financing Mechanisms	Estimated Percent of Capital Good Exports Financed
Canada	Export Development Corporation (EDC)	Direct loans credit lines	7-9%
France	Banque Francaise du Commerce Exterieur (BFCE)	Direct loans rediscounts credit lines	8-10%
Germany	Kreditanstalt fuer Wiederaufbau (KFW)	Direct loans	1%
Italy	Mediocredito	Refinancing interest rate subsidies	4-8%
Japan	Export-Import Bank of Japan	Direct loans credit lines	7-9%
United Kingdom	Export Credit Guarantee Debt (ECGD)	Refinancing interest rate subsidies	15-20%
United States	Export-Import Bank of Washington (Eximbank)	Direct loans refinancing	6-8%

Source: U.S. Department of State, Export Credit Systems of the Major Powers and their Role in Exports of Capital Goods, Washington, D.C., Spring 1977, p. 2.

their mechanisms of financing, and the estimated percentage of capital goods exports financed by these official agencies. The percentage of capital goods exports financed in France, between 8 to 10 percent, is higher than for all other industrial countries, with the exception of the United Kingdom. The comparable figure for the United States is 6 to 8 percent. Still, officially supported export financing in France affects only a small share of its capital goods exports. The use of other sources of international financing (international banks, foreign assistance agencies, and Eurocurrency borrowing) are substantially more important for French exporters (or for foreign importers) than are official export credits.[19] Historically it appears that France has provided relatively cheap credit to its exporters, but differences in comparative term-structures and items and products being financed make it difficult to make difinitive statements.[20]

In a world of fluctuating exchange rates, the advantage given by interest rate differentials in stimulating export sales may sometimes be small relative to movements of exchange rates themselves.[21] Differences in downpayment and maturity requirements also serve to reduce or eliminate the importance of interest rate differentials.

France is unique in that the financing of capital goods exports and public works projects carried out abroad may benefit from a type of work-in-process credit granted during the phase of manufacture or preparation after the order has been placed but before the actual export sale.[22] Reimbursement in this case is normally assured either by medium or long-term loans from abroad or by the foreign exporter's payment, with the help of a buyer's credit accorded by the French Central Bank. Exports of light equipment or consumer goods that do not necessitate the according of such work-in-process credits before or during their manufacture benefit from short-term (18 month maximum) credits.

Chart 3 provides a breakdown of export credits between long, medium, short-term, and work-in-process credits. Total export credits amounted to around 120 billion French francs ($22.5 billion) at the end of 1977, four times larger than the amount at the end of

191

1970. Of this FF 120 billion, medium-term callable credits represented approximately 37 percent, short-term credits 23 percent, work-in-process credits 18 percent and medium-term noncallable and long-term credits 16 percent. The two categories with the largest growth were those of medium-term callable credits and work-in-process credits, which increased nearly fourfold from approximately 5.5 billion francs ($1.2 billion) in 1970 to 20 billion francs in 1977.

The principal products benefiting from export credits are presented in Table II.2. For medium and long-term credits the main beneficiaries are the heavy industry and transport sectors, namely: mechanical equipment and machinery, automobile construction, miscellaneous metal manufactures, electrical and electronic constructions, aircraft, and ships. The main beneficiaries of short-term credits are mineral and organic chemicals followed by automobiles, mechanical equipment and machinery, and electrical/ electronic equipment. The largest increase in short-term credits in recent years has been for aircraft.[23]

Agricultural products are absent from the list; although they are beneficiaries of heavy export subsidization, this is carried out on the European Community level, under the aegis of the Common Agricultural Policy. The picture shown in Table II.2 of the relative volume of exports financed is of course influenced by the maturity dates of the loans and the ease with which rollovers are granted.

The importance of export credits in improving French international competitiveness was evaluated in a recent U.S. State Department report as small, primarily because official financing supports only a relatively modest amount of total French exports. The study asserted that no major shifts in relative market shares could be attributed to export financing and that the performance of France, with one of the most elaborate official export financing systems, was no better than that of the United States or Germany, with the least developed official systems.[24]

Although the overall importance of export financing may be small, its weight in obtaining the award of contracts for French firms for certain products or in certain geographical areas may be

TABLE II.2

PRINCIPAL PRODUCT CATEGORIES BENEFITING
FROM EXPORT CREDITS IN FRANCE

(value, in million French francs, 1976)

	Medium and Long-Term Credits (beyond 5 years)	Short-Term Credits (up to 5 years)
Machinery	4175	1119
Automobiles and Vehicles	3143	1416
Miscellaneous Metal Manufactures	2978	520
Electrical/Electronic Machinery	2262	1074
Aircraft	2122	480
Ships	1900	30
Public Works	1418	--
Parachemical	908	656
Machine Tools	383	234
Rubber	280	528
Metalworks	271	273
Precision Mechanical Products	240	394
Agricultural Machinery	67	311
Mineral/Organic Chemicals	--	2647
Pharmaceutical Products	--	433
Clothing	--	390
Leather	--	380
Plastics	--	190
Hats	--	172
Glassware	--	138

Source: Rapport du Conseil National du Credit, presented in
Problèmes Economiques, 24 August 1977, p. 12.

significant. This appears to be especially true in French export sales to the Third World. A 1978 report of the French Planning Bureau stated that French exports to developing countries had expanded only (emphasis added) due to a very rapid growth in the granting of credits, especially export credits. Half of the total of such export credits (65 billion French francs in 1976) were directed toward trade with developing countries.[25]

Three product areas in particular -- nuclear power plants, commercial jet aircraft, and steel mills -- along with products of heavy industry in general are cited by a U.S. State Department report as those areas in which competition in export financing appears to have played a major role in the award of contracts. This seems to have been the case in the award to a French concern over an American one of a nuclear power plant contract in Spain. The superiority of the equipment, however, is often said to be the determining factor in the export sale rather than the financing terms. The U.S. State Department has argued that, of all major sales of the A-300 Airbus, the only non-American commercial jet that has recently won export orders, most appear attributable to nonfinancial factors, whether they be better equipment or exchange of landing rights.[26]

French Tax-related Export Incentives

Tax-related export incentives increase the competitiveness of French exports by permitting substantial export price reductions, significant increases in export profits, and deductions that are applied to the nonprice determinants of export competitiveness -- or all three. In France, both direct tax incentives and the basic tax structure of the fiscal system itself are said to favor exporters. United States exporters are particularly concerned that tax-related export incentives given in France (as well as in several other West European countries) are providing unfair advantages to foreign exports and that this should be offset by a continuance and strengthening of DISC practices.[27] Principal tax-related practices in France include allowing the retention of export profits in tax-havens, as well as special deductions and credits for export-related expenses.

The question of border tax adjustments was dealt with in the recently concluded Tokyo Round of multi-lateral trade negotiations. In the provisions of the Code on Subsidies and Countervailing Duties, rebates of indirect taxes on exports by countries like France, using value-added tax schemes, are not considered unfair trade practices if such rebates are not in excess of taxes on domestic production and distribution. All export incentives and practices are in fact to be brought under international definition and supervision for those signatories to the Code, beginning with its entry into force on 1 January 1980.

Safe-haven Rules

Under its safe-haven rules, France totally exempts foreign source income from taxable income and defines foreign source income in a very broad way to include any income derived from permanent establishments abroad, from foreign operations of dependent agents, and from operations constituting a so-called "complete commercial cycle" outside France. A French company, under the complete commercial cycle theory, may generate nontaxable income by simply conducting activities outside France but without establishing any permanent facilities abroad. Moreover, a French parent may exclude from its taxable income 95 percent of all dividends received from an offshore subsidiary.

Another facet of foreign taxation that increases the value of French safe-haven rules is that foreign losses are deductible from domestic profits, even though the foreign profits were not subject to tax. This is consequently a great incentive toward the establishment of new operations abroad and substantially reduces the cost of potential losses and the risk of exporting.

Special Deductions

France permits its exporters to constitute special tax-deductible reserves to absorb export credit risks, operational losses, and promotional costs. French companies are permitted to establish reserves for the losses of foreign branches and subsidiaries, even though the profits of such entities are not taxed. In addition, exporting companies are allowed to constitute deductible reserves to cover credit risks; companies that extend two to five-year credit can create a reserve of up to 10 percent of the amount of the credit. If the company continues to sell on such credit terms, it can indefinitely defer a portion of the tax on its export income, assuming its losses are less than its reserves. France also allows exporters to be exempted from the domestic "inflation tax" of 33 1/3 percent it has imposed since 1975 on increases in profit margins over the preceding year's margin.

In addition to the special tax incentives directly tied to exports, there are a number of incentives that indirectly benefit exports. This is the case, for example, of tax incentives to encourage the development of certain industrial sectors or of certain regionally-depressed areas. It seems that such incentives are more readily available for French firms that have plans for substantial export expansion.

Administrative Practices

To the specific tax practices listed above must be added French tax administration practices that provide incentives to French companies with foreign branches or subsidiaries, especially the very liberal rules governing the allocation by transfer prices of profits and income among related companies. According to some U.S. company executives, such an attitude converts the French basic tax structure with respect to taxation of foreign source income into direct export incentives.

Other administrative practices benefiting French exporters include the ability to negotiate tax "agreements" with the French government. Small and medium-sized French firms can form joint ventures for the purpose of expanding their exports and then negotiate favorable tax agreements with the government to obtain substantial tax relief.

The importance of French tax-related export incentives in stimulating export sales and increasing international competitiveness of French firms is difficult to quantify. They most likely affect the structure of exports in the short run when applied differentially among products. In the long run, however, other economic factors such as changes in comparative costs from differing resource endowments, wage rates, productivity, etc., as well as fluctuations in exchange rates may well offset any short-term advantages provided by these incentives.

Foreign Aid and Technical Assistance

Part of the success in selling to developing-country markets, especially former French colonies and the present French franc zone area, probably lies in the substantial volume of development assistance France extends to these countries. The growth of French official aid disbursements has been very rapid, increasing 2.5 times in value terms between 1970 and 1977, surpassed only by Japan whose aid tripled during that period. French aid is the second largest in amount in absolute value terms among all the OECD donor countries. Only the United States ranks higher.[28] In 1977 its overseas development aid disbursements reached $2.3 billion which represented 0.6 percent of its GNP (as compared with aid disbursements representing 0.38 percent of GNP for the United Kingdom, 0.3 percent for West Germany, 0.25 percent for Japan, and 0.22 percent for the United States).[29] Total official loans, private loans, and direct investments in LDCs accounted for $5.2 billion or 1.37 percent of France's GDP in 1977.

France is well ahead of all other countries, including the United States, in the volume of technical assistance provided to developing countries. France has typically provided between one-third and one-half of all technical assistants from developed countries working in LDCs and between two to three times as many as the United States.[30] The bulk of this assistance is directed toward the education sector (France is a major supplier of teachers to French-speaking LDCs), but France is also very active in supporting research in LDCs, particularly in the agricultural sector. This aid, even when not tied, is often an influential factor in encouraging the purchase of French products.

French official aid has been concentrated on those nonoil LDCs to which French exports have grown rapidly over the past years. Such countries include many of France's former colonies in northern and black Africa. In January 1978, a discussion over the purchases by the Ivory Coast of radio and TV networks from France was one of the objects of a five-day visit by President Giscard d'Estaing. Contracts under negotiation were valued at FF 6 billion; the French government had agreed to finance FF 1.5 billion for proposals from French companies and to provide technical assistance in the form of some 2,000 technicians.[31]

In Upper Volta, the French Caisse Centrale de Cooperation Economique (CCCE) agreed to finance extension works of a power station at Bobo-Dioulasso, provide resources to extend the national electricity coverage, and to give aid for projects of rural development and dam construction at Bagre.[32] France was Upper Volta's main trading partner in 1977, exporting primarily steel products and mechanical and electrical equipment.

The CCCE also agreed to sponsor a loan to finance the modernization of the Lomé-Tokoin airport in Togo and to aid in the development of Togo's agricultural sector (cotton growing and cocoa and coffee production). France is Togo's main trading partner, again exporting iron and steel products, heavy equipment, and pharmaceuticals.[33]

An official agreement signed by the French and Moroccan governments in February 1977 provides for soft loans from the French treasury and guarantees suppliers' credits to Morocco. The funds are earmarked to finance purchases of French capital goods, notably for chemicals, steel, shipping, fishing, communications, and public works projects.

French aid to Morocco in 1978 increased by 15 percent to FF 15 billion, of which FF 270 million was in the form of low interest long-term loans and FF 580 million in the form of export credit insurance. The loans helped pay for the Asment cement works at Casablanca, the extension of the Yohammedia oil refinery, the construction of a weaving mill, the development of sugar factories, and large chemical works. In 1977, imports from France accounted for 30 percent of Morocco's import bill, by far the biggest share of any single country.[34] Part of France's success in its export sales to Morocco appears to be in its political support for Morocco's claim to the Western Sahara, in its military cooperation, and in concessions made to ensure the favorable treatment of Moroccan migrant workers in France.

The recent success of French exports in developing countries may be qualified in the future by the occasionally protectionist measures taken by the French authorities to restrict market access of developing country exports. Of all the major industrial countries, France obtains the smallest percentage of its manufactured imports from the developing countries (only 4.3 percent in 1977 and 1978, half of that of West Germany and Great Britain and five times less than that of the United States and Japan).[35] Protectionist measures introduced recently against clothing items have reduced imports in this area by 30 percent in 1978.

Such actions may run counter to the efforts of the French government's export promotion program. Certain developing countries are beginning to demand concessions from their suppliers and to refuse too great an unequal treatment. For example, India broke one order it had placed for an Airbus A-300 in protest against the French position on tightening the Multifiber Accord against textile and clothing products exported by LDCs.[36] The failure to open French markets to developing country imports in the long run could also serve to deny these important customers the financial solvency necessary to increase their absorption of French exports.

III. PROFILES OF PARTICULAR EXPORT SECTORS

Armaments

The armaments industry is one of France's most successful exporters. It is perhaps the most successful in terms of growth, especially in the LDC markets. France is known to be the third largest exporter of arms, after the United States and the Soviet Union (see Table III.1). According to the Stockholm Institute of Peace Research (SIPRI), the great majority of France's half billion dollars of annual arms exports go to less developed countries (see Table III.1). Thus, although yearly French military exports have traditionally been only one-tenth the size of U.S. foreign military sales, French military sales to the Third World may have come to as much as half the size of U.S. military sales to LDCs in recent years, (if sales to Israel, a country not always counted as Third World, are excluded from the U.S. figures).

French military sales are also heavily skewed to military aircraft and missiles. Fighter aircraft, helicopters, missiles, and related products are reputed to have constituted approximately three quarters of French military exports since 1971.[37] This proportion is clearly higher than in the case of U.S. foreign military sales to LDCs, where as much as 15 percent consists of civil engineering work undertaken by the U.S. military for countries such as Saudi Arabia. The proportion is also clearly higher for France than for Great Britain, whose military exports to LDCs include -- as far as one can ascertain -- a much larger proportion of land vehicles and ships.[38] France is evidently the leading noncommunist competitor of the United States in Third World military aerospace markets, with a market share perhaps not far from being two-thirds the size of that of the United States even during the heyday of massive U.S. arms sales to Iran.

Moreover, France continues in an attempt to increase arms sales to Arab countries, especially OPEC, and is concentrating this drive on Iraq, Iran, and Saudi Arabia. Her desire to obtain secured and constant flows of crude petroleum at preferential prices is backed not only by armament exports at

TABLE III.1

INDICATORS OF THE ECONOMIC IMPORTANCE OF MILITARY EXPORTS
TO THE UNITED STATES, FRANCE, THE UNITED KINGDOM, WEST GERMANY
AND THE UNION OF SOVIET SOCIALIST REPUBLICS

	Military Exports 1975 (ACDA Figures)[a] (U.S. $ bn)	Military Exports as Percent of Total Exports	Military Exports as a Percent of GNP
United States	4.85	4.5%	0.32%
France	0.50	0.9%	0.16%
United Kingdom	0.38	1.0%	0.17%
West Germany	0.26	0.3%	0.06%
USSR	2.61	23.0%	0.39%

	Military Exports to LDCs, 1975 (SIPRI Figures)[a] (U.S. $ bn)	Military Exports to LDCs as a Percent of Total Exports, 1975	Military Exports to LDCs, as a Percent of GNP, 1975
United States	1.77[b]	1.6%	0.11%
France	0.47	0.9%	0.15%
United Kingdom	0.50	1.3%	0.23%
West Germany	0.12	0.1%	0.02%
USSR	1.65	14.5%	0.24%

Notes: [a]The ACDA and SIPRI figures are not directly comparable.
Indeed, the SIPRI estimates of UK exports to LDCs
exceeds the ACDA estimates of total UK arms exports.

[b]Includes exports to Israel which amounted to some
$700 million, by U.S. ACDA estimates.

Sources: SIPRI Yearbook 1976, p. 252, Table 6F. SIPRI figures are
in 1973 dollars. World Military Expenditures and
Arms Transfers 1966-1975 Arms Control and
Disarmament Agency, U.S. Department of State.

guaranteed credits but also by offers of technical assistance in other industrial, agricultural, and nuclear areas.

Iraq has agreed to furnish France with 25 million tons of oil in 1979 (an increase of 25 percent over 1978) at preferential prices in exchange for a long list of military hardware including:

- 60 Mirage 2000, of which 20 would be delivered to the Syrian army, 20 would be based in Syria but flown by Iraqui pilots and 20 would be based in Iraq,

- teleguided missiles,

- sophisticated radar systems,

- naval surveillance units equipped with missiles, and

- Puma and Gazelle helicopters equipped with antitank missiles.[39]

Iraqi authorities have also expressed the desire for French construction of a factory to manufacture light and medium arms in Iraq.

A recent defense cooperation agreement signed by the Saudi Defense Minister and the French Defense Minister last July provides for a large increase in French arms sales to Saudi Arabia.[40] The agreement calls for the creation of a permanent joint defense commission covering two areas in which France is already providing hardware, armor and missile defense systems, and in fighter aircraft programs, where Saudi Arabia has previously relied on U.S. suppliers.

Sales to Saudi Arabia of the Mirage 2000 or 4000 are also under discussion, despite the planned delivery in early 1980 of the first of 60 U.S. F-15 fighters. In Egypt a contract has been awarded recently to the French for supply of a missile coastal defense system, at a value of $239 million.[41] One immediate result of the agreement will be the delivery of Thomson CSF/Matra Crotale mobile surface to air missiles for the Saudi Army to be mounted on the bodies of the

French-supplied AMX-30 tank, of which the Saudi Army now has about 400 in service and on order.

The French have also been looking further east to Asia and communist developing markets. On a visit to France in late 1977, China's Deputy Chief of Staff Yang Cheng-wu indicated that China would be interested in purchasing the Mirage 2000 fighter plane.[42] More recently, China has said that it would actually like to buy as many as 1000 of the planes but has not confirmed purchase as yet.

The importance of French military exports in total French exports, however, should be viewed in perspective. Total French military exports are equal to only some 1 percent of total French exports according to the 1975 figures from the U.S. Arms Control and Disarmament Agency (ACDA) cited in Table III.1. These figures serve as a reminder of the proportionately greater importance in total French exports of civilian capital goods.

Aerospace

In 1974, France ranked third behind the United States and just behind the United Kingdom in total world sales of aerospace products. Since then, however, France has moved to second position and provides growing competition.

In this highly successfully export sector most production for sales abroad is of a military nature. In fact, 80 percent of the orders placed for export in France consist of military engines and aircraft. The value of foreign orders in 1977 was at a record high of 20 billion French francs ($4.3 billion) twice as much as the value of orders in 1975.[43] In the civil sector as well, orders have grown enormously for the Airbus, the European consortium-built wide-bodied passenger craft which has seen a take-off in sales over the past year, as well as for the civil carrier Mystere 10 and 20. For the French aerospace industry as a whole, exports are of the most critical importance. Table III.2 shows that exports accounted for 56 percent of total French aerospace industry sales.

TABLE III.2

SALES AND EXPORT FIGURES ON THE
FRENCH AEROSPACE INDUSTRY

SALES (Millions FF)

	1970	1971	1972	1973	1974	1975	1976
Current francs	7,434	7,869	8,861	10,880	12,976	15,500	18,000
Constant francs	12,071	12,212	12,765	15,000	16,000	17,000	18,000

EXPORTS (Millions FF, Current)

	1970	1971	1972	1973	1974	1975	1976
Orders placed	5,507	4,996	3,689	5,470	10,423	9,210	9,709
Deliveries made	2,512	2,720	3,795	4,818	5,350	7,130	10,100

Note: A chart showing the evolution of the French franc/dollar
exchange rate over this period is found on page 12.

Source: Interavia, Geneva, May 1977, p. 419.

204

Private companies in France have succeeded over the past years in competing with nationalized companies in the production of aircraft. These private sector companies -- Morane-Saulnier, Castel-Mauboussin, Breguet and Dassault -- have succeeded in becoming the regular suppliers of the French army and naval-air forces, and along with it, large exporters. So successful have private companies been in the military field that virtually the only role that has evolved for Aerospatiale, the nationalized company, is that of subcontractor. In total, 4,100 combat aircraft, excluding transport carriers, have been built since 1945 by the private companies.

This list includes:

    320 MD 315-311-312 naval aircraft,

    350 MD 450 pursuit aircraft,

    737 Mystere IV and Super Mystere,

    411 Mystere IV A combat aircraft (+176 derived craft),

  1300 Mirage III intercepteur craft (+400 derived craft),

     62 Mirage IV bombers,

    402 Jaguar (Breguet 121) attack aircraft: with the United Kingdom[44] and

    433 Alpha-Jet trainer aircraft: with West Germany.

Several countries count France as the principal supplier of aircraft for their national fleet. Table III.3 shows that (besides France) nine other countries had a majority of Mirage aircraft in their fleet as of 1 December 1978. These aircraft include fighters, bombers, reconnaissance, and training craft. Developing countries who have recently placed major orders for French combat aircraft include: Libya (38), United Arab Emirates (26), Egypt (61), Iraq (72), Morocco (50), Sudan (14), Peru (36), Ecuador (18), Argentina (19), and Gabon (5).[45] Among these

TABLE III.3

PRINCIPAL CUSTOMERS FOR FRENCH FIGHTER AIRCRAFT

1. Countries with Majority of Mirage Aircraft in Fleet*
   as of 1 December 1978

France	672	(of which 200 on order)
South Africa	121	
Libya	112	(plus 38 on order)
Australia	98	
Spain	96	(of which 65 on order)
Belgium	90	
Morocco	50	(all on order)
Switzerland	47	
Peru	36	
U.A.E.	32	(26 on order)

2. Major LDC Orders (As of 1 Dec. 1978) in Addition to
   Those Mentioned Above

Iraq	72
Egypt	61
Argentina	19
Equador	18
Sudan	14
Gabon	5

*Fighters, bombers, reconnaissance, and trainers included.

Source: Interavia, January 1979.

purchasers, the Middle Eastern and Arab countries dominate.

Aerospatiale has an outstanding record, however, in the production and sale of helicopters for export, including the various models of Puma, Dauphin, Gazelle, Alouette, and Ecureuil. An even larger number of countries count a majority of French helicopters in their fleet. As of January 1979 they numbered 38, among them 29 developing countries (of which eight are Arab and twelve African states).

In construction and export of civil aircraft, France's Aerospatiale is one of the four participants in the Airbus-Industrie consortium (along with Germany's Deutsche Airbus, a Spanish firm, and England's British Aerospace) managed by a French director. This program has seen sales shoot up enormously over the past 18 months, providing serious competition to U.S. products, especially the Boeing 767. Although not begun under official EC auspices, the European Commission gives moral and political (if not much financial) support to the consortium as part of its rationalization efforts in major high technology industrial sectors and urges the participation of more EC members as well as consultations to avoid competition between the Airbus program and Britain's BA-146 and Holland's VFW-Fokker projects.[46]

A joint effort has been a success. The two models A-300 and A-310 have been designed as widebodied carriers over short distances and fly lower than their Boeing competitor which has been designed for longer routes.[47] Air India and Eastern Airlines managers who were interviewed stated that because of the Airbus's two-engine configuration, it also offered substantial economies in fuel consumption and maintenance. General Electric and SNECMA, the 50-50 partners in the joint venture that produces the Airbus engine, also claim fuel-saving advantages for their engine. One of the big pluses in the success of the Airbus 300 and 310 is their fuel efficiency in use compared to the U.S. carriers. The best U.S. planes at present designed for medium-length hauls use 40 percent more fuel per passenger than the A-300, and the older crafts built for long-hauls burn double the amount of fuel. Compared specifically to its only present competitor, the Boeing 727, the Airbus consumes 30 percent less fuel per passenger for every mile flown.[48] Purchase decisions by customers have been influenced by these considerations. Financing, however, has been claimed to play a large part in obtaining some export orders (see Table III.4).

Table III.5 shows the roster of airline companies that have ordered and/or placed options on orders of the Airbus A-300 and A-310 craft, as of May 1979. Outstanding orders to develop country airlines for the A-300 total 60 out of 161, or slightly less than a third.

Recent purchasers of Airbus A-300s include Japan which is to buy six planes at a total cost of $225 million, three to be ordered in 1980 and three the following year. The Airbus was chosen in preference to the DC-10 for some inland routes.[49] Singapore Airlines has placed an order for six A-300 craft as well, costing more than $310 million, including spare parts and related equipment. The first two aircraft should be delivered in April 1981 and subsequent ones in 1982 and 1983.[50] Options have been taken on two more craft as well, to be delivered if confirmed in February 1984. The plane was chosen in preference to the Boeing 727.

The Airbus Program, begun in 1969, is scheduled to last until the end of the century. To date, over 350 Airbus planes have been sold. The success of the program is confirmed by orders placed during the past two years: In 1978 around 80 craft were sold or ordered; in the first five months of 1979, 170 A-300 and A-310 models were ordered, for a total value of $10 billion.[51] This sales volume gave Airbus-Industrie one-third of the large carrier market in 1978, with one-third going to Boeing and one-third shared between McDonnell Douglas and Lockheed.

Boeing has claimed that a lack of competitive financing terms has contributed to the loss of several recent sales, especially developing country clients (one-third of its export sales go to developing countries). In 1977, Pakistan International Airlines (PIA) bought the Airbus over a Boeing 747 for which the Eximbank did not provide credits. France also offered to sell nuclear reprocessing equipment, (an offer since rescinded) at about the same time the aircraft were

TABLE III.4
EXAMPLES OF AIRPLANE SALES LOST
(1975-1977)

Customer	Country	Competitive Product Sold	Quantity Ordered	Approx. Price ($ mil)	Competitive Financing			
					Type	Percent Covered	Interest Rate	Maturity (Years)
Cyprus Air	Cyprus	BAC-111	2	$ 13	Unknown, but reportedly very favorable			
Germanair	Germany	A-300	2	$ 40	Debt	85	7.0	12
Indian Air	India	A-300	3	$ 56	Debt	90	8.0	10
Korean Airlines	Korea	A-300	6	$112	Lease	100	6.5	12
S.African Airways	S. Africa	A-300	4	$ 87	Debt	90	8.0	10
Trans-European	Belgium	A-300	2	$ 40	Lease	Unknown	Unknown	Unknown
PIA**	Pakistan	A-300	2	$ 50	Debt	98	Unknown	10
Thai Airways	Thailand	A-300	4	$105	Debt	90	8.0	10
Iran Air	Iran	A-300	10	$250	Unknown			
Eastern Airlines	U.S.	A-300	4	Free				

Customer	U.S. Product Offered (qty)	Approx. Price ($ mil)	Eximbank Terms	Comments
Cyprus Air	727 (2) DC-9	$14	No Eximbank participation	Guarantee acceptable to Eximbank was not available.
Germanair	737 (3)	$24	Standard terms*	Guarantee acceptable to Eximbank was not available.
Indian Air	737 (3) L-1011 DC-10	$30	Standard terms*	Reciprocal trade concessions offered by competition.
Korean Airlines	727 (6) L-1011 DC-10	$60	Standard terms*	Landing rights granted in Paris.
S.African Airlines	747SP (3) DC-10 L-1011	$90	Eximbank guarantee only	French reportedly offered military airplans to S. Africa.
Trans-European	727 (2)	$20	Standard terms*	
PIA**	747SR	($40)	None	France reportedly offered to sell nuclear reprocessing equipment that U.S. refused to sell.
Thai Airways	727 (4) DC-10	$50	Standard terms*	
Iran Air			Standard terms	French reportedly agreed to barter deal and sale of nuclear power plants.
Eastern Airlines	727 L-1011		None	Eastern has no-charge lease for 6 months but pays operational costs.

*Standard terms: 85 percent to 90 percent 10-year term financing with Eximbank providing a direct credit of 30 percent to 55 percent of sales price at a fixed rate of 8.5 percent to 9.0 percent.   Balance of financing is provided by a commercial bank on a variable rate basis.   Eximbank guarantee is rarely offered on commercial bank credit. No Eximbank program for lease financing.
**Pending but believed firm at time of publication.
Source: AIA member company survey, Eximbank.

TABLE III.5

AIRBUS ORDERS AS OF MAY 1979

A-300	ORDERS	OPTIONS
Air France	23	12
Luftansa	11	--
Korean Air Lines	8	
TEA	2	--
Indian Air Lines	8	3
Germanair	4	--
S. African Airways	4	--
Air Inter	6	--
Thai International	8	--
SAS	4	8
Iran Air	6	3
Eastern	23	9
Olympic	2	3
Pakistan	4	6
Hapag Lloyd	2	--
MAS	3	1
Alitalia	8	3
Philippine Airlines	2	2
Iberia	4	4
Garuda	6	6
Laker	10	--
Air Afrique	1	--
Cruzeiro do Sul	2	2
Egyptair	3	4
Aerocondon	1	--
Singapore Airlines	6	6
TOTAL	161	72

A-310		
Lufthansa	25	25
Swissair	10	10
KLM	10	10
Air Afrique	2	--
Air France	5	10
TOTAL	52	55

Source: The Economist, 19 May 1979, p. 94.

under consideration. The United States embargoes the export of nuclear reprocessing equipment on anti-weapons proliferation grounds. Since 1977, however, Eximbank policies have improved. The agency did finance a 747 purchase for use on routes for which the A-300 was less suited due to traffic, frequency, and route requirements.

In 1977, Thai International Airlines purchased four A-300 aircraft for $105 million, instead of four Boeing 727s valued at $50 million: Thai International received debt financing arrangements from European governments and banks. The impact of the loss of the sales was greater than expected: Thai International is using its influence to help persuade other carriers in the region to purchase A-300 aircraft for pooling arrangements. These and other instances involving foreign government support of sales to developing countries are summarized in Table III.4. Five out of nine of the Airbus sales listed were to developing countries.

Nuclear Power Equipment

Both France and West Germany suffered from the cancellation of construction of four nuclear power plants ordered by the Iranian government in 1974. Of the four plants, the Creusot-Loire subsidiary of Framatome (France) was charged with the construction of two on the Karvun river in the south, while the German plants at Bushehor were being built by Kraftwerk Union. The French contact was broken in April and the German one in August of 1979, even though the West German plants were near completion.[52]

This cancellation, for obvious political reasons, is not indicative of the trend of French and German exports in the nuclear field over the past few years. As the major competitors to U.S. suppliers, they have seen their share of the nuclear power plant export market outside the East block rise, as that of the United States has fallen from 80 percent in 1972, to 50 percent in 1977, and to only 14 percent in 1978.[53] Other than the United States, only France, West Germany, the United Kingdom, and Sweden have exported complete nuclear stream supply systems (NSSS). Of

19 export orders for NSSS announced by these four countries from 1971 to 1977, Western Germany won 10 orders, France 6, Canada 2, and Sweden 1. These suppliers also have a thriving business in components and services.

France's sole supplier of NSSS is Framatome, a nuclear design and construction company, the main shares in which are held by Creusot-Loire, the state Commissariat a l'Energie Atomique, and Westinghouse. Framatome has invested in enough production capacity to build eight 900 MW NSSS (or six 1,300 MW NSSS) per year. The current domestic program fills about two-thirds of this capacity and, as domestic orders are expected to decline in the 1980s, the goal is to keep capacity filled with exports.[54]

The concentration of the French on nuclear exports aims both to increase the development of nonoil energy supplies and to push high technology exports. France and West Germany have offered industrial country purchasers not only nuclear power plants but also reprocessing facilities and enrichment services. A list of French reprocessing contracts as of September 1978 shows the majority of these to be with Japan (2,200 tons) followed by West Germany (1,705 tons), Sweden (620 tons), Switzerland (469 tons), Belgium (324 tons), Austria (222 tons), and Holland (120 tons).[55]

In sales to developing countries, financial competition is quite strong. All recent contracts for the construction of nuclear plants in developing countries have involved official export credit and insurance from the supplier country.

Table III.6 shows the world nuclear plant market from 1955 to 1977, with the United State and foreign competitors' share. Of the seven export orders obtained by France since 1955, only three went to developing countries (Spain and Iran). Of the twelve export orders won by West Germany, however, eight were to supply developing countries (Argentina, Iran, Brazil, Spain). West Germany has proved tougher competition than France for the United States, especially in South America where it is to build two reactors in Brazil. In addition, Germany was awarded a

212

TABLE III.6

WORLD NUCLEAR PLANT MARKET: U.S. & FOREIGN SHARE

	1955-70	1971-73	1974-75	1976-77
World nuclear export orders	32	25	19	8
U.S. supplied	24	20	9	4
Exim financed	15	18	8	4
Ratios:				
U.S./World	75%	80%	47%	50%
Exim/U.S.	63%	90%	89%	100%

Foreign Orders:
  (SUPPLIER country in caps, Client country lower case letters)

CANADA	GERMANY	GERMANY	FRANCE
India(2)	Austria	Iran(2)	South Africa(2)
France	Switzerland	Brazil(2)	
		Spain	GERMANY
GERMANY	CANADA	Luxembourg	Spain(2)
Argentina	India		
Netherlands	Korea	FRANCE	
		Iran(2)	
UNITED KINGDOM	SWEDEN	Belgium(2)	
Japan	Finland		
Italy			
FRANCE			
Spain			

Source: Financial Times, 3 October 1978.

213

contract in 1978 to conduct a feasibility study for Argentina's third reactor, a heavy water plant.

France, however, has stressed efforts of technical assistance and collaboration in the nuclear area. An agreement was signed with Indonesia in 1972 providing for the increase in technical assistance for the development of atomic energy for peaceful uses, accompanied by a grant of $300,000 as an aid to Indonesia for the purchase of nuclear equipment.[56] And India's Department of Atomic Energy signed an agreement with Stein-Industrie (of the C.G.E. Group) for technical collaboration concerning certain regenerating equipment and reactors.[57]

Industrial and Transport Equipment

This large sector has been one of the fastest growing in terms of the value of export orders, especially from the Third World. Between 1972 and 1976, exports to developing countries increased by 20 percent annually on average for four broad categories of civil and plant construction (as shown in detail in Table III.7), and were estimated to have created nearly 100,000 new jobs in France. Exports of mechanical and electrical industrial equipment and transport equipment accounted for more than one-fifth of all French exports to developing countries in 1976, and exports of industrial equipment showed the largest growth of all export categories over the 1970 to 1976 period. The three major geographical areas in which the export of French construction and engineering services has been concentrated are the OPEC countries, the other nonoil developing countries, and the eastern bloc countries.

A poll conducted by the Moniteur du Commerce International of French exporters in the industrial equipment, transport equipment, and civil engineering sectors showed that 260 French companies, either as sole or part suppliers (in association with other firms or as sub-contractors) had won 457 foreign orders between November 1976 and November 1977, each worth at least FF 10 million.[58] Although this survey is certainly not exhaustive, the total value of these contracts for the supply of equipment, works, and

TABLE III.7

CONSTRUCTION CONTRACTS WON BY FRENCH EXPORTERS IN
DEVELOPING COUNTRIES, NOV. 1976 - NOV. 1977

	AFRICA	NEAR & MID EAST	NORTH AFRICA	LATIN AMERICA	ASIA
Infrastructure.	21	9	10	7	9
Building construction .	11	22	--	--	--
Technical construction.	21	18	5	7	7
Waterworks.	7	5	4	--	1
Telecommunication; Radio-TV.	7	6	4	3	--
Mines, Nonferrous metals.	3	3	6	--	2
Petroleum extraction, refining, storage equipment	11	15	5	3	1
Light Industry[a]	8	3	1	--	3
Steelworks.	--	--	2	4	2
Construction & storage equipment	--	--	3	6	2
Cement works.	3	2	3	--	1
Chemical plants	1	3	2	1	3
Automobile construction.	4	1	--	--	1
Pulp & paper.	2	--	--	1	--
Technical assistance professional forma- tion, medical and pedagogical material.	--	4	6	1	--
TOTAL	99	91	51	33	32

[a]Includes textile plants, shoe factories, sugar refineries, glass factories, etc.

Source: Moniteur du Commerce International, No. 274, 26 December 1977.

215

services was about 47 billion francs (over $10 billion).

Table III.7 groups the contracts obtained in developing countries by geographical region and according to the branch of industry concerned. The contracts earned in the five developing areas represent two-thirds of those obtained overall.

The value of the 91 contracts earned in the Near and Middle East is far above that of the other areas and amounts to FF 21.6 billion ($4.6 billion). Iran and Saudi Arabia were the largest purchasers, notably in infrastructure construction (dams, highways, etc.), building construction (housing, commercial centers, hospitals, office buildings), in construction of electrical systems, and petroleum extraction and refining equipment.

In Africa, the value of contracts was FF 8.4 billion ($1.8 billion), in Asia FF 3.4 billion ($.72 billion), in North Africa FF 3 billion ($.64 billion), and in Latin America FF 1.8 billion ($.38 billion).[59] The majority of contracts in these four areas went to infrastructure and associated electrical construction.

A special report by the Middle East Economic Digest (MEED) on construction contracts awarded in the Near and Middle East between May 1978 and February 1979, each worth $10 million or more, showed that in the numbers of contracts awarded, French exporters were holding their own against West German, Italian, and U.S. competitors, but were certainly not in the forefront (see Table III.8).[60] All four were substantially behind British and Japanese firms in the number of contracts awarded, although if ranked by value (not available), the order might well be modified. (Data shown in Table III.11 suggest that, in general, the value of French plant exports is greater than that of any country other than the United States.) Total contracts reported numbered 360; however, for a large part of these no contractor was named.

Among the recent contracts awarded to French firms in the Middle East as cited in the MEED special report are those for construction of:

TABLE III.8

CONTRACTS AWARDED IN THE MIDDLE EAST
BETWEEN MAY 1978 AND FEBRUARY 1979

Supplying Country	Number of Contracts Awarded
United Kingdom	49
Japan	40
West Germany	27
United States	26
France	24
Italy	24

Source: Middle East Economic Digest, April 1979, pp. 39-49.

TABLE III.9

PUBLIC WORKS CARRIED OUT IN FOREIGN MARKETS
BY FRENCH FIRMS & SUBSIDIARIES

(Current prices, million FF, $1 = 4.48FF in 1975)

	1973	1974	1975	Percent Change 1976 over 1975
Roads & Airports	1500	2205	3266	+ 48
Maritime Works	739	631	1844	+ 19.2
Electric power lines	1017	849	1525	+ 79
Oil & gas pipelines	507	957	1206	+ 26

Source: Problemes Economiques, "Les Entreprises Francaises de travaux publics sur les Marches Exterieurs," 25 May 1977, p. 4.

217

- a power station for $60 million in Turkey (in a Belgian-Swiss-French consortium) along with two aluminum mills for $18 million,

- development of a gas field, construction of grain silos, fruit processing and pasta factories for $174 million in Algeria,

- a fertilizer plant and a medical institute in Jordon for $46 million,

- a 136 mile road in Libya for $140 million,

- telephone equipment in Syria for $12 million, and

- part of a university, a palace, high-rise commercial complex, civic center, office complex, and supermarket in Saudi Arabia for a combined value of $414 million.

Egypt, particularly, has been a frequent purchaser, and has just signed a $95 million economic and technical cooperation agreement with France that calls for installation of a French air traffic control system at Egyptian airports and French participation in improving Cairo's urban transport system. France will also build a sulphuric acid factory in Egypt, construct railway signalling equipment and supply turbines and relay stations for the Egyptian power network.[61]

Public Works

French strengths in plant and building construction have been complemented by the securing of many public works contracts. French public works firms have been very successful in exporting and, in real, inflation-adjusted terms, their foreign activity grew more than twice as fast as that in the domestic market over the period 1962 to 1975.[62] Table III.9 provides detailed data on the four categories of public works that together represented nearly two-thirds (65.3 percent) of all public works carried out abroad by French firms, and that demonstrated the strongest percentage increase in 1976. All four categories require the use of heavy equipment and machinery, both metal and electric, much of which is presumably obtained from France, and shows up as French goods exports. These categories include road and airport construction, port and maritime construction, electrical power installations, and oil and gas pipelines.

Consulting Engineering Services and Related Capital Equipment Exports

A relatively new element of the perennial concern in France for increasing the value and competiveness of exports has been the attention to the role played by the French consulting engineering industry. A dynamic consulting engineering sector whose services are increasingly in demand outside the national frontiers has become a major factor in the export of French capital equipment.[63] Export of industrial plants, for which consulting services have acted as the motor, accounted for an estimated 44 percent of total French exports of capital equipment in 1977. Furthermore, this figure has grown steadily in the 1970s rising from 8 percent in 1971. The compounded annual growth rates from 1971 to 1976 for exports of capital goods and industrial plant were 20.4 percent and 47.0 percent respectively (see Table III.10).

Although data directly bearing on the demand for engineering services are not available, data relating to major industrial complexes are indicative. Table III.11 shows that in 1975, although the United States was by far the largest exporter, France, accounting for over a quarter of European exports, was second.

The French consulting engineering industry is composed of some 900 firms, of which over 800 do not belong to a manufacturing group an equipment supplier. Sales of services alone (equipment excluded) by the 800 autonomous firms amounted to 8 billion francs in 1977 ($1.7 billion) of which nearly 40 percent or 3 billion ($.64 billion) francs were exports.

219

TABLE III.10

FRENCH EXPORTS IN THE CAPITAL GOODS SECTOR

Year	Exports of Capital Goods (billion francs) (col. 2)	Exports of Industrial Plant (billion francs) (col. 3)	Col. 3 as Percent of Col. 2 (col. 4)	Data Presented by the M.O.I.C. Comparable to those in Col. 4 (col. 5)
1971	28.887	2.369	8.2%	8%
1972	32.263	2.659	8.2%	--
1973	38.327	4.604	12.0%	11%
1974	51.999	10.269	19.7%	--
1975	62.135	15.716	25.3%	--
1976	73.055	16.241	22.2%	--
1977	--	--	--	44%

Source: For colume 5: Moniteur de Commerce International,
(M.O.I.C.), Dec. 1978.
For columns 2 to 4: Les Usines Clefs en Main:
Realité et Perspective pour la France, Etudes de
Politique Industrielle No. 18, Ministère de
l'Industrie du Commerce et de l'Artisanat, 1978.

TABLE III.11

ORDERS FOR EXPORT OF MAJOR INDUSTRIAL COMPLEXES
BY EXPORTING COUNTRY, 1975

($ million, current)

Western Europe	34.2	
United Kingdom		8.5
France		9.2
Italy		6.5
Germany		6.0
Other		4.0
Japan	5.2	
United States	23.6	
Other	3.0	
TOTAL	66.0	

Source: EuroFinance, 1978.

IV. CONCLUSION

One of the factors with which U.S. exporters have had to contend since 1974 has been sharp competition from French suppliers. The success of the French in displacing U.S. exports in markets in the Third World in certain OPEC countries (Saudi Arabia, Iraq, Nigeria) and in several of the advanced developing nonoil LDCs, (Brazil, Mexico, Argentina, and certain of the more advanced developed countries in Central Asia and the Far East) has taken place despite a somewhat higher domestic rate of inflation in France and the appreciation of the French franc against the dollar on foreign markets.

With these two strikes against French exporters and a traditionally more narrow geographical orbit for their exports -- most having been absorbed by their EC partners and associated countries in Western Europe -- what has accounted for the substantial French success in its reoriented export drive? Part of the answer is aggressiveness on the part of French suppliers, who appear to have realized better than their U.S. counterparts that in today's world of expensive energy supplies, selling to those countries with increased purchasing power is the only way to afford necessary imports of petroleum. In addition, however, this individual effort has been supported by an impressive range of French governmental policy tools for export promotion. The use of financial incentives -- both tax and nontax measures -- has been backed by an active political campaign tying French military and technical assistance as well as aid disbursements and support for foreign policy positions to the purchase of French exports.

The importance of these nonmonetary factors cannot be stressed too strongly, and it suggests that excessive concentration by U.S. analysts on price competitiveness and the availability of other official facilities alone in the two countries misses the main point. Indeed, the role of indicative planning and the cooperative relationship between business and government that certainly exists in France, and to a lesser degree in other Western European competitor countries, points to an identification of strategic, commercial, and political interests as integrated parts.   As such, the mere matching of export credits and insurance guarantees by the United States is a feeble and inadequate response to an aggressive world wide drive for export markets.

APPENDIX I

FRENCH EXPORTS TO LDC MARKETS:
GROWTH, DESTINATIONS, AND PRODUCTS

The Geographic Pattern of French Exports to LDCs

French trade with the Third World on the whole follows the traditional pattern of trade between regions of differing levels of economic development. The Third World supplies energy, industial raw materials, foodstuffs, and more recently, certain light consumer products, against which they receive consumer goods and various forms of capital equipment, transport equipment and machinery, for which the Third World represents an important outlet.

The pattern of French exports, however, has altered in response to the commercial strategy mapped out in 1974 by the French government. Geographically, the distribution of French exports has shifted from traditional, developed country markets to an increasing concentration on Third World customers.

Table A.1 shows that French exports to developed countries increased by 99 percent in dollar value terms between 1973 and 1978, while French exports to developing countries grew by 171 percent over the same period. Exports to oil-exporting countries grew 259 percent, followed by Asia at 168 percent, the nonoil Middle East at 149 percent, and Africa at 140 percent. Table A.2 shows in more detail the progression of French export growth to major developing countries. The most spectacular increases were registered with a number of oil exporting countries, followed by several nonoil Middle-Eastern and African countries.

French export performance to OPEC in fact varied widely by country, as can be seen from Table A.2. Although France's exports to OPEC as a whole increased less rapidly than did those of the United States, Japan, and Germany, French exports to Iraq, Nigeria, and Saudi Arabia in fact grew much faster than U.S. exports to these countries after 1973. (See Table A.3 for U.S. comparisons.) In Iraq and Algeria, total French exports also absolutely exceeded those of the

TABLE A.1

CHANGES IN THE GEOGRAPHICAL DESTINATION
OF FRENCH EXPORTS
INCREASE FROM 1973 to 1978 PERCENT

(in value terms)

Exports to:	Percent Increase '73-'78	Changes Against Average Increase
TOTAL EXPORTS	+116	
DEVELOPED COUNTRIES	+ 99	--
Industrial Countries	+ 99	-
Other Europe	+ 93	-
Australia, New Zealand, South Africa	+149	+
SOCIALIST COUNTRIES	+113	
DEVELOPING COUNTRIES	+171	+++
Oil Exporting	+259	++++
Nonoil LDCs	+139	+
Latin America	+100	-
Nonoil Middle East	+149	+
Asia	+168	++
Africa	+140	+

Note: The positive and negative signs indicate the direction
and magnitude of change in French export performance to
the various geographical areas as measured against the
average increases of 116 percent over the period in
question. Their assignment is made by the authors'
judgment.

Source: IMF, Direction of Trade, Annual 1971-1977 and May 1979.

TABLE A.2

CHANGES IN THE GEOGRAPHICAL ORIENTATION
OF FRANCE's EXPORTS TO LDCs

Importing Region or Country	Percent Increase 1973-1978	Weight in each Category, 1978
OIL EXPORTING COUNTRIES	259%	100%
of which: Algeria	104	25
Iran	330	14
Nigeria	676	13
Saudi Arabia	1466	14
United Arab Emirates	133	4
Venezuela	122	5
Kuwait	354	3
Iraq	510	8
LATIN AMERICA	110	100%
of which: Brazil	91	22
Argentina	124	9
Mexico	171	14
NONOIL MIDDLE EAST	149	100%
of which: Egypt	226	37
Israel	72	19
Syria	337	18
AFRICA	141	100%
of which: Cameroon	179	7
Gabon	149	5
Ivory Coast	174	15
Morocco	156	17
Tunisia	200	13

Source: Calculated from IMF, Direction of Trade, Annual 1971-1978.

United States in 1977 by considerable amounts. In Algeria, however, U.S. export growth was slightly faster, helped by major U.S. plant construction projects (such as Bechtel's gas liquification plant in Arzew), and by growing political tensions since 1975 between France and Algeria over France's lack of support for the Algerian position in the Polisario Front's war with Morocco over the former Spanish Sahara.

French exports to non-OPEC LDCs in Latin America and the Caribbean have been growing more rapidly than those of the United States in a number of important markets such as Mexico, Brazil, and Argentina (see Table A.2 and A.3). The growth, however, has come on top of a very small base, and total French exports to most of these markets -- except to the French Caribbean isles -- are still very small compared to the absolute level of U.S. exports. The situation is similar with respect to the LDCs of Asia and the Far East: low absolute levels of French exports, but a considerable higher rate of growth in French, as compared to U.S. exports.

Nonoil, less developed Africa presents a mixed picture of French strength, relative to the U.S. position (see Tables A.2 and A.3). In general, French exports grew faster than did those of the United States: 141 percent compared to 106 percent for the United States. Contrary to the diversification away from France which might have been expected for political reasons in the post colonial era (and which in part is occurring in Algeria and to a much lesser extent Morocco), French-speaking African countries such as the Ivory Coast and Tunisia have become, if anything, better customers of France than in the past. In 1977, 40 percent of all French exports to LDCs still went to former colonies or protectorates.[64]

The notion that France has been particularly competitive in Africa is further borne out by an analysis presented in Table A.4 of the degree to which major OECD countries would have exported manufactured goods had their share of exports to various regions remained constant during several recent time periods. The table shows that Africa was one of two areas of the world in which France increased her market share of manufactured exports in value terms relative to that of

227

TABLE A.3

CHANGES IN THE GEOGRAPHICAL ORIENTATION
OF UNITED STATES' EXPORTS TO LDCs

Importing Region or Country	Percent Increase 1973-1978	Weight in each Category, 1978
OIL EXPORTING COUNTRIES	365%	100%
of which: Algeria	132	2
Iran	377	23
Nigeria	511	6
Saudi Arabia	889	27
United Arab Emirates	307	3
Venezuela	261	23
Kuwait	521	5
Iraq	466	2
LATIN & SOUTH AMERICA	106	100%
of which: Brazil	55	16
Argentina	87	5
Mexico	127	37
NONOIL MIDDLE EAST	151	100%
of which: Egypt	404	30
Israel	100	50
Syria	581	4
AFRICA	106	100%
of which: Cameroon	247	3
Gabon	410	5
Ivory Coast	36	5
Morocco	259	23
Tunisia	38	5

Source: Calculated from IMF, Direction of Trade, Annual
1971-1977 and May, 1979.

TABLE A.4

DEVIATIONS FROM CONSTANT-SHARE NORMS FOR MANUFACTURING
EXPORTS TO LDCs BY TRADING PARTNERS:
1970-73, 1973-76 and 1970-76

($ millions)

	Period	United States	Germany	Japan	United Kingdom	France
Developing	1970-73	- 462	129*	- 9	- 293	209*+
Europe	1973-76	169	24	333	- 125	- 122
	1970-76	- 498	212*	318	- 547	179*
Eastern	1970-73	36	1154	- 40	- 386	- 55
Europe	1973-76	310	-1236	1202	- 411	111
	1970-76	379	846	1144	-1102	3
Africa	1970-73	- 237	122*	428	- 422	5*
	1973-76	171	- 41	- 176	230	407*+
	1970-76	- 268	183*	636	- 555	403*
Caribbean	1970-73	- 43	76*	450	- 173	- 109
	1973-76	19	- 260	229	- 108	23*
	1970-76	- 65	- 127	1055	- 416	- 182
South	1970-73	- 559	126*	479	- 119	139*
America	1973-76	704	- 496	18	- 113	- 137
	1970-76	- 239	- 274	796	- 317	120*
Middle	1970-73	- 117	92*	391	- 248	- 392
East	1973-76	1058	255	1977	-1319	-1468
	1970-76	677	587	3267	-2171	-2624
Central Asia	1970-73	- 287	54*	931	- 298	70*
and	1973-76	164	- 203	- 10	- 648	439*+
Far East	1970-76	- 234	- 142*	1418	-1122	548*
Other	1970-73	128	- 5	- 210	175	21
	1973-76	-1580	789	- 100	-1904	- 387
	1970-76	-1355	788	- 805	- 866	- 181

Note: The table compares the export performance of manufactured
goods of various industrial countries. It shows, in millions
of dollars, the deviations from constant share norms. The
dollar figure represents the extent to which exports in a
category exceed (+) or fell short of (-) the amount needed
to maintain a constant market share over the period. A
positive figure indicates that market share was increasing.

Source: Export Policy Hearing before the Subcommittee on International Finance of the Committee on Banking, Housing and
Urban Affairs, U.S. Senate, 95th Congress Second Session,
23 February 1978, pp. 94-95.

229

the United States, Japan, and Germany in the 1973-1976 period. The other was Central Asia and the Far East excluding Japan, but those increases occurred from a very small base. (Prudence, of course should be exercised in the interpretation of all figures on changes in market share or growth of French exports expressed in dollar terms because of the disparities that the effect of exchange rate changes may introduce.)

French Exports by Industrial and Product Categories

Roughly one third of French exports consists of consumer goods, one third of semifinished products and intermediates, and one third of capital goods and materials. According to one French analysis, capital goods and material exports increased by 136 percent over the 1972-1976 period, while sales of the other two groups increased by less than the average of all export sales (by 106 percent for semifinished, intermediary goods and by 85 percent for consumer goods).[65]

The product categories in which exports increased by more than the 111 percent average increase in total exports between 1972 and 1976 are listed below, where the percentages in parenthesis indicate the importance of each sector in the total of manufactured exports in 1976. Most of these sectors are capital and technology-intensive:

- metal works, not including armaments + 154 percent (3.6 percent),

- chemical products +150 percent (9.1 percent),

- electrical power generation equipment +150 percent (9 percent),

- machines +125 percent (17.4 percent),

- paperboard +117 percent (1.6 percent), and

- manufactured rubber +115 percent (2.2 percent).

Particularly competitive sectors therefore appear to be: metal works, electrical apparatus/ equipment, and machines. Armaments, especially fighter aircraft, helicopters, and missiles, would appear among the top categories, indeed perhaps first of all, if the figures were included in the standard OECD trade data, but they are not.

Trade with the Third World is vital for certain French industries. Table A.5 shows the importance of French exports to LDCs as a percentage of French output in 1970 and in 1976. By 1976, LDC markets took nearly 15 percent of all French arms, aircraft, and ship-building output, as well as a similar proportion (12 percent) of electrical and nonelectrical machinery.

Table A.5 shows that France has become a net importer of labor-intensive goods such as textiles, clothing, wood, furniture, leather, and footwear. French net exports as a percentage of production have been declining in the food industry. Those industries that are increasingly oriented to LDCs are primarily technology and capital-intensive, and concentrated in four categories: mechanical and electrical equipment, armaments, aeronautic and naval construction; metals (iron and steel products and nonferrous metals); and construction material.

In certain product areas, French exports and production are oriented to LDC markets to a degree considerably above general industry levels. Table A.6 shows, for example, that more than half of all French exports go to LDCs in products such as high tension electrical material, railway material, utility vehicles, metal construction, electronic equipment, and steel tubes. In three out of six of these product groups, LDC markets take more than one-quarter of total French output.

Table A.7 shows a breakdown of French exports in 1977 to developing countries by broad commodity group. The majority of French exports to LDCs (70 percent) are made up of two categories: manufactured goods and machinery and transport equipment. (Manufactured goods include various leather, rubber, wood, cork, paper and paperboard products, textile yarn and fabrics, and ferrous and nonferrous metal manufacturing. For a detailed breakdown see Table A.8. Machinery and

TABLE A.5

FRENCH EXPORTS* TO LDCs AS A
PERCENT OF TOTAL FRENCH PRODUCTION
1970 and 1976

	1970	Rank	1976	Rank	Trend
Armaments, aeronautic and naval construction	7.7%	1	14.8%	1	++
Mechanical & electrical machinery	4.9%	3	12.2%	2	+++
Transport material	6.7%	2	9.3%	3	+
Glassware	4.6%	4	6.1%	4	+
Chemicals	3.5%	5	5.1%	5	+
Iron & steel works, nonferrous metals	1.5%	8	3.2%	6	++
Construction material	-0.2%	12	1.6%	7	++
Printed material	1.5%	9	1.6%	8	=
Paper board	0.9%	11	0.9%	9	=
Argo-food industry	1.3%	10	0.8%	10	-
Textiles/clothing	2.8%	6	-1.1%	11	---
Wood & furniture	2.7%	7	-1.8%	12	--
Leather, footwear	-1.1%	13	-3.0%	13	---

*Net of any imports from LDCs

Note: The positive and negative signs indicate whether French exports to developing countries as a percentage of total French production have increased or decreased over the period in question. Any positive growth less than 100 percent receives a + indication; above 100 percent ++ or +++. No or little change is shown by =; negative growth by -; over 100 percent decline by -- or more.

Source: Commissariat General du Plan, "Rapport du Groups Chargé d'Etudier l'Evolution des Economies du Tiers-Monde et l'Appareil Productif Francais," January 1978, Paris, p. 18.

TABLE A.6

PRODUCTS FOR WHICH FRENCH EXPORTS
TO DEVELOPING COUNTRIES ARE OF PARTICULAR
IMPORTANCE (1976)

Product Areas	Share of Exports going to Developing Countries out of Total Exports	Share of Exports going to Developing Countries out of Domestic Production
Steel tubes	50%	26%
Metallic construction	55%	32%
High-tension electrical material	65%	28%
Electronic equipment	55%	8%
Utility vehicles	60%	18%
Railway equipment	65%	30%

Source: Commissariat General du Plan, "Rapport du Groupe Chargé, d'Etudier l'Evolution des Economies du Tiers-Monde et l'Appareil Productif Francais," January 1978, Paris, p. 19.

TABLE A.7

FRENCH EXPORTS BY COMMODITY GROUP
TO DEVELOPING COUNTRIES* IN 1977

(U.S. $ millions)

	Exports to Third World	Percent Share in Total	Trade Balance
Food & Live Animals	1,382	9%	- 1,816
Beverages & Tobacco	281	2%	184
Raw Materials (except fuel)	161	1%	- 1,550
Minerals, Fuels, Lubricants	183	1%	-11,399
Animal & Vegetable Oils & Fats	103	0%	- 174
Chemicals	1,507	9%	1,338
Manufactured Goods	3,085	19%	2,071
Machinery & Transport Equipment	8,114	51%	7,812
Miscellaneous Manufactured Articles	1,191	7%	579
Commodities & Transactions not classified according to kind, including Firearms of war	3	0%	- 1
TOTAL	16,011	100%	- 2,957

*includes OPEC

Source: OECD Statistics of Foreign Trade, Series B - 1977.

234

transport equipment alone comprise 51 percent of the total. This category includes power-generating machinery, metalworking machinery, machines for special industries, electric power machinery and switchgear, telecommunication equipment, passenger motor cars, ships, aircraft, and trucks. France's positive trade balance with the developing countries in machinery and transport equipment is especially large ($7.8 billion in 1977) and the surplus in manufactured goods is also substantial at $2.1 billion.

The third major export category is that of chemicals, where exports of medical and pharmaceutical products, chemical elements and compounds, plastic materials, and essential oil and perfume material are important items. France's positive trade balance with the LDCs in chemicals was $1.3 billion in 1977.

Table A.8 shows the growth of French exports of manufactures by product group (at the two-digit SITC level of classification) between 1974 and 1977. The most spectacular increases were recorded in machinery and transport equipment where exports to LDCs of electrical machinery and apparatus increased by 147 percent during this period, nonelectrical machinery by 137 percent, and transport equipment by 129 percent. The categories under the chemical sector showed smaller increases; that of manufactured fertilizer actually declined by 58 percent over this period.

Table A.9 shows the pattern of exports to LDCs in Africa, Latin America, and Asia (as well as for OPEC) by detailed product group for 1977. The proportion of French exports going to OPEC countries was particularly large for wood and cork manufactured items (60 percent to OPEC customers), for nonelectrical machinery (44 percent), for electrical machinery and apparatus (42 percent), and transport equipment (40 percent). Also 40 percent of explosives and pyrotechnic products exports were purchased by OPEC countries. A large part of these sales most likely accompanied armament sales; however, the available statistical sources do not provide an item breakdown.

Table A.10 shows the detailed product categories of French exports ranked by their weight in total exports to LDCs. French exports are (absolutely) strong in the following fields:

FRENCH EXPORTS OF MANUFACTURES TO LDCs
(INCLUDING OPEC), BY PRODUCT GROUP

($ millions)

		1974	1977	Percent Change 74-77	Trend
CHEMICAL		1075.0	1507.0	40%	+
51	Chemical elements & compounds	181.7	226.8	25%	
52	Mineral tar & crude chemical	.7	.7	-	
53	Dying, tanning & colouring	63.8	81.9	28%	
54	Medical & pharmaceutical products	246.8	391.8	59%	++
55	Essential oil & perfume material	133.1	230.4	73%	++
56	Fertilizer, manufactured	102.1	42.5	-58%	--
57	Explosive & Pyrotechnic products	14.9	25.0	68%	++
58	Plastic materials, regenerated	165.1	230.1	39%	+
59	N.E.S.*	124.8	215.9	73%	++
MANUFACTURED GOODS		1957.0	3085.0	58%	++
61	Leather & dressed fur skins	15.8	32.5	106%	+++
62	Rubber manufactured	135.6	191.3	41%	+
63	Wood & cork manufactured	24.2	62.3	157%	+++
64	Paper, paperboard manufactured	135.5	180.7	33%	+
65	Textile yarn, fabrics	287.5	359.3	25%	
66	Nonmetallic mineral manufactured	180.2	321.6	78%	++
67	Iron & steel	687.7	891.2	30%	+
68	Nonferrous metals	119.5	166.7	39%	+
69	N.E.S.	371.5	879.6	137%	+++
MACHINERY & TRANSPORT EQUIPMENT		3440.0	8114.0	136%	+++
71	Machinery (nonelectric)	1316.1	3118.2	137%	+++
72	Electrical machinery, apparatus	724.3	1788.8	147%	+++
73	Transport equipment	1399.7	3206.6	129%	+++
MISCELLANEOUS MANUFACTURED ARTICLES		638.0	1191.0	87%	++
81	Sanitary, plumbing, heating	39.3	87.9	124%	+++
82	Furniture	41.1	100.2	144%	+++
83	Travel goods, handbags	8.0	17.2	115%	+++
84	Clothing	128.3	218.1	70%	++
85	Footwear	36.0	66.2	84%	++
86	Professional, science & control instruments, photo	147.4	289.2	96%	++
89	N.E.S.	237.5	412.5	74%	++
OTHER (Firearms of War)		7.0	3.0	-57%	--

*Not elsewhere specified

Note: The categories underlined are those that have registered the most rapid change in exports (50 percent or more growth) over the period in question.

Source: OECD Statistics of Foreign Trade, Series B - 1974 and 1977.

GEOGRAPHICAL PATTERN OF FRENCH EXPORTS TO LDCs
BY PRODUCT GROUP AND REGION, 1977

(Percent to Third World [total=100 percent])

	AFRICA	AMERICA	ASIA	OTHER[a]	(OF WHICH OPEC)
CHEMICAL					
51 Chemical Elements & compounds	34%	28%	29%	9%	19%
52 Mineral tar & crude chemical	71	--	29	--	29
53 Dying, tanning & colouring	42	26	24	8	27
54 Medical & pharmaceutical products	74	9	14	2	35
55 Essential oil & perfume material	30	24	36	10	27
56 Fertilizer, manufactured	53	24	20	3	21
57 Explosive & Pyrotechnic products	55	5	37	3	40
58 Plastic materials, regenerated	43	19	31	6	23
59 N.E.S.*	58	17	18	6	20
MANUFACTURED GOODS					
61 Leather & dressed skins	55	6	30	8	25
62 Rubber manufactured	68	8	19	4	37
63 Wood & cork manufactured	46	6	40	8	60
64 Paper, paperboard manufactured	59	17	20	5	29
65 Textile yarn, fabrics	62	7	24	7	30
66 Nonmetallic mineral manufactured	48	15	31	5	41
67 Iron & steel	50	19	24	8	32
68 Nonferrous metals	43	18	34	4	20
69 N.E.S.	59	9	29	3	51
MACHINERY & TRANSPORT EQUIPMENT					
71 Machinery (nonelectric)	50	12	33	6	44
72 Electrical machinery, apparatus	49	14	33	4	42
73 Transport equipment	65	13	18	4	40
MISCELLANEOUS MANUFACTURED ARTICLES					
81 Sanitary, plumbing, heating	64	5	28	3	46
82 Furniture	44	17	33	6	43
83 Travel goods, handbags	28	20	38	13	16
84 Clothing	29	18	42	12	31
85 Footwear	53	19	9	8	34
86 Professional, science & control instruments, photo	43	14	33	10	30
89 N.E.S.	52	16	22	10	27

[a]OTHER includes developing countries in Europe and Oceania.

*Not elsewhere specified

Source: OECD Statistics of Foreign Trade, Series B - 1977.

TABLE A.10

IMPORTANT SECTORS FOR FRENCH EXPORTS TO LDCs
SHOWING SUBSTANTIAL GROWTH BETWEEN 1974 AND 1977

	Weight in French Exports to LDCs in 1977	Growth Between 1974 & 1977
Nonelectrical machinery; appliances	10.8	63%
Heating & cooling equipment	2.3	73%
Pumps & centrifuges	2.5	66%
Materials handling equipment	2.1	61%
Passenger motor cars	5.2	42%
Ships & boats	4.3	83%
Electric power machinery & switchgear	4.1	64%
Special industrial machinery (Printing, bookbinding, construction, etc.)	3.4	55%
Power generating machinery (other than electric)	3.0	55%
Telecommunications apparatus	3.0	60%
Lorries & trucks	2.7	46%
Aircraft	2.6	66%
Medical & pharmaceutical products	2.4	37%
Electrical measuring & controlling instruments (valves & tubes, photo-cells, transistors, etc.)	2.2	49%
Bodies, chassis, frames & parts of vehicles	2.1	50%
Essential oil & perfume material	1.4	42%
Plastics	1.4	28%
Scientific, medical instruments	1.2	48%

Source: OECD Trade Statistics, Series B.

- nonelectrical machinery and appliances,

- passenger motor cars,

- ships and boats, and

- electrical power machinery and switchgear.

Although German exports to LDCs are strongest in special industrial machinery such as construction, printing, and bookbinding machinery, French exports are more competitive in nonelectrical machinery and appliances. This category consists of heating and cooling equipment, pumps and centrifuges, materials handling equipment, and miscellaneous items. It represented more than one-tenth of French exports to LDCs in 1977, by far the most important category. Both French and German exporters are strong in sales of elecric power machinery and switchgear. Such exports constribute to the expansion of public infrastructure in LDCs. French export growth to LDCs has been fastest in:

- ships and boats,

- heating and cooling equipment,

- pumps and centrifuges,

- aircraft,

- electric power machinery and switchgear,

- nonelectrical machinery and appliances,

- materials handling equipment, and

- telecommunication apparatus.

Table A.11 shows a more explicit breakdown of some machinery and transport equipment exported by France to the LDCs in the product categories having the fastest growth over the 1974-1977 period.

TABLE A.11

SOME MACHINERY AND TRANSPORT EQUIPMENT
EXPORTED FROM FRANCE TO LDCs

($ million)

	1974	1977
Ships & Boats	115.3	690.4
Heating & Cooling Equipment	96.0	361.3
Pumps & Centrifuges	137.2	404.9
Aircraft	142.6	415.5
Electrical Power Machinery & Switchgear	240.3	661.5
Equipment for Distributing Electricity	66.1	182.5
Materials Handling Equipment	133.1	342.4
Telecommunications Apparatus	193.6	481.6

Source: OECD Trade Statistics, Series 13.

APPENDIX II

REVEALED COMPARATIVE ADVANTAGE AS A
MEASURE OF FRENCH EXPORT COMPETITIVENESS

French export performance as discussed in Appendix I can be evaluated in several ways. All appropriate measures are necessarily dynamic since they must be related to indicators of change in export performance over a given time period. Export price competitiveness, used as the basis for the statistical table and discussion in Appendix I, is only one measure of export performance, and can provide only one possible explanation of why France's share of world exports going to the Third World in any particular sectors or products has increased or decreased.

The competitiveness of French exports to developing countries may also be evaluated through examining its "revealed comparative advantage" in various product categories.[66] Examining the observed pattern of trade according to this criterion allows all influences determining comparative advantage -- differences in relative costs as well as differences in nonprice factors --to be taken into account without testing them directly.

Trade data used to derive the index of export competitiveness for the two years 1973 and 1976 were the value figures for French exports and for OECD exports to developing countries, on a three-digit SITC basis. An index of French export competitiveness was obtained by dividing France's share of exports of a given commodity by its share in combined OECD exports of all goods, and expressing this as an index number. For example, for a given export item, an index number of 150 will mean that France's share in this commodity's exports to developing countries is 50 percent higher than its share in total OECD exports to LDCs.

French export performance can be evaluated either by: (1) comparing the relative share of French exports in total OECD exports for the various product categories in a recent year, or (2) indicating the change in the relative share of French exports in total OECD exports over time. Each method has its advantages and disadvantages: Taking relative export performance in

241

any one particular year neglects the trend factor, although taking French export growth rates relative to OECD total growth rates can be misleading -- since high growth rates are compatible with small exports in absolute terms. Because of these limitations, both indications of French export performance have been used to illustrate the pattern of revealed comparative advantage in France's trade with developing countries. Table A.12 shows the ordering of product groups in which French export performance with the developing country market is generally high (average index 1973-1966 of 150 or over). Table A.13 shows the ordering of product categories in which a positive rate of growth of 20 percent or more in export competitiveness occurred over the 1973-1976 period.

Three remarks must be made concerning the presentation of these indices of export competitiveness. First, SITC Sections 0 and 1, agricultural products and beverages, are likely to portray a distorted image of export performance, as most of these products are highly subsidized under the European Community's Common Agricultural Policy. Secondly, statistics on sales of armaments are not included in standard international trade data, so one of the key sectors of French exports sales to the Third World is missing. Also, the complications introduced by the fluctuations in exchange rates when calculating these indices are of importance.

On the basis of the product categories ranked by index numbers of export competitiveness (from high to low, including all categories in which the average index, 1973/1976, was above 150) in Table A.12, French exports are strong in the following areas (when agricultural products are excluded): metal products, railway vehicles and equipment; light manufactures (clothing, footwear, handbags), glassware, rubber, and plastic materials; and in two interesting miscellaneous categories --explosive and pyrotechnic products (most likely to accompany armament sales) and equipment for distributing electricity. Thus the pattern of revealed comparative advantage in sales to the Third World follows the general pattern of success of French export sales to the world as a whole taken in terms of percentage growth in nominal value outlined above, with the exception of the inclusion here of some labor-intensive, light manufactured consumer products. The

TABLE A.12

PRODUCT GROUPS IN WHICH FRENCH EXPORT
COMPETITIVENESS IS HIGH IN OECD EXPORTS
TO DEVELOPING COUNTRIES

SITC NO.	Product Description	Average index of export competitiveness 1973-76 (column a)	Value of exports (76) $ millions (column b)
061	Sugar & honey	507.1	237.2
553	Perfumery & cosmetics	457.3	41.4
212	Fur skins, undressed	419.6	8.1
112	Alcoholic beverages (e.g. wine)	370.6	181.3
665	Glassware	340.7	83.4
851	Footwear	291.8	51.0
024	Cheese & curd	289.4	42.6
676	Rails & railway track construction material	285.5	92.2
84	Fur clothing	271.9	152.7
046	Metal & flour of wheat	250.8	159.4
111	Nonalcoholic beverages	243.7	14.0
013	Meat in airtight containers	239.4	31.0
551	Essential oils, perfumes	222.6	36.7
043	Barley, unmilled	218.4	33.1
731	Railway vehicles	217.0	202.7
023	Butter	214.8	97.4
892	Printed matter	211.1	104.6
697	Household equipment of base metals	210.1	44.0
692	Metal containers	209.8	73.3
571	Explosives; pyrotechnic products	199.7	14.7
541	Medicinal & pharmaceutical products	198.1	339.3
841	Clothing	195.8	151.0
642	Articles made of paper, pulp or paperboard	194.6	82.2
895	Office & stationery supplies, m.e.s.	192.2	29.4
692	Articles of rubber	189.0	143.5
821	Furniture	187.7	81.3
048	Cereal preparations	180.4	84.2
831	Travel goods, handbags	175.9	12.0
621	Materials of rubber	174.4	29.1
812	Sanitary, plumbing, heating & lighting fixtures	169.5	57.6
863	Developed cinematographic film	168.1	5.4
422	Other fixed vegetable oils	166.8	6.0
532	Dyeing & tannings extracts	163.5	3.9
893	Artificial plastic articles	162.3	61.3
656	Textile made-up articles	161.8	28.6
694	Nails, screws, nuts, bolts, rivets of iron, steel or copper	160.5	30.1
632	Wood manufactures, n.e.s.	159.2	13.7
896	Works of art & antiques	154.6	7.2

243

SITC NO.	Product Description	Average index of export competitiveness 1973-76 (column a)	Value of exports (76) $ millions (column b)
264	Jute	154.1	.1
723	Equipment for distributing electricity	152.1	149.6
062	Sugar confectionary & preparations	150.8	8.9

Notes: The formula used to calculate export competitiveness for any product category is the following:

$$\frac{x_{F_i}}{x_{OECD_i}} \quad \frac{x_{F_t}}{x_{OECD_t}} \quad = \quad \frac{X_i}{X} \quad = \quad \text{index number}$$

where:

    x = exports
    X = relative share of exports
    t = total
    i = product i
    France, OECD

The formula is taken from B. Balassa, "Trade Liberalization and 'Revealed' Comparative Advantage," The Manchester School of Economic and Social Studies, vol. 33, no. 2, May 1965.

Source: The indices of export competitiveness were calculated on the basis of French exports to developing countries, value in millions of dollars, f.o.b., for the years 1973 and 1976. Data were taken from the OECD, Statistics on Foreign Trade, Series B.

value of French exports in 1976 ($ million) for each of these product categories is also shown to give some indication of the relative importance of each in total exports to developing countries.

Table A.13 presents a somewhat different picture. Those categories in which a strong increase in export competitiveness occurred between 1973 and 1976 were strongly capital-intensive manufactures, notably: metals (iron and steel products as well as nonferrous metals, both semifinished and finished), transport equipment (ships and boats), railway equipment, agricultural machinery, and electrical apparatus. These categories of increasing relative competitiveness correspond by and large to the general pattern of capital intensive exports mentioned above. The most important categories in value of exports were those of ships and boats, metals, rails and railway track construction, agricultural machinery, and pipes.

TABLE A.13

RANKING OF PRODUCT GROUPS WITH SUBSTANTIAL
GROWTH IN FRENCH EXPORT COMPETITIVENESS IN LDCs MARKETS
1973-1976

SITC No.	Product Description	Percentage growth over period (+) (column a)	Value of Exports (76) $ millions (column b)
679	Iron & steel castings	190	10.2
735	Ships & boats	165	722.6
521	Mineral tar & crude chemicals from coal, petroleum & natural gas	152	.8
052	Dried fruit	150	1.0
681	Silver, platinum	141	7.2
411	Animal oils & fats	120	7.8
011	Meat, fresh, chilled or frozen	114	98.3
613	Fur skins tanned or dressed	113	2.4
283	Ores & concentrates of nonferrous base metals	88	.7
691	Metals: finished structural parts	63	306.1
266	Synthetic fibres	62	21.8
284	Nonferrous metal scrap	60	.4
275	Natural abrasives	58	.7
273	Stone, sand & gravel	56	3.9
023	Butter	47	53.2
633	Cork manufactures	47	.5
676	Rails & railway track construction	45	92.2
712	Agricultural machinery	30	91.3
726	Electrical apparatus for medical purposes and radiological apparatus	25	35.0
212	Fur skins undressed	24	8.1
678	Tubes, pipes & fittings of iron & steel	23	313.3
262	Wool & other animal hair	19	15.2

Source: Same as for Table A.12.

FOOTNOTES

[1] IMF, _Direction of Trade_, January 1980. In October 1979, France even surpassed Japan, moving (perhaps temporarily) into third place.

[2] _Le Nouvel Economiste_, 1 December 1976, p. 73.

[3] OECD Industry Committee, _Report to the Council on Positive Adjustment Policies in the Industry Sector, Annex 1_. Inventory of Measures Taken by Member Governments since 1974, OECD, 25 April 1979, IND (79) 3 Annex 1.

[4] The French franc trading zone is composed of countries or territories that were France's former colonies in northern and black Africa, in the French West Indies and in northern South America (French Guyana). These countries settle their commercial transactions with countries outside the zone through the intermediary of the exchange market in Paris or the exchange rate stabilization fund. France reports its foreign trade statistics in the _Annuaire Statistique de la France_ along a division of transactions with zone countries and transactions with all others.

[5] _Le Nouvel Economiste_, 1 December 1976.

[6] U.S. Congress, House of Representatives, International Relations Committee, _Export Stimulation Programs in the Major Industrial Countries: The United States and Eight Major Competitors_. Prepared by Congressional Research Service, October 1978.

[7] See Franko, Lawrence G., "Industrial Policies in Western Europe: Solution or Problem", _The World Economy_, January 1979, especially pp. 33-35. And _Industrial Policy in Western Europe, Past, Present and Future_, The Conference Board in Europe, Brussels, 1979.

[8] U.S. Congress, Senate, Report by the Subcommittee on International Finance to the Committee on Banking, Housing, and Urban Affairs, _U.S. Export Policy_, Washington, D. C., February 1979.

[9] Interviews. See also Christian Stoffeas, _La Grande Menace Industrielle_, Calmann-Levy, 1977.

[10] Commission des Relations Economiques et Financières avec l'Exterieur; _Preparation de l'Orientation Preliminaire du 7'ème Plan_, Paris, March 1975, p. 40.

[11] _Le Monde_, 4 October 1978.

[12] _Africa Confidential_, 31 January 1979.

[13] _Le Monde_, 11 April 1979.

[14] Export insurance may act as a substitute for export financing since such insurance allows an exporter to refinance any credit he wishes to extend to a foreign buyer with the banking system at prime or near prime interest rates.

[15] _Investment, Licensing and Trading in France_, Business International Corporation, June 1978, p. 31.

[16] U.S. Department of State, Bureau of Intelligence and Research, _Investment Insurance Programs of the Industrial Countries_, Report No. 799, 18 May 1977, p. 17.

[17] Boston Consulting Group, 1978.

[18] Ibid.

[19] U.S. Department of State, _Export Credit Systems of the Major Powers and Their Role in Exports of Capital Goods_, Washington, D.C., Spring 1977.

[20] Ibid.

[21] Ibid. p. 6.

[22] _Statistiques et Etudes Financières_, Trente-deuxieme Rapport Annuel du Conseil National du Credit, no. 340, Ministère de l'Economie et des Finances, Paris, 1977, p. 181.

[23] _Problèmes Economiques_, "Le Problème des Exportations Industrielles," 24 August 1977, p. 12.

[24] U.S. Department of State, _Export Credit Systems of the Major Powers and Their Role in Export of Capital Goods_, op. cit., p. 13.

[25]Commissariat General du Plan, Rapport du Groupe Chargé d'Etudier l'Evolution des Economies du Tiers-Monde et l'Appareil Productif Francais, January 1978, Paris, p. 21.

[26]U.S. Department of State, Export Credit Systems of the Major Powers and Their Role in Exports of Capital Goods, op. cit., p. 8.

[27]Such a view is reflected in the statement by Richard Hammer of Price Waterhouse made before the Senate Committee on Banking, Housing and Urban Affairs, headed by Senator Adlai E. Stevenson, from which much of the factual material in the following section is drawn. (U.S. Senate, 1978; 115 et. seg.)

[28]OECD, Development Co-operation 1978 Review, Paris, p. 191.

[29]Ibid, pp. 136-147.

[30]Ibid. p. 253.

[31]Economist Intelligence Unit (EIU), Quarterly Economic Review (QER), 1, 1978, p. 6.

[32]Ibid. pg. 27 and Annual Summary 1978.

[33]EIU, QER, 4, 1977, p. 11.

[34]EIU, QER, 2, 1977 and 2, 1978.

[35]Le Monde, 21 March 1979.

[36]Ibid.

[37]Franko, Lawrence, "Restraining Arms Exports to the Third World: Will Europe Agree?" Survival, Jan. - Feb., 1979.

[38]Ibid.

[39]Journal de Genève, 11 March 1979.

[40]Financial Times, 27 July 1979 and Le Monde, 17 July 1979.

[41]Middle East Economic Digest, April 1979, p. 39.

[42]Newsweek, 5 March 1979, p. 7.

[43]Moniteur du Commerce International, No. 274, 26 December 1977, p. 17.

[44]Le Nouvel Economiste, No. 79, 2 May 1979, p. 61.

[45]Intervia, No. 1, 1979, pp. 51-67.

[46]Europe, 3 March 1979.

[47]Journal de Genève, 18 January 1979.

[48]Air Transport, May 1977.

[49]Europe, 9 February 1979.

[50]Aerospatiale No. 94, June-July 1979, pp. 6-9.

[52]Europe, 9 April 1979 and Financial Times, 13 August 1979.

[53]Financial Times, 13 October 1978.

[54]Financial Times, 3 October 1978.

[55]Ibid.

[56]ATEN, No. 95, May-June 1972.

[57]Energie Nucléaire, vol. 15, March-April 1973.

[59]Moniteur du Commerce International, No. 274, 26 December 1977.

[59]Ibid.

[60]Middle East Economic Digest, April 1979, pp. 39-49.

[61]Financial Times, 11 April 1979.

[62]Problemes Economiques, 25 May 1977, p. 4.

[63]Moniteur du Commerce International, December 1978.

[64]Yves Berthalot and Gérard Tardy, _Le Défi Economique du Tiers Monde_, La Documentation Francaise, Paris, 1978, p. 35.

[65]_Problèmes Economiques_, 1977, p. 4.

[66]This concept, along with its measurement as used here, was developed by Bela Balassa. See B. Balassa, "Trade Liberalization and 'Related' Comparative Advantage", _The Manchester School of Economic and Social Studies_, vol. 32, no. 2, May 1965, pp. 99-123.

4

JAPAN'S EXPORT COMPETITIVENESS IN THIRD WORLD MARKETS

Eleanor G. Hadley

CONTENTS

I. INTRODUCTION

Japan is gaining market share in trade with Third World countries for the same reasons it is gaining market share in trade with industrialized countries. Japan has a strong line of products to sell, produced with quality workmanship, competitively priced, and aggressively marketed. Moreover, Japan regards all export markets -- small as well as large -- as opportunities. Many of the export markets seen as marginal by Europe and the United States, but cultivated by Japan, are of growing significance.

From past lessons, Japan has come to realize that export opportunities are often shaped by import behavior. Japan now imports increasing quantities of labor-intensive products in which it used to specialize. This practice was made politically possible through a massive restructuring of the Japanese economy. As the export goods it produced before World War II -- textiles, apparel, earthenware, cutlery, rubber-soled footwear -- were the very products that the newly independent countries would manufacture to begin their industrializing process, Japan's leaders sought to regain Japan's competitive position in world trade through the restructuring of the economy. Such restructuring was geared to product lines that Japan could sell to the world -- avoiding product areas that the developing countries would be producing themselves. In this writer's judgment, this massive restructuring of Japan's economy was the single most important factor in the country's development of a highly competitive export sector.

Third World countries now import approximately one quarter of the world's exports of manufactures when the "universe" is market economies.[1] Given the impressive

*Statistical assistance from Joseph Natalicchio and typing assistance from Sheila Murphy are gratefully acknowledged.

growth rates of the newly industrializing countries, these markets are gradually being recognized as important export opportunities for industrialized countries. Japan especially has developed trade with these markets not only as a consequence of traditional trading patterns and its need for large quantities of raw material imports, but also because of Japan's need to secure markets for developing further scale and expertise before taking on competition in industrialized countries.

Close to half -- 46 percent in 1978 -- of Japan's manufactures are exported to less developed countries (LDCs), while over one third of the manufactured exports of the United States -- 37 percent in 1979 -- are sent to these countries. Five years prior to 1978, Japan sold 42 percent of its manufactured exports to LDCs.[2] Thus, these countries represent a major and rising proportion of the market for manufactured exports from Japan.

By whatever measure one chooses for comparison, Japan has been gaining position in manufactured exports to Third World markets, the United States losing. If one looks at the ranking of the two countries among OECD exporters to LDCs over the 15-year period, 1962-1977, Japanese exports rose from 11 percent to 25 percent of total OECD exports of manufactured products to these countries; the U.S. share declined from 36 percent to 22 percent of total exports. For the shorter period, 1970-1977, Japanese exports increased from 21 percent to 25 percent of total manufactured exports; the U.S. share declined from 27 percent to 22 percent.[3]

According to the Mikesell and Farah study in the U.S. Export Competitiveness Project of the Center for Strategic and International Studies, which ranks the market share in manufactures of 15 exporting countries (ten industrialized countries, four newly industrializing countries (NICs), plus Australia) in the LDCs, during the 1970s, Japan gained in relative position while the United States lost in relative position.[4] In the two regional groupings of greatest export significance, OPEC and the "Far East and Southeast Asia,"[5] the change in position of the two countries in these regional groupings between 1970 and 1978 was sizeable. During this period, Japan's exports to OPEC countries rose from 15 percent to 21 percent of the total of the 15 countries and its exports to the Far East and Southeast Asia increased from 42 percent to 47 percent. In these years, the U.S. share of manufactured exports to OPEC declined from 23 percent to 18 percent, to the Far East and Southeast Asia from 21 percent to 18 percent.[6]

Other trade details and comparisons of the export performance of Japan and the United States (and other industrialized countries) are found in Appendices A-D. Here this writer wishes merely to underscore the importance of Japan's exports to Third World markets, a number of which have had growth rates above those of the industrialized countries (see Table 1), and Japan's rising competitiveness in these markets.

Manufactured exports going to LDCs represent the full range of such exports by industrialized countries. Obviously LDCs will be importing goods more sophisticated than they are capable of producing themselves, but one might have thought such imports would be largely "low technology" items. Table 2 presents the leading products the 15 exporting nations of the Mikesell and Farah study are sending to LDCs together with the amount of these goods exported from Japan and the United States. This table of leading products reveals the amount of sophisticated goods -- aircraft, telecommunications, metal working machinery, and so forth, as well as lower technology items -- that LDCs are importing.

In steel, the most important export to LDCs, Japanese exports exceed U.S. exports by over 5:1. Clearly, the strength of Japanese exports lies in steel, ships, trucks, buses, and electrical power machinery, while the United States exports mostly aircraft, chemical elements and compounds, fork-lift trucks, and construction and mining machinery. The table omits a significant category of manufactured exports -- military arms. Japan, by interpretation of its constitutional renunciation of war (Article IX), does not export military arms. The United States, of course, is a major exporter -- in this circumstance with no troubling Japanese competition.

Japan must rely on exporting manufactured goods. With grossly insufficient energy supplies (a

TABLE 1

REAL GROWTH RATES OF SELECTED DEVELOPED, ASIAN,
AND OPEC COUNTRIES, 1964-1979
(percentage change in gross domestic product)

COUNTRY	1964-69	1970	1972	1974	1976	1977	1978	1979
Selected Developed Countries								
Japan[a]	10.4	10.9	9.1	-1.3	6.5	5.4	6.0	5.9
United States[a]	4.3	-0.3	5.7	-1.7	5.9	5.3	4.4	2.3
Germany	4.4	5.8	3.4	0.5	5.3	2.6	3.5	4.3
United Kingdom	2.3	2.3	2.7	-0.05	3.7	1.0	3.5	0.9
France	5.4	5.8	5.7	3.8	5.0	2.8	3.8	3.2
Selected Asian Countries								
Korea	10.6	8.6	7.3	8.8	13.9	10.1	11.3	7.4
Philippines[a]	5.3	5.6	4.9	6.0	6.1	5.7	6.3	5.8
Thailand	8.8	6.6	3.8	5.0	9.3	7.3	11.7	6.7
Selected OPEC Countries								
Saudi Arabia	8.7[b]	14.4	19.7	3.1	8.6	15.1	5.6	--
Iran	11.2	11.8	5.5	35.6	13.1	-4.1	--	--
Venezuela	4.3	7.1	3.0	5.8	7.8	7.6	4.8	--
Ecuador	4.9[c]	-1.2	8.4	13.6	7.1	6.0	5.3	5.3
Libya	--	--	--	--	25.2	10.1	--	--
Nigeria	8.1	7.0	6.3	2.6	10.8	9.9	--	--
Indonesia	4.6	1.9	5.1	0.2	6.9	7.4	7.2	--

Notes: a) Gross National Product
        b) 1966-69
        c) 1965-69

Source: For 1964-74, IMF, International Financial Statistics, May 1977; for
         1976-79, ibid., October 1980. Rates for 1964-74 calculated in 1970
         prices; 1976-79 rates in 1975 prices.

100 percent dependence on imported oil and a 77 percent dependence on imports of energy overall),[7] with few industrial raw materials,[8] Japan has an industrial economy out of its trade with the world. With a land area the size of the state of California, five sixths of which is mountainous, Japan is the world's largest agricultural importer.[9] As Ezra Vogel observes, more acres are devoted to agricultural production for Japan in the United States than in Japan.[10] Consequently, manufactured goods make up 98 percent of Japan's exports.

With its rich farm land, its endowments of industrial materials, and its manufacturing industries, the United States in contrast to Japan has a diversified pattern of export. In 1979, agricultural goods made up some 20 percent of U.S. exports, industrial materials about 10 percent, and manufactured goods roughly 70 percent.[11]

Many persons believe that the importance of foreign trade to an economy can be judged by the proportion of trade to GNP,[12] usually measured by merchandise trade (i.e. exports and imports). By this measure the Japanese ratio falls between that of the United States and the much higher ratios for the European countries. In 1979, the ratios were:

Merchandise Trade to GNP[13]

United States	16.6%
Japan	20.9%
West Germany	43.6%

This is not a reliable measure, however, because without merchandise trade the Japanese economy would shrivel. From childhood to adulthood, the Japanese are taught that to exist, Japan must export. Even in the fifth grade children are introduced to the importance of foreign trade.

As we have learned, a characteristic of Japan's foreign trade is to import raw materials and to process them domestically and export industrial products in turn. We call this pattern of trade a 'processing trade.'

TABLE 2

LEADING MANUFACTURED EXPORTS[a] TO LDCs BY 15 EXPORTING NATIONS,[b] 1978
ARRANGED BY DESCENDING SIZE OF SHIPMENTS
(in millions of dollars)

	Total Exports by 15 Nations	Exports from Japan	Exports from U. S.
Steel	11,139	5,732	1,018
Ships, boats	6,741	4,445	176
Trucks, buses	6,648	2,322	1,417
Electrical power machinery	6,608	1,705	1,467
Aircraft	4,249	22	2,529
Telecommunications	4,053	926	978
Motor vehicle parts	4,035	964	580
Fork lift trucks	3,771	515	1,834
Construction, mining machinery	3,431	452	1,711
Plastic materials	3,346	890	776
Pumps, centrifuges	3,308	636	964
Heating, cooling equipment	3,192	916	922
Textile fabrics	3,083	1,647	278
Nonelectric power machinery	2,785	883	536
Internal combustion engines	2,717	692	775
Medicinal and pharmaceutical products	2,359	81	379
Metal-working machinery	2,250	603	457
Watches, clocks	2,080	715	126
Paper, cardboard	2,030	292	587
TOTAL	93,867	27,130	20,571

Notes: a) For SITC concordance, See Appendix Table II-B of Mikesell and Farah.

b) For a listing of these 15 countries, cf. footnote 4.

Source: Raymond F. Mikesell and Mark G. Farah, U.S. Export Competitiveness in Manufacturing in Third World Markets, Significant Issues Series, Vol. 2, No. 9, Center for Strategic and International Studies, 1980, Appendix Table II-C.

Why is Japan engaged in a 'processing trade'?
Some answers to this question are: shortage
of industrial raw materials which came about
as industry grew; availability of a high
level of technology and high quality labor
making production of high quality products
possible.

We have seen that our industry is closely
related with foreign trade.... Thanks to our
efforts, exports have grown markedly in
recent years. Lately, [mid-Seventies] we
have more exports than imports....It is
important that our future foreign trade be
conducted with exports and imports kept in
balance.[14]

Although export competitiveness in market
economies is primarily a consequence of private
entrepreneurship, government policies affect results.
It is the purpose of this study to identify Japanese
government policies that affect its export competitiveness. Because comparison often sharpens understanding,
Japanese policies will frequently be contrasted with
U.S. policies.

Third World developments posed a much sharper
challenge to Japan than to the United States, France,
and Germany, not only because such a large proportion
of Japan's exports had traditionally been directed to
Third World countries but because the goods that these
countries would in time export to the world would be
directly competitive with goods from Japan.

It was evident that LDCs would begin their
industrialization process in the products in which the
civilian sector of Japan's prewar economy had specialized: cotton cloth, apparel, rubber-soled shoes,
cutlery, ceramics, and toys. As Ragner Nurkes observed
in his excellent study, Problems of Capital Formation
in Underdeveloped Countries, demand shapes supply.
Countries begin industrialization in products where
demand is firm, and in country after country, this has
been textiles and other consumer products of light
industry.

Accordingly, Japan saw no choice but to respond to what it has come to call "chasing up" competition. Inasmuch as the LDCs would have much lower labor costs than Japan, the Japanese would not be able to compete in the same product categories. Consequently the leadership of Japan believed it essential to move out of the labor intensive products in which it had engaged and into higher value-added and income elastic goods. Thus, Japan did not perceive its adoption of industrial policy in optional terms. Circumstances were compelling.

It is noteworthy that Japan made the decision to reorient its economy in the early 1950s. LDC exports were not yet on its shores, nor were they on third country shores. Industrial production in LDCs was only under consideration. Americans consider improved import statistics as an "early warning." Japan's conception of "early warning" is careful economic analysis projecting events ten to fifteen years hence.

The present significance of Third World markets to Japan's major manufacturers is clearly seen in Table 3. (For the historical pattern, see footnote 15.) Note that for many Japanese firms today, the Southeast Asian market is of comparable or greater importance than the American market -- for example Hitachi's exports of electrical equipment, Nippon Steel's and Kawasaki Steel's steel exports, and for all of the chemical firms listed in the table. The table is taken from the President Directory which annually publishes the breakdown of export markets for individual Japanese firms. The companies shown in Table 3 represent firms better known to American readers.

Illustrative of the type of export analysis in which the Japanese government continually engages, is the following chart comparing the growth performance of Japanese exports to the U.S. market with the growth performance of exports of the newly industrializing countries to this same market. Japanese growth rates are plotted on the vertical axis and the growth rates of the newly industrializing countries are shown on the horizontal axis. If growth rates from the two sources were the same for a particular product, product entries would fall on the 45° helping line. Product entries shown under the 45° line indicate product categories where export growth rates for the newly industrializing

262

TABLE 3

REGIONAL MARKET SHARES OF JAPANESE CORPORATIONS
SELECTED EXAMPLES, 1976
(percent)

Company	ASIA		NORTH AMERICA	
	Southeast	Middle East	USA	Canada
Electrical Equipment				
Sanyo Electric	8	11	40	5
Hitachi	41	7	-----16-----	
Tokyo Shibaura Electric	14	6	-----39-----	
Nippon Electric	16	18	-----15-----	
Mitsubishi Electric	20	21	9	1
Chemicals				
Mitsubishi Chemicals Industries	54	3	3	-
Fuji Photo Film	20	1	35	5
Sumitomo Chemical	47	3	5	3
Mitsubishi Petrochemical	57	15	1	-
Showa Denko	38	5	19	4
Mitsui Petrochemical	73	-	------3------	
Transport Equipment				
Nissan	4	12	46	3
Toyota	7	12	-----40-----	
Honda	10	5	40	5
Mitsubishi Heavy Industries	14	11	------4-----	
Machinery				
Sumitomo Heavy Industries	16	2	1	-
Toyoda Automatic Loom	38	12	5	2
Chiyoda Chemical Engineering and Construction	1	12	4	-
Steel				
Nippon Steel	35	11	-----22-----	
Sumitomo Metal Industries	-------31--------		18	-
Nippon Kokan	10	17	15	1
Kawasaki Steel	23	10	21	1
Textiles				
Toray	30	9	18	4
Mitsubishi Rayon	40	10	12	3
Glass, Ceramics				
Noritake	18	9	48	1
Asahi Glass	35	9	-----19-----	
Onoda Cement	45	41	1	-
Rubber				
Bridgestone Tire	10	30	20	5
Yokohama Rubber	11	31	20	4
Pulp, Paper				
Jujo Paper	29	-	-	-
Mitsubishi Paper Mills	62	4	9	-

Source: President Directory, (Tokyo: Diamond-Time Publishers, 1978).

countries are higher; products plotted above the line represent product categories where Japan has higher export growth rates. The chart underscores Japan's continuing sensitivity to LDC competition. It underscores that LDC competition is a dynamic process, that as one challenge is met, a new one is faced.

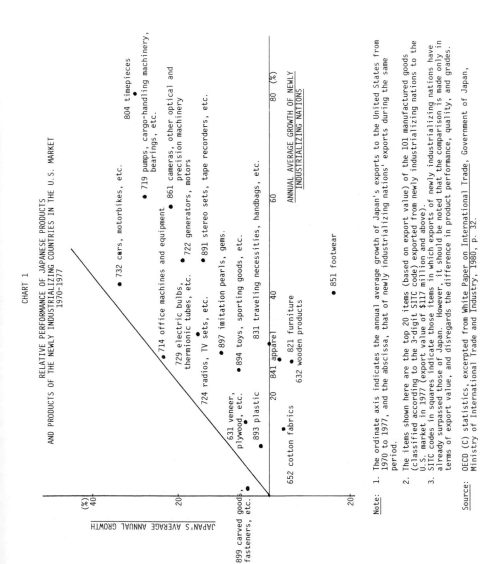

CHART 1

RELATIVE PERFORMANCE OF JAPANESE PRODUCTS
AND PRODUCTS OF THE NEWLY INDUSTRIALIZING COUNTRIES IN THE U.S. MARKET
1970-1977

JAPAN'S AVERAGE ANNUAL GROWTH

ANNUAL AVERAGE GROWTH OF NEWLY
INDUSTRIALIZING NATIONS

804 timepieces

719 pumps, cargo-handling machinery, bearings, etc.

861 cameras, other optical and precision machinery

732 cars, motorbikes, etc.

722 generators, motors

891 stereo sets, tape recorders, etc.

714 office machines and equipment

729 electric bulbs, thermionic tubes, etc.

897 imitation pearls, gems.

724 radios, TV sets, etc.

894 toys, sporting goods, etc.

831 traveling necessities, handbags, etc.

631 veneer, plywood, etc.

893 plastic

841 apparel

821 furniture

632 wooden products

851 footwear

652 cotton fabrics

899 carved goods, fasteners, etc.

Note:
1. The ordinate axis indicates the annual average growth of Japan's exports to the United States from 1970 to 1977, and the abscissa, that of newly industrializing nations' exports during the same period.
2. The items shown here are the top 20 items (based on export value) of the 101 manufactured goods (classified according to the 3-digit SITC code) exported from newly industrializing nations to the U.S. market in 1977 (export value of $117 million and above).
3. SITC codes in squares indicate those items in which exports of newly industrializing nations have already surpassed those of Japan. However, it should be noted that the comparison is made only in terms of export value, and disregards the difference in product performance, quality, and grades.

Source: OECD (C) statistics, excerpted from White Paper on International Trade, Government of Japan, Ministry of International Trade and Industry, 1980, p. 32.

265

II.   INDUSTRIAL POLICY AS A TRADE INSTRUMENT

The product mix of an economy can be either a deliberate or inadvertent part of trade policy. When the mix is a result of a deliberate policy, the economic leadership of a nation assesses the present and potential international competitiveness of its industries and takes action accordingly. When it is an inadvertent part of policy, the economic leadership of the country is likely to believe that there is no role for government in providing information on probable trends in world production, facilitating changes in the mix where needed, or ensuring modernization of plant and equipment, but that government does have a responsibility to protect existing industries. Even if one assumes comparable entrepreneurial ability, industries may be below internationally competitive levels through the prices of the factors required in their production -- land, labor, and capital -- or because their output is not produced by modern plant and equipment.

In our Anglo-American heritage we have grown up with a static conception of comparative advantage. Some of us believe that Americans have a "right" to compete in high technology products whereas Japan, and certainly the newly industrializing countries should compete in less sophisticated products. But as Joseph Schumpeter observed, capitalism itself involves "creative destruction" with those coming from behind shoving those ahead. Today the world has several emerging "new Japans." Tomorrow it will have more.

Many Americans believe it is unfair to use government as an instrument of trade policy except for tariffs, quotas, and the like. But this is scarcely a realistic approach; elsewhere governments will use the tools at their disposal for trade purposes. Japan and the newly industrializing countries have already demonstrated this, and there will be many more demonstrations to come. Governments are going to do everything possible to promote economic development which characteristically means industrial development.

The General Agreement on Tariffs and Trade (GATT) establishes broad ground rules for its members. It should be noted that in the countervailing duty code, adopted in the recently concluded Tokyo Round, a distinction is made between government support of domestic industrial development and the export sector. It is when government programs apply only to exports that the products become liable under the countervailing duties code.

As observed earlier, faced with what would in a decade or more be "chasing up" competition, Japan set about in the early 1950s to effect changes in its manufacturing sector. On the basis of economic analysis the government of Japan used an array of policy instruments to attract private investment into lines of production perceived to be prospective for GNP growth and exports. The Japanese kit of tools has included policies affecting tax, credit, trade, competition, investment, and foreign exchange.

Japanese industrial policy has also given major emphasis to rationalization, that is, to promoting production, whatever the line of product, in modern plants employing the most advanced technology. Tax and credit policies have been the principle instruments toward this end. A profile of the resulting changes in the Japanese economy is seen in Table 4. As should be noted, whereas textiles had been the overwhelmingly dominant prewar industry, this sector declined sharply in relative importance in the postwar period as emphasis shifted to steel and machinery. Changes in the relative importance of Japan's export mix were also sharp. Although cotton cloth made up 12.3 percent of Japan's exports in 1965, it constituted but 3.7 percent in 1978; and although automobiles made up only 1.4 percent of Japan's exports in 1965, they accounted for 10.9 percent in 1978.[16] As the American economist Terutomo Ozawa observes, "No other industrial country...is so bent on transforming...[its] industrial structure as is Japan."[17]

Masahisa Naitoh, the Japanese economist, vividly contrasts the views toward industrial structure in the two economies. He observes, "In the United States, industrial structure...is described and expressed statistically. [In Japan] industrial structure [is viewed] as a system for setting and implementing goals."[18]

TABLE 4

THE ROLE OF SELECTED INDUSTRIES IN JAPAN'S
MANUFACTURING OUTPUT, 1920-1970

(Percent)

	Textiles	Iron & Steel	Chemicals	Machinery
1920	34.3	4.6	12.4	14.5
1925	39.3	4.4	10.1	7.2
1930	30.6	6.2	12.8	11.2
1935	29.1	9.98	14.4	16.3
1955	16.8	11.9	18.9	14.2
1960	12.1	13.75	17.4	25.2
1965	10.1	12.98	17.1	26.2
1970	7.6	14.1	15.3	32.1

Source: Kazushi Ohkawa and Shinohara, Patterns of Japanese Economic Development, Yale University, 1979. Tables A-19 and A-20 where the figures are given in current yen.

268

Because industrial policy has a variety of meanings it will be helpful to clarify Japanese usage of the term.[19] From the foregoing statistics it is obvious that the Japanese economy has undergone dramatic transformation in the postwar period. Specialists on the Japanese economy know that a significant part of the change was the product of market forces. There were not that many special measures laws. In terms of the rapid development of such key industries as steel, automobiles, machine tools, and, more recently, semiconductors and computers, however, government stimulus measures were clearly important and could be said to represent "Japan Inc.," with all the foreign misperceptions thereto attaching. Although Japan targeted such industries, much of its postwar industrial policy was simply rationalization measures available to most of the economy. It is important to note that virtually all of the measures since 1952 -- rationalization or target industries -- have been "elective." Business has not been compelled to operate in particular ways. The government's approach has been, "We will make it to your advantage to do what in our analysis represents national advantage." The Ministry of International Trade and Industry (MITI) has been the key ministry in most of Japan's postwar architecting of the economy.

The tools with which the Japanese government has effected industrial policy have varied sharply over time, depending on the authority of the Japanese government and business' acceptance of government assistance. In the disruption of the immediate postwar years, the Japanese government possessed powers to compel business to take specified action. With supply and demand conditions approximating normalcy in 1952, the government lost such powers, but because of its critical balance of payments position, the government continued to possess the power to allocate foreign exchange, a powerful tool. Until roughly 1970 all foreign investment in Japan required Japanese government approval. Importation of foreign technology was administered under this law, giving the government authority to review proposed technology transfer agreements. When Japan became an Article VIII nation at the International Monetary Fund (IMF) in 1964 -- under outside pressure and with enormous self-pity -- the government lost this potent authority. Further, its ability to provide nearly water-tight tariff protection diminished under successive rounds of tariff negotiations. On being admitted to the OECD in 1964, the government was under strong foreign pressure to allow unrestricted foreign direct investment in Japan. Liberalization of investment became significant in the early 1970s.

To repeat, the tools with which industrial policy has been effected in Japan have varied significantly over time. Some observers divide these changes into three periods. Between 1945-52, the government could compel business to take action under the Temporary Supply and Demand Law which expired in 1952. The second phase, 1952-64, ended with Japan becoming an Article VIII nation in the Fund. The third and current phase began in 1964. As any careful student of Japanese affairs knows, the "internationalization of the economy," as the Japanese refer to the third phase, scarely occurred overnight.

The success of industrial policy requires a superior performance on the part of both business and government. Since Japanese industrial policy represents an emphasis on investment that the government believes will bring national advantage, the success of the policy rests not only on the skill with which desirable investment lines have been perceived, and the readiness of business in a market economy to give it translation, but also on the entrepreneurial vigor and imagination with which it is carried out.[20]

III. THE JAPANESE OBJECTIVE

Generally, MITI has sought to encourage production in industries that have high value-added content and are income elastic. By selecting industries where there is a large difference between the cost of the raw materials and the selling price, GNP is maximized and export earnings are improved. By choosing industries with income elastic products Japan is assured of expanding markets as its own and foreign GNP grows. In the early postwar years, the industries meeting these criteria were the heavy industries and chemicals, the same industries that have characterized production in the industrialized countries.

But among the heavy industries and chemicals, which ones should the government emphasize, or "grow"? The importance of an internationally competitive steel industry was recognized in the immediate postwar years, for steel is the basic building material for all industrial production. Its price and quality affect the price and quality of everything made of it. It is instructive to compare the performance of Japanese and American steel industries over the last thirty years, for there have been differences not only in depreciation provisions, in the sources of outside capital, and export stimulation measures in the two economies, but also in management style. The business consultants, Magaziner and Hout, highlight the case of Japanese and American steel this way (note the contrast in the role of exports in management decisions):

> In 1950, the United States produced over 70 percent of total world steel, and imported virtually none. It had the world's largest steel producing facilities and thus, while it had the world's highest wage rates as well, was still the lowest-cost producer. In 1958, the U.S. steel industry was estimated to be three times more productive per manhour than Japanese producers. Modernization of the Japanese steel industry proceeded rapidly during the 1950s and output increased at 15 percent per year; nevertheless Japanese companies remained high-cost producers relative to the United States and exported less than 5 percent of their production.

271

During this period, the U.S. industry invested far less in physical capital than the Japanese and had a higher profit margin. Increases in productivity in the U.S. steel industry were less than one quarter of those of the Japanese industry. American companies were not as quick to take advantage of new technology....

...Throughout the 1960s and early 1970s, although the rate of growth of Japanese domestic demand slowed down, the Japanese industry continued to expand production. This greater volume was absorbed by an increasingly aggressive export programme and allowed Japanese steelmakers to build large, modern, efficient mills. Eleven new facilities constructed between 1952 and 1978 now account for over 80 percent of Japanese steel production.... [one was built in 1952, the others were: 1958, 1; 1959, 1; 1960, 1; 1961, 2; 1965, 2; 1967, 1; 1968, 1; 1971, 1.] These mills are on average larger and more modern than their U.S. and European counterparts, and give the Japanese industry a cost advantage. In many steel processes, the cost per unit declines systematically with increasing volume. In blast furnaces, for example, this scale advantage amounts to a 30 percent reduction in production cost for every doubling in scale. In 1977, Japan had twenty-five blast furnaces capable of producing over two million annual tons in volume; the United States had none and the EEC only seven.... ...during this period... only one greenfield facility was constructed -- [in the United States]....

Thus, Japan built the world's most efficient steel industry. The venture required both massive capital investment and aggressive pursuit of export markets to support continued rapid growth despite decreases in the rate of home consumption. In the crucial years when Japan gained its productivity advantage over the United States, the Japanese steel industry increased its physical capital by over 23 percent a year compared to only 4 percent for the United States, despite a lower average rate of return on capital....

The U.S. steel industry's underlying assumptions about the business prevented it from making the aggressive investments in modernization that would have been needed to match the pace of Japanese investment. From the U.S. company's point of view, the discounted cash flow return from a new low-cost greenfield steel mill could not justify its construction. Levels of debt as high as the Japanese industry's were unthinkable, and, since no attempts were made to export in large quantities, growth rates were too slow to justify the large additions to capacity....

The increase in exports of the Japanese steel industry did not come easily. Japanese companies made large investments in more than 50 finishing facilities in developing countries in order to establish a base for steel exports....

Although the success of the Japanese steel industry thus reflects a combination of valid assumptions, appropriate attitudes and intelligent decisions, it is also due in part to the sluggishness of its competition. In industries where U.S. and European producers have responded more alertly, the Japanese approach has been less successful.[21]

Louis J. Mulkern, recently Vice-Chairman of American Security Bank National Association, Washington, D.C., observes:

The loss of world leadership in steel by the [U.S.] industry to Japan in the 1960s was perhaps the most significant single development in the postwar history of either country.[22]

The Case of Automobiles

Since the price and quality of steel affect the price and quality of steel products, the decision to target this commodity was easy. The case of the automobile industry was more difficult. As is well known, the debate in the early 1950s over whether Japan should attempt to build a passenger car industry was long and sharp. Prewar Japan had had an extensive truck industry, but the dominance of General Motors and Ford in the passenger car market virtually precluded Japanese production. MITI saw automobiles as an especially desirable industry not only because automobiles are a high value-added and income elastic product, but also because of the stimulus which this industry has on other industries, such as rubber, glass, road building machinery, and so forth. Other government officials contended there was no way that Japan could successfully compete in passenger cars with the United States and thus stimulative measures would be poorly used. Mr. Ichimada, then governor of the Bank of Japan, contended, "Since Japan should develop its foreign trade on the basis of the international division of labor, efforts to develop the automobile industry will be futile." MITI, arguing the industry position, however, won the debate and automobiles became one of Japan's "target" industries.

How did Japan proceed to build an automobile industry?[23] The government began by providing foreign exchange to this industry more freely than for most other industries during years when foreign exchange was far short of market demand, and approved technology transfer agreements for this industry more liberally. Initially the government provided some credit to automobile manufacturers through the Japan Development Bank at below market rates,[24] but, more important, such credit served to provide the industry access to commercial credit when the amount of credit business needed was far in excess of what commercial banks could lend.[25] (It should be borne in mind that the greater part of outside capital in postwar Japan has been supplied by bank credit, and because it was government policy to keep the interest rate below market-clearing levels, credit was, in effect, rationed.) The Japanese government provided the industry water-tight protection against imported cars and foreign companies establishing production facilities in Japan. Furthermore, the industry enjoyed the various accelerated depreciation schemes and foreign market development support discussed below.

The Japanese Computer Industry

When Japan decided in the late fifties that a domestic computer industry was essential to its future international competitiveness, the prospects of success were considerably bleaker than for the automobile industry in the early fifties. GM's share of the world's automobile market did not approach the commanding 60 percent world market share that IBM held in computers. Furthermore, the challenge of the computer industry, a high technology sector, was far more formidable than Japan's quest in the lower technology industry of automobiles. Also, as a new industry, there was no earlier Japanese production to serve as a base.

By 1979, however, while IBM held over a 60 percent market share position in Germany, France, and Italy, and a 50 percent position in the United Kingdom, its position in Japan was 27 percent.[26] The foreign share of Japan's market (IBM plus other U.S. companies) in that year was just over 40 percent.[27] How did Japan, which has not been strong in high technology industries successfully challenge IBM? It did so through industrial policy.

In the case of computers, industrial policy consisted not only of tariff protection and quotas but also of government financial assistance with R & D, joint corporate research, government-sponsored leasing arrangements for users of computer equipment, government incentives for business to upgrade the computers already in use, and exemptions from provisions of the Antimonopoly Law.[28]

Japan was obliged to structure its approach to growing domestic capacity in this industry quite differently than in automobiles. IBM was already in computer production in Japan with a 100 percent held subsidiary. Accordingly, there was no way to keep foreign production out of the domestic market. Japan

275

was obliged to live with IBM in its domestic market. This inescapably had an effect on pricing practices within the Japanese market. IBM could "race" Japanese companies on pricing, thus denying them the profit position they might have otherwise enjoyed.

Furthermore, not only did Japan have to live with foreign competition in its domestic market, it had to have licenses under certain of IBM's patents in order to advance. IBM had achieved its 100 percent subsidiary position in Japan only by agreeing to be a "yen company," that is, by agreeing not to remit profits in dollars. IBM used Japan's dependence on its technology to gain permission to remit profits in dollars. Notwithstanding these concessions, Japan surged ahead of Europe as the challenger to the U.S. position in the computer industry.

In current discussions on industrial policy in the United States, picking "winners" is often thought to be a statistical exercise in which growth rates of different industries for the last decade or decade and a half are compared and then assistance made available to those with the highest record.[29] By contrast, Japan's approach to industrial policy has rested on economic analysis. Japan sees the role of computers in the postindustrial society as it views steel in industrial production, that is, an industry capable of affecting the competitiveness of a whole array of other industries.

IV. TAX MEASURES USED IN JAPAN'S INDUSTRIAL RECOMPOSITION

Tax policy has been a major instrument for encouraging new industries as well as rationalizing existing ones. (As mentioned earlier, other instruments used have included credit policy, commercial policy, inward investment policy, and competition policy.) Japan has used tax policy with the deliberate intent of effecting change in market behavior. Japan has not had tax neutrality as a goal (disregarding whether any tax system ever has achieved tax neutrality).

Furthermore, tax policy has been used not only to stimulate production but also to stimulate demand. This is to say, users of equipment which it is the government's desire to promote have also enjoyed special tax write-offs.

In addition to promoting new lines of production, Japan has used tax policy to promote rationalization, that is, ensuring production in modern plant and equipment. For some 20 years Japan's tax laws provided for a "rationalization allowance" that permitted in addition to regular depreciation, a 25 percent first-year depreciation charge for approved equipment and approved industries.[30] The legislation was written in general terms allowing the ministries to determine the specifics. The qualifying industries varied somewhat year to year, but by 1971 they were:[31]

1. Spinning
2. Weaving
3. Dyeing and finishing
4. Fertilizer
5. Petrochemicals
6. Industrial sharpening equipment
7. Pulp
8. Fiber board
9. Nonferrous metal refining
10. Nonferrous metal rolling
11. Electric wire and cable
12. Wholesale, retail trade
13. Steel
14. Forging
15. Casting
16. Nonferrous metal casting
17. Power metallurgy
18. Atomic furnace
19. Construction machinery
20. Industrial machinery
21. Hydraulic machinery
22. Bearings
23. Electronics
24. Automobiles
25. Aircraft
26. Agriculture and forestry

Thus, by 1971, this important tax boon was available to virtually the whole of the producer-goods sector of the economy and agriculture. When a first-year rationalization allowance of 25 percent is added to first-year depreciation -- on an assumed life of 11 years using the double-declining balance method -- first-year depreciation could be as great as 43.2 percent.

Former Export Stimulation Tax Measures (Now Available to Medium/Small-Scale Companies)

Prior to 1972, additional depreciation allowances were available to Japan's large companies whatever the line of production for strong export performance. Because Japan's biggest economic problem in the postwar period up to the mid-sixties was to produce exports sufficient to pay for imports, a stimulus program was devised for any company with any product for export. Part of the calculation for additional depreciation rested on the ratio of export sales to total sales, the other portion rested on improvement in this ratio. Details varied in different years, but by this route companies could earn from four to nine additional percentage points of depreciation, bringing the total of first-year depreciation to over 50 percent at times.[32]

Former Reserve for Overseas Market Development (Now Available to Medium/Small-Scale Companies)

The government also provided Japanese business a reserve for overseas market development, eliminated in 1972 for large businesses but still available for medium and small businesses. Through this arrangement, the extra expense involved in initial market penetration could be spread over a five-year period for tax purposes. Deductible amounts were to be restored to income in equal installments over the five years following the year in which the deduction was taken. The purpose of the arrangement was to increase the cash flow available to management.

Like the tax provisions that had rewarded strong performance, the reserve for market development was divided into two parts, a basic rate and a supplemental rate awarded for improvement. The rates distinguished between manufacturing companies and trading companies, providing higher rates to the former. Although the rates appeared low -- for example, in 1974, for manufacturing companies 1.5 percent for the basic rate and 2.4 percent if the supplemental rate was included -- these rates applied to gross foreign sales, not net income, and thus very large amounts of money were at stake. Data on the amounts claimed under the reserve for overseas market development by industries indicate that prior to 1973 two industries stood out -- steel and automobiles.[33]

V. CAPITAL FORMATION, SAVINGS RATES

In the context of intense rivalry for market position, the tax measures greatly stimulated capital formation. Andrea Boltho reports,

It was estimated that in the mid-1960s two thirds of the capital in manufacturing, and over half of the total private capital stock, excluding housing, were less than five years old.[34]

By contrast, in the United States there has been a dismaying lack of capital formation which is at the root of the international competitiveness problem. In 1978, absolute capital formation in industry in Japan and the United States was extremely close notwithstanding the fact that the American economy is twice that of Japan. In that year, Japan invested $148 billion and the United States $153 billion.[35] Thus, proportionately, Japan was putting up industrial capital equipment at essentially twice the rate of the United States. The 1978 gross fixed investment statistics are listed below with breakouts:

	Gross Fixed Investment	Transport, Machinery, & Equipment	Residential Construction
Japan	30.2	10.9	7.3
United States	18.1	7.3	5.0
Germany	23.8	8.1	8.4
France	21.5	9.1	6.9
United Kingdom	18.1	9.2	3.2
Italy	18.8	7.8	5.0
Canada	22.2	7.6	5.7

Source: OECD, "Basic Statistics: International Comparisons," found in back of all OECD Economic Surveys. This table taken from Economic Survey: Japan, 1980.

As noted, the United States ties for last place with the United Kingdom on overall investment as a proportion of GDP and is lowest for transport, machinery, and equipment.

Table 5 presents the ratio of gross fixed capital formation to GDP, 1970-1978, for Japan, the United States, and selected other countries. Capital formation in turn rests on savings. Table 6 presents the ratio of personal savings to personal disposable income, 1970-1978. There it will be noted that no industrial country compares to the paucity of personal savings found in the United States. Even Canada whose economy is so heavily influenced by the U.S. economy, had twice the rate of personal savings than the United States, the United Kingdom close to three times the U.S. rate, and France over three times the U.S. rate. Thus, although the U.S. government is currently being accused of spending too much, the American consumer is equally guilty.

The OECD publishes a broader comparison of national savings. The formula employed is:[36]

$$\frac{GNP - (private\ consumption + public\ consumption)}{GNP} \times 100$$

By this formula, savings rates for 1978 as a percentage of GNP are:[37]

	Percent
Japan	32.6
West Germany	25.1
France	23.7
Italy	22.2
United Kingdom	21.1
Canada	20.6
United States	18.5

Saving in the Economy and the Burden of Defense

Most Americans regard defense expenditures as a stimulus to the economy, and, in particular instances, they can be. In the sixties, my own conventional thinking was challenged by Japanese businessmen frequently saying to me, "Oh, what it is to be freed from the burden of defense!" They were, of course, referring to the levels of defense expenditure in their

TABLE 5

RATIO OF GROSS FIXED CAPITAL FORMATION
(EXCLUSIVE OF RESIDENTIAL) TO GROSS DOMESTIC PRODUCT, 1970-1978

Year	Japan	U. S.	Germany	France	U. K.	Italy	Canada
1970	27.7	13.7	20.0	16.7	15.2	14.3	16.8
1971	27.3	13.2	19.1	16.8	15.0	14.4	16.7
1972	26.9	13.3	17.9	16.8	16.0	14.0	16.2
1973	27.8	13.6	16.6	16.6	16.8	14.9	16.4
1974	27.8	14.1	15.4	16.9	16.0	16.1	17.1
1975	23.0	13.0	15.1	16.0	15.4	14.7	18.5
1976	21.7	12.3	15.1	15.9	14.5	14.5	16.7
1977	23.2	10.0	15.0	15.7	15.0	14.6	16.9
1978	23.4	10.4	15.5		14.9	13.7	16.8

Source: Organization for Economic Cooperation and Development, National Accounts of OECD Countries, 1961-1978 and Quarterly National Accounts Bulletin, Third and Fourth Quarters, 1978.

TABLE 6

RATIO OF PERSONAL SAVINGS TO DISPOSABLE
PERSONAL INCOME, 1970-1978

Year	Japan	U. S.	Germany	France	U. K.	Italy	Canada
1970	18.1	7.4	14.6	16.7	8.8	18.8	5.3
1971	17.5	7.7	14.3	16.8	8.5	20.6	5.9
1972	18.0	6.2	15.5	16.8	10.4	21.4	7.4
1973	20.5	7.8	14.9	17.3	11.9	20.9	9.1
1974	23.7	7.3	16.1	17.4	14.4	19.2	9.9
1975	22.5	7.7	16.4	18.6	15.0	23.0	10.9
1976	22.4	5.7	14.7	16.0	14.6	21.8	10.8
1977	21.2	5.1	13.7	17.1	14.2	23.1	10.7
1978	-	5.3	13.7	17.2	14.4	-	10.9
1979	-	4.5	14.6	-	18.5	-	10.3

Source: For 1970-1977, U. S. Department of Commerce, International Economic Indicators, June 1979, p. 44; for 1978-1979, Ibid., December 1980, p. 12, with the exception of the U.K., where 1975-1979 is taken from the December 1980 issue.

economy in the thirties and forties. With the "no war clause" in their postwar Constitution, enthusiastically endorsed (if not conceived) by General MacArthur,[38] defense expenditures in the postwar period have been low while Japan has "enjoyed" security commitments from the United States. Thus one otherwise very large item of the government budget has been kept to very modest proportions. Inasmuch as most defense expenditure is for consumption items, this has freed resources in the Japanese economy for capital formation. Many American advocates of increased defense expenditure do not realize the burden placed on the economy by their proposals.[39]

VI. DOMESTIC COMPETITION IN THE JAPANESE AND U.S. ECONOMIES

Competition encourages entrepreneurial vigor and imagination. Many Americans have the mistaken image of Japan as a land of concentration and cartels. In fact, rivalry within markets is intense in Japan, frequently in the form of price competition.

Similarly, many Americans hold the image that the U.S. economy is highly competitive, and there are frequent calls for relaxing U.S. antitrust statutes. In certain instances, there may be merit in considering modification of such statutes (extraterritorially for example), but the popular belief that competition is strong in the U.S. economy may come from assuming that one can measure national competitiveness from concentration ratios and antitrust statutes. Tougher U.S. antitrust statutes than Japan's antimonopoly law and similar concentration ratios in key sectors of the two economies do not demonstrate, however, that the U.S. economy is more competitive. In fact, it is this writer's strong guess that the opposite is true.

Domestic competition in Japan was transformed when the holding companies of the prewar zaibatsu (conglomerate groupings) were dissolved. This action freed the former subsidiaries to act on the basis of their own self interest rather than in the interest of the zaibatsu group as a whole as had previously been the case. Market concentration as defined by concentration ratios changed very little as a result of the Occupation deconcentration program, but market behavior was transformed.[40]   Rivalry for market share became intense.

In addition, there is a sociological factor which strengthens competition, a factor that, in the author's view, has emerged only since the liquidation of the prewar holding companies. The Japanese typically define themselves in terms of a group, most commonly their place of employment. In Japan, companies are ranked not by return on investment but by market share. If another person's company has 20 percent of the market whereas the company for which I work has only 10 percent, the other person is of higher standing than I. Thus, for white and blue collar workers alike, there is a keen drive to improve self-definition by improving the company's market share. Prewar zaibatsu groupings were too entrenched and immense for there to be any chance of improving relative rankings.

For those who believe that in all situations the "learning curve" supplies an economic rationale for expanding market share, a sociological factor seems unnecessary. If the learning curve, however, is universally applicable, it is puzzling why Japanese businessmen should be so much more adept at perceiving this. The disparity in business behavior is sufficiently striking that in my view one needs to add this sociological factor. Further, high growth is in itself a procompetitive phenomenon and no economy has matched Japan's earlier average per annum real growth of 10 percent for some 20 years.

Nobuyoshi Namiki, a former leading MITI official now with one of Japan's major research organizations, makes the point that competition is vital to the success of industrial policy. He writes,

> In Brazil, a Japanese shipbuilding company has a subsidiary with a capacity for building 500,000-ton tankers. But it lacks competitive power due to excessive protective measures. In... [LDC] countries, there is a vicious circle between heavy protection and lack of competitive power. Because of deficient competitiveness, governments feel obliged to apply protective measures, and then due to the existence of protective measures, the industry cannot become competitive.[41]

Furthermore, the effect of entrepreneurial timeframes on competitiveness is an important factor increasingly noted by scholars of the Japanese economy. Business judgements made in terms of the profits shown in the next annual report as opposed to decisions on where the company expects to be in five years, may result in immediate gain but longterm regret. Robert H. Hayes and William J. Abernathy of the Harvard Business School discuss this point in their article, "Managing Our Way to Economic Decline."[42] The issue is similar to the one Joseph Schumpeter emphasized:

A system -- any system, economic or other -- that at <u>every</u> given point of time fully utilizes <u>its</u> possibilities to the best advantage may yet in the long run be inferior to a system that does so at <u>no</u> given point of time, because the latter's failure to do so may be a condition for the level or speed of longrun performance.[43]

VII. GOVERNMENT ASSISTANCE TO THOSE LEFT BEHIND

Adjustment Measures

The foregoing discussion has revealed how Japan has pulled resources into desired paths. What is the other side of the coin? What has happened to firms and workers left behind in the recomposition of the economy? What industries are no longer viable because of the revolution in the price of energy?

Prior to 1973, firms, workers, and industries left behind did not represent a problem of such magnitude that government action was necessary. The very "exuberance" of the economy provided so many alternative opportunities that enterprise resources and workers were absorbed. The post-1973 picture has been different. Although the real growth rate of GNP averaged 10.6 percent between 1965 and 1972, annual real growth between 1973 and 1979 was:[44]

1973	9.9%		1977	5.4%
1974	-1.2		1978	6.0
1975	2.1		1979	5.9
1976	6.5			

Further, the oil price hikes have called for the disengagement from certain industries previously viable. Japan's energy costs are now estimated to be four times those of the United States and two times those of the European countries.[45]

For Japan's medium and small manufacturers, these last years have been an incredibly difficult period. As is often the case, those least able to bear the burden bear a disproportionately large portion. Large Japanese manufacturers extensively subcontract to medium and small businesses which often constitute the lower half of Japan's dual economy,[46] where wages are lower, credit higher, and business riskier.[47] In downturns of the economy, large businesses, until recent legislation restricting such practices, have passed on much of the adjustment process to the smaller firms, cancelling or delaying orders, extending the time period in which they will make debt settlements and so forth. With the economy plunging, as previously noted, from a growth rate of 9.9 percent in 1973 to -1.2 percent in 1974, bankruptcies occurred in staggering numbers. To meet this situation, the government has extended low interest and interest-free loans as well as various tax incentives to medium and small business through the Small and Medium Enterprise Modernization Promotion Law (enacted in 1963 with amendments in 1969, 1973, and 1975), the Temporary Law for Small and Medium Enterprises (enacted in 1971), and the Law on Extraordinary Measures for the Conversion of Small and Medium Enterprises (effective in December 1975). These measures have only modestly met the problem.

A solution chosen by certain members of Japan's more labor-intensive industries has been to re-establish their businesses outside of Japan in low-wage countries, especially Asia. Professor T. Ozawa writes,

> ...Asian countries account for about 40 percent of Japan's overseas investment in manufacturing. The manufacturing activities transferred to this region are mostly those labor-intensive, low-technology sectors in which Japan used to enjoy decisive trade advantages but in which she can no longer compete internationally if production is continued at home.

> This newly evolving ...trade system [with ...Japan, advanced industrialized countries, and LDCs] enjoys not only the low-cost production available in developing countries but, and more important, the marketing networks so extensively developed by Japanese firms, notably the trading companies, in the world market. The global marketing channels that Japan established initially for her own exports are thus evolving into outlets for exports produced in developing countries with Japanese capital and technology.[48]

Professor Ozawa contends that it is easier to relocate abroad than to shift industries.

In 1977, MITI identified 12 industries severely impacted by slower economic growth and the higher production costs associated with higher raw material costs and higher energy costs. The 12 industries were:

open hearth and electric
   furnace steel
nonferrous metals
aluminum refining
chemical fertilizers
machine tools
textiles

sugar refining
polyvinyl chloride
   resin (PVC)
shipping
shipbuilding
plywood
corrugated paper

Firms in these industries through industry advisory councils work with the pertinent ministry (all except shipbuilding and shipping are under MITI jurisdiction) in drawing up "Basic Stabilization Plans." These plans, conceived in five-year timeframes, provide as the name implies, measures for meeting the fundamental adjustment problems. To finance scrapping excess capacity and to carry out reconversion programs, the government is prepared to guarantee to firms in these industries loans through the Japan Development Bank and city banks of up to ¥ 100 billion.[49] To persons familiar with the way the United States approaches adjustment assistance problems, it will at once be evident that Japan proceeds differently, that is to say, Japan proceeds on the basis of industry, the United States on the basis of individual firms.

In addition, some firms in these industries have formed recession and rationalization cartels. Japan's Antimonopoly Law generally prohibits cartels. Its two exceptions, recession cartels and rationalization cartels, have been sparingly granted and authorized for fairly short time periods. The recession cartels formed in these industries together with certain of the details can be found in Table 7.

Worker Adjustment Assistance

For male workers fortunate enough to be "regular" or lifetime workers (roughly one third of the workers in manufacturing), much of the brunt of economic adjustment has been assumed by their companies.[50] During the first quarter of 1975, the Bank of Japan

TABLE 7

RECESSION CARTELS FORMED UNDER
THE ANTIMONOPOLY LAW, 1977-1979

Commodity	No. of Firms	Method of Restriction	Time Period Permitted
Yarn		Locking of Equipment	
(cotton, spun	100	Restriction of no. of days	4/9/77 - 6/30/77
rayon, short-	95	" "	7/1/77 - 9/30/77
staple, synthetic)	95	" "	10/1/77 - 12/31/77
	95	" "	1/1/78 - 3/31/78
	94	" "	4/1/78 - 6/30/78
Yarn, worsted		Locking of Equipment	
	39	Restriction of Volume	4/22/77 - 7/21/77
	41	" "	7/22/77 - 10/21/77
(Japanese Wool Spinning Association)		" "	
	(39)	" "	10/22/78 - 1/21/78
	(39)	" "	1/22/78 - 4/21/78
	(38)	" "	4/22/78 - 7/21/78
	(35)	" "	7/22/78 - 10/21/78
	(35)	" "	11/1/78 - 1/31/79
Polyvinylchloride Resins		Locking of Equipment	
	22	Restriction of Volume	5/13/77 - 8/31/77
	22	" "	9/1/77 - 11/30/77
	21	" "	12/1/77 - 2/28/78
	20	" "	3/1/78 - 5/31/78
	18	" "	6/1/78 - 8/31/78
Cardboard			
(kraftliner and		Locking of Equipment	
juteliner)	22	Restriction of No. of days	9/20/77 - 12/31/77
	22	" "	1/1/78 - 3/31/78
	21	" "	4/1/78 - 6/30/78
	20	" "	7/1/78 - 9/30/78
	18	" "	11/15/78 - 2/28/79
Semicorrugated Cardboard		Restriction of No. of Days	
	21	" "	9/20/77 - 12/31/77
	21	" "	1/1/78 - 3/31/78
	22	" "	4/1/78 - 6/30/78
	19	" "	7/1/78 - 9/30/78
	19	" "	10/1/78 - 12/31/78
		" "	1/1/79 - 2/28/79
Asbestos, slate		Restriction of Volume	
	27	" "	3/1/78 - 5/31/78
	27	" "	6/1/78 - 8/31/78
	27	" "	9/1/78 - 10/31/78
Synthetic Fibers		Restriction of Volume	
(nylon, filament,	15	" "	4/1/78 - 6/30/78
polyester fila-	15	" "	7/1/78 - 9/30/78
ment, polyester	15	" "	10/1/78 - 3/31/79
staple, acrylic staple)			
Artificial Graphite Electrode	8	Restriction of Volume	8/1/78 - 10/31/78
Dye Used for Synthetic Fabric		Restriction of Volume	
	5	" "	8/5/78 - 10/31/78
	5	" "	11/1/78 - 1/31/79
	5	" "	2/1/79 - 3/31/79
Polyvinyl Acetate Monomer		Restriction of Volume	
	4	" "	9/1/78 - 11/30/78
	4	" "	12/1/78 - 1/31/78
Aluminum Ingot	6	Restriction of Volume	9/1/78 - 3/31/79
Doublecoated Kraft Paper		Restriction of No. of Days	
	10	" "	11/1/78 - 1/31/79
	10	" "	2/1/79 - 4/30/79

Source: Government of Japan, Fair Trade Commission, Annual Report, (in Japanese), 1978, pp. 305-6.

estimated that Japanese industry had some two million unnecessary workers on its payroll. Adjustment, however, has been so severe in certain industries that exhausting other resources (transfer to affiliated companies, early retirement, and so forth), some companies have dismissed lifetime employees. The government has now made funds available to companies for payments to unnecessary "regular" workers for up to 75 days in a six-month period if the company will retain them on its payrolls. It was estimated in 1975 that the program had saved some 200,000-300,000 jobs.

For the majority of workers in manufacturing -- those who are not lifetime employees -- the government has adopted programs similar to those of other governments. With the customary first line of defense, unemployment insurance, proving insufficient, the government has lengthened the period of coverage. It has instituted retraining programs to encourage worker mobility into stronger lines of production and has made provisions for relocation allowances. It is encouraging firms to increase the retirement age from the traditional age 55 to age 60 when social security begins. Unlike the situation in virtually all other industrial countries, the age group hardest hit by adjustments in Japan has been that of the older workers. The tightest part of Japan's labor market is that of young workers, for under a seniority wage system, they are the cheapest.

The United States and Industrial Policy

Before turning to the other factors in Japan's export competitiveness, two observations on U.S. industrial policy are instructive. With debate beginning as to whether the United States should employ industrial policy in its trade strategy, it is noteworthy that the United States has employed industrial policy for decades in agriculture. The Department of Agriculture (USDA) makes major decisions on key crops in the light of demand within the domestic economy and the world economy. With respect to civilian production, USDA could be said to be America's "MITI" and a force in its own right. USDA does not just respond to grower requests, it architects economic policy. MITI officials are miffed when their ministry is compared to the U.S. Department of Commerce (DOC), for their perception of the DOC is that it merely "responds." We oftentimes are given to describing our culture as "adversarial," yet it is noteworthy that USDA and growers have "consensus" talents.

Like MITI, USDA is keenly interested in export performance. Not only do our embassies have agricultural attaches whose primary responsibility is advancing the growth of American farm exports, but USDA also contributes to "cooperator programs" wherein tax dollars are added to grower dollars for market development.

Secondly, the role of the U.S. Department of Defense (DOD) in American industrial policy should be noted. Certain key American commercial successes have started with DOD procurement; aircraft and computers are two key examples. Although U.S. firms often point to the fact that many foreign governments subsidize R & D, they are reluctant to admit that U.S. research has been significantly supported through DOD funding. These firms discount such funding as a subsidy, using the argument that the research is part of U.S. defense. But where defense work has commercial spillover, trading partners who are not similarly engaged are apt to see it differently. Dispassionately considered, there does not seem to be a conceptual difference between DOD funding of computer research and MITI funding of such research.

Some Americans believe industrial policy may make sense for countries "coming from behind," but question whether government could ever usefully supplement market decisions in an advanced economy. Such persons are likely to be thinking in terms of "positive" industrial policy only, where governments recommend desirable lines of production. There is, however, the other half of the coin, of "where not to be." Governments, with their capabilities for following worldwide production developments, have a stronger knowledge base than is available to the ordinary firm and could contribute in this regard.

This position, however, assumes that Americans have an interest in changing the structure of their economy. Many in the U.S. labor movement as well as in management do not see it this way and opt for protectionist measures such as tariffs and quotas. Because industrial policy for the United States is not the subject of this paper, the author simply wishes to observe that there is both national as well as international advantage in being structurally responsive to developments among the industrializing LDCs. The present machinery in place in the United States -- adjustment assistance to workers, firms, and communities -- does not in any way meet this problem.

VIII. PRICE COMPETITIVENESS

Japan believes in price competition. Much of American business prefers to compete in other terms -- styling, advertising, and service. Many American businessmen find Japan's emphasis on price competition irritating.

Price competition has been a potent tool in Japan's strong export performance. As noted in the discussion of industrial policy, costs are strongly influenced by the modernness of plant and equipment which in turn is strongly influenced by entrepreneurial imagination, tax depreciation and similar provisions, and the general level of savings in the economy. Costs are often a function of scale. Large-scale production often results in items at lower cost than small-scale production. In a number of industries, if not in all, costs are also influenced by the "learning curve." That is to say, with each doubling of cumulative output, costs can be brought down, resulting in reductions of 20 - 30 percent for each such doubling of output. Both the Japanese and U.S. electronic industries have given striking demonstrations of this. Thus, expanding market share can be a means of lowering costs of production.

Production costs are also influenced by the competitiveness of market structure. Competitive markets compel economy; concentrated markets make it elective. As noted in the discussion of industrial policy, competitiveness has been a striking feature of Japan's postwar economy.

Inflationary Trends

Inflation has been considerably more aggravated in the U.S. economy than in the Japanese. Although the consumer price index is commonly used for measuring inflation internationally, it makes a poor measure inasmuch as goods in international trade sell at wholesale, not retail, prices. In Japan, where the consumer and producer price indexes often sharply diverge, the CPI makes an especially poor index.

Furthermore, because of divergent wholesale price trends within the Japanese economy depending upon whether the measure is price performance in the "modern sector" or in the medium and small business sector, wholesale prices (reflecting all business) and export prices (dominated by the "modern" sector) will frequently diverge. Table 8 presents the wholesale and export price indexes together with an index of U.S. producer prices. (It is heartening that the Bureau of Labor Statistics is engaged in constructing export and import price indexes for the United States. Currently the import price index covers 47 percent of imports, the export index, 62 percent.)

Exchange Rates: The Floating World

Although costs and rates of inflation may be different in the United States and Japan, will exchange rates compensate? Exchange rates adjust in part, but they are not determined solely by the merchandise trade balance -- globally, much less bilaterally, much less from trends in a particular product line. Exchange rates are determined by the totality of a country's international transactions. In addition to merchandise trade, services, long-term capital movements, and the volatile short-term capital transactions influence exchange rates. At times, psychological factors can also come into play. Underlying factors do not produce the scale of swings in yen/dollar exchange rates seen in recent years. Table 9 shows the shifts that have occurred in major currencies in 1978 and 1979. It should be noted that the yen/dollar swings are, with the exception of the Swiss franc/dollar rates, overwhelmingly larger than those found in the case of other countries.

Since it is estimated that some three quarters of Japan's exports and almost all imports are quoted in dollar prices, the scale of the yen/dollar swings shown in Table 9 makes it clear that considerable uncertainty is introduced into trade transactions. To meet this situation, the government offers businessmen exchange-rate insurance.

In periods of sharp appreciation of the yen, the resultant Japanese export prices in dollars can be

TABLE 8

PRICE TRENDS IN JAPAN AND THE UNITED STATES
1975=100

| | Japan (¥) | | United States ($) |
Year	Wholesale Price Index Manufactured Products	Export Price Index, All Commodities	Producer Price Index, Finished Goods
1975	100.0	100.0	100.0
1976	104.4	98.4	104.2
1977	106.2	93.5	110.5
1978	104.2	88.0	119.1
1979	110.8	95.8	132.1

Source: For Japan, Bank of Japan, Price Indexes Annual, 1979. Wholesale prices from table, p. 115; export prices from table, p. 249. Japanese wholesale prices are defined as the price of goods at the intermediate selling level, not ex-factory. For the United States, for 1975-78, Economic Report of the President, 1980, Table B-55; for 1979, Monthly Economic Indicators, May 1980, "Producer Prices," p. 22. Both U. S. sources converted to 1975=100.

TABLE 9

SWINGS BETWEEN LOW AND HIGH IN AVERAGE MONTHLY DOLLAR RATES
(in percent)

	1978	1979
Canada	7.17	4.29
Japan	30.96	12.41
Austria	12.87	8.37
Belgium	12.91	5.86
Denmark	12.68	5.85
France	14.56	4.93
Germany	14.89	6.24
Italy	7.37	5.02
Netherlands	13.23	5.12
Norway	10.53	4.12
Sweden	8.75	4.79
Switzerland	29.31	7.02
United Kingdom	10.41	12.77

Source: Cited in United States-Japan Trade Report, prepared by the United States-Japan Task Force for the Subcommittee on Trade of the House Ways and Means Committee, September 5, 1980, p. 9, where the original source is shown to be Frank A. Southard and William McC. Martin, "The International Monetary System in Transition." The Atlantic Council, Washington, D. C., May 1980, p. 44.

quite handsome, as will be noted in Table 10 which shows the disparity between price trends in automobiles in yen and dollars. While the high prices reduce pressure on American manufacturers, the resultant high Japanese profits can lead to more investment in plant and equipment to the further competitive advantage of Japan.

TABLE 10

AUTOMOBILE PRICE TRENDS, JAPAN AND THE UNITED STATES
1975=100

Year	Japanese Export Price Index for Passenger Cars		U. S. Producer Price Index for Motor Vehicles & Equip.
	In Yen (1)	In Dollars (2)	(3)
1975	100.0	100.0	100.0
1976	103.3	108.1	106.4
1977	102.2	130.0	113.2
1978	100.5	157.8	121.6
1979	113.4	144.3	--

Source: Column 1, Bank of Japan, Price Indexes Annual, 1979, p. 267; column 2, converted to dollar base using IMF, International Financial Statistics, October 1980, "Japan" country section; column 3, President's Economic Report, 1980, p. 249 with the index recalculated to a 1975 base. Inasmuch as U. S. producer price indexes include imported goods, the disparity between the imported producer and domestic prices may be greater than that shown. Currently Japanese imports constitute roughly 1/5 of the market.

IX. QUALITY COMPETITION

Increasingly, Japanese-American competition involves quality competition, a remarkable fact considering only 30 years ago Japanese products were thought of as cheap and shoddy. Taking seriously the management lessons on statistical quality control that Deming and Juran offered in the early 1950s, the Japanese focus on preventing defects in the first place rather than subsequently inspecting them out.[51] This approach has at times produced striking differences in the products manufactured in the two economies.

Richard W. Anderson, general manager of the Data Systems Division of Hewlett-Packard, which boasts of being "the world's largest manufacturer of electronic instruments" and "one of the three largest manufacturers of mini-computers," gave striking statistics of his own corporate experience to a seminar on Quality Control sponsored by the Electronic Industries Association of Japan in Washington, D. C., in March 1980. Explaining that his company both produced integrated circuits itself and bought them from the "merchant market," Anderson described the hesitancy that he and his colleagues felt in turning to Japanese producers to supplement shortages in the American market. Chronicling the company's experience with Japanese integrated circuits, he explains:

> We soon began to see that not only was the quality good, it was actually superior to what had been our experience with domestic suppliers in either 4K or 16K RAMS [Random Access Memories].[52]

Anderson presented the table reproduced below summarizing the Hewlett-Packard experience with three major American suppliers and three major Japanese merchant suppliers with respect to the quality of 16K bit dynamic RAMS.

Supplier	Sample Testing Incoming Failure Rate (%)	Field Failure Rate (% per 1,000 hrs)	Composite Quality Index (%)
J 1	0.0	0.01	89.9
J 2	0.0	0.019	87.2
J 3	0.0	0.012	87.2
A 1	0.19	0.09	86.1
A 2	0.11	0.059	63.3
A 3	0.19	0.267	48.1

Explaining the table, Anderson commented:

This table covers approximately 300,000 memory chips; almost exactly half were produced by three Japanese suppliers, the other half produced by three American suppliers. The [second] column is "Sample Testing Incoming Failure Rate." In other words, as we open the shipping cartons coming from the manufacturers, we sample test to see if we have a bad lot. ... In that four-month period, we had from the three Japanese suppliers essentially zero incoming inspection failures. From the American suppliers, the reject rate has been running between 0.1 and 0.2 percent, which, by historical semiconductor acceptance standards, is in fact very, very good.

The [third] column is probably even more significant. This is "Field Failure Rate" -- the rate with which we see them fail after they've been installed into a system....The best American record is ...approximately six times as many failures in the same time interval as we experienced with the best Japanese supplier, and the poorest performance is about 27 times as many failures per thousand hours.

The last column is a composite of other factors that we use in qualifying the vendor. It includes the quality parameters that you see here. It also includes some things like service, cost, and other factors. There were ten parameters, each weighted with ten points, so a perfect score should be a hundred. You will notice that all three Japanese suppliers are about 87 percent. There was one American supplier that fell in the 80 percent category, one fell in the 63 percent category, and at 48 percent... There is nothing unusual about this time period.[53]

In a report on automobiles prepared by staff of the International Trade Subcommittee of the House Ways and Means Committee released September 1980, quality emerges as a significant factor in Japanese automobile competition:

When imported car buyers are asked why they purchased an imported car, the answer invariably involves the high quality of the product....According to an annual survey conducted by Ward's Auto World, even automotive engineers from the five domestic automobile companies were of the opinion that the best quality cars in the world are produced in Japan.[54]

How does Japan compete with the United States in Third World markets? It competes not only in price, but also in quality.

X. MARKETING

Economists are apt to shortchange marketing techniques and assume that costs of production alone are important. (Quality control is not yet a topic in economic textbooks.) In markets that are competitive, low costs are a necessary but not sufficient condition for success.

The Japanese apply marketing strategy with intensity. Typically they begin by noting general characteristics of the market before addressing the circumstances surrounding their particular product. Thus they are likely to heed the overall GNP growth rate, income distribution, age distribution, and other general characteristics before taking up the competitive circumstances of their product. Magaziner and Hout note that Japanese exporters frequently focus upon weak spots in export markets.

> The market and product entry strategies of Japanese companies have often targeted the weak spots of competitors. Japanese companies commonly begin exporting to Third World markets which are peripheral to their large U.S. or European competitors. These markets represent a small portion of Western sales but can add significantly to the Japanese company's volume base. When entering these markets, Japanese companies generally cut prices.

> Often the Western company's manager in these markets is concerned about his current profitability and does not look beyond a two or three year period after which he can return to the home office. He is likely to sacrifice market share to a new, aggressive competitor rather than see a decline in current profits. As market share is often taken from market growth and thus does not affect current sales levels, this is safer than sacrificing profitability. In this way, Japanese competitors replace Western companies in these small but growing markets and gain a stronger overall volume base with

which to enter European or American markets.[55]

Furthermore, the Japanese are quick to note local preferences and build these into their products. Again and again one hears complaints that U.S. manufacturers operate on that old dictum of Mr. Ford, "the customer can have any color so long as it is black." To engage in competition with those who are highly conscious of designing products for the market in question when one is not so oriented makes for an obvious competitive disadvantage.[56]

In the winter of 1978-79, in a collaborative effort between the Department of State, the Asia Pacific Council of American Chambers of Commerce (Japan, Korea, Okinawa, Taiwan, Hong Kong, Singapore, Malaysia, Thailand, Philippines, Indonesia, and Australia), and the American missions in these countries, questionnaire information was sought from U.S. businesses in the region on the factors responsible for reduced U.S. competitiveness. Price competitiveness and marketing skills were especially noted. Over half of the respondents identified better foreign company price, price-negotiating flexibility, and greater ability to deliver promptly, as factors which win business away from U.S. suppliers.[57]

Summarized by officers in the Department of State the overall conclusions submitted by American businessmen were as follows:

Japan clearly sets the pace in the race for East Asian exports...[T]he single most effective factor in the Japanese market position throughout Asia is price and price flexibility in negotiating of business transactions....

[Marketing was seen as the next major factor explaining Japanese competitive strength.] "Local sales representation and support for agent training,"... "knowledge of the market," "commitment to long-term development," "advertising," "agressive sales force," "better attitudes toward marketing," "absence of legal/political burdens," "close relationships with local officials," "ability

303

to offer total project sales packages," "foreign government aid in advertising," [were most frequently cited.]

Thus, almost 50 percent of Japanese competitiveness is attributed to tough price competition and more effective marketing strategies.

Many respondents also identified as an important attribute the Japanese ability to deliver quality products with short lead times, to train operators in their uses, to service them, to maintain readily available spare parts suppliers, to provide uninter-rupted supply, and to provide simple designs and/or to modify their products for the market.

.... [Certain] responses noted the advantages of Japanese ability, particularly by the large trading companies, to offer attractive financing, suppliers' credits, assistance in financing, and direct sale by manufactures. European firms were frequently also credited with such advantages.[58]

The Joint Economic Committee of Congress held follow-up hearings in the Far East in January 1980 in the Philippines, Hong Kong, Taiwan, and South Korea at the request of the State Department and the partici-pating chambers.[59] In the testimony presented to the East Asia "Study Mission" of the JEC, the focus of business presentations was apparently not on economic factors affecting competitiveness nor on marketing, but on U.S. government practices deemed inimicable to export performance.

In situations where several factors are involved, assigning appropriate weights to these elements is difficult indeed. Often the participants themselves have as much difficulty as others. In 1971 when the then U.S. Tariff Commission (now International Trade Commission) held several months of hearings on the lack of U.S. competitiveness, only one witness mentioned currency misalignment as a significant factor, glaring as that factor was. While obviously aware of economic considerations the Study Mission focused its recommendations on tax relief, tax stimulation, a restructuring of the Foreign Corrupt Practices Act, amendment of the Webb-Pomerene Act, and an expanded role for the Export-Import Bank. In this writer's judgment, pertinent as these topics are, they are not at the root of the U.S. export competitiveness problem. It is important not to let valid reasons efface more basic reasons.

Generally, Americans have not been eager traders, have not grown up thinking in export terms, and have not displayed foreign language competency. In assessing the advantages of entering into a joint venture with a Japanese automobile producer, one U.S. "Big Two" auto manufacturer noted:

> They help to establish a U.S. presence in other Far East markets with Japanese-made cars bearing U.S. names, with U.S. models through Japanese outlets... [and] they allow U.S. manufacturers to take advantage of Japanese overseas marketing, including language skills and knowledge of Asian cultures.[60]

In contrast, it would be very difficult to imagine Japanese auto producers willing to export to central and South America, for example, by putting Japanese names on U.S. produced goods, or to rely on U.S. expertise in these markets.

XI. GOVERNMENT EXPORT FINANCING

Like other governments, Japan has an Export-Import Bank (ExIm) to handle government assistance on commercial transactions with a separate organ to handle aid, the Overseas Economic Cooperation Fund (OECF). Much to the disapproval of the Development Assistance Committee (DAC) of OECD, a considerable proportion of Japan's aid has taken the form of concessionary loans rather than grants as DAC would prefer. For trends in the composition of Japan's official development assistance, see Appendix Table E. (If the results of DAC grants were more impressive, one would be more inclined to join in criticism of concessionary lending.)

In using concessionary loans more than other DAC members, Japan has been charged with mixing OECF and ExIm funds to produce preferential credit for its business. In 1976, OECD members agreed to abstain from offering mixed credits. Japan's ExIm officials deny that there has been mixed Japanese financing since the agreement, though they do point to a few circumstances of "coincidence" where ExIm and OECF separately supplied funds to one project. They illustrate such a circumstance with the example of a dam where the OECF grant for its construction was untied. Subsequently, Japan's ExIm Bank supplied credit to a Japanese exporter of power equipment who ostensibly obtained his order under international competitive bidding. The U.S. Export-Import Bank's March 1979 report to the Congress on export credit competition for the period 1 April 1978 through 30 September 1979 states:

> The Japanese government has denied reports of mixing OECF and Eximbank of Japan funds to yield the longer repayment terms and lower interest rates that characterize mixed credits. There is, however, some evidence that contradicts this claim and indicates that the Japanese government allows its exporters to offer attractive terms and subsequently decides which parts of a project to fund through OECF or Japan Eximbank funds.[61]

In a report of the same series issued January 1980, the U.S. states:

> Since the July 1976 implementation of the International Arrangement, Japan has abstained from offering mixed credit financing. Japanese foreign aid funds are used, however, to finance national resource projects in developing countries where the output is sold back to Japan. Technically, these aid funds are untied to Japanese procurement although it is increasingly alleged that orders for the necessary equipment and capital goods are placed with Japanese firms as a condition for obtaining the aid. During the twelve-month period ending 31 March 1979, there were two transactions in which U.S. suppliers, supported by Eximbank financing commitments, lost sales to Japanese competition primarily because the latter were offering concessionary aid financing.[62]

Although the conditions surrounding the extension of government credit warrant careful ongoing scrutiny, this practice does not constitute the core of the United States' competitive problem in Third World countries, in this writer's judgement.

XII. TRADING COMPANIES

Many tend to associate Japan's marketing with its trading companies. In his admirable monograph, Sogoshosha, Yoshi Tsurumi describes the functions of Japan's general trading companies as:

1) providing a network of foreign and domestic market intelligence;
2) providing both static and dynamic economies of scale;
3) being able to put together, out of the scale and diversity of their operations, deals that otherwise would be impossible; and
4) being able to borrow worldwide in the most advantageous markets and lend such funds to clients.[63]

The largest of Japan's trading companies constitute unparalleled centers of commercial intelligence. Information from around the world is fed into headquarters offices which build composites showing developments and trends oftentimes well in advance of their perception by others.

The largest trading companies conceive both supply and demand in global terms. Not only are such companies prepared to search the world for the best prices on purchases and sales, an important part of their business does not involve Japan at all. Referred to as their "entreport" trade, trading companies have a sizable business in transferring products between third countries. To have a worldwide commercial intelligence capability demands a giant volume of business over which to spread costs and the greater the business volume the easier it is to secure intelligence.

In competition for Third World Markets much attention is necessarily focused on the terms and conditions of government financing through export-import banks. Little attention, however, is given the competitive advantages that may occur through trading company financing. Trading companies are positioned to tap credit resources throughout the world and to finance transactions with such funds. Volatile floating exchange rates, however, add much uncertainty to such operations.

Japan's trading companies not only trade, they invest. They are active investors in natural resources projects and manufacturing establishments, especially in Third World countries. It was a Japanese trading company that saw extraordinary opportunity in Brunei's natural gas. Although in such situations, the government of the host country, the Japanese government, and other private investors may become involved, it is often the trading company that initially perceives the fuller range of commercial advantages for the project.

Trading companies have frequently been facilitators of Japan's manufacturing investments in Asia as well has handlers of their products. As earlier noted, much of Japan's manufacturing investment in Asia comes from the medium/small business companies unable to continue traditional lines of output at home in the face of rising wages. Trading companies have advised on locations, assisted in financing the transition, and have marketed the output -- in the host country, in third countries and even as imports to Japan.

Japan's trading companies had their genesis in the country's shortage of persons with foreign language skills when the country was opened to foreign trade in the middle of the last century -- a problem for a country that had isolated itself from the world for over 200 years. Under the zaibatsu system that emerged as Japan industrialized, trading companies grew into critical control instruments for the zaibatsu families. All purchases and sales of their vast subsidiary network were required to be handled through the trading company in order to insure that the weight of the entire zaibatsu grouping would be brought into each transaction.[64] This procedure was ensured through "sole agency contracts" signed between the various subsidiaries and trading company that bound such companies to make all purchases and sales through the trading company. Under Japan's Antimonopoly Law such contracts are now outlawed.

The postwar growth of trading companies reveals that such exclusive arrangements were not necessary to trading company success. By their extraordinary commercial intelligence networks, their ability to put together deals in unrelated products and often in

TABLE 11

JAPAN'S TOP GENERAL TRADING COMPANIES, 1978
(money amounts in billions of yen)

COMPANY	Annual Turnover (Sales)			Number of Japanese Employees	Profits after Taxes
	Amount	Domestic %	Foreign %		
Class A					
Mitsubishi	9,300	46	54	9,645	16.0
Mitsui	8,700	50	50	10,382	10.0
Class B					
C. Itoh	6,700	50	50	8,120	2.0
Marubeni	6,500	44	56	7,961	4.0
Sumitomo	5,900	56	44	6,062	7.5
Nissho-Iwai	4,500	49	51	6,627	3.5
Class C					
Kanematsu-Gosho	2,300	50	50	3,079	0.8
Tomen	2,250	50	50	3,330	1.0
Nichimen	1,850	39	61	3,664	1.5

Source: Y. Tsurumi, Sogoshosha, Institute for Research on Public Policy, Montreal, 1980, p. 6.

unrelated parts of the world, as well as more conventional arrangements, and the advantageous financing they bring clients, trading companies have proved their worth.

Although there are thousands of Japanese trading companies, the most important are the top general trading companies, the sogoshosha. These are listed in Table 11 taken from the Tsurumi study.

In the 1970s both Brazil and Korea established trading companies,[65] and bills have been introduced in the Congress to authorize U.S. trading companies. Some proponents of the U.S. legislation see it as a way of bringing medium and small businesses into export trade. It should be noted, however, that notwithstanding its trading companies, large companies account for roughly the same proportion of Japan's exports as is presently the case in the United States.[66]

XIII.   TECHNOLOGY TRANSFER AND PLANT EXPORTS

Japan has a positive attitude toward technology transfer to the LDCs. Since 1959, provisions have been made in Japan's tax laws to stimulate technology transfers.[67] And, while Japan was still struggling with its own industrial recomposition, a nonprofit association, "The Japan Association for Plant Exportation," was formed in 1955 to promote plant exports.[68] Since the 1950s, Japan has assiduously pursued plant exports to the LDC markets. With recent dramatic energy price hikes, and further tightening of domestic pollution standards, plant exports may come to play an expanded role in Japan's trade.

Plant exports and technology transfer frequently have significance beyond the immediate transaction. Masaharu Hishida describes "technology exchange between Japan and China" as more than technology transfer. He holds, "from the Japanese perspective, it is an ignition key to start business transactions and trade."[69]

Assessing the economic implications of technology transfer and plant exports for the Japanese domestic market, Japanese economists have emphasized the necessity of Japan moving into more sophisticated areas of production to avoid the "boomerang" effect. For example, in an April 1979 "Memo on the Transfer of Technology from Japan to the LDCs," Kiyohiko Fukushima of the Nomura Research Institute bluntly states, "The parent company in Japan must always move forward into a more sophisticated area in technology through heavy R & D spending; otherwise...if the company fails to move forward, it will be hit by the boomerang."[70]

IX.   CONCLUSION

Industrial policy has been the single most important policy shaping the export performance of Japan. Instead of allowing its industrialists to be pitted against those in the industrializing LDCs who were operating with much lower labor costs, the government and large scale businesses jointly developed a strategy whereby Japan became the "chasing up" competition to the industrialized countries.

Japan's emphasis on production in modern plant and equipment, utilizing the latest technology, is the result of both government policy and private sector behavior. Japanese tax policy has been structured to provide rapid write-offs, used by the private sector for new plant and equipment investments -- not for acquiring other companies. (In Japan, except in rare circumstances, corporations are not for sale.) Furthermore, the high rate of personal savings in Japan has enabled the country to enjoy a large capital supply for plant and equipment investments.

The vigor with which management seeks new plants and equipment -- new technologies generally -- reflects the competitive climate of the economy. Notwithstanding concentration ratios very similar to those in the United States and a government antimonopoly policy not as strong as in the United States, domestic competition in Japan is considerably keener than in the United States. It would appear that the explanation for this anomoly lies in a sociological factor. The Japanese define themselves by their place of employment, and companies are ranked not according to returns on investment but by their market share. This produces keen rivalry between corporations. In the prewar zaibatsu system, companies were too immense and too entrenched for this sociological factor to emerge.

U.S. businessmen doing business in the Far East and Southeast Asia believe that Japan's classical price competition is a major factor in Japan's competitive success. The use of longer time frames in managerial decision making, emphasis on quality, and aggressive export marketing are equally important factors affecting Japan's competitive strength.

Government export financing is not a major determinant in Japan's successful export performance. Of greater significance is the credit financing used through Japan's trading companies, which borrow worldwide in the most advantageous markets and lend to their customers.

Underlying Japan's practices in the export sector is the perception that comparative advantage is a dynamic phenomenon, one capable of being shaped by public policy. Japan's record provides a dramatic demonstration of the advantages attached to operating under such an approach.

APPENDIX TABLE A

AREA DISTRIBUTION OF TRADE OF INDUSTRIAL COUNTRIES AND MANUFACTURED EXPORTS, 1963, 1973, 1977, AND 1978
(Percentage Share)

	Year	North America			Japan			EC and EFTA		
		Total	Engineering Products	Textiles, Clothing	Total	Engineering Products	Textiles, Clothing	Total	Engineering Products	Textiles, Clothing
World Total[a]	1963	100	100	100	100	100	100	100	100	100
	1973	100	100	100	100	100	100	100	100	100
	1977	100	100	100	100	100	100	100	100	100
	1978	100	100	100	100	100	100	100	100	100
North America	1963	30	29	21	30	26	26	9	9	11
	1973	41	44	27	20	33	21	9	10	6
	1977	38	41	25	27	30	18	7	8	4
	1978	36	38	23	28	31	18	8	8	4
Japan	1963	4	4	1	x	x	x	1	1	1
	1973	6	4	7	x	x	x	2	1	2
	1977	4	3	2	x	x	x	1	1	1
	1978	4	3	4	x	x	x	1	1	2
EC and EFTA	1963	24	23	26	9	10	8	56	53	65
	1973	22	21	25	16	18	6	62	58	74
	1977	20	18	30	14	16	6	59	53	75
	1978	21	19	29	14	16	7	59	54	76
Other Developed Countries[b]	1963	7	7	11	7	7	11	9	11	7
	1973	6	6	10	8	8	11	8	9	6
	1977	6	5	7	7	7	7	7	8	5
	1978	5	5	7	6	6	7	6	7	4
OPEC	1963	6	6	6	7	5	11	4	4	4
	1973	5	5	3	7	6	14	4	5	2
	1977	11	14	7	15	15	18	10	13	5
	1978	11	13	7	15	14	18	9	12	4
Other Developing Countries	1963	28	29	34	34	34	39	16	18	11
	1973	20	18	26	28	23	43	10	11	6
	1977	20	20	27	26	22	41	10	11	5
	1978	21	20	30	28	24	41	10	12	5
Eastern Trading Area	1963	-	-	-	5	5	2	4	4	2
	1973	1	1	2	6	3	6	5	5	4
	1977	1	1	1	6	3	10	6	5	4
	1978	1	1	1	7	4	7	5	5	4

Notes: a) Including trade of unknown origin or destination.
       b) Australia, New Zealand, S. Africa, Greece, Spain, Turkey, Yugoslavia.

Source: GATT, International Trade, 1978-79, Geneva.

AREA DISTRIBUTION OF TRADE OF INDUSTRIAL COUNTRIES AND MANUFACTURED IMPORTS, 1963, 1973, 1977, AND 1978
(Percentage Share)

	Year	North America			Japan			EC and EFTA		
		Total	Engineering Products	Textiles, Clothing	Total	Engineering Products	Textiles, Clothing	Total	Engineering Products	Textiles, Clothing
World Total[a]	1963	100	100	100	100	100	100	100	100	100
	1973	100	100	100	100	100	100	100	100	100
	1977	100	100	100	100	100	100	100	100	100
	1978	100	100	100	100	100	100	100	100	100
North America	1963	42	52	10	52	59	21	13	16	4
	1973	40	49	11	36	54	8	9	12	3
	1977	39	47	10	37	49	5	9	11	3
	1978	35	42	8	35	47	5	9	11	3
Japan	1963	13	10	21	x	x	x	1	1	2
	1973	17	19	13	x	x	x	3	5	1
	1977	19	23	10	x	x	x	4	7	1
	1978	20	25	9	x	x	x	4	7	1
EC and EFTA	1963	36	38	36	36	36	70	79	80	79
	1973	28	25	24	33	33	22	78	79	74
	1977	23	20	16	32	37	24	76	76	67
	1978	24	21	16	33	40	22	76	75	68
Other Developed Countries	1963	1	1	1	2	1	-	1	1	2
	1973	2	1	2	3	1	1	2	2	5
	1977	2	-	1	4	1	1	3	2	6
	1978	3	-	1	4	1	1	3	2	6
OPEC	1963	-	-	-	-	-	-	-	-	-
	1973	-	-	-	-	-	-	-	-	-
	1977	-	-	-	-	-	-	-	-	-
	1978	-	-	-	-	-	-	-	-	-
Other Developing Countries	1963	7	1	30	6	4	6	3	1	9
	1973	13	7	47	22	7	57	4	1	12
	1977	16	9	60	23	13	57	5	2	17
	1978	17	10	61	24	12	60	5	2	16
Eastern Trading Area	1963	1	-	1	4	-	2	2	1	2
	1973	1	-	2	5	1	12	2	1	4
	1977	1	-	4	4	1	11	3	1	4
	1978	1	-	4	4	-	12	3	1	4

Notes: a)   Including trade of unknown origin or destination.
         b)   Australia, New Zealand, S. Africa, Greece, Spain, Turkey, Yugoslavia.

Source: GATT, International Trade, 1978-79, Geneva.

316

APPENDIX TABLE C

JAPAN, U.S., AND EC TRADE WITH CHINA BY PRODUCT GROUP, 1973, 1977, AND 1978
(billion dollars)

| | | Reporting Country | | | | | |
| | | Japan | | United States | | EC | |
Project Group	Year	Exports	Imports	Exports	Imports	Exports	Imports
All Commodities	1973	1.04	0.97	0.69	0.06	0.73	0.67
	1977	1.94	1.55	0.17	0.20	0.90	0.99
	1978	3.05	2.06	0.82	0.32	1.89	1.21
Primary Products	1973	0.06	0.60	0.61	0.03	0.11	0.42
	1977	0.12	1.22	0.09	0.08	0.07	0.50
	1978	0.11	1.56	0.63	0.11	0.15	0.62
of which:							
Food	1973	-	0.26	0.47	0.01	-	0.17
	1977	-	0.31	0.05	0.03	0.02	0.19
	1978	-	0.42	0.42	0.03	0.04	0.24
Fuels	1973	-	0.04	-	-	-	-
	1977	-	0.68	-	-	-	-
	1978	-	0.82	-	-	-	0.01
Manufactures	1973	0.98	0.37	0.08	0.03	0.62	0.24
	1977	1.80	0.32	0.08	0.12	0.82	0.50
	1978	2.92	0.46	0.19	0.21	1.73	0.59
of which:							
Iron and Steel	1973	0.51	-	-	-	0.26	-
	1977	1.03	-	-	-	0.26	-
	1978	1.58	-	-	-	0.87	-
Engineering	1973	0.20	-	0.07	-	0.21	0.01
Products	1977	0.26	-	0.06	-	0.31	0.02
	1978	0.72	-	0.12	-	0.48	0.03
Textiles	1973	0.04	0.15	-	0.01	0.02	0.08
	1977	0.13	0.12	-	0.04	0.02	0.15
	1978	0.13	0.22	-	0.06	0.02	0.18
Clothing	1973	-	0.05	-	-	-	0.02
	1977	-	0.06	-	0.03	-	0.06
	1978	-	0.09	-	0.06	-	0.08
Other Consumer	1973	-	0.11	-	0.01	-	0.05
Goods	1977	-	0.05	-	0.04	-	0.13
	1978	0.01	0.06	-	0.04	0.01	0.16

Source: GATT, International Trade, 1978-79, Geneva.

JAPAN'S SHARE OF IMPORTS AND EXPORTS WITH ASIAN COUNTRIES
Imports, CIF; Exports, FOB
(percent)

Country	1970 Imports: % of Total	1970 Exports: % of Total	1975 Imports: % of Total	1975 Exports: % of Total	1978 Imports: % of Total	1978 Exports: % of Total
Korea	1.2	4.2	2.3	4.0	3.6	6.1
China	1.3	2.9	2.6	4.0	2.8	3.1
Taiwan	1.3	3.6	1.4	3.2	2.4	3.6
Hong Kong	0.5	3.6	0.04	2.4	0.7	3.1
India	2.1	0.5	1.1	0.8	1.1	0.7
Indonesia	3.4	1.6	5.9	3.3	7.4	2.1
Malaysia	2.2	0.9	1.2	1.0	4.6	1.2
Singapore	0.5	2.2	0.7	2.7	1.2	2.3
Philippines	2.8	2.3	1.9	1.8	1.5	1.5
Vietnam	0.02	0.8	0.2	0.6	0.07	0.2
TOTAL	15.3	22.6	17.3	23.2	25.3	23.9

Source: For 1970, U.N. Yearbook of International Trade Statistics, 1972-73; except Taiwan, taken from OECD, Overall Trade by Countries, January 1971; for 1975, U.N. Yearbook, 1976; except for Taiwan and Vietnam taken from OECD, Statistics of Foreign Trade, July 1976; for 1978, OECD, Statistics of Foreign Trade, July 1979. OECD statistics converted to yearly figures from "average monthly."

APPENDIX TABLE E

TRENDS IN COMPOSITION OF OFFICIAL DEVELOPMENT ASSISTANCE, CLASSIFIED BY TYPE
($U.S. millions)

Items \ Year	1961	1962	1963	1964	1965	1966	1967	1968	1969	1970	1971	1972	1973	1974
Total official development assistance	106.9	86.8	140.3	115.9	243.8	285.3	385.3	356.2	435.6	458.0	510.7	611.1	1,011.0	1,126.2
Reparations	65.0	67.0	62.0	57.8	62.8	55.6	81.7	46.4	41.3	18.2	21.8	34.6	66.9	27.5
Other grants	0.4	4.0	10.2	5.1	13.4	41.5	45.7	56.9	63.2	81.4	75.9	100.4	96.0	107.6
Technical assistance	2.4	3.6	4.5	5.8	6.0	7.6	11.0	13.4	19.0	21.6	27.7	35.6	57.2	63.5
Direct loans	27.7	5.0	51.5	37.5	144.1	130.0	202.2	190.5	216.2	250.3	306.7	307.2	545.1	681.8
Contributions to multilateral agencies	11.4	7.2	12.1	9.7	17.5	50.6	44.7	48.8	95.9	86.5	78.7	133.3	245.8	245.8

Source: Ministry of International Trade and Industry, Japan, The 1975 White Paper on the Current State of Problems of Japan's Economic Cooperation, 16 January 1976, (NR-83; 76-1), processed, p. 45.

FOOTNOTES

[1]Raymond E. Mikesell and Mark G. Farah, U.S. Export Competitiveness in Manufactures in Third World Markets. Significant Issues Series, vol. 2, no. 9. (Washington D.C.: Center for Strategic and International Studies, 1980), p. 1. In the Mikesell and Farah study, "world" refers to the "free" world and accordingly excludes the trade of centrally planned economies.

[2]The Japanese figures are taken from GATT, International Trade, 1978-79, Geneva, 1979, p. 8. The U.S. figures are given in absolute form in the Twenty-Fourth Annual Report of the President of the United States on the Trade Agreements Program, 1979, p. 21. The percentage of total exports that are manufactures, is taken from the U.S. Department of Commerce, International Economic Indicators, June 1980, pp. 21 and 28, where the trade figures are expressed in dollars. In the case of Japan, "46 percent of its exports of manufactures" means virtually 46 percent of its total exports. In the case of the United States where some 70 percent of its exports are manufactures, "one third of its exports of manufactures" means approximately one fifth of its total exports.

[3]Mikesell and Farah, op. cit., Table I-1.

[4]The 15 countries that Mikesell and Farah use are: the United States, Japan, Federal Republic of Germany, United Kingdom, France, Italy, Canada, Netherlands, Sweden, Switzerland, Australia, Brazil, South Korea, Mexico, Hong Kong. It will be noted that Taiwan has not been included. The market share of exports of manufactured goods by the four "newly industrializing countries" shown is small though sharply rising. Collectively they accounted for 2.2 percent of the total in 1970, and for 3.9 percent in 1978. In International Economic Indicators, the Department of Commerce also presents trade statistics for 15 countries, but 15 industrial countries. Eleven of the countries in the Mikesell and Farah study are identical. The Mikesell and Farah 15 include Australia and four newly industrializing countries. They omit from the Commerce list Austria, Belgium, Denmark, Luxembourg, and Norway.

[5]OPEC includes Saudi Arabia, Iraq, Iran, Kuwait, United Arab Emirates, [Qatar is not included] Algeria, Libya, Nigeria, Gabon, Indonesia, Venezuela, and Ecuador; "Far East and South Asia" includes South Korea, Taiwan, Hong Kong, Philippines, Malaysia, Singapore, Thailand, Bangladesh, India, Pakistan, Sri Lanka. It will be noted that Indonesia, because of its OPEC membership, is not treated as part of Asia.

[6]Mikesell and Farah, op. cit., Table I-A.

[7]Economic Planning Agency, Economic Outlook: Japan, p. 80. The statistic is for 1978. The brochure carries no date, but since it is a "review of economic management for fiscal year 1979," it was definitionally published after 1 April 1979.

[8]U.S. General Accounting Office, United States and Japan Trade: Issues and Problems, ID-79-53, see table p. 12.

[9]Fred Sanderson, Japan's Food Prospects and Policies, (Washington, D.C.: The Brookings Institution, 1978), p. 1.

[10]Ezra Vogel, Japan as Number One, (Cambridge: Harvard University Press, 1979), p. 9.

[11]U.S. Department of Commerce, Highlights of U.S. Exports and Import Trade, December 1979, Table E-6, where the data are presented in absolute figures.

[12]For a discussion of foreign trade ratios and how little we know about their determination apart from the fact that geographically small nations have higher ratios than large ones, cf. Simon Kuznets, Six Lectures on Economic Growth (Free Press of Glencoe, 1959). Kuznets computes his trade ratios using national income plus imports as the divisor. In speaking of foreign trade ratios, two points should be borne in mind. We speak of foreign trade but mean two different things by the term: merchandise trade on the one hand, and goods and services, on the other. Depending on what usage is being employed, the ratio will, of course, differ. Secondly, it is to be borne in mind that in comparing exports and imports to GNP, we are comparing total values to value-added figures. Interestingly, postwar Japan's foreign trade ratios have been

appreciably smaller then prewar, as will be seen in the following statistics showing merchandise exports and imports as a percentage of GNE (GNE = GNP); but recently they have been rising.

	Exports	Imports
1920	13.8%	16.9%
1925	17.1	19.9
1930	11.5	12.3
1935	17.9	17.88
1955	8.3	8.6
1960	9.2	8.6
1967	8.4	7.5
1979	10.1	10.8

Source: For the years 1920-67, Kazushi Ohkawa and Miyohei Shinohara, eds., Patterns of Japanese Economic Development, (Yale University Press, 1979). Prewar merchandise exports and imports, Table A-31; postwar, Table A-33. GNE for the prewar years is from Table A-1; postwar years, Table A-2. Figures in source are given in current yen. For 1969, foldout table entitled, "Basic Statistics" in OECD Economic Surveys: Japan, 1980.

[13]U.S. Department of Commerce, International Economic Indicators.

[14]Translation from a textbook in use in 1976.

[15]Japan's trade patterns in 1913 and 1936 were as follows:

	1913 Exports	1913 Imports	1936 Exports	1936 Imports
Asia	50.3%	51.9%	63.1%	53.2%
Colonies: Korea, Formosa	11.7	8.1	24.9	24.1
China including Manchuria+ Hong Kong	34.4	11.7	20.0	10.9
India	4.1	22.8	7.2	10.2
Southeast Asia	3.4	10.2	8.4	6.5
United States	26.4	15.3	16.8	23.3
Europe	20.5	27.7	8.6	9.1
British Dominions	2.0	2.1	3.9	8.2

Source: W. W. Lockwood, The Economic Development of Japan, Princeton University Press, 1954, p. 395 where the figures are given in millions of yen.

It was the scale of this earlier trade with China that made the American-imposed ban on such Japanese trade after 1949 onerous and led U.S. foreign policy officers to feel an obligation to facilitate other trading arrangements. It would be unwarranted to suppose the PRC trade could be extrapolated from the earlier patterns, but nevertheless there is every reason to believe that Japanese trade would have been substantial had it not been for U.S. policy. It is these circumstances that made Nixon's breaking the many-times reiterated U.S. government pledge of prior notification before opening discussions with China a "shock."

[16]Kazuo Sato, "The Japanese Economy at the Crossroads," paper given at Columbia University Japan Seminar, 11 April 1980, p. 20; for detailed but somewhat earlier statistics, cf. Lawrence Krause and Sekiguchi, "Japan in the World Economy," in Patrick and

Rosovsky, eds. <u>Asia's New Giant,</u> (Washington, D.C.: The Brookings Institution, 1976), p. 408.

[17]Terutomo Ozawa, <u>Multinationalism, Japanese Style,</u> (Princeton University Press, 1979), p. 234. This Ozawa assertion is given statistical corroboration by Professor Kenichi Imai in his article, "Japan's Industrial Organization" in Kazuo Sato, ed., <u>op. cit.,</u> p. 32. There he compares changes in the industrial composition among industrial countries for two time periods, 1954-1961 and 1960-1970. In the first period Japan is shown with 18.4 as its variation coefficient, the United States with 5.6, and Germany with 7. For the second period, Japan is shown with 19.3, the United States with 10.9, and Germany with 10.6.

[18]Diane Tasca, ed., <u>U.S.-Japanese Economic Relations,</u> (Pergamon Press, 1980), p. 62.

[19]For a discussion of industrial policy, cf. among other sources, Ira C. Magaziner and Thomas M. Hout, <u>Japanese Industrial Policy,</u> (London: Policy Study Institute, 1980), (The University of California Press expects to bring out an American edition in 1981.); Kazuo Sato, ed., <u>Industry and Business in Japan,</u> (M. E. Sharpe, 1980); William Diebold, Jr., <u>Industrial Policy as an International Issue,</u> (New York: McGraw-Hill, Inc., 1980), (paperback ed.); Nobuyoshi Namiki, "Japanese Subsidy Policies," in Steven J. Warneck, ed., <u>International Trade and Industrial Policies,</u> (New York: MacMillan, Inc., 1978), pp. 123-43; Masahisa Naitoh, "American and Japanese Industrial Structure," in Diane Tasca, ed., <u>U.S.-Japanese Economic Relations,</u> (Elmsford, N.J.: Pergamon Press, Inc., 1980); William V. Rapp, "Japan's Industrial Policy," in Isaiah Frank, ed., <u>The Japanese Economy in International Perspective,</u> (Baltimore: Johns Hopkins Press, 1975), pp. 37-66; OECD, <u>The Aims and Instruments of Industrial Policy,</u> Paris, 1975; MITI, <u>Japan's Industrial Structure: A Long-Range Vision,</u> 1975 (an English summary of the 1980 version has recently been released); Philip H. Trezise and Suzuki, "Politics, Government, and Economic Growth," in Patrick and Rosovsky, eds., <u>Asia's New Giant,</u> (Washington, D.C.: The Brookings Institution, 1976).

[20]For a challenging discussion of the trade effects of different styles of entrepreneurship, cf. Robert H. Hayes and William J. Abernathy, "Managing Our Way to Economic Decline," Harvard Business Review, July-August 1980, pp. 67-77.

[21]Magaziner and Hout, op. cit., pp. 14-18.

[22]Louis J. Mulkern, "U.S.-Japan Relations: Economic and Strategic Implications," in U.S.-Japan Economic Relations, A Symposium on Critical Issues, Institute of East Asian Studies (Berkeley: University of California Press, 1980), p. 28.

[23]Among other sources, cf. Magaziner and Hout, op. cit., pp. 54-64; appendix chapter, "Automobiles," prepared by the Boston Consulting Group, in Eugene Kaplan, Japan: The Government-Business Relationship, U.S. Government Printing Office, 1972; Hiroya Ueno and H. Muto, "The Automobile Industry of Japan," in Kazuo Sato, ed., Industry and Business in Japan, op. cit.; GAO, U.S.-Japan Trade, chapter on "Automotive Trade," op. cit.

[24]Ueno and Muto, in Sato, (ed.), op. cit., Industry and Business, p. 152.

[25]In his Japan chapter in Foreign Tax Policies and Economic Growth, A Conference Report of the National Bureau of Economic Research and the Brookings Institution, 1966, p. 83, R. Komiya observes, "Japanese bankers say that they are more willing to make loans on investments for which accelerated depreciation applies, since they can recover the loans within a shorter time period and with more certainty."

[26]GAO, U.S.-Japan Trade, op. cit., p. 22, where the original source is shown to be Financial Times of London, World Business Weekly, March 12-18, 1979, p. 30.

[27]Ibid., U.S.-Japan Trade. p. 22.

[28]Among other sources, cf. Boston Consulting Group appendix chapter in Kaplan, op. cit.; the computer chapter in the GAO study, U.S.-Japan Trade, op. cit.; Magaziner and Hout, op. cit., pp. 82-88.

[29]Cf. for example, Wall Street Journal account of a recent exercise in the Department of Commerce, "Chemical, Tobacco Industries Are Rated as 'Winners' by U.S.," November 7, 1980.

[30]The Enterprise Rationalization Law, 1952-76 when it was suspended.

[31]Japanese Ministry of Finance.

[32]For the details of such computation, cf., for example, GAO, U.S.-Japan Trade, op. cit., pp. 178-84; also, Yoichi Okita, "Japan's Fiscal Incentives for Exports," in Isaiah Frank, ed., op. cit., pp. 207-230.

[33]This underscores a larger point that must be borne in mind: because a tax provision exists does not mean that it is necessarily used. Cf. for example, Table 5-13 by Joseph A. Pechman and Tamura in Asia's New Giant, p. 358, which demonstrates the extent to which tax provisions were not utilized.

[34]Andrea Boltho, Japan: An Economic Survey, (Oxford: Oxford University Press, 1975), p. 77, where it is attributed to the Economic Planning Agency, Economic Survey of Japan, 1965-66, p. 61; and the OECD Economic Survey: Japan, 1970, p. 39.

[35]William V. Rapp, now vice president of Bank of America, originally pulled together this comparison. He used $144 billion for Japan and $148 billion for the United States. The text figures are from the Japan Development Bank (fiscal year 1978) for Japan and the Survey of Current Business for the United States.

[36]OECD, Economic Surveys: Japan, 1980, fold-out "Basic Statistics" table. Exports, FOB, imports, CIF.

[37]Ibid.

[38]Cf. for example, Justin Williams, Sr., Japan's Political Revolution Under MacArthur, (Athens, Ga.: University of Georgia Press, 1979), pp. 107-08, and Theodore McNelly, "The Origins of Article Nine," Horitsu Jiho, vol. 51, no. 6, May 1979, pp. 260-256.

[39]Although the primary economic burden of large defense expenditures comes from increasing consumption

and hence decreased savings in the economy, there are managerial ramifications. Defense work can draw off a corporation's top managerial talent, leaving lesser management for commercial production. Prominent Japanese economists and businessmen see this as a factor in the U.S. weakened trade performance. In Japan's case, one sees an additional economic dimension to the low defense posture. Many of those who would have gone into the officer corps have gone into business. Before World War II the Army and Navy attracted many of "the best and the brightest." Today the officer corps is a fraction of the level of the thirties and furthermore, the Self-Defense Forces have not enjoyed the prestige that was part of the Imperial Army and Navy. In the judgment of many, for the first time in Japan's history, business begins to approach government in prestige.

[40]Cf. for example, Eleanor M. Hadley, Antitrust in Japan, (Princeton: Princeton University Press, 1970), p. 424 and Table 14, p. 345.

[41]Nobuyoshi Namiki, "Japanese Subsidy Policies," in Steven J. Warnecke, ed., International Trade and Industrial Policies, op. cit., p. 133.

[42]Hayes and Abernathy, op. cit.

[43]Joseph Schumpeter, Capitalism, Socialism, and Democracy (New York: Harper and Row, 1975).

[44]For average, OECD, Economic Surveys: Japan, 1976, p. 6; for individual years, 1973-75, ibid; for 1976-79, OECD, Economic Surveys: Japan, 1980, p. 9.

[45]James Abegglen, address to the Federal Bar Association, Washington, D. C., October 10, 1980.

[46]Among various studies, P. Seymour Broadbridge's classic study, Industrial Dualism in Japan, (New York: Aldine, 1966).

[47]And, it is frequently observed, where profit is higher! Cf. for example, Ryutaro Komiya, "Monopoly Capital and Income Redistribution Policy" in Sato, Industry and Business, op. cit., p. 4. Is this difficult-to-believe fact the product of the

underdeveloped state of accounting among small and medium businesses?

[48]T. Ozawa, op. cit., pp. 24-25.

[49]OECD, Economic Surveys: Japan, July 1978, p. 50.

[50]Female workers may begin their employment as "regular" workers, but they have been expected to resign on marriage. In today's world, women have not taken quite so easily to losing "regular" status with marriage. There have been court cases and the courts have sustained the women's position that it is denial of constitutional rights to force her to resign on marriage. Japan's courts, however, operate on code law, not case law, therefore successful suits do not result in legal precedent. For citation and discussion of court cases, cf. Alice H. Cook and Hiroko Hayashi, Working Women in Japan, (Ithaca: Cornell University Press, 1980), pp. 45-63.

[51]Cf. for example, W. Edwards Deming, "What Happened in Japan?," Industrial Quality Control, August 1967, pp. 89-93; J. M. Juran, "The Japanese Revolution in Product Quality" in proceedings of Electronic Industries of Japan Seminar, Quality Control: Japan's Key to Higher Productivity, March 25, 1980, Washington, D. C., processed, pp. 7-10.

[52]Richard W. Anderson, "The Japanese Success Formula" in proceedings of Electronic Industries of Japan Seminar, Quality Control: Japan's Key to Higher Productivity, p. 18.

[53]Ibid., p. 19 (though I have chosen to use the form and punctuation of an earlier "verbatim" copy which I received).

[54]U.S. Congress, House of Representatives, Subcommittee on Trade of the Committee on Ways and Means, Auto Situation: 1980, Committee Print, June 6, 1980, p. 47.

[55]Magaziner and Hout, op. cit., p. 13.

[56]In the Yamaha piano factory in Hamamatsu, Japan, one will find those pianos bound for the United States on one production line and those bound for Europe on

another. Although the wood for the cabinetry must be comparably cured for the two markets, preferences on graining are different: Europeans prefer graining to be vertical, Americans prefer horizontal graining. When the Japanese began exporting cars to the U.S. market, they noted that in the United States the front seat is the most important seat. This contrasted with the Japanese preference for the back seat as the prestige position. Nonetheless, Japan's export cars were adjusted to accommodate U.S. preferences. In the machine tools industry, lack of sensitivity to adapting products to the export market was a significant factor affecting the U.S. lack of competitiveness in the Japanese market, according to the GAO study, U.S.-Japan Trade, op. cit., pp. 117-18.

[57]Quoted in the Executive Summary of the Project, processed.

[58]Ibid.

[59]U.S. Congress, Joint Economic Committee, East Asia Study Mission, January 5-14, 1980, Committee Print, June 26, 1980.

[60]GAO, U.S.-Japan Trade, op. cit., p. 45.

[61]U.S. Export-Import Bank, Report to the U.S. Congress on Export Credit Competition and the Export-Import Bank of the United States for the Period April 1, 1978 through September 30, 1979, March 1980.

[62]U.S. Export-Import Bank, Report to the U.S. Congress on Export Credit Competition and the Export-Import Bank of the United States for the Period October 1, 1978 through June 30, 1979, January 1980, p. 10.

[63]Yoshi Tsurumi, Sogoshosha, (Montreal: The Institute for Research on Public Policy, March 1980), pp. 11-14.

[64]Hadley, op. cit., pp. 148-53.

[65]For an account of trading companies in Brazil and Korea, cf. Tsurumi, Y., Sogoshosha, op. cit., pp. 59-72.

[66]William V.   Rapp,   "The   U.S.   and   Japan: Competition in World Markets," speech given at the 1980 Annual Meeting of the Association of Asian Studies, March 21-23, Washington, D.C., p. 4, processed.

[67]Krause and Sekiguchi, op. cit., p. 453.

[68]Ibid.

[69]Masaharu   Hishida,   "Japan's   Experience   in Technical   Exchange   with   China,"   China Newsletter, JETRO, December 1979, p. 3.

[70]Kiyohiko Fukushima,   "Memo   on   the   Transfer   of Technology   from   Japan   to   the   LDCs,"   Nomura Research Institute, April 1979, processed.

5

ADVANCED DEVELOPING COUNTRIES AS EXPORT COMPETITORS IN THIRD WORLD MARKETS: THE BRAZILIAN EXPERIENCE

William G. Tyler

CONTENTS

I. INTRODUCTION

Some of the fastest growing economies in recent years have been those of the newly industrializing countries (NICs). Between 1970 and 1977 such countries as Brazil, South Korea, the Dominican Republic, Hong Kong, Singapore, Taiwan, and Malaysia experienced annual GDP growth rates in excess of 7.5 percent. For newly industrializing countries as a whole the annual rate of GDP growth was 6.1 percent, as compared to 3.1 percent for the industrialized countries.[1] Although many of these countries are still small in economic size, their rapid growth represents both an opportunity and a challenge for the industrial countries.

Growing economies have signified export opportunities and growing markets for the exports of other countries. In fact, the imports of nonoil exporting less developed countries (LDCs) have grown faster than total world imports. Between 1973 and 1978, the current dollar imports of the nonoil LDCs grew 157 percent, as compared to 132 percent for total world imports (Appendix Table 1). Although some of the growth of imports can be attributed to higher oil bills, the growth of LDC imports nevertheless remains impressive. For oil exporting LDCs, enjoying dramatic terms of trade gains during the period, the growth of imports was dramatic --417 percent in current dollar terms for the 1973-1978 period. By 1978 such imports represented 34 percent of all LDC imports.

The major economic challenge presented by the rapid growth of some NICs for the United States and other industrial countries involves competition in world product markets, both in their own domestic markets and in third country markets. In the former, the industrialized countries have been feeling the pressure of competition from LDC exports. This competitive pressure in developed country markets is particularly strong in labor intensive commodities where the developing countries have a clear comparative advantage, given their relative labor abundance and lower wages. These same commodities, involving such goods as textile products, apparel, and shoes, are frequently important sources of employment in the developed countries, and adjustment to cheaper, low wage, labor intensive imports from the LDCs constitute both a major problem and challenge for the industrial countries. Although some countries have adjusted to growing import competition from the LDCs, the reluctance in others to adjust to changing international economic conditions has resulted in an increase in protectionist attitudes and undercurrents.

The increase in import restrictions imposed on LDC products has of course little direct effect on the competition that industrial countries also feel in third markets. The only way the industrial countries can meet this challenge is by increasing their own competitiveness. Some developing countries are emerging as powerful competitors in international markets, not only in the industrial countries but in the LDCs as well. As such, the dominance of industrial country exports in the import markets of LDCs is being challenged by the LDCs themselves. Between 1973 and 1978 the share of imports for nonoil exporting LDCs coming from the major industrial countries declined slightly, from 63 to 61 percent (Table 1). Reflecting their dependence on petroleum imports and rising petroleum prices, the share of oil exporting LDCs in the total imports of nonoil LDCs increased dramatically during the same period -- from 9 to 15 percent. For their part, the nonoil LDCs themselves experienced a very slight decline in their share of total nonoil LDC imports.

In the aggregate the import situation for the oil-exporting LDCs is markedly different. For the imports of such countries the industrial countries have not only maintained their share of the market but have increased it. In 1973 the major industrial countries supplied the oil-exporting LDCs with 74 percent of their imports; by 1978 this share had increased to 79 percent (Table 1). Although the nonoil LDC share of the total imports of the oil-exporting LDCs suffered a decline, falling from 15 to 11 percent, the absolute increase of nonoil LDC exports going to the

TABLE 1

ORIGIN OF IMPORTS FOR NONOIL AND OIL EXPORTING DEVELOPING COUNTRIES
1973-1978

LDC Category	Imports From	1973		1978	
		U.S.$ billion	% of total	U.S.$ billion	% of total
Nonoil LDCs	Major Industrial Countries	50.0	63.3	123.2	60.6
	Other Europe	1.8	2.3	5.1	2.5
	Australia, N. Zealand, S. Africa	2.3	2.9	5.4	2.7
	Oil Exporting LDCs	6.8	8.6	30.1	14.8
	Other Nonoil LDCs	12.0	15.2	30.2	14.9
	Total Imports	79.0	100.0	203.2	100.0
Oil Exporting LDCs	Major Industrial Countries	14.7	73.5	81.8	79.2
	Other Europe	.7	3.5	4.5	4.4
	Australia, N. Zealand, S. Africa	.3	1.5	1.2	1.2
	Oil Exporting LDCs	.3	1.5	1.8	1.7
	Nonoil LDCs	2.9	14.5	11.4	11.0
	Total Imports	20.0	100.0	103.3	100.0

Source: IMF, Direction of Trade Yearbook, 1979.

oil-exporting LDCs was still impressively high -- an increase of 293 percent between 1973 and 1978.

During the 1973-1978 period the export performance of individual countries has of course varied. The United States has fared less well than the average, suggesting a reduction in its competitiveness in international markets. The U.S. share of total world trade has continued to decline, as witnessed by the slower growth rate for its exports than for total world exports. Between 1973 and 1978 U.S. exports grew by 101 percent, in current dollars, as compared to an increase of total world trade by 132 percent. (See Table 2 and Appendix Table 1.) In addition, the United States has lost some ground in the markets of Third World countries. U.S. exports to nonoil LDCs grew by 110 percent, while the total imports of those countries increased by 116 percent. During the same 1973-1978 period, American exports to oil exporting LDCs increased by 389 percent, slightly less than the 417 percent growth in total oil exporting country imports. As seen in Table 2, Japan, Germany, and France all fared better than the United States in their export performance.[2]

If a number of the key industrial countries have out-performed the United States in both total exports and exports to Third World countries, the same can be said for a number of developing countries as well. In recent years the dramatic export success of countries such as South Korea, Taiwan, Singapore, and Hong Kong has been widely recognized and evaluated.[3] Although it is true that these countries have been successful in expanding labor intensive exports to the developed countries, it is equally true that they have experienced success in expanding their exports to Third World markets. In all four of these particular countries, their exports to LDCs grew faster during the 1973-1978 period than their total exports. For South Korea, the country with the most dramatic GNP and export growth, exports to nonoil LDCs increased by over four times; the growth of Korean exports to oil exporting LDCs was even more spectacular (Table 2).

Although the most impressive export growth for developing countries not blessed with exportable petroleum reserves has occurred among Asian countries, generally as a result of explicitly export oriented

TABLE 2

EXPORTS OF SELECTED COUNTRIES TO THIRD WORLD COUNTRIES
($ millions)

	Exports Nonoil LDCs			Exports to Oil Exporting LDCs			Total Exports		
	1973	1978	% Increase in Current Dollars, 1973-78	1973	1978	% Increase in Current Dollars, 1973-78	1973	1978	% Increase in Current Dollars, 1973-78
Industrial Countries									
United States	17,505	36,809	110	3,440	16,013	389	71,347	143,660	102
Japan	11,424	29,434	158	2,689	14,178	427	37,008	98,415	166
France	4,777	11,421	139	1,734	6,231	259	36,659	79,380	117
Germany	5,485	11,539	110	2,225	12,077	443	67,609	142,285	110
South Africa	728	1,319	81	14	7	- 50	6,066	12,162	100
Major Third World Countries									
Argentina	995	1,781	80	80	281	251	3,269	7,016	115
Brazil	907	2,163	138	225	929	313	6,199	12,461	101
Chile	241	533	129	2	102	5,000	1,231	2,493	103
China (Mainland)	1,883	3,512	87	246	814	231	4,099	8,444	106
Colombia	170	189	11	23	161	600	1,177	3,003	155
Hong Kong	1,032	2,322	125	272	926	240	5,052	11,498	128
India	510	1,062	108	166	916	452	2,958	7,092	140
Mexico	235	616	162	45	106	136	2,262	5,572	146
Pakistan	274	343	25	184	409	122	952	1,487	56
Peru	112	231	106	10	29	190	1,052	1,838	75
Singapore	1,566	4,312	175	67	526	685	3,664	9,422	157
Spain	731	1,977	170	321	1,634	409	5,158	13,118	154
South Korea	334	1,727	417	78	1,473	1,788	3,225	12,482	287
Taiwan	771	2,451	218	213	1,020	379	4,377	12,682	190

Source: IMF, Direction of Trade Yearbook, 1979.

policies exploiting comparative advantages, the recent export performance of a number of Latin American countries has also been quite satisfactory. Between 1973 and 1978, Mexico and Colombia have both expanded their exports at faster rates than the total world export growth rate. For its part, Brazil has done less well recently despite very strong export growth in the late 1960s and early 1970s. Between 1973 and 1978, Brazilian exports in current U.S. dollars increased by 101 percent, a rate of growth less than that for the increase of total world trade. Brazil nevertheless continued to sustain high rates of growth for exports to Third World markets. Its exports to nonoil LDCs grew by 138 percent, while exports to the oil-exporting LDCs increased by 313 percent.

Although Brazil's export performance in the last five years has not fulfilled the expectations generated by the rapid 1968-1973 economic and export expansion, the size of its external sector ranks it among the leaders in the Third World in trade. No developing country in 1978 registered appreciably more exports than Brazil. As shown in Table 2, only Brazil, Spain, South Korea, and Taiwan managed to export in the $12-13 billion range in 1978. (All $ figures in U.S. dollars unless otherwise specified.) With the exception of Hong Kong, all other developing countries were far behind. Similarly, Brazil ranks as one of the most significant developing country exporters to the Third World markets.

In examining the performance and prospects of advanced developing countries in Third World markets, Brazil is an important case study on several grounds. First, as noted, the past growth of Brazilian exports to developing countries has made it one of the most significant LDC suppliers in those markets. Second, Brazil's potential for expanding exports to LDCs can only be described as vast. Brazil now possesses a highly diversified industrial sector producing a wide range of goods in what appears to be a reasonably efficient manner. It is capable of supplying LDCs with products that are not directly competitive with current LDC exports. Given Brazil's current economic and balance of payments situation, export expansion is becoming a recognized necessity by economic policy makers.

In focusing on Brazil, the remainder of this study will first provide an overview of the recent Brazilian economic performance with an emphasis on the critical external sector situation. Next, in Chapter III, we will examine Brazil's exports to Third World markets. Chapter IV will present a description and analysis of the various economic policies affecting export behavior and export promotion. To be examined in turn are exchange rate policy, import restrictions, fiscal incentives provided for export, financial incentives and credit subsidies, and promotion and sales efforts undertaken by the Brazilian government. Chapter V will examine the evidence concerning the competitiveness of Brazilian exports in Third World markets. Concluding remarks will be presented in Chapter VI.

II. AN OVERVIEW OF RECENT BRAZILIAN ECONOMIC PERFORMANCE

The Macro Economy

The growth and modernization of the Brazilian economy is not solely a recent phenomenon. Brazil witnessed a great spurt in its industrial and economic growth in the 1930s, and since then, with some fluctuations, the economy has experienced constant, and relatively rapid, expansion. Between 1932 and 1978 the average annual rates of real growth for GDP and industrial output were 6.3 and 9.0 percent, respectively. The period 1968-1974, characterized by the so-called Brazilian miracle, witnessed especially rapid growth, averaging an annual rate of GDP real growth of over 11 percent (Table 3). This accelerated growth in part represented a catching-up process in the wake of the slow, below trend, growth of the early and mid-1960s. To be sure, however, the spurt of growth was accompanied by, and was to a large extent due to, innovative economic policy reforms undertaken by the government. The oil price hikes, first felt in 1974, plus the international recession of 1974-1975, have dampened the euphoria of the 1968-1974 boom period and have added considerable problems of economic adjustment to the Brazilian economy. These international economic events have ushered in a period of slower growth. The rates of GDP growth for the period 1975-1978 have averaged about 6 percent annually, thus approximating the historical trend for the last half century. Despite severe problems in the balance of payments, accelerated inflation, and pressing poverty, the overall, medium term outlook for the Brazilian economy, barring severe economic policy mismanagement, remains favorable.

The leading sector pushing Brazilian economic growth has been industry. Reflecting the consistently higher relative growth rates for industry, the industrial sector's share of GDP has increased steadily, reaching 37 percent in 1977 as compared to 34 percent for the United States.[4] Although still possessing many of the elements of a less developed and poor economy, Brazil has become industrialized. Its industrial

TABLE 3

MACRO PERFORMANCE OF THE BRAZILIAN ECONOMY,
1948-1978

	GDP (%)	GDP per Capita (%)	Industry (%)	Agricul- ture (%)	Exports ($millions)	Imports ($millions)	Annual Rate of Inflation[a] (%)
	Annual Real Growth Rates						
1948-50	6.8	4.3	11.0	4.3	1,210	1,987	12.0
1951-55	6.8	3.7	7.7	5.1	1,488	1,645	15.6
1956-60	6.9	3.7	10.1	3.8	1,333	1,382	20.6
1961	10.3	7.2	10.6	7.6	1,403	1,460	33.3
1962	5.3	2.3	7.8	5.5	1,214	1,475	54.8
1963	1.5	-1.3	0.2	1.0	1,406	1,486	78.0
1964	2.9	0.0	5.2	1.3	1,429	1,263	87.0
1965	2.7	-0.1	-4.7	13.8	1,595	1,096	55.4
1966	3.8	0.8	9.9	-14.6	1,741	1,494	39.5
1967	4.8	1.9	3.1	9.2	1,654	1,667	28.8
1968	11.2	8.1	13.3	4.5	1,881	2,132	27.8
1969	10.0	6.8	12.2	3.8	2,311	2,265	20.3
1970	8.8	5.8	10.0	1.0	2,739	2,849	18.2
1971	13.3	10.2	14.3	11.4	2,904	3,701	17.3
1972	11.7	8.7	13.4	4.2	2,991	4,232	17.4
1973	14.0	10.8	15.8	3.5	6,198	6,192	20.4
1974	9.8	6.8	9.8	8.5	8,568	12,641	31.5
1975	5.6	2.8	6.2	3.4	8,669	12,210	32.7
1976	9.0	6.0	10.8	4.2	10,128	12,383	41.9
1977[b]	4.7	1.8	3.9	9.6	12,120	12,023	44.1
1978[b]	6.0	2.3	8.1	-1.7	12,658	13,683	40.5

Notes: [a]Implicit deflator used in the national income accounts.
[b]Preliminary estimates.

Sources: Centro de Contas Nacionais of the Fundacao Getulio Gargas, Atualizacao Parcial do Sistema de Contas Nacionais, 1971/72, June 1973; IBGE, Anuario Estatistico, 1972; and Fundacao Getulio Vargas, Conjuntura Economica, various issues.

341

sector is large and highly diversified, producing a wide range of consumer and producer goods.

Reflecting Brazil's increased industrial diversification is the change over time in the output composition within the manufacturing sector. The share of intermediate and capital goods in total manufacturing output has increased steadily during the last 50 years at the expense of the consumer goods industries. The textile and food processing industries have been among the slowest growing; their shares of total manufacturing output declined from 19 and 32 percent in 1949 to 9 and 21 percent, respectively, in 1977.[5] For the consumer goods industries as a group the decline was from 66 percent to 37 percent between 1949 and 1977. The fastest growing intermediate goods industries were metal products and chemicals, their shares of manufacturing output increased from 8 and 9 percent in 1949 to 16 percent each in 1977. For the capital goods industries the gains have also been dramatic. By 1977 these industries accounted for 27 percent of total manufacturing output, as compared to 5 percent in 1949.

Government policies have in part been responsible for the diversification, and even fragmentation, of industrial activities. Various policies, designed to protect and promote industries, have affected the relative profitability of different economic activities and in doing so have influenced the pattern of resource usage and investment. High levels of protection have fostered industrial development along the lines of forced import substitution. Various studies have indicated that import substituting industrialization was a major source of Brazil's industrial demand growth until the mid-1960s.[6] By the mid-1960s, however, import substitution was virtually complete in nearly all manufacturing industries. In 1964, the proportion of imports to available domestic supply for total manufacturing industry was only 6 percent, as compared to 70 percent in 1939.[7] Only in three, admittedly important, industries out of 21 did imports in 1964 represent more than 10 percent of total available domestic supply. These three industries -- machinery, chemicals, and miscellaneous manufacturing -- still possessed some latitude for continued import substitution. In all others further substitution was no longer a viable growth strategy.

342

Partly as a result of the exhaustion of import substitution possibilities, economic policies in the mid-1960s began to be more export oriented. As will be described below, various incentive programs for exports, particularly manufactured exports, were initiated. In addition, some measures involving import liberalization were implemented, reducing to some extent tariffs and facilitating the obtaining of tariff exemptions. The results of these various trade liberalization policies were, in addition to spurring impressive export growth, to bring about a cautious opening up of the economy. On an aggregate level, exports grew from about 5 percent of GDP in the mid-1960s to 10 percent in 1974.[8] Liberalized import restrictions, coupled with high, import intensive, investment rates, resulted in a rapid expansion of imports. The proportion of imports to total available domestic supply for all manufacturing grew from 6 percent in 1964 to 10 percent in 1971.

The tentative and cautious opening up of the Brazilian economy was dealt a harsh blow by the petroleum price increases beginning in late 1973. Brazil is dependent upon imported oil for about 80 percent of its petroleum usage, and there was a drastic increase in its international petroleum bill. Oil imports rose from $606 million in 1973 (less than 10 percent of total imports) to $2,558 million in 1974 and then to $4,093 million in 1978 (30 percent of total imports).[9]

The immediate result of the 1973 and 1974 oil price increases was a serious balance of payments problem. Going from a slight trade surplus position in 1973, Brazil ran trade deficits in 1974 and 1975 of $4.7 and $3.5 billion respectively, amounts greater than its total export earnings several years earlier. The terms of trade shock and the concomitant balance of payments difficulties presented a policy dilemma to the Brazilian authorities, involving contraction and adjustment to the new international economic situation, on the one hand, and temporary expedients, delaying tactics, and autarkic retrenchment, on the other. Because of the risks of halting the on-going growth process through contractional macroeconomic policies, the response mostly involved the latter. Two principal measures were employed -- the accumulation of a foreign debt and a dramatic increase in import restrictions.

343

A reduction in Brazil's international reserves, observed between 1973 and 1975, was more than equalled by an increase in international borrowing. Brazil's foreign debt, mostly owed to private lenders, grew from $9.5 billion at the end of 1972 to $21.2 billion by the end of 1975, and then to a staggering $50 billion in 1979.[10] Contracting such indebtedness was facilitated by the high dollar liquidity of the large U.S. and European banks during the 1975 recession and its aftermath. Seen as relative to GDP or exports, the size of Brazil's net international debt has increased markedly. The effect of this borrowing has been to stave off the external adjustment rendered essential by the shocks brought by international economic events.

Brazilian policymakers have also reacted to the balance of payments problems associated with the oil price increases by increasing the restrictions on imports. Beginning in 1974 there were widespread tariff increases, with some tariffs being increased 100 percent. The average nominal legal tariff, based upon import weights, was 31.2 percent in 1972, but this had risen to 43.0 percent in 1977.[11] More important still than the upward drift of tariff levels since 1973 has been the increase in nontariff barriers. In 1975 an import deposit system was established. The nominal tariff equivalent of this measure has been estimated at a possible 50 percent on the import FOB price for 1978.[12] In January 1979, it was announced that the import deposit system would be gradually phased out, but with the December 1979 economic policy reforms it has been eliminated completely. More direct controls over imports also prevail. The tightening up of an elaborate system of controls over imports in the public sector contributed to a reduction of imports by 69 major state enterprises from about $3 billion in 1975 to $1.8 billion in 1977. The ability of firms outside the public sector to obtain tariff exemptions through official programs was made increasingly difficult. Finally, in December 1979, it was announced that all tariff exemption schemes, except those for regional development, were to be eliminated.

Accompanying the balance of payments difficulties in the mid-1970s and the increase in import restrictions was a renewed interest in industrial import substitution as a strategy for Brazilian economic development. Concern about international recession and protectionism in the developed countries coincided with nationalist sentiments about reducing import dependence. Major government efforts and policy initiatives were mounted in the remaining areas of possible import substitution, namely basic intermediate inputs and capital goods. Liberal protection for these activities was provided along with heavy doses of subsidized official credit, mostly channeled through the National Development Bank (BNDE) and its affiliates. Large investments in these industries resulted.

The increase in import restrictions, coupled with the slowdown of economic growth, was effective in dampening the growth of imports. As observed in Table 3, aggregate imports in current U.S. dollars reached a high point in 1974 and then leveled off. Nonoil imports were reduced annually until a spurt in 1978. Nevertheless, even in that year, nonoil imports were still 5 percent below the 1974 level in terms of current dollars, and, of course, much lower in real terms. Taking the significant dollar inflation into account, the reduction in imports become all the more dramatic. In addition to their effort on imports, the increased import restrictions have also had an impact on exports through their effect on the allocation of economic resources. The growth of Brazilian exports has been slowed by such measures along with, quite possibly, the overall growth of the economy. Reflecting the reductions in the openness of the economy, the proportion of Brazilian GDP accounted for by exports fell from 10 percent in 1974 to less than 7 percent by 1978. Had the 1974 international economic shocks been responded to by Brazilian economic policymakers with real exchange rate depreciation and appropriate macroeconomic policies to reduce absorption, instead of by increasing Brazil's foreign debt and import restrictions, the 1979 Brazilian balance of payments problems would have been much less severe.

On 7 December 1979 the Brazilian government announced a series of economic policy reforms, the central thrust of which was to dismantle some policy-induced distortions and provide a greater reliance on economic, market signals. A maxi-devaluation of the cruzeiro was effected, reducing the nominal value of the cruzeiro by 30 percent. At the same time, the fiscal tax credit subsidies for manufacturing exports and the import deposit scheme were eliminated. Steps were also announced to do away with tariff exemptions and rebates, thus indicating the intention to dismantle a highly discretionary, bureaucratic, and distortional system of awarding such tariff exemptions. This particular measure will increase the effective cost of imports by placing a greater reliance on the legal nominal tariffs, that for the most part are quite substantial. Whether the macroeconomic policies of absorption reducing and expenditure shifting deemed essential for an effective devaluation will be undertaken by the government remains to be seen. A current danger, despite some fiscal measures serving to reduce the presently enormous government deficit (4 percent of GDP), is that this will not be the case.

The Export Sector

The slowdown in export growth since 1974 is seen in Table 4. In real terms Brazilian exports grew at an annual rate of 12.6 percent during the period 1964-1974, classifying Brazil as one of those countries achieving most rapid export growth.[13] Yet for the 1974-1978 period the real growth rate for total exports fell to 5 percent annually. The sharpest fall occurred with a primary product export growth that fell from an annual real growth rate of 8.2 percent for 1964-1974 to nil between 1974 and 1978. Industrialized product exports continued to grow strongly in the later period although at greatly reduced rates.

Brazil's international image is that of a primary product exporter, most notably of coffee. To be sure, throughout the postwar period up until the mid-1960s coffee accounted for over one-half of Brazil's export earnings.

Table 5 shows that primary product exports, including coffee, are indeed still important for Brazil, but such exports are becoming less important relatively as further export diversification occurs and the growth of manufacturing exports continues. In 1964 primary product exports accounted for a full 85 percent of Brazil's exports, with coffee alone accounting for over 50 percent. By 1978, however, exports were considerably diversified. For that year, coffee accounted for only 18 percent of total exports, while

TABLE 4

ANNUAL GROWTH RATES OF BRAZILIAN EXPORTS,
1964-1974 and 1974-1978
(Percent)

	1964-1974	1974-1978
Total Exports		
in Current U.S. Dollars	18.7 %	12.3 %
in Constant U.S. Dollars	12.6	5.0
Primary Product Exports		
in Current U.S. Dollars	14.1	7.0
in Constant U.S. Dollars	8.2	.04
Industrialized Product Exports		
in Current U.S. Dollars	31.6	19.6
in Constant U.S. Dollars	24.8	11.8

Note: The U.S. wholesale price index was used to deflate current dollar export receipts. In all cases the annual compounded growth rates are reported.

Source: Author's computations from Table 5 and from U.S. wholesale price information published in IMF, International Financial Statistics, various issues.

the share of industrialized products exports had grown to 51 percent of the total.

Within the industrialized exports category the fastest growing component has been manufactured exports. The real growth rate of manufactured exports, as calculated from constant U.S. dollars, was 14.5 percent annually for the 1974-1978 period, as compared to 4.3 percent for semimanufactured products. Brazilian manufactured exports cover an enormous variety of products, ranging from sewing machines to ready-made clothing, from processed vegetable oils to heavy armaments, and from canned hearts of palm to buses. Every Brazilian manufacturing industry classified at the two-digit commodity code level exports at least some of its output. Although no single product predominates in Brazilian manufactured exports, the most important export items include soluble coffee, shoes, office machines, spun cotton fibers, machinery, automotive products, metal products, and orange juice (Appendix Table 2).

Despite the very rapid expansion of manufacturing exports, especially during the late 1960s and early 1970s, exports remained small in proportion to total manufacturing output. In no industry, defined at an aggregate two digit level, did exports amount to more than 11 percent of output in 1971.[14] The proportion of exports in total manufacturing production for that year was still only 4 percent. The Brazilian Institute of Geography and Statistics (IBGE) industrial survey for 1974, the latest year for which information is available, indicates export sales for manufacturing amounting to 5 percent. Although the proportion of output exported is increasing for nearly all industries, the continued relatively small ratio indicates that manufactured exports in Brazil have not yet exercised a quantitatively important role in accounting for the expansion of total demand and output in the manufacturing sector.[15]

TABLE 5

BRAZILIAN EXPORTS FOR SELECTED PRODUCTS
AND PRODUCT GROUPS, 1964, 1974, AND 1978

Products and Product Groups	1964		1974		1978	
	U.S.$ Million	% of Total	U.S.$ Million	% of Total	U.S.$ Million	% of Total
PRIMARY PRODUCT EXPORTS	1,220.6	85.4	4,576.7	57.6	5,999.6	47.4
Meat and Meat Products	23.1	1.6	192.3	2.4	255.8	2.0
Coffee	759.9	53.2	980.4	12.3	2,294.7	18.1
Sugar and Sugar Products	33.1	2.3	1,385.8	17.4	395.9	3.1
Cocoa	45.8	3.2	326.5	4.1	750.5	5.9
Fruits and Fruit Products	24.0	1.7	134.9	1.7	453.2	3.6
Cane	2.9	0.2	139.0	1.8	2.2	0.0
Soybean and Soybean Paste	3.0	0.2	889.3	11.1	1,220.0	9.6
Tobacco	3.8	0.2	99.0	1.2	238.9	1.9
Cotton	109.8	7.7	92.4	1.1	53.5	0.4
Sisal	37.4	2.6	114.1	1.4	34.2	0.2
Iron Ore	80.6	5.6	571.1	7.1	1,027.7	8.1
INDUSTRIALIZED PRODUCT EXPORTS	204.5	14.3	3,179.7	40.0	6,504.0	51.4
Natural Fiber Textile Products	–	–	345.8	4.3	441.6	3.5
Metal Products	17.2	1.2	219.0	2.7	621.5	5.0
Machinery and Electrical Materials	10.8	0.8	454.6	5.7	1,091.0	8.6
Transportation Equipment and Materials	7.4	0.5	191.4	2.4	832.6	6.5
TOTAL EXPORTS	1,429.8	100.0	7,951.0	100.0	12,659.0	100.0

Source: Banco do Brasil, Comercio Exterior: Series Estatisticas, 1978
         and CIEF, Comercio Exterior, 1964.

III. BRAZILIAN EXPORT MARKETS AND EXPORTS
TO THE THIRD WORLD

Like the products Brazil exports, its export
markets are also increasingly diversified. During
1948-1964 the market destination of Brazilian exports,
along with their product composition and total amount,
underwent very little in the way of change. Beginning
in the mid-1960s with the initiation of the sustained
growth of exports, the market composition of Brazilian
exports began to change as well. Two features of this
change are especially noteworthy. First, the importance of the U.S. market for Brazilian exports as a
whole has been greatly reduced. Although a full
40 percent of Brazil's exports went to the United
States in 1960, the U.S. share had been reduced to
18 percent by 1973 (Table 6). Although Brazilian
exports to the United States again increased to
23 percent of total exports in 1978, there has nevertheless been a significant reduction of the Brazilian
dependence on U.S. markets during the last 10 years.
During the 1960s and early 1970s, the decrease in the
percentage of exports going to the United States was
partly offset by the growing importance of the European
Common Market countries and Japan as export markets for
Brazil. In 1960 the present EEC countries and Japan
accounted for 25 and 2 percent respectively of Brazil's
exports.[16] By 1973 these respective shares had grown
to 37 and 7 percent, but fell again during the
1973-1978 period.

The second discernible feature concerning Brazil's
changing export market composition is the increasing
importance of Third World markets. Until the
mid-1960s, Brazil exported very little to other
developing countries and of that amount, exports were
primarily to neighboring countries. The subsequent
growth and diversification of Brazil's exports,
assisted initially in part by the formation of the
Latin American Free Trade Association (LAFTA), has
brought about fundamental and important changes in its
international economic interactions. By 1973 exports
to Latin American countries accounted for 10 percent
of Brazil's total exports, and by 1978 the comparable
figure had grown to 14 percent (Table 6). In absolute
terms this growth in the relative importance of Latin
America as a market represented a current dollar export

TABLE 6

BRAZILIAN TRADE BY DESTINATION AND ORIGIN, 1973 AND 1978

(U.S. $ million FOB)

| | 1973 | | | | 1978 | | | |
| | EXPORTS | | IMPORTS | | EXPORTS | | IMPORTS | |
	U.S. $ million	% of Total	U.S. $ million	% of Total	U.S. $ million	% of Total	U.S. $ million	% of Total
INDUSTRIALIZED COUNTRIES								
United States	1,122	18.1	1,818	29.4	2,869	22.7	2,884	21.1
Canada	69	1.1	109	1.8	152	1.2	357	2.6
European Economic Community	2,297	37.1	1,766	28.5	3,735	29.5	2,517	18.5
W. Germany	555	9.0	812	13.1	1,062	8.4	1,106	8.1
Netherlands	621	10.0	150	2.4	783	6.2	196	1.4
European Free Trade Association Countries[1]	287	4.6	395	6.4	500	4.0	510	3.7
Other Western European Countries	365	5.9	136	2.2	509	4.0	146	1.1
Japan	425	6.9	492	7.9	650	5.1	1,242	9.1
Australia & New Zealand	21	0.3	16	0.3	74	0.6	101	0.7
South Africa	34	0.5	15	0.2	37	0.3	16	0.1
USSR	147	2.4	11	0.2	179	1.4	16	0.1
Eastern European Countries	192	3.1	76	1.2	550	4.3	174	1.3
SUBTOTAL	4,960	80.0	4,834	78.1	9,255	73.1	7,961	58.4
THIRD WORLD COUNTRIES								
Latin American Free Trade Association	557	9.0	557	9.0	1,619	12.8	1,424	10.4
Argentina	198	3.2	321	5.2	349	2.8	544	4.0
Bolivia	37	0.6	18	0.3	134	1.1	36	0.3
Chile	35	0.6	33	0.5	191	1.5	226	1.7
Mexico	50	0.8	52	0.8	178	1.4	196	1.4
Paraguay	61	1.0	23	0.4	224	1.8	47	0.3
Uruguay	40	0.6	16	0.3	133	1.1	130	1.0

TABLE 6 CONTINUED

| | 1973 | | | | 1978 | | | |
| | EXPORTS | | IMPORTS | | EXPORTS | | IMPORTS | |
	U.S.$ million	% of Total	U.S.$ million	% of Total	U.S.$ million	% of Total	U.S.$ million	% of Total
THIRD WORLD COUNTRIES Continued								
Venezuela	63	1.0	66	1.1	219	1.7	126	0.9
Other Latin American & Hemisphere Countries	77	1.2	71	1.1	167	1.3	102	0.7
OPEC²	160	2.6	574	9.3	686	5.4	3,854	28.3
Algeria	52	0.8	2	***	106	0.8	54	0.4
Saudi Arabia	1	***	265	4.3	357	2.8	3,663	26.9
Kuwait	1	***	67	1.1	14	***	473	3.5
Iran	55	0.9	38	0.6	121	1.0	519	3.8
Iraq	38	0.6	143	2.3	85	0.7	1,226	9.0
Libya	1	***	53	0.9	63	0.5	83	0.6
Nigeria	4	0.1	6	0.1	234	1.8	68	0.5
Other Middle Eastern Countries	77	1.2	13	0.2	99	0.8	14	0.1
Africa³	95	1.5	91	1.5	195	1.5	184	1.3
China	65	1.0	**	***	129	1.0	4	***
Other Asian Countries	164	2.6	49	0.8	250	2.0	90	0.7
India	7	0.1	1	***	111	0.9	4	***
Others	35	0.6	0	***	145	1.1	**	***
SUBTOTAL excluding OPEC	1,077	17.4	782	12.6	2,715	21.5	1,822	13.4
SUBTOTAL	1,237	20.0	1,356	21.9	3,401	26.9	5,676	41.6
TOTAL	6,197	100.0	6,190	100.0	12,656	100.0	13,637	100.0

Notes: [1] Includes Austria, Norway, Portugal, Sweden, and Switzerland.
[2] Excludes Venezuela and Equador.
[3] Excludes Algeria, Libya, Nigeria, and South Africa.
**Indicates less than U.S. $ 500,000.
***Indicates less than 0.05%.

Source: CACEX, Relatorio, 1977 and CACEX, Brasil: Comercio Exterior, 1978.

growth of 182 percent between 1973 and 1978. Imports from other Latin American countries, while roughly balancing exports, have grown less rapidly. As demonstrated in Table 6, within the Latin American area Brazilian trade with the LAFTA countries is most significant.

A regional bilateral trade balance is clearly not the case with the Middle Eastern and African OPEC countries. Brazil's imports from those countries have of course increased enormously with the oil price increases, and exports to those countries, although attaining impressive growth, still remain small in relation to either Brazil's total exports or its imports from the OPEC nations. By 1978 Brazilian exports to the OPEC countries amounted to $686 million, or 5 percent of Brazil's exports, as compared to $160 million in 1973.

Brazil's exports to other Third World countries, although still relatively small, have also increased rapidly in recent years. Non-OPEC African country markets have received much publicity and official attention in view of existing cultural ties especially after the independence of the former Portuguese colonies. Brazilian exports to these countries have grown along with the overall expansion of Brazilian trade. Exports to Asian countries, as a whole, excluding Japan and China, have grown less rapidly. The major individual country exception has been India, to which exports have grown rapidly to $111 million in 1978.

Taken as a whole, Brazilian exports to Third World markets totaled $3.4 billion in 1978, accounting for 27 percent of total exports (Table 6). Since the industrialized countries account for the remaining 73 percent of Brazil's exports, it is clear that the developed markets are by far the most important for Brazil in its international economic relations. Nevertheless, it is important not to understate the significance of the Third World in Brazil's trade relations. First, in absolute amounts the export revenues earned from exporting to the developing countries are large -- exceeding the total exports of all but a few developing countries. Second, the proportion of Brazil's exports going to Third World markets has been growing rapidly, increasing from

20 percent of the total in 1973 to 27 percent in 1978. Finally, the growth of the OPEC markets along with Brazil's increased dependence on imported petroleum has served to focus attention on those markets. This attention will continue to grow and may eventually result in bilateral trading agreements.

The products Brazil exports to Third World countries run the gamut of Brazil's export product composition.[17] One important generalization, however, can be made. Brazil's exports to the Third World are heavily concentrated in manufactured products, the category enjoying the fastest growth among its exports. A full 64 percent of those products exported to Third World markets in 1978 were manufactures. For the LAFTA country markets providing some preferential treatment for Brazilian exports, the comparable figure was even higher; 80 percent of LAFTA imports from Brazil consisted of manufactured products.

Reflecting this concentration of exports to Third World countries in manufactured products, these countries are disproportionately important as markets for Brazil's manufactured exports. In 1978, 43 percent of its exports of manufactured products went to developing countries (Table 7). For their part, the LAFTA countries were among the most important markets for Brazilian manufactured exports. In 1978, together they accounted for 25 percent of such exports.

Despite the growth in Brazilian exports since the mid-1960s, Brazil accounts for a minute part of total world trade; its exports in 1978 represented only 1 percent of total world exports. One should be very careful, however, in concluding that Brazil's role in the world economy is one of a minor participant unable to affect world trade patterns or influence international prices. For one thing few countries do have large shares of total world exports. Even the United States accounts for only about 14 percent of the total. Moreover, in some international product markets, such as those for coffee, soybeans, and cocoa, Brazil is an important supplier and exercises some influence in the market. Finally, all countries do not import goods from different countries in the same proportions. Brazil, for example, is an important supplier of imported goods for some countries, although its share in the total imports of others is negligible. Those

TABLE 7

BRAZIL'S MANUFACTURED EXPORTS BY MARKET DESTINATION, 1977-1978

	1977		1978	
	U.S. $ Millions	% of Manufactured Exports	U.S. $ Millions	% of Manufactured Exports
INDUSTRIALIZED COUNTRIES				
United States	1,032	26.9%	1,445	28.4%
Canada	106	2.8	108	2.1
European Economic Community	844	22.0	954	18.8
W. Germany	292	7.6	308	6.0
Netherlands	142	3.7	153	3.0
United Kingdom	199	5.2	264	5.2
European Free Trade Association Countries[1]	78	2.0	91	1.8
Other Western European Countries	60	1.6	65	1.3
Japan	94	2.4	103	2.0
Australia	24	0.6	60	1.2
South Africa	15	0.4	21	0.4
USSR	28	0.7	18	0.4
Eastern European Countries	82	2.1	55	1.0
SUBTOTAL	2,363	61.5	2,920	57.4
THIRD WORLD COUNTRIES				
Latin American Free Trade Association	973	25.3	1,289	25.3
Argentina	145	3.8	167	3.3
Bolivia	137	3.6	129	2.5
Chile	108	2.8	175	3.4
Colombia	53	1.4	107	2.1
Equador	21	0.5	43	0.9
Mexico	83	2.2	162	3.2
Paraguay	177	4.6	223	4.4

TABLE 7 CONTINUED

	1977		1978	
	U.S. $ Millions	% of Manufactured Exports	U.S. $ Millions	% of Manufactured Exports
THIRD WORLD COUNTRIES Continued				
Peru	48	1.2	33	0.6
Uruguay	67	1.7	74	1.5
Venezuela	135	3.5	174	3.4
Other Latin American & W. Hemisphere Countries	78	2.0	151	3.0
Asia & Middle East[2]	154	4.0	221	4.3
Taiwan	2	.0	6	0.1
Hong Kong	14	0.4	20	0.4
Israel	5	0.2	15	0.3
Pakistan	1	.0	2	.0
Africa[3]	260	6.8	493	10.1
Algeria	35	0.9	80	1.6
Morocco	3	.0	4	.0
Sudan	3	0.2	1	.0
Tunisia	5	0.2	2	.0
China	11	0.3	18	0.4
Others	1	.0	4	.0
SUBTOTAL	1,478	38.5	2,176	42.7
TOTAL	3,841	100.0	5,096	100.0

Notes: [1]Includes Australia, Norway, Portugal, Sweden and Switzerland.
[2]Except Japan and China.
[3]Except South Africa.

Source: CACEX, Brasil: Comercio Exterior, 1978.

countries where imports from Brazil are significant relative to total imports include, as to be expected, the neighboring countries with good communications systems with Brazil. In 1978, Paraguay purchased a full 20 percent of its imports from Brazil, while the comparable figures for Uruguay and Bolivia were 12 and 14 percent, respectively (Appendix Table 4). Although reflecting Brazil's competitiveness and influence in these countries, further export expansion there may very much depend upon the growth of those markets themselves. On the other hand, in markets where Brazil's share of total imports is very small, rapid increases in Brazilian exports may be easier to affect, depending upon the competitiveness of Brazilian goods in those markets.

Although Brazil's economic interactions with the Third World center on trade in commodities, an active trade in services is also developing. As a result of the industrialization of the Brazilian economy, a considerable stock of industrial know-how and technology has been acquired. Brazil is now taking advantage of this development to export industrial services to less technologically advanced countries. Frequently, the sale of Brazilian services abroad, mostly of a technical engineering variety, is accompanied by the export of Brazilian capital goods. The provision of these services, almost entirely focusing on Third World countries, has grown rapidly. In the past three years, Brazilian firms have been contracted to advise on and construct hydroelectric facilities (Paraguay, Venezuela, Algeria, Equador, Peru), highways (Mauritania, Saudi Arabia), port facilities (Uruguay), railways (Iraq), hotels (Iraq), low-cost housing (Algeria), sewage systems (Costa Rica, Libya), and telecommunications systems (Nigeria). Services for agro-industry projects have also been contracted with Nigeria, Costa Rica, and the Ivory Coast. These contracts, plus others under negociation with the assistance of the Brazilian Ministry of Foreign Relations, total $3.6 billion.[18]

IV. ECONOMIC POLICIES AFFECTING EXPORTS

The performance of Brazilian exports is closely linked to the administration of economic policies in Brazil. Of the various types of economic policies some are referred to as export promotional or export incentive policies. Other policies, undertaken for varying objectives, also affect export behavior, although frequently in a more indirect manner. Just as some economic policies can have the effect of expanding exports, others serve to retard export growth or even reduce exports. Of primary importance, however, is the net effect of the various policies on export performance.

Such policies are important because they affect the profitability of different productive activities in international markets. Exports will simply not take place unless they are profitable for producers. Facing international prices for their products, producers can only compete in world markets if they can match or better the prevailing international prices. Economic policies affect the domestic currency remuneration for exports and therefore profitability. Unless economic policy incentives are conducive to export profitability, no amount of promotional efforts or cajoling of potential exporters by government will be effective. Easing policy discrimination against exports and adjusting prices through the administration of appropriate economic policies is a necessary condition for exporting. Only then can export sales and promotional efforts on the part of the government be fully effective and successful. Even then their primary effects are to provide information about export opportunities and assure exporters that government policies undertaken in the future will not prejudice exporter interests.

In Brazil, beginning in the early 1960s, economic policymakers began to be more concerned about the export sector and its problems. The stagnation of exports and the exhaustion of the opportunities for continued import substitution led to a cautious reorientation of economic policies and the adoption of more outward looking policies. For the most part these policies simply reduced the discrimination against export activities by providing some specific incentives for exports, primarily for manufactured products. The growth of exports has been directly related to these economic policies. Even though considerable biases still exist against exports and in favor of production for the domestic market in many sectors of the economy, the reduction of these biases has been instrumental in expanding Brazilian exports.

One feature of Brazilian policies affecting export behavior is that, with two relatively minor exceptions, such policies are not product market or region specific. In other words, Brazil has done little to intentionally increase its exports to Third World countries vis-a-vis other countries. The incentives and policies affecting exports apply equally to exports to all country and regional markets. There is no discrimination with respect to markets, nor is there any apparent grand design on the part of Brazilian economic policymakers to increase exports to any particular region. What is prevalent is the desire to simply increase exports, taking into account, naturally, the fact that some countries may offer better market prospects than others.

The exceptions to the market uniformity of Brazilian policies affecting exports deal with sales and promotional efforts by the government and Brazilian participation in LAFTA. Beginning in the late 1960s the Brazilian government, mostly through the Ministry of Foreign Relations and the Banco do Brasil, has taken an increasingly active interest in helping Brazilian producers market their products abroad. These activities, to be discussed in some detail below, do not necessarily have to possess a country or regional export market concentration. In fact attention has been devoted to markets on a worldwide basis. Yet, to the extent that a bias in markets exists, particularly on the part of the Ministry of Foreign Relations, it is one toward providing proportionally more attention to Third World markets.

The Brazilian participation in LAFTA is a visible economic commitment to Latin America. After the establishment of LAFTA in the early 1960s and the extension of the relatively easy first concessions, there were substantial increases in Brazilian trade with Latin American countries. Moreover, the appearance of LAFTA and its early successes raised considerable expectations about future prospects and market potential. Yet these expectations, for the most part, were not realized. Trade liberalization within LAFTA broke down, and the LAFTA trade preferences remain small. Geographic and communications proximity may very well provide Brazil with a stronger advantage over imports from third countries in Brazil's neighboring countries than the LAFTA preferences.

Exchange Rate Policy

The Brazilian government has pursued an exchange rate policy to attain multiple economic objectives. Although industrial development and commercial policy considerations have at times been included, the administration of exchange rate policy has not in general been favorable to exporting activities. As of early December 1979, the prevailing exchange rate was heavily overvalued, as it had been more or less continuously in recent years, and as such it has discriminated against the export sector and against substituting sectors. Estimates vary as to the extent of the exchange rate overvaluation but are generally in the 25 to 35 percent range.[19] These are rather rough estimates, necessarily involving assumptions about capital flows, the measurement of protection, changes in other policies, tariff and trade restrictions external to Brazil, and price elasticities. What gives rise to the possibility of supporting an overvalued exchange rate is protection and other distortions and taxes affecting a country's trade. Attempts to estimate a shadow exchange rate are thus in fact attempts at measuring the distortions imposed by economic policies. In any case, the Brazilian exchange rate has been clearly overvalued.

Changes in exchange rate policy over time can affect the degree of overvaluation, as can changes in trade distortions or external prices. Until the adoption of the so-called mini-devaluation policy in 1968, there were substantial oscillations in the degree of exchange rate overvaluation, as reflected through movements in the real exchange rate.[20] These fluctuations in real local currency remuneration for exports were decidedly prejudicial for developing Brazilian exports, as a large degree of uncertainty was apparent for exporters. Since the establishment of the mini-devaluation policy, however, there has been little change in the administration of exchange rate policy. The expressed government policy has been to devalue the currency regularly in general accordance with domestic inflation and inflation in Brazil's major trading partners. The objective has been to maintain the real purchasing power parity for the currency.

Table 8, presenting information on Brazil's exchange rate movements, indicates that the real exchange rate, reflecting the nominal exchange rate adjusted for domestic and international inflation, did not undergo substantial change from 1973 until December 1979. There was a slight real depreciation of the cruzeiro in terms of other currencies. Yet, when an adjustment is made for the deteriorated terms of trade, reflecting mainly the petroleum price increases for Brazil, it is apparent that there was a slight appreciation. In other words, although the real value of the currency has not changed appreciably, the nominal exchange rate had become slightly more overvalued. Yet these changes are minor, and, as such, changes in exchange rate policy in recent years, until December 1979, have not been significant in altering the profitability and competitiveness of Brazilian manufactured exports. With the 30 percent nominal devaluation of December 1979, the future directions of Brazilian exchange rate policy have become unclear. If a real depreciation of 30 percent is in fact effected, Brazilian competitiveness in international markets will have been increased.

Import Restrictions

The existence of import restrictions affects exports and export behavior in two basic ways. First, the existence of a domestic market protected by import restrictions means that prices will be higher in the domestic market than abroad. It therefore becomes more profitable in the absence of other measures to produce for the domestic market than for exports. Economic resources are thus pulled into those sectors receiving protection from import competition and out of export activities.

TABLE 8

PURCHASING POWER PARITY EXCHANGE RATE MOVEMENTS, 1973-1979

Year	Nominal Exchange Rate (CR$/U.S.$)	Real Exchange Rate[1] (in constant terms of 1973)	Barter Terms of Trade Index (1973=100)	Real Exchange Rate Adjusted for Changes in the Terms of Trade
1973	6.126	6.126	100.0	6.126
1974	6.790	6.328	81.8	5.176
1975	8.126	6.309	79.4	5.009
1976	10.670	6.554	88.8	5.820
1977	14.138	6.707	104.3	6.995
1978	18.063	6.655	91.4	6.083
1979[2]	26.300	6.939	84.6	5.870

Notes: [1]Nominal exchange rate deflated by the Brazilian wholesale industrial price index and adjusted for inflation in Brazil's leading 11 trading partners with convertible currencies.

[2]Preliminary estimates as of November 1979. These figures do not reflect the 30 percent maxi-devaluation of 7 December 1979.

Sources: IPLAN/IPEA, "Consideracoes a Politica Cambial Brazileira Pos-1973," unpublished paper, November 1979.

Export activities are further hindered by the price raising effects that protection may have on their intermediate inputs. Protection is rarely selective, and attempts to import substitutes in the intermediate goods industries through import restrictions will have the effect of raising the production costs of all user industries. If the protection provided for the domestic production of intermediate inputs is great, the discrimination against exporters using those inputs can be substantial. Protection from imports of finished products for the inputs using industries, while helping in the domestic market, will be of no avail in international markets. Other economic policy instruments must be used to provide offsetting incentives to restore competitiveness and export profitability.

Throughout the postwar period in Brazil the industrial sector has received generous tariff protection. Yet in the late 1960s some liberalization of import restrictions was observed. In 1965 and 1966 considerable import liberalization occurred through changes in the then prevailing exchange premium system. In March 1967 a commercial policy reform was instituted with large tariff reductions and the abolition of a special, and highly restrictive, category for imports. As a result, the average tariff for manufacturing products fell from 99 percent in June 1966 to 48 percent in April 1967.[21] The import liberalization, intensified by a real appreciation of the cruzeiro, proved to be politically unsustainable, however, and tariffs were revised upward. By December 1969 the average tariff for manufacturing was back up to 66 percent. Subsequent piecemeal reductions brought the level to 59 percent by November 1973.[22]

The general easing downward of tariff levels was also accompanied by a liberalization and increase of the tariff exemptions granted to importers under government industrial incentive programs. Especially favored under the tariff exemption schemes were machinery and other capital goods. Reflecting the increased importance of the various tariff exemption programs, the realized tariff rate, i.e., actual tariff collections divided by total imports, fell from 12 percent in 1969 to 7 percent in 1974. The effect of these cautious import liberalization measures was to reduce the bias against export production in the industrial economy, and as a result exports increased markedly.

The pendulum, however, was about to swing back the other way. As has been referred to earlier, tariff levels were increased sharply in the mid-1970s as a response to balance of payments pressures brought on in great part by the petroleum price increases. The increase in tariff levels is demonstrated in Table 9. The simple average of all items in the Brazilian tariff schedule rose from 55 percent in 1971 to 82 percent in 1977 -- a 50 percent increase. Compounding the protective effect of the tariff increases were a number of nontariff import restrictions, briefly described earlier. The system of advance deposits for imports, direct controls on import purchases of government firms, and a tightening up of the tariff exemptions and reductions under industrial incentive programs all had the effect of increasing import restrictions and the protection for domestic production from imports. Since there was no appreciable change in the export incentives during the 1974-1978 period, the profitability of production for the domestic market increased vis-a-vis that for the export market. Consequently, the increase in import restrictions served to draw marginal economic resources out of export activities in favor of the domestic market. Thus, in part, the slower growth of Brazilian exports during the 1974-1978 period can be attributed to the increase in import restrictions, a measure that served to brake the rapid export growth of the 1965-1974 period.

In addition to the allocational, resource pull effect of the increase in import restrictions, export growth was also dampened by the increase in costs because of increased protection for Brazilian industries producing intermediate goods. Beginning in 1975 a major government effort was initiated to import substitutes in the capital goods and basic inputs industries. In addition to massive credits to those industries at highly subsidized interest rates, greater protection from import competition was also provided through more traditional commercial policy instruments. The tightening up in tariff exemptions was felt most for capital goods and intermediate product imports, thus serving to increase protection for those products made in Brazil. Moreover, as seen in Table 9, considerable tariff increases were granted for raw

TABLE 9

NOMINAL LEGAL TARIFF RATES[1] BY PRODUCT GROUP
1971, 1975, and 1977

(in percentages)

PRODUCT GROUP	1971	1975	1977
Nondurable Consumer Goods	109.0%	96.0%	134.0%
Durable Consumer Goods	108.0	112.0	146.0
Combustible and Lubricants	14.0	16.0	61.0
Raw Materials and Intermediate Products for Agriculture	9.0	16.0	19.0
Raw Materials and Intermediate Products for Industry	34.0	44.0	63.0
Construction Materials	54.0	66.0	86.0
Capital Goods for Agriculture	36.0	32.0	38.0
Capital Goods for Industry	35.0	40.0	55.0
Parts and Transportation Equipment	37.0	55.0	83.0
TOTAL	54.7	58.1	81.6

Note: [1]Calculated as a simple average over all items listed in the tariff manual.

Source: Joal de Azambuja et al., "Alguns Aspectos da Politica Tarifaria Recente", Fundacao Centro de Estudos do Comercio Exterior, unpublished paper, November 1979, pp. 19-20.

365

materials, intermediate goods, and capital goods between 1973 and 1978.

Fiscal Incentives

The most significant, as well as best known, direct incentives for export in Brazil are the fiscal incentives. Coming into existence in the mid and late 1960s and remaining essentially unchanged until December 1979, the fiscal incentives for export have included: (1) exemption from the Imposto Sobre Produtos Industrializadas (IPI) federal industrial product tax on exports; (2) a tax credit based upon the IPI for exported products; (3) exemption from the Imposto de Circulacao de Mercadorias (ICM) state taxes on exports; (4) a tax credit based on the ICM for exports; (5) an income tax exemption for profits earned from exports; (6) exemption from the payment of various minor taxes for exported products; and (7) drawback provisions allowing duty free import of materials used to produce finished export products. With the exception of the drawback incentives, the receipt of the fiscal incentives for an exporting firm is automatic. There is no room under the regulations for a discretionary awarding of the fiscal incentives on a case by case basis. All firms exporting manufactured products receive the fiscal incentives regardless of export destination.

Although formally a value of product tax, the IPI in effect operates as a tax on value, added because of the allowance of tax credits for taxes paid on inputs purchased by the firms. The IPI export incentives are based upon the IPI tax rates that vary by product. Since agricultural products are not subject to the IPI, in effect only manufactured exports can receive the IPI export incentives. In addition, some products are not covered, e.g., soybean oils; thus the failure to exempt these exports from the payment of the IPI constitutes the administration of an export tax. Although the IPI tax rate averages around 10 percent for the entire manufacturing sector, the variation over products is considerable. In general, the more heavily a product is taxed by the IPI in the internal market, up to a limit, the greater are its IPI fiscal incentives if it is exported.

It has been the tax credit mechanism in the IPI export incentives that incorporates the subsidy element of the IPI incentives. The mere exemption of the IPI for exported products is not an export subsidy according to GATT provisions. The tax credit component of the IPI does constitute a pure subsidy, however. The subsidy can range up to 15 percent of the value of tax product exported.[23]

The ICM export incentives are quite similar to those involving the IPI. Payment of the ICM is exempted for manufactured product exports. This tax varies from state to state but is currently set at a uniform 14 percent in the more developed South-Central states. As is the case with the IPI incentives, it is only the tax credit arrangement that constitutes a pure export subsidy. The combined fiscal subsidy for exports for the IPI and ICM subsidy mechanisms ranged from -7.9 percent (an export tax) to 35.5 percent in 1977 (Table 10). Although the products of many industries fall in the 20-30 percent range, the 1977 mean for manufacturing, weighted by 1970 value added, was 18.8 percent in nominal value of product terms.[24]

In January 1979 the Brazilian government announced that the IPI and ICM fiscal subsidies for export would be phased out over a five year period with uniform reductions occurring annually. Except in a couple of cases, these subsidies have not been of sufficient magnitude to offset even the discrimination against Brazilian exporters because of exchange rate overvaluation. Yet, because of its export successes Brazil was increasingly subjected to complaints about the subsidies and to countervailing duty actions by the developed countries. These pressures were in part responsible for the decision to phase out the fiscal subsidies. To compensate for the reduction of local currency remuneration for exports because of the elimination of the fiscal subsidies, the Brazilian authorities also announced in January 1979 that the cruzeiro would be depreciated in real terms by 4.5 percent annually for the next five years on a pari passu basis with the phasing out of the fiscal subsidies. The December 1979 economic policy reforms have eliminated the gradual phasing out of the fiscal subsidies with an immediate one step removal accompanying the compensatory devaluation. Because of the inequality of the fiscal subsidies, the main beneficiaries from these favorable policy changes will be those industries receiving the smaller subsidies. Agricultural exports and food product exports particularly will benefit. Conversely, one might expect relatively slower export growth in the future of those products with the higher fiscal subsidies. Disproportionately large amounts of these products in the past have gone to Latin American and other Third World markets.

A third category of fiscal incentives for manufactured exports is the income tax exemption for export sales. Dating back to 1967, this incentive stipulates that the portion of a firm's profits earned through exports of manufactured goods is not subject to the business income tax. In actual practice this has meant that a firm is allowed to deduct from its taxable income an amount of its total profits proportional to the amount of its total sales from exports. This particular provision in the tax laws is subject to periodic renewal with the next renewal decision to be made in 1980. In addition, an exporter is allowed to deduct promotional expenses abroad and the costs connected with the firm's overseas sales operation. As a whole, the nominal effect of the income tax incentives for export, seen on a value of product basis, is rather small. In very few industries do the income tax incentives represent more than 2 percent of the value of the products exported (Table 10). The 1977 manufacturing average, again weighted by value added, was 1 percent.

There are several other miscellaneous tax exemption incentives for manufactured exports in Brazil, the total magnitude of which is quite small. These incentives involve the exemption of various taxes where manufactured exports are concerned. Among the taxes exempted for manufactured exports are a financial operations tax, a tax on exchange operations, taxes for export credit insurance and transportation insurance, the tax on combustible materials, a fee for port improvement, and a fee for the renovation of the merchant marine. These fees and minor taxes were more of a nuisance than anything else, and their exemption for manufactured exports primarily represents an attempt of the government to simplify export procedures and generate exporter good will.

TABLE 10

NOMINAL TARIFF PROTECTION AND EXPORT SUBSIDIES BY INDUSTRY, 1977

	Nominal Tariff Protection		Nominal Export Subsidies			
	Legal Rate[1] (%)	Realized Rate[2] (%)	Fiscal IPI & ICM Subsidies (%)	Income Tax Incentives (%)	Credit Subsidies (%)	Total (%)
Mining	4.0	16.0	- 7.7	5.4	0.0	- 2.3
Extraction of Combustible Minerals	1.0	0.0	0.0	0.0	0.0	0.0
Cement	35.0	8.9	16.2	2.2	7.6	26.0
Glass & Glass Products	96.0	39.6	18.9	1.4	6.4	26.8
Other Nonmetallic Mineral Products	75.0	47.0	15.8	0.8	6.0	22.7
Cast Iron and Basic Steel	24.0	40.6	13.7	2.3	5.6	21.6
Rolled Steel	26.0	21.3	25.0	0.9	4.0	30.0
Steel and Iron Foundry Products	78.1	20.8	20.0	1.2	2.8	24.0
Nonferrous Metals	20.0	21.4	8.3	0.5	2.4	11.3
Other Metals Products	53.0	37.1	22.5	1.7	4.6	29.0
Pumps & Motors	52.0	26.7	25.9	0.8	3.4	30.0
Machine Parts	47.0	52.3	26.8	0.9	4.8	32.4
Industrial Equipment & Machinery	39.0	33.0	24.1	1.5	7.7	30.4
Agricultural Equipment & Machinery	28.0	25.1	16.2	1.4	4.1	21.8
Office & Domestic Equipment & Machinery	67.0	28.6	27.9	1.6	4.9	24.3
Tractors	28.0	30.1	23.4	0.2	2.6	26.7
Equipment for Electric Energy	73.0	44.8	20.0	0.7	8.7	29.3
Electrical Conductors	67.0	36.1	20.0	1.7	7.0	28.7
Electrical Equipment	62.0	54.9	20.5	1.2	4.4	26.0
Electrical Machinery	27.0	26.9	25.2	0.3	3.7	29.2
Electronic Equipment	47.0	25.5	20.7	0.6	3.9	25.1
Communications Equipment	86.0	52.2	26.1	0.3	5.4	32.0
Automobiles	112.0	5.7	26.0	1.0	5.4	32.5
Trucks and Buses	31.0	33.6	26.3	0.4	4.6	31.3
Motors and Vehicle Parts	91.0	22.0	25.9	1.2	3.8	30.9
Shipbuilding	9.0	21.3	24.0	1.1	8.7	32.8
Railway & Aircraft Equipment	42.0	24.6	24.4	2.1	5.7	32.3
Lumber & Wood Products	140.0	8.1	10.1	1.0	1.5	12.6
Furniture	83.0	11.4	28.0	1.0	9.0	38.1

TABLE 10 CONTINUED

	Nominal Tariff Protection		Nominal Export Subsidies			
	Legal Rate (%)	Realized Rate[2] (%)	Fiscal IPI & ICM Subsidies (%)	Income Tax Incentives (%)	Credit Subsidies (%)	Total (%)
Pulp Products	20.0	21.8	0.0	0.0	6.2	6.2
Paper and Paper Board	25.0	24.1	26.1	0.9	7.2	35.3
Paper Products	84.0	71.9	27.6	0.3	7.0	34.9
Rubber	98.0	66.8	27.7	1.7	2.1	31.4
Leather Products	155.0	28.4	9.1	0.7	1.4	11.2
Chemical Products	18.0	33.9	8.0	2.6	4.8	15.3
Petroleum Refining	7.0	17.9	2.1	1.4	0.0	3.9
Coal Products	19.0	1.4	0.0	0.0	0.0	0.0
Resins and Synthetic Fibers	42.0	19.8	25.2	4.7	4.6	30.1
Vegetable Oils	64.0	8.0	8.0	3.9	3.9	4.0
Paints and Varnishes	54.0	19.1	15.3	4.4	4.4	20.6
Miscellaneous Chemical Products	20.0	4.6	17.0	3.6	3.6	21.9
Pharmaceutical Products	18.0	17.2	7.5	6.2	6.2	14.5
Perfumery and Soaps	55.0	20.9	21.5	4.4	4.4	26.0
Plastics	122.0	60.7	25.2	3.7	3.7	29.9
Natural Fiber Preparations	53.0	9.0	8.2	1.5	1.6	11.2
Synthetic Fiber Textile Mill Products	63.0	15.6	35.5	4.1	4.1	41.0
Natural Fiber Textile Mill Products	184.0	35.6	31.6	6.4	6.4	39.3
Other Textile Products, Inc. Knitting	64.0	26.5	31.5	9.4	6.4	42.1
Apparel	176.0	12.6	27.8	8.3	8.3	37.5
Footwear	170.0	37.3	12.0	9.4	9.4	23.0
Food Products	55.0	1.5	6.1	3.1	3.1	10.1
Sugar Refining	84.0	0.0	5.0	0.0	0.0	5.7
Refined Vegetable Oil Products	65.0	22.3	6.3	13.7	13.7	20.1
Other Food Products	115.0	15.1	21.2	2.7	2.7	25.2
Beverages	187.0	80.0	25.1	5.6	3.7	31.4
Tobacco	154.0	63.6	- 5.3	4.1	0.0	- 1.2
Printing & Publishing	5.0	5.1	20.2	5.5	0.4	26.1
Miscellaneous Manufacturing	42.0	15.1	22.1	1.3	1.3	28.9
Manufacturing Average[3]	67.9	33.3	18.6	1.1	5.0	24.8

TABLE 10 CONTINUED

[1] Import weighted averages.

[2] The realized tariff rate is equal to the tariff collection divided by the CIF value of imports. In their case it also includes the realized import deposit tariff equivalents.

[3] Value added weights from the 1970 input-output table were used.

Source: FUNCEX Materials. Jose Augusto Arantes Savasini et al., "Acompanhamento da Quantificacao da Estrutura de Incentivos as Exportacoes: Efeitos da Politica Protecionista Apos 1975," Fundacao Centro de Estudos do Comercio Exterior, unpublished paper, 1979, p. 9, and Joal de Azambuja Rosa et al., "Alguns Aspectos da Politica Tarifaria Recente," Fundacao Centro de Estudos do Comercio Exterior, unpublished paper, November 1979, p. 92.

Another, and more important, fiscal incentive for exports is the drawback provision, which for Brazil dates back to the early 1960s. The idea of the drawback is to permit the duty free importation of materials used in the manufacturing of export products. Essentially it is an exemption or rebate for tariffs and other import restrictions to allow the export producer to obtain his tradable inputs at world prices instead of the higher domestic prices brought about through protection for the intermediate goods industries. By effectively establishing a free trade regime for export production, a functioning drawback system short circuits the discrimination against exports from protective commercial policy. As such, in a heavily protected economic environment, a drawback scheme can constitute a very important export promotional instrument. Without drawbacks, the exports of some finished goods for many developing countries would not be possible. If an overvalued exchange rate is part of the economic policy environment, as is generally true in developing countries with protective commercial policies, the ability of a firm to purchase imported inputs duty free at the overvalued official exchange rate seems to be a subsidy element.

The functioning of the Brazilian drawback system, applicable for all manufactured exports, operates through the suspension of import duties and other border taxes on inputs. Unlike the experience with the drawback in some countries, there are few complaints about the actual administration of the Brazilian drawback.[25] The approval process is routine and practically automatic. Although there are some minor complaints by exporters about the red tape, the system is evidently run honestly and reasonably efficiently.

With the apparent increase in protection for intermediate products in recent years, the drawback system becomes more important as a mechanism to assure the continued competitiveness of Brazilian manufactured exports. Accordingly, one might expect a relative increase in inputs brought into the country under the drawback system. That evidently has not occurred. Such imports amounted to 16.4 percent of total manufactured exports in 1973, but by 1978 the comparable figure had fallen to 12.8 percent.[26] In any case, the drawback system remains an important instrument in Brazilian export promotion policies.[27]

Related to the drawback scheme are two other formalized mechanisms permitting the nonpayment of import duties for export production. These are the Special Export Programs, namely the BEFIEX (Comissao para Concessao de Beneficios Fiscais e Programas Especiais de Exportacao) and the CIEX (Comissao de Incentivos as Exportacoes). Under the BEFIEX system a firm can submit a project for approval to the Commission, which is administered by the Ministry of Industry and Commerce with the collaboration of other government agencies. The projects must include long run plans (usually 10 years) committing the applying firm to a certain amount of exports. If approved, a project can benefit from some income tax advantages but, most importantly, from import tax reductions of 70 to 90 percent for imported capital goods and up to 50 percent for all imported inputs.

Initiated in late 1972, the BEFIEX program is beginning to show important export results undertaken under its aegis.[28] Table 11 demonstrates the growth of exports undertaken with BEFIEX incentives. By 1978 such exports had grown to over $1 billion, an amount equal to 20 percent of Brazil's manufactured exports or 8 percent of its total exports. Although it is true that some of these exports, perhaps most of them, would have taken place without the BEFIEX program, BEFIEX incentives have been significant in stimulating exports. To date most of the projects approved under the program have been concentrated in the automotive industry and, accordingly, have involved foreign firms.[29]

The de facto emphasis of the BEFIEX program on large projects led to the establishment of the CIEX program, as it is now administered, in 1976. The CIEX, operating through the Ministry of Finance, can reduce tariffs and border taxes up to 90 percent for capital goods imports for firms that have an export plan and are willing to assume an export commitment. The project approval process for CIEX is less elaborate than that for the BEFIEX program and is designed primarily for small projects. There are more stringent restrictions on the capital goods imported under the CIEX program; they must be new and not be available from Brazilian producers. These restrictions, along with the availability of similar incentives through other official industrial investment incentive schemes,

TABLE 11

BEFIEX PROGRAM EXPORTS, 1972-1978

Year	(1) BEFIEX Program Exports (U.S. $ millions)	(2) Manufactured Exports (U.S. $ millions)	(3) Total Exports (U.S. $ millions)	Ratio of BEFIEX Program Exports to Total Manu- factured Exports	Ratio of BEFIEX Program Exports to Total Exports
1972	2	898	3,991	0.3	0.1
1973	70	1,434	6,199	4.9	1.1
1974	214	2,263	7,951	9.5	2.7
1975	368	2,585	8,670	14.2	4.2
1976	492	2,776	10,128	12.7	4.9
1977	708	3,845	12,139	18.4	5.8
1978	1,015	5,083	12,659	20.0	8.0

Source: CACEX data and Conselho de Desenvolvimento Industrial, Relatorio de Atividades, various years.

374

have kept the CIEX program relatively small. From the beginning of the CIEX program in 1976 through 1978, 39 projects were approved amounting to $19 million of imports in return for commitments to export $268 million over the next four years. With the economic policy reforms of December 1979, the government announced its intention to consolidate CIEX into BEFIEX's administrative framework.

Credit Incentives

In Brazil two major types of official financing for exports are credit for export sales and financing for export production. Both types of credit, along with a few others of lesser magnitude, are administered through the Foreign Trade Department (CACEX, or Carteira de Comerio Exterior) of the Banco do Brasil through a facility called FINEX (Fundo de Financiamento a Exportacao). In all cases, the origin of these funds is the Brazilian Central Bank or Central Bank mandates.

In the mid-1960s direct financing for Brazilian export sales was begun for selected manufactured products in an attempt to make such exports competitive in international markets. Following the practices of other exporting countries, credits were made available for the export sales of Brazilian capital goods and some durable consumer goods. Under current arrangements CACEX can finance, through the FINEX facility, up to 85 percent of the FOB value of exports in dollars at an interest rate of between 7 and 8.5 percent annually. These rates of interest are slightly less than those prevailing for official suppliers' credits from most industrialized countries. The permitted maturities range from five years to eight to ten years depending upon the size and type of transaction, with large capital goods exports receiving the most privileged terms.

The official direct financing of export sales has grown steadily from $8 million in 1969 to $424 million for the first ten months of 1978. As is shown in Table 12, about one half of all the official export credits extended have gone for transportation equipment. Reflecting the concentration of Brazil's exports of transportation equipment, capital goods, and durable

TABLE 12

DIRECT EXPORT FINANCING PROVIDED BY FINEX, 1974-1978

(U.S. $ millions)

Sector	1974	1975	1976	1977	1978[1]
Power, Telecommunications	-	-	-	41.7	36.3
Food Processing	11.0	11.2	6.6	17.8	34.0
Construction	11.4	41.6	30.1	36.3	28.2
Paper	2.9	-	5.4	12.1	0.9
Leather, Plastics	-	-	-	-	1.7
Metal Products	-	-	-	-	1.3
Transportation Equipment	41.1	124.9	136.1	198.7	167.7
Machinery	-	4.1	-	13.4	4.2
Food Products	-	-	13.6	19.1	5.5
Textiles	-	-	-	-	4.0
Wood Products	-	-	-	-	1.2
Aircraft	-	6.4	-	-	18.3
Refrigeration Equipment	-	-	-	-	0.9
Other Industries	-	16.5	19.9	7.6	31.1
Miscellaneous	24.1	31.9	60.2	28.8	10.0
TOTAL	90.5	236.6	271.9	375.5	345.3

[1]First eight months of 1978 only.

Source: CACEX.

consumer goods to Third World markets, it is not surprising to learn that most of Brazil's long-term export sales credits involved exports to developing countries. In 1978 Bolivia, Algeria, and Chile alone accounted for 16, 13, and 11 percent, respectively, of financed exports.

An extension of the system for financing export sales was established in the end of 1978. Sometimes referred to as FINEX II, these arrangements permit an exporter to secure privileged credit terms through the commercial banking system. Borrowing is undertaken at a commercial rate of interest, and the difference between the commercial and official rates of interest (i.e., the subsidy) is provided by the Banco do Brasil through a discounting operation. CACEX in effect guarantees the equalization of the commercial and official rates of interest for an exporter to finance his sales abroad. To date (November 1979) there has been little experience and use of this facility. Presumably, it will most benefit Brazilian exports to Third World markets.

The availability of official, i.e., subsidized, credits for financing export production concentrates in providing working capital to exporting firms and dates back to 1971. Under this system -- now called the Central Bank Resolution 398 system -- credits are provided through the commercial banking system in local currency for a one year period. Since the nominal interest rate for these credits is currently set at 8 percent per annum, the subsidy element is considerable, with nominal market interest rates in 1979, reflecting the inflation rate, running about 55-60 percent. Moreover, with an acceleration of the rate of inflation, such as has been experienced in Brazil during the past few years, the subsidy element becomes greater still. With such heavily negative interest rates the rationing of credit to potential borrowers becomes important in the commercial banks. Although there are restrictions on eligibility for credits according to the value of exports and export increases, the demand for the subsidized Resolution 398 credits far exceeds the available supply.

In part to further stimulate exports at a time when fiscal export subsidies are being eliminated, the Brazilian government has recently substantially

377

increased the pool of funds available to the commercial banks for lending. During 1979 the total credit available grew to CR $50 billion (approximately U.S. $1.7 billion).[30] Although current government plans are to keep expanding these credits, the subsidy element will probably be reduced through an increase in the effective cost of credit for borrowers.

The credit subsidies for exports, in view of their magnitude, have been quantitatively significant, and the immediate prospects are that they will become still more important as an export promotional device for Brazil. In 1977 the average nominal credit subsidy, expressed as a percentage of export FOB values, was 5.0 percent for the manufacturing sector (Table 10). Yet, the variance over industries was very great. Some industries, such as refined vegetable oils, shoes, and furniture, received relatively high credit subsidies for export, while the credit subsidies for others was quite small, e.g., wood products and leather. There appears to be no economic rationale for such differences. Furthermore, it appears that there is little consistency from year to year on credit subsidies received by different industries. One can only surmize that the variance of the credit subsidies over exporting firms is also very high. This is evident from the way in which the Resolution 398 credits are rationed by the commercial banks among firms. Small firms, to be sure, are at a disadvantage in receiving the subsidized credits.

Government Promotional and Export Marketing Efforts

Key elements in any attempt to expand exports are information about export marketing possibilities and the overall support of the government for export activities. In recent years the Brazilian government has done much to assist producers exporting abroad and, in doing so, has increased the confidence of the business sector in government policies affecting exports.

The export promotional activities of the Brazilian government, although perhaps not striking in comparison to those of other industrial countries, are in marked contrast to the past activities of the Brazilian government. During the 1950s and early 1960s discrimination against exports through economic policies was great.[31] Prior to the mid-1960s the prevailing philosophy appears to have been that exports were necessary but basically prejudicial to the national interest, to be controlled and regulated rather than promoted. According to many exporting firms interviewed, exporters were frequently viewed by the government with suspicion and mistrust. Fortunately for Brazil, this attitude has changed. Export procedures, once a labyrinth of redtape, have been drastically simplified, and the government has been increasingly engaged in export promotional activities.

Within the government the primary operational responsibility for promotional activities and exporter assistance is divided between CACEX and the Ministry of Foreign Relations (Itamarati), with CACEX ostensibly responsible for activities within Brazil and Itamarati responsible for handling promotional activities abroad. In practice the spheres of responsibility are not well defined, and there exists considerable overlap, organizational jealousy, and even conflict between the two institutions. To provide a greater amount of coordination the National Council of Foreign Trade (CONCEX) was reorganized and given new powers in September 1979. Its new role, however, is not yet clear.[32]

CACEX has greatly expanded its own activities to promote exports. It organizes seminars, conferences, and trade expositions in Brazil and works on a day to day basis with exporting firms. There is a special office within CACEX for export promotion that publishes widely disseminated export opportunity information and frequently serves as an advocate in resolving the individual problems of exporting firms. In addition, CACEX is active abroad through some 52 agencies of the Banco do Brasil scattered throughout the world but concentrated in developed countries.

The trade and export promotion activities of Itamarati possess more of a Third World orientation. Although it has very effectively organized trade firms and trade missions all over the world, Third World countries have received disproportionate attention. Itamarati has patiently and conscientiously sought export opportunities in the developing country markets.

There seems to be a special interest on the part of Itamarati, related to overall Brazilian foreign policy, to extend Brazilian influence in the Third World through an increase in Brazilian exports to those countries. This has been the case for Latin America, where Itamarati has been one of the major Brazilian institutional supporters of LAFTA, and it is increasingly true for the Middle East in response to Brazil's dependence on imported petroleum. In its dealings with prospective importers, Itamarati has frequently assumed the posture of an intermediary. For example, in many of the recent arms sales to developing countries Itamarati has fulfilled an important negotiating role.

The element of confidence in government policy for the exporter or potential exporter is crucial. A major risk in export activities is that government policies will change and export profitability will be adversely affected. Investment decisions depend greatly upon profit expectations, and to invest for export production is especially risky if there is great uncertainty as to future profitability. To reduce uncertainty the government must convince exporters that policies will not be capricious. Exporters must be confident that the government has their interests at heart, reflecting the overall public interest in expanding exports.

Numerous moves by the Brazilian government have served to bolster exporter confidence since the mid-1960s: policies more conducive to exports were implemented and the policy bias against exports was reduced. At one point in the early 1970s the government adopted the slogan "To Export is the Solution." In recent years, however, the rhetoric has grown stale and various economic policies have been undertaken prejudicial to export activities. With the announcement in January 1979 of the gradual phasing out of the fiscal export subsidies, uncertainty among exporters has increased. A greater public relations effort on the part of the government, accompanied by economic policies fostering export growth, appears to be in order.

The Net Effect of Economic Policies

All of the policy measures described above have affected Brazilian exports, as has been demonstrated both through econometric analysis and interviews with exporting firms.[33] The question raised here is to what extent there exists discrimination against export activities as a result of various economic policies. Do existing economic policies favor production for the domestic or for the export market? To the extent that the prevailing policy incentives for domestic market production exceed those for export production there does exist an antiexport bias in economic policies.

The first question is whether or not export subsidies have been sufficient to offset the discrimination against exports resulting from an overvalued exchange rate. The answer is that for the most part they have not. This can be demonstrated by comparing the estimated exchange rate overvaluation, at approximately 30 percent, with the nominal export subsidies presented in Table 10. The average nominal export subsidy for the manufacturing sector in 1977, calculated with value-added weights, was 24.8 percent -- less than the approximate 30 percent exchange rate overvaluation. Looking at individual manufacturing industries, it is apparent that in only 19 out of 58 industries did the combined nominal export subsidies exceed 30 percent. In the remaining industries -- the majority -- there was apparent net discrimination against exports as a result of the exchange rate overvaluation. Moreover, the antiexport discrimination is understated because it does not include the cost raising effects of protection for input supplying industries. The incorporation of effects of protection on inputs would imply that even larger export subsidies would be required to offset the discrimination against exports coming from exchange rate policy and commercial policy.

The discrimination against exports is even more striking for the agricultural sector. Unlike manufacturing industries as presented in Table 10, agricultural activities do not receive subsidies for export. In fact they are all subject to export taxation, deriving de facto from the nonexemption of the ICM for exports and the existence of elaborate export taxation schemes for some products such as coffee. Export taxes have become quite explicit with the December 1979 economic policy package. Immediate export taxes of 30 percent, exactly matching the 30 percent devaluation, were announced for some 75 primary products. To curtail immediate domestic price increases, the government has indicated that these export taxes will be phased out in a relatively short period of time. Consequently, with an effective, real devaluation the predictable result, barring harvest failures, is that Brazilian agricultural exports will increase markedly in the next few years.

The discrimination against exports can also be seen through a comparison of the protection afforded to production for the domestic market and the subsidization provided to export production.[34] If domestic market protection exceeds nominal export subsidization, the incentives imply greater profitability for domestic market production. Accordingly there is an antiexport bias.[35]

For the Brazilian case, suggestive evidence is again provided in Table 10. Using value-added weights, the average full legal tariff for manufacturing in 1977 was 67.9 percent. Comparing this figure with the average nominal export subsidy of 24.8 percent, it appears that a substantial antiexport bias exists. The antiexport bias is apparent in 52 out of 57 manufacturing industries.[36] It can be argued that the full legal tariffs overstate protection in the domestic market because of various tariff exemption schemes and widespread tariff redundancy. Using realized tariffs as a measure of protection provides a less dramatic, but still convincing, story. The average realized tariff for manufacturing in 1977 was 33.3 percent -- still larger than the 24.8 percent average export subsidy. Comparing the individual industry realized tariffs with the industry export subsidies indicates the existence of an antiexport bias in 36 out of 59 industries. This, it is felt, is a conservative indication of the discrimination against exports because of the understatement of protection for domestic market production apparent with the use of the realized tariff rate. With the elimination of the fiscal subsidies for export and the reduction of tariff exemptions, it is evident the antiexport bias will increase. The overall conclusion is inescapable. The

382

current constellation of economic policies discriminates against exports and, as a result, export growth has been retarded.

V. THE COMPETITIVENESS OF BRAZILIAN EXPORTS IN THIRD WORLD MARKETS

Although Brazilian economic policies have generally discriminated against exports, Brazilian industrial growth has been accompanied by productivity increases and gains such that, despite adverse commercial policies, many manufactured goods produced in Brazil are now competitive in international markets. This is in part demonstrated de facto by the growth and diversification of Brazilian exports, especially of manufactured products, since 1964. These products have surely benefitted from export subsidies. Yet, as pointed out above, such subsidies have for the most part not compensated for the discrimination against exports resulting from the exchange rate overvaluation. Consequently, these products would be internationally competitive in a nondiscriminatory, free trade policy environment. Changes in economic policies have indeed been very important in bringing about the growth of manufactured exports, but they alone are not a sufficient explanation. A country's international competitiveness is determined both by its economic policies and its productivity. In the Brazilian case, economic policies since the mid-1960s have become more conducive to exports, and productivity in the industrial sector has grown rapidly since 1950.[37]

Wage comparisons between countries provide some indirect suggestive evidence on possible international competitiveness and the prospects facing individual countries. As seen in Table 13, average wages in Brazilian manufacturing are considerably lower than those for the United States and Japan. The same can be said for all other developed countries. On the other hand, Brazilian wages are higher than in either Korea or Taiwan -- two of its principal developing country competitors. Although wage comparisons are suggestive, differences in productivity preclude drawing comparative cost and price conclusions from the wage information.

Some direct evidence of Brazil's international competitiveness is available from price comparisons between Brazilian goods and the products of other countries. Table 14 presents price information from a recent BNDE (The National Development Bank) study for

TABLE 13

AVERAGE WAGES IN MANUFACTURING FOR SELECTED COUNTRIES

1977

Country	Average Wages,[1] U.S. $/month
Brazil (1976)	266
Japan	748
South Korea	143
Mexico	249
Taiwan	144
United States	983
Venezuela	336

[1] Includes basic salary and wage payments. Conversions were made on the average length of the work week and based upon the average exchange rates during the year.

Sources: ILO, Yearbook of Labor Statistics, 1977 and IMF, International Financial Statistics, April 1979.

Brazilian and internationally produced capital goods -- products important in Brazil's exports to Third World markets. Direct price quotations in U.S. dollars in international bidding were the source of the price information. The Brazilian price quotations include the effects of the export subsidies and were provided at the prevailing overvalued exchange rate. Out of the 17 product price comparisons listed in Table 14 in only three cases were Brazilian prices more than 30 percent greater than the price of the comparable foreign product. In most cases the prices were quite close. Similar evidence of the international competitiveness of many Brazilian manufactured products is available in an international comparison of prices for road building machinery and equipment.[38] With the exception of heavy, crawler tractors, most of the price comparisons showed great similarities between Brazilian and international export prices. Further comparisons of ex-factory quoted prices for such products as diesel engines, electric motors, tractors, and textile spinning equipment indicate that the Brazilian products are competitive with comparable items produced in the industrialized countries.[39]

If under existing economic policies many Brazilian products have attained a reasonable degree of international price competitiveness, the question then becomes one of the elements of nonprice competition. Two such important elements are product quality and the terms of sale. In neither case does Brazil appear to possess either a distinct disadvantage or advantage relative to its competitors for Third World markets. Interviews with firms have suggested that the quality of exported Brazilian manufactured products is acceptable by international standards; in some cases it is superior. Export financing is important for the sale of manufactured products, especially capital goods, in international markets. Although the amount of such financing available for Brazilian exports is limited, but growing, the terms of financing are quite competitive by international standards. Brazil does not lose many international bids because of noncompetitive financial arrangements. Similarly, the speed of potential delivery appears to be no more of a problem for Brazil than for other countries.

Nevertheless, in competing with other countries, mostly developed countries, for LDC markets,

TABLE 14

SELECTED PRICE COMPARISONS BETWEEN BRAZILIAN AND
FOREIGN PRODUCED CAPITAL GOODS

Industry & Product	(1) Price Quotations of Brazilian Product (U.S. $ FOB)	(2) Price of Comparable Foreign Product (U.S. $ FOB)	(3) Country of Origin for Foreign Product	(4) Ratio of Brazilian Price to Foreign Price (1)/(2)
Machine Tools				
Bench Lathe				
Case A	850	820	Taiwan	1.03
Case B	1,550	1,380	United States	1.12
Universal Lathe				
Case A	16,811	11,806	Czechoslovakia	1.42
Case B	9,422	9,925	Argentina	.94
Drill Press				
Case A	386	363	Rhodesia	1.06
Case B	862	1,363	United States	.60
Textile Machinery				
Spinning Machine				
Case A	40.968	40,000	Europe	1.02
Case B	41,735	40,000	Europe	1.04
Looms				
Case A	3,661	3,000	South Korea	1.22
Case B	7,674	9,500	Europe	.81
Agricultural Machinery				
Automated Harvester				
Case A	29,411	23,000	Europe	1.27
Case B	32,866	23,000	Europe	1.42
Case C	29,330	23,000	Europe	1.27
Case D	24,203	23,000	Europe	1.05
Wheeled Tractors				
Case A	7,083	8,900	Europe	.79
Case B	9,608	10,404	United States	.92
Case C	9,383	7,658	Europe	1.22

Source: EMBRAMEC, "Competitividade da Industria Brasileira de Bens de Capital," unpublished paper, 1978.

Brazil does possess several unique disadvantages. First, other than the products of some multinational firms, Brazil suffers from poor name recognition. Brazilian manufactured products are not widely known, and Brazil is penalized by its LDC image. As a result of limited experience, there is generally little confidence in Brazilian products. In the same way that some Brazilian consumers harbor a preference for goods produced in the advanced, technologically sophisticated industrial countries, other Third World purchasers possess similar preferences. With the passage of time and the growth of Brazilian manufactured exports it is likely that such prejudices will lessen. Second, because of the relatively little trade between Brazil and other Third World countries, shipping schedules frequently present a problem; these are less of a difficulty for the industrial countries than for Brazil. Brazilian exporters also have complained of shipping rates for shipments to LDC markets, especially those outside of Latin America.[40]

A final disadvantage Brazil faces in Third World markets is the relatively underdeveloped state of its sales networks in those markets. The multinational firms operating in Brazil generally have marketing outlets at their disposal if they believe it is useful to promote the products of their Brazilian subsidies in those markets. Domestically owned firms, however, do not have such advantageous networks. It is for this reason that Brazilian governments export promotion efforts, especially those of the Foreign Ministry, have been employed, sometimes quite successfully, in LDC markets. As Brazilian export experience grows, the sales and marketing infrastructure for Brazilian products can also be expected to expand.

Partially offsetting these disadvantages, Brazil possesses to some extent a political advantage in its competition for the markets of the Third World. Being an ostensibly developing country carries a certain advantage -- as well as the disadvantage of low product confidence. As a Third World country itself, Brazil can play on the theme of Third World solidarity and nonalignment, although this approach is more likely to impress diplomats and bureaucrats than it is business customers. Yet, many Third World countries are trying to reduce their dependence on the industrialized nations and one way to achieve this objective is to switch import purchases from the developed countries to other LDCs. To the extent that such objectives are considered important by policymakers, Brazil is in a good position to increase its own exports to Third World markets. There is less stigma in purchasing certain types of products from a less powerful country than from a world power. Brazilian arms exports have definitely benefitted from this as well as from the Brazilian policy of "no questions asked" for armaments sales.

Brazil's situation in the world economy, although not unique, is considerably different from that of either the leading industrial nations or the very poor countries. It possesses both a sophisticated industrial economy and relatively low wages. As such, it is in a good position to exploit the international product cycle by either mass producing new products developed in the technologically leading countries or quickly adopting and adapting new production processes. Technological adaptation is relatively easy in Brazil, given the increasing technological sophistication of the economy.

VI. CONCLUDING REMARKS

Brazil has experienced substantial growth in its exports and GDP since the mid-1960s. Manufactured exports have led the export growth. Brazil's exports to Third World countries, mainly involving manufactured products, have also increased proportionately. The reasons for this expansion in Brazilian exports lie mainly with economic policies that have provided the necessary environment to enable and induce Brazilian producers to begin or expand their exports.[41] Those policies have had the effect of reducing exporter uncertainty and lessening the degree of policy discrimination against export activities. Other than some promotional efforts by the Foreign Ministry, the policies undertaken to expand exports have not been market specific. In other words, Third World markets have not been especially favored through the exercise of government policies. Since the mid-1970s economic policies have been less conducive to export expansion than during the 1966-1973 period, and, as a result, export expansion has proceeded less rapidly.

The prospects for continued export growth and continued market penetration in Third World countries remain favorable for Brazil. As of December 1979, the balance of payments situation and outlook were quite serious. It appears, however, that Brazilian policy-makers will be farsighted enough to adopt economic measures that will serve to increase the rate of export growth.

APPENDIX TABLE 1

IMPORTS OF MAJOR COUNTRY GROUPS, 1973-1978

	1973	1978	Percent Increase in Current Dollars, 1973-78
Principal Industrial Countries	386.8	836.9	116
Nonoil LDCs	79.0	203.2	157
Oil Exporting LDCs	20.0	103.3	417
TOTAL WORLD	535.0	1,241.9	132

Source: IMF, Direction of Trade Yearbook, 1979.

MAJOR INDUSTRIALIZED PRODUCT EXPORTS, 1974 AND 1978

(U.S. $ millions)

Products	1974	1978
Semi-Manufactured Products	917.0	1,421.2
Crystallized Sugar	283.3	32.8
Carnauba Wax	25.2	18.1
Tin in Bulk	21.4	21.0
Hewed Iron and Steel Parts	12.6	43.6
Rough Cast Iron	31.0	111.5
Rough Alloy Iron	49.0	125.0
Sawed Pine Timber	50.0	23.3
Sawed Timber (except pine)	35.7	22.0
Cocoa Butter	100.0	83.0
Peanut Oil	30.5	56.8
Babassu Oil	36.8	6.5
Castor Oil	128.4	110.0
Soybean Oil in Bulk	1.9	283.1
Other Vegetable Oils	9.3	6.4
Paper Making Paste	36.8	57.5
Prepared Skins and Hides	38.0	100.0
Other Semimanufactured Steel Products	0.1	2.0
Other Semimanufactured Products	27.1	320.0
Manufactured Products	2,263.0	5,082.0
Refined Sugar	60.3	121.3
Manufactured Rubber	13.0	53.4
Soluble Coffee	116.0	348.2
Shoes	120.2	280.9
Beef Products	81.0	97.4
Steel Plates	10.2	42.1
Wooden Construction Materials	16.3	35.0
Sisal Cordage	40.1	37.4
Cutlery	10.0	14.4
Meat Extracts	18.3	6.2
Tools	11.3	25.0
Cotton Fibers	66.4	117.1
Synthetic Fibers	15.5	30.2
Silk Fibers	16.3	19.1
Jewelry	21.3	7.3
Laminated Rosewood	6.0	1.8
Laminated Woods, except Rosewood	17.0	23.0
Leather Products	22.7	40.5
Electrical Machinery and Apparatus	183.1	315.2
Office Machinery	96.3	127.4
Earth-moving Machinery and Equipment	10.5	48.0
Machinery Tools	11.7	27.8

Products	1974	1978
Machinery and Boilers	150.5	565.6
Transportation Equipment	186.5	827.7
Menthol	46.5	19.0
Furniture	13.2	18.1
Combustible Petroleum Oils	33.1	46.3
Vegetable Oil Essences	37.5	21.5
Purified Soybean Oil	0.9	11.8
Paper and Paper Products	18.0	53.3
Cut Gems	16.7	24.3
Metal Products	62.2	171.5
Textile Linen Products	29.2	61.0
Fruit Juices, except Orange Juice	6.0	13.7
Orange Juice	59.1	332.6
Cotton Fabrics	59.4	67.3
Knitted Fabrics	77.6	4.6
Synthetic Fiber Fabrics	31.6	46.0
Apparel	52.2	31.7
Glass and Glass Products	16.8	26.4
Other Manufacturing Products	402.2	878.1
Total Industrialized Product Exports	3,199.7	6,504.0

Source: CACEX: Comercio Exterior: Series Estatisticas, 1978.

APPENDIX TABLE 3

EXPORTS TO SELECTED THIRD WORLD COUNTRIES, BY PRODUCT GROUP, 1978
(U.S. $ millions)

NBM Chap.	Group	Argentina	Bolivia	Chile	Columbia	Equador	Mexico	Paraguay	Peru	Uruguay	Venezuela	LAFTA TOTAL	Algeria	Saudi Arabia	Iran	Iraq	Libya	Nigeria	India	Angola	18 LDC Country Total	Total Brazilian Exports
01	Live Animals	0.2	2.1	3.2	-	-	-	0.1	-	.0	.0	3.0	-	-	-	-	-	-	-	-	3.0	3.2
02	Meats and Offals	0.1	-	2.6	-	-	-	2.4	-	.0	2.7	0.6	-	6.1	9.0	15.0	-	17.0	-	-	47.3	128.8
03	Seafood	1.7	-	-	-	-	.0	.0	-	.0	.0	1.8	-	-	-	-	-	-	-	-	1.8	91.3
04	Dairy Produce, Eggs & Honey	0.6	.0	.0	-	-	-	-	-	0.8	0.1	1.0	-	-	-	.0	-	-	-	-	1.0	8.7
05	Other Animal Origin Products	0.2	.0	.0	-	-	-	.0	.0	.0	-	0.2	-	.0	.0	-	-	.0	-	-	0.2	19.0
06	Trees and Plants	-	.0	.0	-	-	-	-	.0	-	.0	.0	-	-	.0	-	-	-	-	-	.0	6.6
07	Edible Vegetables	1.3	.0	-	-	-	-	-	.0	.0	-	1.3	-	-	-	-	-	-	-	-	1.3	2.8
08	Edible Fruits & Nuts	26.5	.0	.0	.0	-	1.0	.0	-	2.4	7.3	30.8	-	-	-	-	-	-	-	-	30.8	102.1
09	Coffee, Teas & Spices	45.0	0.8	5.2	0.3	-	1.8	.0	0.2	12.2	0.3	65.3	16.5	-	-	-	-	1.3	.0	-	83.0	2,035.3
10	Cereals	0.7	.0	-	-	-	-	-	-	-	-	0.8	-	-	1.2	-	-	4.3	-	1.9	8.1	48.0
11	Milling Industry Products	-	-	0.3	.0	-	-	-	-	-	0.2	0.8	-	-	-	-	-	-	-	-	9.4	2.5
12	Oil Seeds & Misc. Grains	.0	.0	.0	-	-	-	-	-	-	.0	0.7	.0	.0	-	11.0	-	-	.0	0.1	11.6	182.2
13	Industrial Vegetable Materials	.0	-	.0	-	-	0.3	0.2	-	0.3	.0	0.5	-	-	-	-	-	-	.0	-	0.4	11.0
14	Other Veg. Prod.	.0	.0	.0	-	.0	-	-	.0	-	-	.0	-	-	-	-	-	-	-	-	.0	1.1
15	Animal & Vegetable Fats & Oils	1.0	4.9	5.7	3.0	.0	4.0	0.1	0.1	1.6	23.6	39.6	-	-	60.6	-	-	2.0	106.5	-	208.7	514.6
16	Meat & Seafood Preparations	-	.0	.0	-	-	-	-	-	-	-	0.8	-	-	-	2.7	-	-	-	-	5.3	110.8
17	Sugar & Sugar Prod.	-	1.3	6.8	.0	2.6	-	3.4	-	.0	13.7	27.9	3.0	1.1	34.5	22.3	.0	0.6	-	.0	97.0	395.9
18	Cocoa & Cocoa Prod.	13.0	0.6	1.1	-	-	-	0.4	-	1.9	-	16.9	0.7	0.2	-	-	-	9.7	-	-	17.5	834.1

APPENDIX TABLE 3 CONTINUED

NBM Chap.	Group	Argentina	Bolivia	Chile	Columbia	Equador	Mexico	Paraguay	Peru	Uruguay	Venezuela	TOTAL LAFTA	Algeria	Saudi Arabia	Iran	Iraq	Libya	Nigeria	India	Angola	18 LDC Country Total	Total Brazilian Exports
19	Cereal Products	.0	0.6	.0	-	-	.0	0.6	-	.0	-	1.3	-	.0	-	-	-	-	-	-	-	1.4	2.2
20	Vegetable Preparations	1.2	.0	1.2	-	-	.0	1.7	-	.0	7.1	11.4	-	1.4	-	.0	-	1.3	-	-	-	14.1	359.8
21	Miscellaneous Edible Preparations	0.6	0.4	0.5	.0	.0	0.1	1.0	.0	.0	.0	2.8	2.1	0.2	.0	1.4	-	.0	-	-	-	6.6	367.0
22	Beverages	.0	.0	0.3	.0	-	-	3.1	-	.0	-	3.6	-	0.1	-	-	-	.0	-	-	-	3.7	8.7
23	Residues & Food Wastes	.0	0.2	0.6	-	-	-	1.1	-	0.1	12.2	14.3	5.8	-	-	10.8	5.7	0.2	-	-	-	31.1	1,136.3
24	Tobacco	.0	0.7	.0	-	-	-	4.7	-	2.2	.0	7.8	-	-	-	-	-	0.8	.0	-	-	13.7	249.3
25	Salt, Sulphur, Lime & Cements	0.8	2.7	0.4	.0	.0	0.2	5.7	0.7	0.3	0.8	11.8	-	-	-	.0	-	2.0	-	-	-	13.8	33.9
26	Metallic Ores	43.8	-	-	-	-	4.3	-	-	.0	1.8	50.0	-	-	-	-	-	-	-	-	-	50.0	1,096.7
27	Mineral Fuels & Oils	20.0	1.0	0.1	34.9	.0	0.2	9.3	1.8	33.7	-	101.2	-	-	.0	-	-	54.9	-	-	-	156.1	195.1
28	Inorganic Chemicals	5.0	-	0.4	4.8	-	2.3	0.3	0.1	0.5	0.6	10.0	-	-	-	-	-	-	-	-	-	10.0	16.3
29	Organic Chemicals	8.4	.0	1.8	1.2	0.2	7.1	.0	1.0	0.8	4.1	25.0	0.2	-	.0	-	-	-	.0	-	-	25.1	86.6
30	Pharmaceutical Prod.	0.1	1.3	0.7	0.1	0.5	4.0	8.8	-	0.3	0.9	5.4	-	-	-	-	-	0.1	-	-	-	5.8	7.9
31	Fertilizers	1.0	.0	-	-	-	-	8.0	-	0.5	-	1.7	-	-	-	-	-	-	-	-	-	1.6	1.7
32	Tanning & Drying Extracts	0.6	1.5	1.1	0.6	.0	0.5	1.8	0.1	0.4	0.1	6.8	.0	.0	-	0.1	.0	0.2	3.3	.0	10.6	16.4
33	Essential Oils & Cosmetics	.0	1.2	.0	0.2	.0	0.8	2.9	.0	.0	0.2	5.4	-	-	.0	-	-	-	-	.0	5.6	27.6
34	Soaps & Waxes	0.4	0.8	0.7	.0	.0	0.4	3.5	0.1	.0	0.3	5.8	-	-	-	.0	-	.0	-	.0	5.9	25.4
35	Albuminoidal Substances & Glues	.0	0.2	0.7	.0	0.2	-	0.4	0.3	.0	0.1	1.7	-	-	-	-	-	-	-	-	1.7	8.4
36	Explosives	0.3	0.4	0.1	-	.0	0.5	0.4	-	.0	-	1.8	-	-	-	-	-	-	-	-	1.8	5.4
37	Photographic Prod.	0.3	0.1	0.6	1.9	.0	9.3	0.2	0.4	0.3	1.7	18.0	-	-	-	-	-	-	-	-	18.0	18.6
38	Misc. Chemical Prod.	7.0	4.3	1.1	0.7	.0	0.9	1.2	0.1	0.9	2.4	18.7	0.6	.0	.0	0.4	-	.0	-	.0	19.7	43.3

NBM Chap.	Group	Argentina	Bolivia	Chile	Columbia	Equador	Mexico	Paraguay	Peru	Uruguay	Venezuela	TOTAL LAFTA	Algeria	Saudi Arabia	Iran	Iraq	Libya	Nigeria	India	Angola	18 LDC Country Total	Total Brazilian Exports
39	Artificial Resins & Plastic Materials	3.0	1.2	2.4	0.5	0.1	0.8	3.8	0.2	3.3	0.5	15.2	.0	.0	.0	.0	.0	0.3	-	.0	15.7	26.0
40	Rubber & Synthetic Rubber	1.8	2.5	2.4	2.3	0.1	1.2	9.9	0.4	1.3	5.9	27.8	1.3	1.3	.0	0.5	0.5	0.5	.0	0.1	30.9	55.2
41	Raw Hides & Skins	.0	.1	.0	.0	-	.3	.0	-	.0	-	0.1	-	.0	.0	-	-	-	-	-	0.2	100.7
42	Leather Products	.0	.1	0.1	.0	-	-	0.3	-	.0	0.1	1.0	-	.0	-	-	-	-	-	-	1.1	47.6
43	Furs & Fur Prod.	.0	.0	.0	-	-	-	.0	-	-	-	.0	-	.0	.0	.0	-	.0	-	-	.0	19.2
44	Wood & Wood Prod.	17.6	.0	.0	0.2	.0	-	0.2	0.1	0.5	9.9	33.1	.0	.0	.0	0.6	.0	0.9	-	.0	34.7	194.8
45	Cork & Cork Prod.	.0	.0	.0	.0	.0	-	.0	-	.0	.0	0.1	.0	-	.0	.0	-	.0	-	-	1.2	1.3
46	Basketware & Wickerwork	-	-	-	-	-	.0	.0	-	-	.0	.0	-	-	-	-	-	-	-	-	.0	.0
47	Paper-making Materials	5.7	-	.0	0.2	.0	-	-	0.2	1.0	1.2	8.5	-	-	-	-	-	0.8	-	0.5	9.9	57.4
48	Paper, Pulp & Paper Board	2.3	2.1	3.4	0.3	1.4	1.2	3.4	0.1	0.3	0.6	15.3	-	2.5	0.5	0.5	-	6.3	-	5.0	25.7	88.2
49	Books & Graphic Materials	3.3	0.1	0.1	3.0	0.1	.0	0.3	.0	0.2	0.4	5.1	-	.0	.0	-	-	.0	0.4	.0	5.2	10.5
50	Silk	2.0	.0	0.1	-	-	.0	.0	-	.0	.0	0.3	-	.0	.0	-	-	-	.0	-	0.7	27.3
51	Synthetic Fibers (continuous)	.0	3.3	0.2	-	0.9	-	2.9	.0	.0	.0	7.4	-	-	.0	.0	-	0.4	.0	-	8.0	12.3
52	Metallic Textiles	-	-	-	-	-	-	-	.0	.0	-	-	-	-	-	-	-	-	-	-	.0	.0
53	Wool	-	.0	.0	.0	-	.0	.0	-	0.4	-	0.5	-	-	1.7	-	-	-	-	-	2.2	69.3
54	Flax and Ramie	.0	.0	.0	-	-	-	0.1	-	.0	.0	0.3	-	-	-	-	-	-	-	-	0.3	14.1
55	Cotton	.0	2.2	4.1	.0	.0	-	6.4	-	1.4	.0	14.4	-	-	0.5	0.2	-	19.3	-	7.7	35.2	238.6
56	Synthetic Fibers (discontinuous)	0.2	6.6	3.2	0.6	0.1	-	4.4	0.2	1.0	.0	16.0	-	-	-	-	-	15.0	-	0.6	31.9	50.5

NBM Chap.	Group	Argentina	Bolivia	Chile	Columbia	Equador	Mexico	Paraguay	Peru	Uruguay	Venezuela	TOTAL LAFTA	Algeria	Saudi Arabia	Iran	Iraq	Libya	Nigeria	India	Angola	18 LDC County Total	Total Brazilian Exports
57	Other Vegetable Textile Materials	3.2	.0	0.1	-	-	-	0.4	-	0.1	0.3	4.2	-	-	-	-	-	.0	-	-	4.2	38.6
58	Carpets	.0	0.6	0.1	-	.0	.0	0.1	-	0.9	0.1	2.9	.0	.0	.0	.0	-	.0	-	.0	2.9	6.3
59	Cordage	0.1	1.0	2.0	0.3	0.1	.0	1.6	.0	0.9	0.1	6.5	-	.0	0.2	-	-	.0	-	.0	6.7	47.1
60	Knitted Goods	0.2	3.9	1.5	.0	.0	.0	16.9	.0	0.2	10.0	23.7	-	.0	.0	.0	.0	.0	-	0.3	24.0	46.0
61	Apparel	.0	2.4	1.3	.0	-	.0	12.2	-	.0	0.8	16.9	-	-	-	.0	.0	.0	-	.0	16.9	51.6
62	Other Textile Articles	.0	0.9	1.3	-	.0	0.1	7.5	.0	-	7.1	17.9	-	.9	.0	0.4	0.2	.0	-	-	18.7	69.1
63	Old Clothing & Rags	-	0.4	2.0	-	-	.0	1.7	-	.0	-	4.3	-	-	-	-	-	.0	-	-	4.3	0.1
64	Footwear	.0	0.8	.0	-	.0	-	.0	-	.0	0.1	1.1	-	-	-	-	-	-	-	-	1.1	292.0
65	Headgear	-	.0	-	-	-	-	0.1	-	-	-	0.1	-	-	-	-	-	-	-	-	0.2	1.7
66	Umbrellas	-	-	-	-	-	-	-	-	-	-	-	-	-	-	-	-	-	-	-	-	0.1
67	Feather & Hair Products	-	.0	.0	-	-	-	.0	-	-	-	0.	-	-	-	-	-	-	-	-	0.1	0.1
68	Stone, Plaster & Cement Products	0.3	0.9	1.1	0.3	0.3	0.1	1.9	.0	0.3	0.2	5.6	.0	.0	0.4	.0	.0	.0	-	.0	5.8	13.4
69	Ceramic Products	3.6	3.1	9.6	0.2	.0	-	5.0	0.1	0.4	0.6	14.0	-	0.2	-	-	-	0.4	-	-	15.0	30.0
70	Glass & Glassware	4.8	1.5	1.1	2.5	0.4	7.1	0.8	0.7	0.5	3.8	23.6	.0	0.1	.0	.0	.0	0.2	0.3	-	24.0	26.4
71	Jewelry	0.1	.0	.0	.0	.0	.0	.0	.0	.0	.0	0.3	-	.0	-	-	.0	.0	.0	-	0.7	48.3
72	Coins	-	-	-	-	-	-	0.3	-	.0	-	0.3	-	-	-	-	-	-	-	-	3.4	3.4
73	Iron & Steel & Their Products	14.9	17.6	2.3	10.2	1.0	6.2	13.1	1.4	14.4	6.5	87.7	3.0	3.6	3.5	8.7	1.3	11.4	.0	0.4	119.6	496.0
74	Copper & Copper Products	.0	0.2	.0	1.4	.0	0.1	0.3	.0	0.8	0.2	3.4	-	.0	-	.0	.0	.0	-	.0	3.5	8.2
75	Nickel & Nickel Products	.0	-	-	-	-	-	0.2	-	-	-	0.3	-	-	-	-	-	-	-	.0	0.3	0.3

APPENDIX TABLE 3 CONTINUED

NBM Chap.	Group	Argentina	Bolivia	Chile	Columbia	Equador	Mexico	Paraguay	Peru	Uruguay	Venezuela	LAFTA TOTAL	Algeria	Saudi Arabia	Iran	Iraq	Libya	Nigeria	India	Angola	18 LDC Country Total	Total Brazilian Exports
76	Aluminum Products	0.3	0.9	0.7	0.1	0.1	.0	1.4	.0	.0	2.5	6.3	-	-	-	-	-	0.1	-	.0	6.5	11.9
77	Magnesium & Beryllium Products	-	-	-	-	-	-	-	-	-	-	-	-	-	-	-	-	-	-	-	-	.0
78	Lead Products	-	-	-	-	-	-	-	-	-	.0	.0	-	-	-	-	-	-	-	-	-	0.1
79	Zinc Products	.0	-	-	0.1	-	-	-	.0	-	-	0.1	-	-	.0	-	-	-	-	-	0.1	0.1
80	Tin Products	4.5	.0	0.3	-	-	0.1	.0	.0	.0	-	5.4	-	-	-	-	-	.0	-	-	0.5	54.3
81	Other Products	-	-	-	-	-	-	-	-	0.5	-	0.1	-	-	-	-	-	-	-	-	0.1	5.0
82	Tools & Cutlery	2.6	1.3	2.5	1.2	0.4	-	2.3	4.5	.0	4.0	20.7	-	-	0.4	-	-	0.1	-	-	21.7	40.8
83	Miscellaneous	.0	2.1	0.3	.0	0.2	1.0	1.9	-	0.7	0.7	5.4	.0	.0	.0	-	.0	0.2	-	0.3	5.7	9.3
84	Boilers, Machinery & Mech. Appliances	64.5	20.3	19.8	19.7	16.6	66.7	30.5	10.4	15.2	42.2	304.1	0.5	3.4	7.2	1.9	4.1	19.7	.0	.0	346.9	772.6
85	Elec. Machinery & Equipment	11.6	7.8	7.3	4.1	2.7	21.2	11.8	2.4	4.4	12.0	85.3	.0	0.3	0.3	-	.0	2.4	.0	1.2	91.3	318.3
86	Railway Equipment	0.8	8.3	0.6	-	-	0.3	-	-	.0	.0	10.3	1.3	.0	-	0.7	0.8	-	.0	0.1	12.6	25.1
87	Vehicles	14.2	16.0	66.4	21.9	14.0	30.4	29.5	7.6	19.8	41.4	261.3	66.0	3.3	0.3	6.9	50.3	59.4	.0	1.0	462.0	656.8
88	Aircraft & Parts	1.9	.0	3.5	0.4	-	.0	-	-	-	-	-	-	1.0	-	-	-	-	-	14.4	8.0	35.9
89	Ships & Boats	.0	.0	19.4	-	-	-	0.1	-	0.9	-	20.6	-	-	-	-	-	-	-	-	20.6	114.8
90	Optical & Photographic Equipment	1.4	0.6	3.1	1.4	0.7	4.2	0.7	0.1	0.4	1.4	14.3	-	-	-	-	-	-	-	-	14.7	37.1
91	Clocks & Watches	0.2	.0	.0	.0	.0	0.4	.0	.0	.0	0.4	1.1	.0	.0	.0	.0	0.2	.0	.0	.0	1.1	3.0
92	Musical Instruments & Recording Devices	-	0.3	-	-	.0	0.9	-	-	.0	0.2	2.5	-	-	-	.0	-	.0	-	-	3.0	7.7
93	Arms & Munitions	0.5	0.2	0.4	0.1	-	-	0.8	.0	.0	.0	4.5	-	.0	-	0.4	-	-	-	-	4.6	21.1
94	Furniture	.0	0.8	3.3	.0	-	.0	3.2	.0	-	0.3	5.0	-	0.1	-	0.1	-	.0	-	.0	5.5	18.7
95	Carving Products	-	.0	0.5	-	-	.0	.0	-	-	-	.0	-	-	-	.0	-	0.2	-	-	.0	.0

APPENDIX TABLE 3 CONTINUED

NBM Chap.	Group	Argentina	Bolivia	Chile	Columbia	Equador	Mexico	Paraguay	Peru	Uruguay	Venezuela	LAFTA TOTAL	Algeria	Saudi Arabia	Iran	Iraq	Libya	Nigeria	India	Angola	18 LDC Country Total	Total Brazilian Exports
96	Brooms	.0	0.1	.0	.0	.0	.0	0.3	.0	.0	.0	0.7	-	.0	-	-	-	.0	-	-	0.7	1.0
97	Toys & Sports Eqmt.	0.2	1.1	0.6	.0	0.1	0.2	0.9	-	.0	1.3	4.5	-	.0	.0	-	-	-	-	.0	4.6	8.3
98	Misc. Manufactured Products	1.1	0.5	0.3	0.3	.0	.0	1.0	.0	0.4	0.3	4.0	.0	.0	-	.0	-	.0	-	.0	4.0	5.1
	TOTAL	349.0	133.8	191.1	113.2	43.9	178.0	224.3	34.2	133.2	218.6	1619.3	106.1	25.7	121.1	85.0	63.5	233.5	110.7	22.6	2387.4	12536.5

Source: CACEX, Comercio Exterior: Exportacio, 1978

APPENDIX TABLE 4

BRAZIL'S SHARE IN THE TOTAL IMPORTS OF BRAZIL'S
MAJOR IMPORTING COUNTRIES, 1978

	Imports from Brazil (U.S.$ millions)	Total Imports (U.S.$ millions)	Share of Imports Originating from Brazil (%)
Major Industrial Country Markets			
United States	3,035	183,136	1.7
Canada	218	44,806	0.5
W. Germany	1,144	121,807	0.9
Netherlands	460	53,840	0.9
United Kingdom	546	78,605	0.7
Italy	337	56,065	0.6
France	761	81,792	0.9
Japan	790	79,900	1.0
South Africa	5	7,422	0.1
USSR	174	13,391	1.3
Major Third World Country Markets			
LAFTA			
Argentina	335	4,505	7.4
Bolivia	102	867	11.8
Chile	134	2,793	4.8
Colombia	110	3,030	3.6
Equador	39	1,659	2.4
Mexico	127	7,560	1.7
Paraguay	63	319	19.7
Peru	47	1,659	2.8
Uruguay	109	788	13.8
OPEC Country Markets			
Algeria	94	7,843	1.2
Saudi-Arabia	20	22,060	0.1
Kuwait	22	5,184	0.4
Iran	148	19,964	0.7
Iraq	88	5,842	1.5
Libya	62	5,986	1.0
Nigeria	220	11,086	2.0
Angola	27	780	3.5
Tunisia	12	2,120	0.6
Singapore	50	12,992	0.4
Philippines	71	5,297	1.3
India	111	8,333	1.3
Indonesia	78	6,916	1.1
Total World	12,461	1,241,900	1.0

Source: International Monetary Fund, Direction of Trade Yearbook, 1978.

[1]For low-income developing countries the comparable figure for the 1970-1977 period was 3.2 percent. When per capita income figures are examined it is apparent that the absolute and relative income gap between the rich and very poor has widened. Per capita GNP between 1960 and 1977 for the industrialized countries grew at 3.4 percent annually, while that for the low-income developing countries grew at a very low 1.4 percent. For the newly industrializing countries as a whole a slight narrowing of the gap is apparent, with an annual rate of per capita GNP growth 3.6 percent for the 1960-1977 period. If recent growth rates can be sustained into the future, it is evident that some of the more advanced and rapidly growing developing countries will be able to join the club of industrialized countries. For a presentation of the basic data, see the World Bank, World Development Report, August 1979.

[2]For exports to oil exporting LDCs, only France did more poorly than the United States. Yet, total exports from France to Third World countries grew more rapidly (171 percent) than U.S. exports to those same countries (152 percent).

[3]See, for example, Bela Balassa, "Export Incentives and Export Performance in Developing Countries: A Comparative Analysis," Weltwirtschaftliches Archiv, vol. 114, no. 1(1978), pp.24-61.

[4]World Bank, World Development Report, 1979, p.131.

[5]James Riedel and William G. Tyler, "Export Oriented Industrialization and National Economic Integration in Brazil and Taiwan," Viertel Jahres Berichte, no. 75 (March 1979), p.38. Regis Bonelli and Dorothea Werneck, "Desempenho Industrial: Auge e Desaceleração nos Anos 70," Wilson Suzigan, editor, Industria: Politica, Instituicoes e Desenvolvimento, Monograph No. 28 (Rio de Janeiro: INPES/IPEA, 1979), p.190.

[6]See Samuel A. Morley and Gordon W. Smith, "On the Measurement of Import Substitution," *American Economic Review*, vol. 60, 1970, pp. 728-735; and William G. Tyler, *Manufactured Export Expansion and Industrialization in Brazil*, (Tubingen: J. C. B. Mohr, 1976).

[7]Riedel and Tyler, *op. cit.*

[8]Computed from Banco do Brasil, *Comercio Exterior: Series Estatisticas*, 1978.

[9]Banco do Brasil, *Comercio Exterior: Series Estatisticas*, 1978, p. 1. In comparison total petroleum imports in 1968 amounted to only $138 million.

[10]*Boletim do Banco Central*, various issues.

[11]Author's calculations based upon CIEF information. A simple unweighted average, calculated from the tariff schedules, rose from 54.7 percent in 1971 to 81.6 percent in 1977. See Table 9 and Joal de Azambuja Rosa et. al., "Alguns Aspectos da Politica Tarifaria Recente", Fundacao Centro de Estudos do Comercio Exterior, unpublished paper, November 1979.

[12]William G. Tyler, "Import Restrictions and Tax Incentives for the Brazilian Capital Goods Sector," *Pesquisa e Planejamento Economico*, forthcoming in 1980. Because of exemptions the actual weight felt from the import deposit is less than its possible tariff equivalent. The realized tariff equivalent of the import deposit for 1977 was estimated to be 16.2 percent. See Azambuja, *op. cit.*

[13]During the postwar period until 1964, Brazilian exports were virtually stagnant.

[14]Tyler, *Manufactured Export Expansion*, *op. cit.* p. 143.

[15]For 1967-1971, a period involving very rapid export growth, it has been estimated that exports

accounted for only 6 percent of total manufacturing demand growth. In only leather products and food products did export increases contribute to more than 15 percent of demand growth. See Tyler, Manufactured Export Expansion, op. cit. pp.73-81.

[16]Tyler, ibid., p. 143.

[17]For a detailed product group breakdown of Brazil's exports to its major Third World country markets, see Appendix Table 3.

[18]Jornal do Brasil, 4 November 1979.

[19]Some estimates can be found in Frank J. Earwaker and Peter T. Knight, "Brazil -- Shadow Exchange Rate," unpublished paper, 28 December 1977 and Claudio R. Contador, "A Taxa Social de Cambio," unpublished paper, 1979.

[20]For an examination of Brazilian exchange rate policy the reader is referred to the author's "Exchange Rate Flexibility under Conditions of Endemic Inflation. A Case Study of the Recent Brazilian Experience," in C. Fred Bergsten and William G. Tyler, editors, Leading Issues in International Economic Policy: Essays in Honor of George N. Halm (Lexington, Massachusetts: D.C. Heath, 1973), pp. 19-49. See also Roberto Fendt Jr., "The Brazilian Experience with the Crawling Peg," in John Williamson, editor, The Crawling Peg: Past Performance and Future Prospects (London: MacMillan, forthcoming in 1980).

[21]Joel Bergsman, Brazil: Industrialization and Trade Policies (New York: Oxford University Press, 1970), p. 42.

[22]Tyler, Manufactured Export Expansion, op. cit. p. 239.

[23]In some cases, e.g., various textile products, the IPI export subsidy rate has slightly exceeded 15 percent.

[24]The largest single weight -- more than double that of any other industry -- was for the food products industry. This particular industry has received fairly low (6.2 percent) fiscal subsidies for export.

[25]A good example of a country possessing a drawback system plagued with administrative problems is the Philippines. There import duties for imports used in export production are reimbursed under the drawback system, but exporters claim that, because of necessary extra-legal administrative expenses, they are rarely able to recover 100 percent of the reimbursable import duties paid. A description is provided in William G. Tyler, "The Industrial Incentive System and Policies in the Philippines," unpublished paper, March 1979.

[26]By way of comparison it can be noted that in 1970, imports exempted from import duties under the drawback system equaled 14 percent of Brazilian manufacturing exports. The data are from CACEX, Relatorio, 1978.

[27]There also exists a similar scheme involving duty free imports of intermediate goods for exporters that relates the amount of permissible duty free imports to a proportion of the previous year's increase in the firm's exports. This mechanism, however, is no longer widely used.

[28]For a good analysis of the experience with the BEFIEX program see Regis Bonelli and Wilson Suzigan, "State, Domestic Private, and Foreign Firms in Brazilian Manufacturing Industries," an unpublished paper prepared for the OECD, September 1979.

[29]This tendency may be changing. In 1978 BEFIEX approved a large steel mill project involving planned investments of more than $2.2 billion and committing the firm to exports of $5.5 billion over an extended period. See CDI, Relatorio de Atividades, 1978.

[30]By way of comparison, the total credits extended through the program for the first 10 months of 1978 amounted to only U.S. $3.5 billion. See CACEX, Relatorio, 1978, p. 141.

[31]See, for example, Bergsman, op. cit. and Tyler, Manufactured Export Expansion, op. cit.

[32]In the first two months of its existence the new CONCEX met only once.

[33]Tyler, Manufactured Export Expansion, op. cit. pp. 254-271.

[34]Conceptually, it is preferable to measure an antiexport (or proexport) bias in terms of the difference between the effective rate of protection for domestic market production and the effective rate of subsidization for exports. In the Brazilian case, however, the inadequacy of information on protection, especially affecting inputs, precludes meaningful estimates of either measure.

[35]In a free trade situation, with an equilibrium exchange rate, the absence of either domestic market protection or export subsidization indicates the presence of neither a pro or antiexport bias. Economic policies do not affect trade in their allocational effects.

[36]In two of the remaining industries -- rolled steel and shipbuilding -- substantial nontariff import restrictions exist. It thus appears that an antiexport bias may also exist in those industries.

[37]See Regis Bonelli, "Technology and Growth in Brazilian Manufacturing," Brazilian Economic Growth, No. 2, (1976), pp.35-72.

[38]EMBRAMEC, "Competitividade da Industria Brasileira de Bens de Capital," unpublished paper, 1978.

[39]For a further description see Tyler, "Import Restrictions," op. cit.

[40]Shipping schedules and rates are not a difficulty for Brazilian exports to some of its major

Third World markets. Nearly all Brazilian exports to Bolivia, Paraguay, Uruguay, and Argentina are transported by truck.

[41]The overall growth of world trade was a contributing factor, but one must not overstate its importance. The period of the 1950s was also a period of rapid expansion in world trade, yet during this period Brazilian exports were stagnant. The reason for this stagnation was an export impeding and discriminatory economic policy.

REFERENCES

Azambuja, Joal de, et al. "Alguns Aspectos da Politica Tarifaria Recente," Fundacao Centro de Estudos do Comercio Exterior, unpublished paper, November 1979.

Balassa, Bela. "Export Incentives and Export Performance in Developing Countries: A Comparative Analysis." Weltwirtschaftliches Archiv. vol. 114, no. 1 (1978). pp. 24-61.

Bergsman, Joel. Brazil: Industrialization and Trade Policies. (New York: Oxford University Press, 1970).

Bonelli, Regis. "Technology and Growth in Brazilian Manufacturing." Brazilian Economic Studies. no. 2 (1976). pp. 35-72.

Bonelli, Regis and Suzigan, Wilson. "State, Domestic Private, and Foreign Firms in Brazilian Manufacturing Industries." unpublished paper prepared for the OECD. September 1979.

Bonelli, Regis and Werneck, Dorthea. "Desempenho Industrial: Ague e Desaceleracao nos Anos 70," in Wilson Suzigan, editor. Industria: Politica, Instituicoes e Desenvolvimento. Monograph No. 28 (Rio de Janeiro: INPES/IPEA, 1979). pp. 167-226.

Contador, Claudio R. "A Taxa Social de Cambio." unpublished paper. 1979.

Earwaker, Frank J. and Knight, Peter T. "Brazil-Shadow Exchange Rate." unpublished paper. 28 December 1977.

Fendt, Roberto Jr. "The Brazilian Experience with the Crawling Peg." in John Williamson, editor. The Crawling Peg: Past Performance and Future Prospects (London: MacMillan, forthcoming in 1980).

Morley, Samuel A. and Smith, Gordon W. "On the Measurement of Import Substitution." American Economic Review. vol. 60. (1970). pp. 728-735.

Riedel, James and Tyler, William G. "Export Oriented Industrialization and National Economic Integration in Brazil and Taiwan." Viertel Jahres Berichte. No. 75. (March 1979). pp. 35-60.

Savasini, Jose Augusto Arantes, et al. "Acompanhamento da Quantificacao da Estrutura de Incentivos as Exportacoes: Efeitos da Politica Protecionista Apos 1975." Fundacao Centro de Estudos do Comercio Exterior. unpublished paper. 1979.

Tyler, William G. "Import Restrictions and Tax Incentives for the Brazilian Capital Goods Industry." Pesquisa e Planejamento Economico. forthcoming in 1980.

Tyler, William G. Manufactured Export Expansion and Industrialization in Brazil (Tubingen: J. C. B. Mohr, 1976).

6

CHANGING FORMS OF COMPETITION AND WORLD TRADE RULES

Harald B. Malmgren

CONTENTS

I.   INTRODUCTION

The world marketplace of the 1980s will pose even harder tests for the U.S. economy and U.S. competitiveness than the 1960s and 1970s. We enter the 1980s after a decade of slow capital formation, flagging R&D efforts, inflationary corrosion, and massive energy shocks. The capital stock was not renewed and adapted at the pace required by the new, rapidly changing economic environment, and much of the existing capital stock was rendered obsolete by the energy shocks. At a time when the U.S. economy was becoming more dependent upon the world market than ever before and global forces of change required accelerated structural adjustment, the U.S. economy restructured its productive system more slowly than at any time since World War II.

The cumulation of the effects of slow adjustment for a decade make the task of adjustment in the 1980s even harder than would have been the case if U.S. growth and capital formation had kept up with the earlier trends of the 1950s and 1960s. Moreover, the prolonged maladjustment of the economy is itself a source of chronic inflationary pressure, as a relatively inefficient and unadapative production system is put under the growing strain of an unusually high relative level of consumption.

II. INTERACTION OF MARKETS

The interdependence of the U.S. economy with the global economy became an important factor in the 1970s, as various measures of trade in relation to domestic economic activity (especially the ratio of exports or imports to domestic production of goods) doubled or more than doubled.[1] Not only did domestic energy prices have to adjust, but domestic grain prices as well as domestic prices for steel, autos, and many other products came to reflect world competitive pressures and exchange rate adjustments. In the 1970s this resulted in strong price turbulence in some key sectors, whereas in other sectors investment was discouraged by the unanticipated scale of the domestic effects of changes in world market conditions.

The trade effects of increasing interdependence, especially on the import side, have become increasingly visible to domestic producers. The management of the domestic monetary system, however, also came to be heavily influenced by international market forces, with domestic policy periodically driven by external considerations. This has been much less widely perceived and understood by the public as well as by high level economic officials and members of Congress.

The intertwining of our domestic capital markets with the rest of the world has become highly intricate. Banks not only lend globally, they also source funds throughout international capital markets. The range of financing options to a corporation are now so wide that the Federal Reserve during the 1980 credit squeeze felt compelled to ask non-U.S. banks, and their respective national monetary authorities, to discourage lending to U.S. enterprises outside the guidelines imposed on the U.S. banks. (The monetary authorities of several other nations did not agree to the Fed's request, and the problem would no doubt have become serious had the credit squeeze continued inside the United States.)

The growing, relatively unregulated Eurocurrency market has assumed a scale that brings into question many traditional instruments of monetary control. According to the Bank for International Settlements (BIS) statistics on this market, the scale had by the end of 1979 reached about $1 trillion gross or about

$650 billion net of interbank deposits.[2] New figures have now emerged in the work of the International Monetary Fund (IMF) and in recent research by an American banker, J.F. Sterling, Jr.,[3] that suggest that the actual scale may be even greater -- that the gross figure at the end of the 1970s may have approached $1.8 trillion.   This pool, primarily dollars, is sufficiently large and liquid that its potential volatility threatens national monetary management. Moreover, the scale of that pool itself has a significant effect on the level of exchange rates. Large holders of dollar-denominated assets throughout the world must increasingly concern themselves with the potential volatility of the dollar, and of other currencies as well.

This intense interaction of financial markets and the consequent potential volatility, have a great effect on exchange rate determination. The traditional conception of exchange rate markets is that they were driven by the demand for each currency in order to carry out transactions. The current account of a nation would therefore suggest certain conclusions about the transactions demand for that currency. The nature and scale of capital outflows or inflows can also affect exchange rates, of course. When capital outflows, however, or inflows for major trading nations became large relative to trade balances in the 1960s and 1970s, some economists found their theories about purchasing power and the structure of comparative advantage in production and trade of goods losing conceptual strength.

Now, as we enter the 1980s, with persistently high rates of inflation still with us for the foreseeable future, the dollar holders and other asset holders must concern themselves with preserving and enhancing their assets against the ravages of inflation. In this environment of persistent inflation and intense interaction of markets and national economies, as I have noted elsewhere,[4] the asset management motivations may often overwhelm the transactions motivations, in which case the primary determinants of exchange rates are expectations about future values and yields of different potential positions in different currencies. These expectations may be partially based on the recent current account experience of a nation, but they will also reflect expectations about inflation, productivity, political safety, national politics, economic policies, and especially interest rate policy. As with equity markets, expectations are also greatly conditioned by what one thinks other buyers and sellers expect. Under these circumstances, it is quite possible in relation to the trade performance of a country for currencies to rise to undesired heights or fall to illogical depths on the basis of many factors other than the current account outlook. With asset managers in the United States and throughout the world more and more alert to changes in the tide of expectations, strong currencies can move great distances in relatively short periods of time -- as was the case in the markets in the 1978-1980 period for such currencies as sterling, the deutsche mark, yen, the Swiss franc, the Canadian dollar, as well as the U.S. dollar.

The present desire of many large asset holders (e.g., the Organization of Petroleum Exporting Countries (OPEC) surplus cumulators) to diversify their holdings, decreasing the share held in dollar positions and diffusing assets among short, medium, and long-term positions in other economies and currencies, will add to the political volatility. The markets may well become even more volatile in the 1980s as domestic asset managers increasingly learn that they too can manage their portfolios on an international scale and as the markets become even more interlinked globally by technological advances in communications and information processing.

Thus, exchange rates will not necessarily behave in a manner consistent with underlying competitiveness. One key factor, for example, will be the willingness of U.S. authorities to adjust on a continuing basis their domestic monetary policy objectives to international interest rate requirements. This is not just an abstract intellectual point. Chancellor Helmut Schmidt raised this question publicly after the initial announcement of the Reagan administration economic policy and expressed fear that U.S. credit policies could greatly aggravate Europe's recession and disrupt normal trade adjustment processes.

The high and growing degree of interdependence of national economies, through interaction of trade and capital markets, constitutes one set of forces to which the U.S. economy must adapt. Another fundamental set of forces, not well recognized in our basic macro-economic theories or in our national economic policies, is the interdependence of the various specific markets: the financial markets, commodity markets, property markets, bond and equity markets, and other asset markets. The worldwide runup of prices in the early 1970s, culminating in the global commodity boom that preceded in the 1973-1974 oil price shock, for example, was a harbinger of the 1980s. Parties interested in capital gains joined in frantic speculative competition with commodity producers, users, and traders, as other forms of assets turned towards the commodity markets. This crossover among markets became quite intense in 1980, to such an extent that the U.S. Federal Reserve, as part of its credit squeeze, made explicit admonitions about credit granted to speculative activity. (The silver market crunch in 1980 was symp-tomatic.) In the 1980s we shall have to view commodity markets and the financial and currency markets as inextricably intertwined.

Thus these interactions are making obsolete many of our economic theories and concepts about trade competitiveness and exchange rate determination. Much economic theory is built around consideration of specific changes in particular market sectors or par-ticular countries while all other market conditions are assumed to hold steady. The supply and demand for copper, or for sugar, or for bonds, are usually analyzed as if they were separate markets. Financial portfolio theorists in recent years have widened their perspective to look at the greater interaction among different financial markets, but this thinking is not well integrated into the mainstream of economics. In the volatile economic environment of the 1980s, lurches from one asset or market to another can be expected. The possibilities for great swings and disruptions are great.

The consequent movement of exchange rates and their direct effect on competitiveness are important. Beyond these effects, however, is a more fundamental consequence. The sheer uncertainty about the relative strength of the various market segments and the direct-ion of transnational financial flows tends to discourage long-term capital commitments and long-term market development efforts related to trade, as contrasted with short and medium-term capital expenditures and product modifications aimed at improving near-term financial performance. In such an environment, the seemingly safer course is to stay with what one knows, and to keep a short-term orientation in business decisions. U.S. industry, as well as U.S. government policymakers, could easily become more inward-looking and more nationalistic in this context, even though a far more transnational, transmarket perspective may be called for. There is already considerable evidence that this has happened in relation to long-term technological and market development when compared with Japanese performance.[5]

III. OBSOLESCENCE OF THE INSTITUTIONAL FRAMEWORK

The United States has in the last 50 years or so sought a world economic system based on the rule of law, on internationally agreed rights and obligations, and on multilateral consultative mechanisms for conflict resolution and dispute settlement. The institutional mechanisms that have been developed in recent decades, however, are not well suited to cope with the environment of the 1980s. The international institutions were built to reflect the traditional economic compartments: trade, monetary affairs, economic policy harmonization, financial flows, basic industrial and agricultural development, etc.

We devised in recent decades different institutions for each compartment of thought and activity: the General Agreement on Tariffs and Trade (GATT), the IMF, the Organization for Economic Cooperation and Development (OECD), the BIS, the World Bank, and others. We have in addition an array of bilateral arrangements and regional groups that further reflect compartmentalization. Trade people in government as well as in the international institutions rarely talk to the monetary people; the international institutions rarely, and then reluctantly, consult each other and coordinate their efforts. Consequently, as the institutional rules and mechanisms have become perceived as inadequate, a variety of experimental, new institutions were added, especially in the 1970s. Many new committees, task forces, global commissions, and new institutions were initiated. There was a proliferation of organizations and meetings to the point that governments had serious difficulty staffing out these activities and finding adequate representation. Even heads of government became involved, and the economic summit idea from 1975 onwards became an ongoing process of policy reconciliation -- not only among the United States, Canada, Japan, and the larger European countries, but also among the European Community (EC) countries, the Arab League, and others.

At the beginning of the 1980s, even the UN General Assembly itself has been looking at the concept of "global negotiations," reflecting the widespread perception that nothing else has worked and the problems transcend all the existing institutional mechanisms.

One of the motivations behind this global approach is to overcome the problem of proliferation of institutions and to restructure the balance of power among them by giving the General Assembly an oversight role, including the ability to modify or overturn decisions by the other bodies or agencies.

At the end of the Kennedy Round in 1967 a handful of trade officials and members of the GATT Secretariat realized that what had been done in tariff liberalization was not enough and that if nothing were done about the nontariff interventions of governments, the rule of law in trade would break down. Yet another round of global negotiations was thus conceived in the autumn of 1967 in the form of a ministerial conference in Geneva to initiate a new GATT Work Program. This process, spurred by the August 1971, U.S.-induced shocks that resulted in a new exchange rate regime and given further impetus by a ministerial meeting in Tokyo of more than 100 countries and by a new U.S. Trade Act in 1974, nonetheless took 12 years to complete. Trade agreements were not reached until the spring of 1979. The agreements, including the codes of conduct in the nontariff area that were negotiated as part of the multilateral trade negotiations (MTN), constituted a vitally needed reform and adaptation of the GATT to the changing role of governments in world trade.

Yet even the new MTN codes also reflect a narrowness of perspective. They were drawn up by trade officials looking at trade problems. The broader interactions with finance and other aspects of the global economy were generally not taken into account. This should not be surprising, inasmuch as it takes quite a few years to develop international political consensus on any new rules or procedures. International negotiations by their nature tend to produce results that lag behind current needs. The problems that were perceived in the late 1960s were the focus of the agreements reached at the end of the 1970s.

At the start of the 1980s, the existing institutional framework does not readily lend itself to resolution of the problems that are now faced. The interactions of trade, finance, aid, capital flows, financial and commercial markets, etc. are not being addressed in this framework -- and the improvisation of governments in guiding their own national economies is further threatening the relevance of the existing international framework.

The United States is finally coming to grips with its internal economic difficulties, with new policies aimed at shifting the bias of the U.S. economy away from current consumption toward savings and investment and aimed at allowing a combination of growth and market forces to restructure the economy to fit the new global competitive realities.

The United States is not alone, however, in focusing on its domestic problems. Fundamental rethinking is taking place in most capitals of the world in the light of new realities. Developing countries are embarked on domestic austerity programs, supported by new restrictions on imports and new export drives in every case. Eastern European economies are also retrenching and planning to cut imports and boost exports to help relieve the pains of restructuring. Several Western European nations are making major efforts to reorient their economies, to modernize or rationalize their basic industries and attempting to shield this process from imports, hoping to build demand on the export side. The upshot of these efforts to restructure on the basis of national concepts, while insulating economies from international disturbances and promoting exports, is that every nation is trying to export more and import less. These policies are mutually negating, and because of this they could generate a further slowdown of world growth and capital formation.

IV.   THE GLOBAL TRADE ENVIRONMENT

The sheer scale of international payments adjustments required in the early 1980s constitutes a major challenge to world trade. In 1974-1975, there was a crisis of confidence in most official and financial circles concerning the ability to recycle the then foreseen OPEC surpluses. Subsequently, the world economy adjusted reasonably well to the energy price shocks of 1974-1975, as well as to the 1974-1975 recession, and many authorities concluded that the present system was adequate to handle the current and potential stresses. Yet the new round of energy price adjustments at the end of the 1970s, combined with growing recognition that the present institutional framework is somehow inadequate to the needs of the early 1980s, has brought about yet another crisis of confidence among governments and in the global marketplace.

The recycling problem of the mid-1970s was resolved through a combination of high OPEC country purchases and heavy medium-term commercial lending by Western banks of the OPEC surpluses that had been deposited short-term with them. At the start of the 1980s, the scale of national borrowing in international markets is already high, and bank exposure limits in various countries have already been met. National monetary authorities are restraining banks from perceived excesses. The profitability of much international lending has fallen off. The syndication market has been greatly weakened by a variety of events -- ranging from the methods used by the United States in seizing Iranian assets to the falling out of smaller banks from international syndication. The OPEC surplus is increasingly diversified among currencies and asset positions, much of it now wending its way to capital markets of the richest countries rather than to the developing nations. At the same time, because of new policies of national budget austerity in most of the industrialized countries, aid funds are also becoming constricted.

Does this matter to world trade and to U.S. trade? The answer is yes, very much so. The share of U.S. total exports destined for OPEC and the nonoil developing nations is well over one-third. The share for Japan is approaching one-half. For various European countries, the share is also high. At a time when the growth of Western industrialized countries has slowed and capital formation is especially sluggish, the developing countries and Eastern Europe appear to be an important outlet for existing capacity. The developing countries have in recent decades had an average growth rate higher than that of the developed, industrialized West -- about half again as fast. Some of them have grown at startlingly high rates.

Developing and keeping these newly emerging markets requires some agility, however. Because these nations are only able to buy if the financing is available externally, the role of commercial and official finance and aid is crucial. Competition in official trade finance is an area not well regulated by the present institutional framework. The recently negotiated GATT code on subsidies which emerged from the MTN process did not cover export credits, and the old OECD arrangements on export credits do not begin to meet the scope and complexity of the problem.[6] This new era of competitive tension encompasses a number of other borrowing nations, including the centrally planned economies of Eastern Europe and China.

The new environment poses other challenges too. The rapid development and export growth of some of the developing countries, the emergence of Eastern European countries in world trade, and the rapid progression of other nations, especially Japan, up the ladder of technological competitiveness, pose a fundamental challenge for the United States and other slower-adjusting economies in Europe and Canada. The scope and intensity of international competition is growing, in number of competitors, in the quality of products offered, and in financing arrangements available to buyers.

Compounding these structural challenges is another change in market structure brought about by national and regional policies. The EC in particular will in the 1980s be digesting a broadened membership. Greece has now become a full member. Spain, Portugal, and even Turkey will gradually have more intimate arrangements with the EC, with Spain likely to become a full member quite soon -- with the timing depending primarily upon French attitudes. These countries can supply labor-intensive products, as well as labor, for the EC. They, and the other nations "associated" with the EC, especially in Africa, can supply raw materials as well. The EC will have all it can do to assimilate the growing economic role of these nations in the community and will be reluctant to involve itself in further trade liberalization toward the rest of the world. In this context, the relative roles of the markets in the Asian Pacific, Latin America, and, eventually, Africa are likely to prove more important to countries like the United States.

The role of developing countries as "the growth markets" of the 1970s and 1980s is well recognized in official circles in Europe and Japan, compared with a much lower level of awareness in the United States. Another factor, however, is also behind the interest of European nations and the Japanese in expanding commercial relationships with the developing world and the centrally planned economies. That is the fear of inadequate resource and energy supply in the latter 1980s.

It is well recognized that the world faces a tight fit in global energy supplies and that unhappy political developments in oil-supplying nations can dramatically disrupt the world market and the process of adjustment to the new energy realities. This potential for disorder has led several countries to seek out special arrangements and diversified sourcing to ensure supplies in time of crisis.

There is also a tight fit for raw materials supply in the 1980s, although this is less widely recognized. Global investment in basic resources especially mining, slowed to a trickle in the 1970s. If in fact the Western industrialized economies do get back onto a faster growth, faster adjustment path, bottlenecks in raw materials in the 1980s are expected in the basic resource industries. With slower growth, these bottlenecks will simply come later in the decade. In addition, the main sources of many industrial raw materials are in politically volatile or uncertain areas such as Southern Africa and the Soviet Union. This situation of potential constriction and dependence on uncertain sources cannot be quickly corrected. Lead times for new mining and processing facilities range from five to seven years.

These fears of resource and energy constraints are encouraging a new emphasis on bilateralism in Europe and Japan. They are a spur to innovative trade arrangements with Eastern Europe, China, OPEC, and other nonoil developing nations. They have prompted broader political efforts, too, as in the current evolution of the Euro-Arab dialogue, which encompasses not only political initiatives but also bilateral trade agreements. Another example was the push given to a European initiative in the resolution of the Rhodesia-Zimbabwe transition and in peacekeeping in Southern Africa. The German interest in detente is not only political, but involves supply of energy and resources from Eastern Europe and the Soviet Union. The Japanese pursuit of liberal financing arrangements in development of Chinese projects has been directly related to long-term Japanese export and import objectives.

V.   CHANGING FORMS OF COMPETITION

In the context outlined above, a number of governments have felt compelled to become more directly involved in trade and in dealing with problems of changing comparative advantage and competitiveness. Among the industrialized Western economies, after decades of gradual liberalization of markets, governments are again being drawn into a growing range of trade-related intervention activities including:

- government-private cooperation and coordination with both producers and banks in selling military supplies, large turnkey projects, and materials and services for infrastructure and other development projects;

- aggressive innovations in public financing, guarantees, and insurance schemes for exports;

- "mixing" of official credits with aid funds to soften the financing terms of various export transactions, with a gradual "retying" of aid;

- domestic intervention to assist troubled sectors in dealing with import competition (not only various domestic incentives or subsidies, but also production and price planning for troubled sectors like steel and increased government participation in equity positions of companies as well as in financing);

- domestic intervention to assist industries to develop plants with export capabilities; and

- selective domestic intervention to promote R&D and production in new areas of technological promise aimed at enhancing global competitiveness.[7]

The developing nations and the centrally planned economies are placing growing emphasis on the public or government role in trade -- both in managing imports and exports. Some of the responses include:

- growing attention to barter possibilities;

- frequent use of buy-back requirements in agreeing to purchase capital goods and turnkey projects;

- aggressive shopping among alternative developed country suppliers, with special attention to financing terms and availability of parallel soft loans;

- aggressive use of export subsidies and import restrictions to promote domestic industrialization and export capabilities; and

- extensive use of state enterprises for trading.

At the end of the 1970s the developing countries and the centrally planned economies were pressed by commercial lenders and multilateral financial institutions to import less, export more, and limit external borrowing. Entering the 1980s, a number of these countries face even tighter constraints: They have already squeezed out nonessential imports; they have pushed exports; and they have slowed domestic growth. They now have growing import bills for oil and food and must cope with the reluctance of lenders to expand credit, with tougher commercial borrowing terms, and with high debt service commitments. The aid or soft loan flows to them are severely circumscribed and they are faced with slow growth in the industralized Western economies -- which will inevitably slow down growth of demand for imports from the developing world.

One LDC response to the tightening global constraints has been further pursuit of "global bargaining" on a North-South basis. The 1980 General Assembly session reflects this approach, as does the work of various specialized UN bodies such as the United Nations Conference on Trade and Development (UNCTAD).

Another response has been innovation in dealing jointly with the government and the traders of some of the Western nations. This "packaging" approach may involve bringing in Western enterprises and governments to develop resources, energy, or industrial projects, with a package including sale of equipment and services, supply of commercial and official financing as well as aid funds, transfer of technology, development of related local industries and infrastructure, and sale of materials back to the Western industrialized supplier. President Lopez Portillo has recently personally tried such resource diplomacy with the heads of government of Canada, France, the Federal Republic of Germany, Sweden, and Japan. The package concepts he proposed have included requests for additional aid flows to blend in with official export credits and commercial loans.

International cooperative arrangements are becoming even more complex. The Germans, for example, have not only developed a strong relationship with Brazil in nuclear energy production and reprocessing technology, but they are now assisting Brazil in joint efforts with Iraq, under a Brazil-Iraqi nuclear technology agreement.

Such packaging is much easier on a government-to-government basis, especially where there is a tradition of public-private cooperation in trade promotion, as in Japan, France, or Germany. It is rather difficult in the U.S. context, where public-private cooperation is limited, and where government selection of private participants in a large project would give rise to charges of favoritism. It is most difficult where, as in the United States, the commercial banks and the government work at a distance from each other, and much easier where, as in France, the demarcation between banks and government is blurred.

VI. LINKAGE OF TRADE AND FINANCE

The new MTN code on subsidies should have placed further limits on national discretion in assisting exports, but in reality little was done to constrain domestic aids that have a trade effect and creative official assistance in financing exports. In 1979 and 1980 the United States tried to negotiate a tightening of the understandings among the OECD countries on export financing, but the results were meager. In 1979, the U.S. Treasury sought (1) an increase in minimum interest rates, (2) an elimination of financing of local costs, (3) greater restraint in the use of "mixed credits" (aid funds combined with export finance), and (4) broadened coverage of sectors presently excluded, such as aircraft, military hardware, agricultural commodities, and nuclear power plants. These objectives proved nonnegotiable. In the meantime, governments made continuing innovations to promote or facilitate exports, including wider use of mixed credits (with cases of up to half a project on aid terms as low as 3 percent for 25 years, with a grace period as well), inflation risk insurance, exchange risk insurance, financing of local production costs, and greater financing of foreign content.

Building on the foundation of an extensive OECD inquiry in 1979-1980 (the Axel Wallen Report), the failing OECD negotiations were revitalized by a new U.S. effort to change the basis of the gentlemen's agreement on interest rates from a common fixed-rate formula to floating rates of interest geared to the individual capital market circumstances of each nation. This technical approach based on economic concepts, while bearing considerable logic, has held little political appeal for several key governments. An effort was made by the United States to take up this matter at the Venice summit, and the heads of government declared their intention to find by 1 December 1980 a new formula to contain official export credit growth. In spite of this commitment, the talks broke down at the end of 1980. Moreover, as noted above, the present orientation of the negotiations scarcely touched the recent areas of innovation in finance and public-private cooperation.

The present policy trend seems to be moving away from the pursuit of tighter international rules and toward greater national freedom of action. Because aid funds are increasingly difficult to secure from budget-conscious parliaments and trade finance is more popular, the use of aid funds to support trade deals has been growing recently. At times the long-term aid loans may be provided for balance of payments support in parallel with trade credits and commercial loans for a project, but the recipient knows they are related to the sale. In effect, we are witnessing the retying of aid after several years of effort by many donor and recipient countries to reduce aid tying.

The United States has tried threats of official credit counteraction to get the cooperation of other governments, but these threats have been widely per-ceived as not capable of implementation. The U.S. Eximbank did in a few, selective cases successfully match the mixed credit terms of the French, and this was held up as evidence of a U.S. willingness to meet and beat competitive excesses by other nations. At the end of 1980, when the most recent credit talks failed, the United States threatened to lengthen credit terms beyond 10 years and then carried out this threat in a few cases before the end of the Carter administration. On the other hand, President Carter personally instructed Eximbank President John Moore to main-tain a "restrained credit program," and in particular he denied the bank new flexibility in terms of addi-tional funds. This soon became known to the French and other governments. Moreover, the Europeans anticipated that U.S. budgetary circumstances would eventually act to circumscribe any aggressive U.S. posture, and this has been proven correct by the early proposals of the Reagan administration to cut back Eximbank activities.

Thus, the U.S. bargaining threats of 1979 and 1980 were never taken seriously by many other governments, and it is doubtful that Congress will override the president and make available additional funds on the scale required, on favorable terms, to sustain serious U.S. participation in an export credit war. Looking back on 1979 and 1980, the executive branch and the Congress together kept the brakes on the Eximbank, and in so doing they undertook little real debate on the changing character of global competition and on the interaction of trade and finance in world growth markets.

The U.S. competitive position in global commercial banking is also slipping, although this has not so far been widely recognized outside the top management of the leading U.S. banks. In global international lending to nonbanks, i.e., to corporations and governments, the U.S. bank market share dropped from 33 percent in 1976 to under 7 percent in 1978. It is highly unlikely that the U.S. banks' share will rebound to the share held in the 1960s and 1970s (which was in the 25 to 40 percent range at that time). Most U.S. banks experienced net repayments on Eurocurrency loans in 1978, and 1979 preliminary data suggest that this falling back is continuing. Among the reasons is a structural problem: The capital-assets ratio for U.S. banks requires a pretax spread of 100 basis points (one percentage point) or more on lending to obtain a satisfactory rate of return on capital. A French bank can accept a pretax spread of about 45 basis points, a German bank 55 basis points, a Swiss bank 60 basis points, and a Japanese bank about 65 basis points.[8] Moreover, a German bank can fatten its return by providing a range of services for fees by buying into a deal, by taking a position in the project or in the trading operations derived from it, and by drawing fees or dividends, since involvement of banks in operating enterprises or trading companies is not proscribed by German law or regulations.

The regulatory environment and the capital structure of U.S. banks mean that the profit dynamics of the 1980s work against U.S. banks in global competition. On top of this, U.S. banks already have high exposure in many countries and are cautious about expanding their country lending limits. U.S. regulators are also sensitive on this point. The international loan syndication market has also been made more uncertain by recent shocks -- notably the methods used in the U.S. seizure of Iranian assets and the subsequent scramble of U.S. banks to cover themselves with a series of essentially unilateral actions. U.S. regional banks have been falling out of the international market, and risk diversification is becoming more difficult within the U.S. context.

But the international commercial lending climate is now also less bright for banks of other nations, even though they can accept smaller spreads and still make satisfactory profits on their capital. Therefore increasing attention is being given throughout the Western world to official help to exporters and to banks -- to clinch deals in countries where financing is crucial and the borrowing capacity limited. The array of aids, including official export finance, guarantees, local cost financing, inflation and exchange risk insurance, and even use of direct aid funds, is growing. Governments and banks and sellers of big-ticket projects are working more and more closely in most of the OECD countries.

Large U.S. banks have learned to work with multiple sources of credit, without national loyalty. They have developed relationships with the export assistance agencies of other governments, especially through the branch networks of U.S. banks in Europe. Regular dealings are common with Hermes (Germany), Export Credit Guarantee Dept (ECGD) (United Kingdom), Compagnie Francaise d'Assurance pour le Commerce Exterieur (COFACE) (France), and other such institutions. For example, according to British government statements, U.S. banks do more than 20 percent of the foreign currency financing of the ECGD -- and foreign currency financing has lately been the main form of ECGD assistance to British exporters. They have come to prefer sourcing and financing of trade from the U.K., France, and some other Western European countries, as against U.S. exports. This is because the flexibility of the European official institutions and possibilities for related soft-terms assistance (aid money) insure higher success ratios for bids and often allow wider margins or higher fees on the banks' own commercial financial arrangements -- all of which spell higher profits for each transaction. At a time of narrow spreads, this appeal is strong indeed.

In addition, the distinction between trade financing, balance of payments financing, and large-scale project financing is becoming blurred in the new market environment. For big-ticket projects, financing of imports required for the project is often arranged by general lines of credit and package loans to be drawn against when imported. Moreover, if the buyer were to ask for help in putting together the right package of supplies -- taking into account both price and financing terms -- and asked a lead U.S. bank for help, the U.S. bank might not only offer to put together a syndicated loan, but also offer to assist in choosing among German, French, British, U.S., and other sources for various parts of the project to secure favorable official financing and guarantees from other nations. In such a case, some of the bigger U.S. banks now seem to favor sourcing from non-U.S.-based suppliers, and in the event large U.S. multinational enterprises are involved, they will be encouraged to source from their overseas subsidiaries if possible.

Without elaborating on the intricacies of contemporary trade finance, the generalization can be made that further innovations will be developed; they will increasingly be related to government export assistance policies as well as regulatory policies; and the countries where banks and governments are close or where banks are allowed greater leeway in participating in projects or in trade will have a competitive advantage in the actual trading transactions.

It is not easy, within the present GATT and OECD framework, to tackle the trade and finance issues together. The present codes do not provide meaningful constraints. The bureaucratic compartmentalization of issues, keeping trade questions removed from financing questions, ensures continued inability to come to grips with the evolving nature of trade competition.

Taking into account the enormous scale of the recycling problem of the early 1980s and the consequent search by many purchasing countries for favorable financing terms, the situation cries out for action and creative negotiating approaches. The elements of any new deal among governments, however, would have to encompass not only official credits, guarantees, insurance, and other forms of assistance, but also development aid and commercial lending operations that are built around government-assisted projects.

To meet these altered market circumstances, the United States needs to rethink the role of its commercial banks as well. Does, for example, the Glass-Steagall separation of banks from operating enterprises make sense in the face of German bank practices or the extensive financial operations of Japanese trading companies with help from their sister banks? The trading company bill is one modest answer, since it would allow bank participation in the equity of U.S. trading firms, and by the latter part of 1980 it had finally earned some executive branch support. Even then, it faced continued resistance from the Federal Reserve Board and key congressmen, who were looking at international banking and trading as it once was, not as it is becoming in the 1980s. The proposal died at the end of the 1979-1980 congressional session and it is now being reconsidered in the new session. But doubts are already being expressed by some influential congressmen, and the Federal Reserve Board has renewed its criticisms and active opposition.

VII. INDUSTRIAL POLICIES AND TRADE COMPETITION

The response of most of the industrialized Western economies to their own serious industrial adjustment problems has tended to be defensive. Troubled sectors have been the focus of political efforts to keep employment up and to provide for "orderly adjustment" -- which in most cases is a euphemism for maintaining the status quo, for keeping troubled, high-cost enterprises afloat, and utilizing public funds, thereby placing burdens on more efficient, more profitable enterprises. Indeed, I have tended to describe the policies as "adjustment resistance policies" inasmuch as they impede rather than accelerate adjustment.

Pressures for expanded use of import restrictions, particularly against Japan and the less developed countries (LDCs), were on the whole kept under control in the 1970s. A key area of contention in the MTN, however, was the negotiation of an international safeguard code. It was widely felt in the latter 1970s that import-restrictive "safeguard" action would be more frequently resorted to in the 1980s as problems of certain industries in the OECD countries grew with expanding industrial imports from Japan and the newly industrializing countries (NICs). This particular effort to negotiate a new import safeguard code failed, and the MTN was completed without it. The negotiating objective ostensibly was to develop common rules for import-restrictive arrangements which might be taken in the spirit of Article XIX of the GATT.[9] In this way, it was argued, the ad hoc responses of individual countries to special import pressures could be contained and made subject to multilateral surveillance.

In reality, the EC industries and their negotiators sought to free governments from some of the strictures of Article XIX, especially the condition that import restrictive action be nondiscriminatory. The logic put forward for selectivity in the application of import restraint was that if country A's exports were disruptive but other countries' exports were more moderate, the other countries should not be penalized for the excesses of country A. Selective action against those causing injury seems on its

433

face to be fairer. In practice, it allows an importing nation to pressure particular exporters directly, with the objective of obtaining a voluntary restraint agreement (VRA) or a bilateral orderly marketing agreement (OMA) without the government of the exporting interests claiming the right of compensation or retaliation. This selectivity approach gave rise to objections from Japan and the LDCs. The United States formally opposed it, but behind the scenes encouraged the EC's efforts and gave assurance of support for the EC's position at the appropriate negotiating moment.

Although this effort to introduce an international sanction for selective action failed, it is symptomatic of the growing feeling in industrial circles in Europe and North America that Japan and the LDCs will pose a serious threat to their basic industrial structure in coming years. Arguments that exports to the LDCs far outstrip imports from them have so far carried little political weight.

Despite the fact that these fears have been growing in key developed countries (DCs), the multilateral development banks and the LDCs have been striving to achieve diversification of their exports away from reliance on a few commodities toward exports of manufactures. The tightening constraints posed by rising import bills for oil and food and by rising debt service obligations are spurring this drive to industralize, to diversify, and expand exports. In the 1980s, the number of LDCs able to export industrial products will no doubt grow. The export successes of Taiwan, Korea, Hong Kong, and a few other LDCs will be emulated. The range of products will expand well beyond textiles, apparel, and footwear (the DC import problems of the 1960s and 1970s), to electrical and electronics products, steel, shipbuilding, chemicals, and other sophisticated areas. Korea's already apparent global success in shipbuilding, steel, electronics, and even engineering services are but an example of what is to come. Brazil's great progress in aircraft production and international sale is another.

Although the World Bank, GATT, IMF, and various reports have decried a perceived trend toward greater protectionism against these countries, the LDCs themselves have been active protectionists, using protection to build up their new infant industries.

Many of them have resisted strongly the full application of GATT rules and, even more strongly, the application of the new MTN codes to them on the grounds that it would unfairly limit their freedom of action in promoting industrialization.

Moreover, they have increasingly resorted to strict conditions on foreign business sales and operations in their countries to bring about greater local enterpreneurial efforts, more local jobs, more R&D and technical training, etc. Local content, coproduction, licensing, and other requirements have been used to induce foreign businesses to become full participants in their industrial development, and performance requirements are increasingly being used to force foreign enterprises to export from the newly established bases inside the developing countries.

This trend is not, however, unique to the LDCs. It has been widespread in Europe as well, most noticeably in the aerospace and defense systems area, but also in other key industrial areas where government policies and procurement are vital. In 1980, there has been a resurgence of this kind of industrial development policy in Canada, which is now insisting on greater R&D efforts, job creation, and training in Canada by foreign enterprises.

What about the United States? For some years, the AFL-CIO and other labor spokesmen critized the outflow of U.S. direct investment and technology transfer in response to such nationalistic pressures in other areas around the world. Yet in 1977-1978, when Japanese exports of televisions to the United States came to be perceived as a vital threat to the U.S. television industry, the U.S. position reversed. When an OMA was negotiated limiting the level of television exports to the United States, the OMA included a "side letter" stating the intention of the Japanese government (MITI) to give guidance to certain Japanese companies to bring about direct investment in production facilities inside the United States (with the expected level of domestic labor content specified).[10] This marked a change in underlying trade policy thinking, although it probably was not perceived as such in 1978 when the OMA package was worked out. In 1979-1980, the same theme was played out in public policy debate about Japanese automotive exports to the United States. The executive branch resisted talk of import restrictions for many months, but strongly encouraged Japanese investment in new production facilities and greatly increased parts procurement in the United States. Many members of Congress supported this policy approach and threatened domestic content legislation if it failed.

In this new environment, the competitiveness of nations may increasingly depend on the adaptability of companies to changing national industrial development policies in their own nation and the industrial policies of other nations. Tariffs and overt trade restrictions have over decades of negotiation been considerably liberalized. The MTN in a sense marks the culmination of that drive. In the 1980s, the types of policies and policy instruments that affect trade patterns may be rather different. The present international rules may not readily encompass the new forces at work. Marina Von Neumann Whitman, in a perceptive and politically realistic comment about autos, put it this way:

> A major challenge of the 1980s, then, will be to find ways of achieving the economic efficiencies of worldwide specialization of production and development within the political constraints imposed by national policies. The structure of automotive trade will shift from exporting finished products toward exporting parts and components, as manufacturers 'trade off' the right to import some components into a particular nation for local assembly in return for a commitment to produce other parts for export.
>
> Finally, rapid changes in production patterns and product characteristics require enormous amounts of capital. Thus, with the worldwide industry in a state of transition and companies facing rising cost pressures, intensified political constraints and accelerating capital requirements, the trend toward pooling of resources -- in the form of mergers, joint ventures and cooperative agreements -- will continue in the 1980s.[11]

Her conclusion is that there will be "a stepped-up pace of innovation and competition in an increasingly global -- rather than national -- automotive industry." A cautionary note, however, is in order: Global industry may have to be structured to fit national industrial policy preoccupations, and it is unlikely to match what world market forces would otherwise have brought about.

VIII.   GLOBAL TURBULENCE AND POLICY RESPONSES

In a global environment of economic turbulence and intensifying competition, the industries characterized by heavy fixed costs or intensive labor use can be expected to seek defensive measures to shield them from the buffeting.   They can also be expected to move slowly in making new, long-term, capital commitments in light of the great uncertainties.   Restructuring or adapting to meet the new market circumstances will therefore prove difficult.   Moreover, capital will tend to flow to the larger, more successful enterprises and away from those firms that become troubled.   This will tend to promote consolidation and greater concentration of industry within the Western industrialized countries, as the weaker firms fail or are absorbed by the stronger.   National competition and antitrust policies may resist such changes in the structure of industry -- but if so, then the present structure may only be sustainable by restricting the effects of foreign competition.   This agonizing dilemma has not yet become a central issue of trade policy debate, but it will probably emerge during the 1980s.

The cumulative effect of other industrial changes in recent decades will also converge in the 1980s. Prominent among these changes is the growing role or direct involvement of governments in trade in Europe, the OPEC countries, Eastern Europe, China, and most LDCs.   Ironically, the government role in trade in Japan will probably phase down, while it is likely to increase in some of the relatively free market economies such as Canada.

What will be the U.S. response to a growing recognition that this increased government participation in trade matters is not simply a matter of subsidies or government procurement policies, now covered by MTN codes, but of more far-reaching changes? If such trends in the rest of the trading world continue on the present path, and if there is a resurgence of economic bilateralism, the global market will take on a different character from that envisaged in the establishment of the initial framework of trade and payments in the late 1940s.

These trends reflect our times. They are a response to slow growth, slow capital spending, international shocks, and consequent economic adjustment problems. Governments are responding to internal pressures, focusing primarily on sector-by-sector adjustment difficulties. The consequent policies inevitably conflict with one another, within nations, and, especially, among nations.

IX. NEED FOR A NEW FRAMEWORK OF COOPERATION

U.S. economic policies and international negotiating objectives have usually been developed with past experiences in mind -- focusing on the problems of yesterday rather than the problems of tomorrow. This tendency to construct solutions on the basis of exper- ience reflects characteristic American pragmatism. It has made sense in the last few decades, given that a key objective of post-World War II international economic policies has been to open up the global economy. The negotiations to reduce national restrict- ions on trade and capital flows and to build multinational institutions based on nondiscrimination have been dramatically successful. Each stage of trade liberalization and of enhancement of financial cooper- ation has facilitated further growth of world trade and world capital flows. The multilateral institutions that were developed to guide this process of liberalization have on the whole worked quite effectively.

The process of liberalization of the kinds of restrictions that prevailed after World War II has nearly run its course, however, and new problems are emerging of a different character. As this essay has noted, success in liberalization, together with the growth of the world economy, have resulted in an acute interdependence of markets. Global competition is intensifying, not only as advanced countries like Japan move up the technological ladder, but also as the NICs enter more and more fields of resource development, industry, and agribusiness.

Inflation, energy shocks, and other forces of disturbance, together with greatly intensified compe- tition on a global scale, call for accelerated adjustment or restructuring of the older industrialized nations -- especially in North America and Europe. Instead of accelerating growth and capital spending to facilitate adjustment, these industrialized nations have slowed down; capital spending has declined and become more oriented toward short-run benefits; and policies have been adopted to assist troubled sectors remain viable -- thereby retarding adjustment.

As we enter the 1980s, the responses of governments to the new circumstances have involved such a high degree of active intervention that the forms of competition are changing. National policies are altering the relative competitiveness of the various sectors of each economy. Policies are increasingly aiming to bias economies toward exports, utilizing innovative combinations of domestic and international policies and of public and private cooperation. Given the vital interaction of trade and finance, governments are increasingly seeking the means to manipulate that interaction to promote their national exports.

At the beginning of the 1980s the response to global inflation and slow growth -- stagflation, as some call it -- is a worldwide effort to induce austerity at home, insulate national markets from foreign competition, and stimulate exports. If nearly every country follows this kind of policy, however, the combined effect will be self-cancelling, further depressing global economic activity.

Positive alternatives are needed. If governments insist on activist policies to help correct the malfunctions of national economies, then some means must be found to reconcile and bring into concert on an international level the various national policies. Because of the intense interaction of markets and of national economies in the 1980s, purely national policy prescriptions are likely to fail. Not even monetary policies can any longer be managed on a purely domestic basis.

As has been observed above, the existing framework for international consultation, dispute settlement, and financial assistance is not well structured to deal with the new realities. The existing institutions are too compartmentalized, and there is too little cooperation and cross-fertilization among them.

Replacement of the various existing international institutions with some new, comprehensive single institution is not practicable, however. The existing institutions each reflect a mutuality of interests among those nations directly involved, but not all nations have the same sets of interests. The problems of the Western industrialized nations are different from those of the NICs, of the nonmarket industrialized

441

economies of Eastern Europe, and of the poorest developing nations.

The idea of bringing together all of the issues into one comprehensive management system, such as the General Assembly of the UN, is not a useful pre-scription. If such a body were to monitor and overrule other bodies, it would have to have universal member-ship and act either on the basis of voting or on the basis of consensus. Given the fundamental differences of interest among the many nations, such a universal body would probably become impotent, and its decisions, if made at all, would be reached slowly and ponderously, often generating ineffective remedies and coming too late to be relevant.

To start up entirely new, broadly based institutions that have some powers and that are based on rights and obligations would require elaborate international negotiations among scores of countries. The kinds of negotiations that generated the IMF, the World Bank, and the GATT systems after World War II were possible because only a few countries (really only two -- Great Britain and the United States) dominated the world economy, and they could work out a framework without considering the political, social, and economic aspirations of 100 or more other nations. Such a situation no longer exists. It is highly doubtful that a new international economic conference could generate a new institution that would have any meaningful powers.

In the second half of the 1970s another mechanism was created to coordinate policies -- the so-called economic summits. This process of annual, brief encounters of leaders of governments can hardly be expected to cope with the wide array of ongoing prob-lems requiring action. Something else is therefore needed, and a more pragmatic starting point would be to work with existing institutions, supplementing them with ad hoc groups on specific issues (as is often done in international financial crises or debt rescheduling).

It is not the purpose of this essay to analyze or recommend specific institutional changes or procedures. Rather, the orientation here is to suggest the types of problems that need to be addressed in the 1980s and to suggest the need for new approaches to them involving far greater international consultation and reconciliation of policies that exist at the beginning of the 1980s.

The turbulence we can expect in the world economy in the 1980s will tend to generate short-sighted responses, as public and private decisionmakers respond to events rather than anticipating them. Just as it has become vital within the U.S. economy to stabilize expectations about the future economic environment and to circumscribe the ad hoc responses of government, the same holds true internationally.

Moreover, if the United States is to get its own economy in order, with the new economic concepts and policies of 1981, it is imperative that the new approach be reconciled with global, economic, and political realities. Domestic analyses and prescriptions will increasingly have to recognize that their soundness and efficacy depend on world market forces and not just on domestic market forces. The same kind of interaction holds true for other nations.

To cope adequately with the competitive problems of the 1980s and thereafter, we need to take action both internationally and domestically. Several international objectives seem to be essential:

1. To bring international order into the growing disarray of instruments of intervention, new international rules and consultative procedures need to be worked out. Governments will need to develop a framework to reconcile and bring into concert their domestic sectoral policies on the international level. This means going beyond their trade policies to subject their domestic industrial and agricultural policies to international consultation. (It is increasingly difficult, for example, to develop a purely national policy for the steel or automotive sectors, and, although this is beginning to be recognized, international consultations in the OECD are only of the most simplistic kind.) This may initially have to be done among like-minded and economically comparable

443

countries in a limited membership context such as the OECD.

2. A new international framework is needed for managing the interactions of trade and finance, including such issues as export finance, development assistance in relation to projects and industrial development, and exchange rate policy in relation to trade. (The expanding credit war at the beginning of the 1980s and its relationship to aid policies is one example of an imperative not covered by existing rules or procedures.) This will probably require some new coordinating mechanism among the IMF, the World Bank, and the GATT, in parallel with more intensive consultations within the OECD.

3. Domestic macroeconomic policies will need to be coordinated internationally even more intensively and in greater detail than in the past to avoid such phenomena as competitive devaluations, escalating interest rates on a global scale, unnecessary international diffusion of inflationary pressures, and mutual negation of policy objectives. The work of the Economic Policy Committee of the OECD, and especially Working Party 3, have only scratched the surface of what needs to be done. Initially, a more limited consultation involving the United States, the United Kingdom, France, and West Germany may be required, followed by a U.S.-EC-Japan triumvirate to consider the mutual effects of their separate policies.

A new domestic framework for the government action is also needed:

1. Far greater public-private consultation and cooperation is needed in the United States to ensure that U.S. responses to the changing global competitive environment are adequate and timely. However, the U.S. formula for public-private cooperation should be uniquely American, with a view to preserving the ultimate economic decision-making autonomy of U.S. enterprises, which has provided so much

444

international long-term capital markets. Trade policies and domestic industrial policies have to become far more coherent. The U.S. economy is part of a global economy and is increasingly interactive with it. Our thinking must now reflect the new realities that flow from that interaction. Otherwise, U.S. competitiveness will continue to erode, and the consequent problems of domestic adjustment will grow increasingly painful.

It is time to set aside old problems and reactions to past feelings of unfairness and to look forward at the changing character of the world economy and deal with it. The institutions, the rules, and decision-making processes we have built in the post-World War II period provide a foundation, but creative, innovative approaches to the new realities are now urgently needed.

of the strength of our economy in the past. The format of the various advisory committees established for trade negotiations by the Trade Act of 1974 may provide lessons for an effective public-private cooperation mechanism for all aspects of U.S. commercial and financial relations with other nations.

2. A fundamentally different orientation for antitrust and competition policy is needed, that recognizes that foreign competition often provides the major force for competition in the United States, and that domestic consolidation of industry, conglomerate risk-spreading, and cooperation in international selling activities may often lead to more, rather than less, effective competition -- and may be essential to improving U.S. competitiveness in key globalmarkets.

3. A fundamental rethinking of the relationship of banks to operating enterprises should be undertaken to take into account such matters as the role of banks in international trade competition, the role of banks and merchant banks in the restructuring of domestic industry, and the interest of the government in insuring that adequate financial resources flow in directions that bring about structural adjustment rather than retarding it.

4. Greater, not less emphasis must be placed on adequate means of competition in trade finance, with expansion, not contraction of the Eximbank essential, and with flexible interplay between trading and financing enterprises allowed -- perhaps through the vehicle of the export trading company bill.

5. Domestic economic policy formulation needs to be carried out in a different framework of analysis that explicitly recognizes the international interactions and that provides for intensive and detailed international consultation on such fundamental questions as the degree of reliance on monetary and interest rate policy, the emphasis placed on investment and savings relative to

consumption, and the objectives of sectoral policies, etc. To provide adequate coordination of domestic and international economic policies, something like the former Economic Policy Council directed by an assistant to the president -- utilized in the Nixon-Ford period -- is needed. The decision system at work at the beginning of 1981 has already demonstrated inadequate cognizance of international constraints on, and effects of, new domestic policies.

6. Much greater emphasis needs to be placed on shifting the biases of the U.S. economy toward savings and investment, with a view to accelerating the rate of capital spending and enhancing the importance of R&D, to ensure much faster restructuring of the U.S. economy to meet global competitive requirements.

7. Development assistance policies should be formulated in clear recognition of the role of aid, both bilateral and multilateral, in sustaining a viable global trade market. To the extent that aid policies are altered, their economic effects must be given far greater attention, especially their effects on banking and trade.

In the U.S. private business sector, the new global realities require some profound changes in the orientation of top level management:

1. Strategic planning needs to be given far greater weight in private-business decision-making, taking into account global market developments and investment plans, public policies of other nations as well as those of the United States, and the turbulence and intense interactions of markets in the years ahead. This also requires changes in many aspects of decisionmaking. For example, capital budgeting decisions need to be increasingly tailored to the strategic planning process and to global competitive circumstances and less and less to the

operating proposals of the various division of an enterprise as presently structured

2. Parallel with 1. above, the self-destructiv American emphasis on short-range financia performance must be replaced by a growin emphasis on meeting global competition over several-year time horizon. Many Americ businessmen have become too shortsighted deal with the kinds of long-term chang needed in the next few years.

3. When businesses call on government to ta action at home or internationally, t should design their proposals for action w far greater preparation and sophisticat to arm the government with the knowledge needs of policies and markets of ot nations and of the objectives it should s for negotiations or countermeasures to carried out effectively. Business complai are useless without practicable proposals action.

In conclusion, we urgently need an impr framework for decisionmaking both at home and abr both public and private, that can cope with turbulence, volatility, and intensive interaction the global economy. The international elements of a new framework cannot solely be based on rigid or codes of conduct. Recent experience has shown the changes in the character of international ad ment problems, and the changes in policy respons them, tend to outpace the negotiation of new r Therefore, because of the enormous time lags imp in complex international negotiation, a new fram of international rights and obligations must heavily on active consultative mechanisms reconciling divergent national policies.

In essence, the global interaction of marke the rapidly growing interdependence of the U.S. e with those of other nations no longer allow the of dealing with internal U.S. problems as if the separable from international developments. Do fiscal, monetary, and sectoral policies cann divorced from international monetary movement global interaction with the markets in goods, a

FOOTNOTES

[1] For appropriate statistical series and international comparisons, see U.S. Department of Commerce, International Economic Indicators, quarterly, tables on trade in relation to production of goods.

[2] Although it is popular to rely on the net figure, one should remember that the loan portfolio of a lending institution is driven by its own gross deposits and not by a statistician's abstraction of global market positions described as net.

[3] J. F. Sterling, Jr., "How Big Is the International Lending Market?," The Banker, January 1980, and J. F. Sterling, Jr., Competitive Advantage in Eurocurrency Lending, (forthcoming dissertation).

[4] "Interaction of Financial and Commercial Markets: Challenge for Policy Makers," The World Economy, November 1980.

[5] See, for example, Jack Baranson, The Japanese Challenge to U.S. Industry, Lexington Books, forthcoming in 1981.

[6] This again is an example of artificial separation of issues along bureaucratic lines. The developed country trade negotiators in the GATT agreed to let national financial officials of the OECD countries try to negotiate separately new undertakings on export credits in the OECD. This latter effort failed in 1980, leaving a gaping hole in the international rules on export aids.

[7] It may also be worth noting that in the early years after World War II, similar types of intervention policies were used to facilitate balance of payments and foreign exchange management, whereas in recent years the efforts are more focused on sectoral difficulties arising out of changing comparative advantage.

[8] J. F. Sterling, Jr., Competitive Advantage, op. cit.

[9]Article XIX recognizes that a government may find that one of its industries is temporarily in grave difficulty and that a period of import relief may contribute to rectifying its difficulties. In such a case, if serious injury to the industry from imports is shown, the government may for a fixed period raise tariffs or otherwise restrict imports, but it should carry out such restrictions on a nondiscriminatory basis. Moreover, the government must offer tariff concessions or other trade compensation or accept trade retaliation by the countries adversely affected during the period of special protection. In practice, restrictions under Article XIX have been applied without full regard to the rules, and there have been frequent efforts to work around Article XIX with ad hoc restrictions imposed by force.

[10]These Japanese companies were expected "to adopt such production processes as add no less labor content in the United States than the Japanese-affiliated color television receiver manufacturers which are operating commercially in the United States at the time when the Notes exchanged entered into force." Letter of 20 May 1977 from Ambassador Togo to Ambassador Robert S. Strauss, accompanying the exchange of documents which constituted the Orderly Marketing Agreement, also dated 20 May 1977.

[11]"Auto Industry's New Challenge," The New York Times, 3 September 1980, page D2.

ABOUT THE AUTHORS

DR. JACK N. BEHRMAN is the Luther Hodges Distinguished Professor at the University of North Carolina Graduate School of Business Administration and an advisor to the U.S. Department of State, the United Nation's Center for Transnational Corporations, and the Fund for Multinational Management Education. He served as assistant secretary for commerce for domestic and international business under the Kennedy and Johnson administrations.

DR. JACK CARLSON is the executive vice president, chief economist, and corporate secretary of the National Association of Realtors. Prior to joining the National Association, he served as vice president and chief economist for the Chamber of Commerce of the United States.

DR. MARK G. FARAH is visiting professor in the College of Business Administration at the University of Oregon. He worked as a research economist at the National Economic Research Associates, Inc. and the Oregon Research Institute.

DR. ROBERT A. FLAMMANG is professor of economics at Louisiana State University and serves as a consultant for the Port of New Orleans and the Gulf South Research Institute. He has been a consultant with the Agency for International Development in the Philippines, Indonesia, and Thailand.

DR. LAWRENCE G. FRANKO is coholder of the U.S. Professorship of the Corporation and Society and director of research at the Centre d'Etudes Industrielles in Geneva, Switzerland. He also is a consultant to the Conference Board (Europe), the OECD, the World Bank, and the International Labor Office. He served as deputy assistant director for international affairs at the U.S. Congressional Budget Office, was a fellow at the Carnegie Endowment for International Peace, and taught at the Georgetown University School of Foreign Service.

MR. HUGH GRAHAM is director of the Forecasting Center at the National Association of Realtors. He was formerly the deputy director of the Forecast Center of the Chamber of Commerce of the United States.

MR. THOMAS R. GRAHAM is adjunct professor of law at American and Georgetown Universities, a resident associate of the Carnegie Endowment for International Peace, and a senior associate of the Southern Center for International Studies in Atlanta. He served as deputy general counsel to Special Trade Representative Robert Strauss under the Carter administration, participating actively in the Tokyo Round negotiations.

DR. ELEANOR M. HADLEY is group director and senior economist in the International Division of the U.S. General Accounting Office, adjunct professor of economics at the George Washington University, and an associate member of the George Washington University's Sino-Soviet Institute. She served with the U.S. Office of Strategic Services, the Department of State, and the U.S. Tariff Commission.

DR. PENELOPE HARTLAND-THUNBERG is director of economic research at the Georgetown Center for Strategic and International Studies and adjunct professor of economics at Georgetown University. Before joining CSIS, she served on the Board of National Estimates of the Central Intelligence Agency, the Council of Economic Advisors, and the U.S. Tariff Commission.

DR. HARALD B. MALMGREN is president of Malmgren, Inc., Washington, chairman of Malmgren, Golt, Kingston, and Company, Ltd, London. He is also adjunct professor at Georgetown University and a director of the Atlantic Council of the United States, the Overseas Development Council, the Council on Science and Technology for Development, and the Trade Policy Research Centre in London. He served as deputy special representative for trade negotiations under the Nixon and Ford administrations.

DR. RAYMOND F. MIKESELL is the W.E. Miner Professor of Economics at the University of Oregon and a consultant to the Department of State, the Office of Technology Assessment, and the Office of Science and Technology. He has served on the Advisory Council of Overseas Private Investment Corporation and on the Council of Economic Advisors.

DR. SIMON SERFATY is director of the Washington Center of Foreign Policy Research and a faculty member of the Johns Hopkins School of Advanced International Studies.

MR. ROGER E. SHIELDS is vice president and head of the International Economic Research Unit of the Chemical Bank. He served as deputy assistant secretary for international economic policy at the U.S. Treasury Department and as deputy assistant secretary for international economic affairs at the U.S. Defense Department. He has also served on the faculty of the University of Texas and the University of Virginia.

MR. R. CRAIG SONKSEN is an international economist at the Chemical Bank, joining the Economic Research Department in 1978 after receiving his M.P.A. from Brigham Young University. His specializations include Eastern European economies, East-West relations, and Asian affairs.

MS. SHERRY STEPHENSON is a research associate with the Centre d'Etudes Industrielles in Geneva, Switzerland and is completing her Ph.D. from the Graduate Institute of International Studies. Before joining CEI, she served as an associate economic affairs officer with the United Nations Conference on Trade and Development.

DR. WILLIAM G. TYLER is senior economist at the Research Institute of the Brazilian Planning Secretariat and a member of the economics faculty at the University of Florida. He has also served as a consultant to the World Bank, USAID, and the Brazilian Institute of Economics.

MR. RICHARD J. WHALEN is chairman and editorial director of Worldwide Information Resources, Ltd., adjunct senior fellow at the Georgetown Center for Strategic and International Studies, and international business editor of the Center's Washington Quarterly. He served as senior editor to Fortune, and was given the American Book Award for his bestseller, Founding Fathers, a biography of Joseph P. Kennedy.